W9-CHL-619

Alice Meynell

PROSE AND POETRY

ALICE MEYNELL AET: 30
An etching (1879) by Tristram Ellis after a
water-colour portrait (1877) by Adrian Stokes

1847 1922

Alice Meynell

PROSE AND POETRY

Centenary Volume

edited by

F.P., V.M., O.S. & F.M.

With a biographical & critical introduction by

V. SACKVILLE-WEST

Essay Index Reprint Series

 BOOKS FOR LIBRARIES PRESS
FREEPORT, NEW YORK

First published 1947 by Jonathan Cape Limited

Reprinted 1970 by arrangement

08-053749-1
HUM

HOUSTON PUBLIC LIBRARY

RO1106 49131

INDEXED IN   EGLI

INTERNATIONAL STANDARD BOOK NUMBER:
0-8369-1983-1

LIBRARY OF CONGRESS CATALOG CARD NUMBER:
76-117824

PRINTED IN THE UNITED STATES OF AMERICA

THE CONTENTS

INTRODUCTION

How enviable appears the task of the biographer whose subject has passed safely beyond the reach of living memory; when one man's interpretation, based on the available documents, is as good as another's. It is then only a matter of selection and of a judicious piecing together to compose the portrait; there can be no true check on the likeness, there can be nothing but a divergence or else a concurrence of opinion. The most that can be demanded is that the portrait shall be convincing in itself; that it shall re-create, with sufficient plausibility, the entity that was once a living man or woman. All must depend upon the inferences drawn according to the particular outlook of the chronicler, and these in turn must largely be based upon the written impressions of others, likewise gone beyond the reach of dispute. Unable to come forward and disagree, these others, whose evidence alone would be worth having, are securely relegated to the region whence can come no refutation. But how different is the case when a multitude of the personally well-informed exists to ululate in protest. Like an army of friends and relations invited to view a posthumous painting, they fill the artist's studio with their cries of objection: the nose is not bad, they say, and you have certainly caught the glint in the hair; but where is that elusive smile we knew so well, that little fleeting look of irony, or that charming glance of amusement which came so seldom and was so precious when it did come? and where is the characteristic gesture of the hand? and where that touching droop of slight tiredness? where, in fact, is the person we knew? Not here. Accurate in every definable particular, something has eluded the brush: this is not wholly he, or she, whom we loved.

I never saw Alice Meynell. Hearing of her from time to time from her friends who were also my friends, I put together a composite image which might bear but little resemblance to the truth. I imagined a rather tall, very willowy woman, swathed in grey voile with a bunch of Parma violets at her breast; a woman gliding rather than walking through life even as she glided rather than walked through the parquet-floored drawing-rooms of her acquaintances. An attractive aloofness, tinged with preciosity, in my conception rendered her somewhat unapproachable if not actually inhuman; a woman who reserved her expansiveness even as she reserved her affections, for her family and a chosen few. It was so impossible to associate anything cheap or cheapening with Alice Meynell, that I had no desire to 'know' her unless it might be in the hope of knowing her well — an honour not likely to fall to the lot of one so young and obscure as I. Thus I never sought to make her acquaintance, although I could easily, through those friends, have done so; and now I cannot be sure if I am sorry or glad.

A legend to me, even then when I was so young, she retains the quality of a legend still. Ethereal, rather than very real, she seemed to live with a nimbus of adoration round her; and if a woman can achieve that, I thought, her personality must indeed hold something authentic and remarkable. She might never have written a word, and yet she would be listened to. People would instinctively get up when she entered the room. Such were my early and half-informed impressions. I now discover that they were not wholly aside the truth. I had not got Alice Meynell quite right, but I had not got her wholly wrong.

Even the mistakes were in some way justified. Thus, I learnt that she was not, in inches, tall, but to diminish that misconception I learnt also that she gave the impression of being taller than she was, and moreover, with an endearing vanity (which came to me as a surprise) took particular pains in the use of draped garments and high heels to make herself appear as tall as possible. I realized that she was far more softly feminine than I had supposed. I realized a fact that I had overlooked: the conscious intention that grace should attend a woman in every region of her conduct. I had heard Alice Meynell

8

called ladylike, and resented the word as slightly belittling to
a woman of her serious distinction; but I now see that, in no
derogatory sense, it might be fitted into the pattern of her per-
sonality. Observe the pose and gesture of her hands in all her
portraits — is it studied? is it natural? or perhaps a little bit of
both? Coventry Patmore, in a charming trifle never destined
for publication, pays a tribute to another feature of which she
was evidently proud: he shall speak for this in his own words,
and shall speak also for the warmth of a presence I had in my
ignorance interpreted as far too cool:

> A rustle on the staircase
>   Gives the heart gay warning;
> With a laugh like many primroses
>   She flies the children's chase;
> And she comes in to breakfast,
>   As light as a May morning,
> All the day's glad duties
>   Shining in her face.
> 'You ARE an early caller!'
>   'I have brought you my review.'
> In haste she takes her coffee;
>   Then she rises, and we two
> Draw our chairs towards the fender,
>   And I read her praise, while, sweet,
> She smiles in contemplation
>   Of her fame and her small feet.

That was not quite the Alice Meynell I had built up for my-
self. Did that remote woman really come down to breakfast,
laughing like many primroses, pursued by many children, and
did she really enjoy admiring her small feet as much as she
enjoyed hearing the praise of her great fame brought to her by
Coventry Patmore at that unsuitable hour of the day, breakfast
time?

We must accept that she did.

A few more details, on inquiry, were revealed. Her voice,

which I had imagined soft, slow, and veiled, was indeed contralto in speech as in song; but her laughter was high and light — another thing to be managed pleasingly, as a lady in those better-mannered days must be careful to manage. Did she herself not write 'A feminine laugh too has to be decorative . . .'? I had not gone very far wrong as yet; but my next question was asked in some apprehension. Was she talkative, I asked? almost fearing to be told that she was. *NO.* She spoke little; and I registered with relief the confirmation of my surmise that she spoke only when she had something to say, and then said it with an air that gave it the weight of considered authority. Her silences, I was glad to learn, were perhaps even more impressive than her pronouncements. That was as it should be.

My few remaining misapprehensions were then charmingly corrected by her daughter Viola's Memoir. My principal error I then saw, lay perhaps in an under-estimation of her humanity; I had thought no sense of fun lay beneath that ladylike demeanour, no lightness within that serious heart. Yet now I read of her packing her children into a large trunk and gaily dragging them through rooms and out on to landings, making them guess where they were before the lid was lifted. There was laughter in that house, even though the children were responsible for most of it. But this is starting at the wrong end, or at any rate in the middle, and a short biography had better introduce these endearing incidents in their proper order.

Alice Thompson and her sister Elizabeth were born in the years 1847 and 1846 respectively. Their father had been an intimate friend of Charles Dickens; their mother, Christiana, appears to have been a somewhat feckless, ecstatic, sentimental, 'artistic' example of Victorian womanhood whose private journal provides an unconsciously vivid picture of the little family's nomadic existence in France and Italy — chiefly Italy. Dickens, who visited them near Genoa, 'living in a beautiful situation in a ruinous palace', found them blissful but in a 'singularly untidy state', the father with a pointed beard, smoking a great German pipe, his feet in slippers, the two little girls with their hair cropped and a bright little bow on top — Christiana said she had invented this as a picturesque thing, adding that perhaps it was, and perhaps it was not. Dickens got the impression that what with her painting and her music, the household affairs went rather to the wall. The children's education was clearly erratic: at the time of Dickens's visit their father was teaching them the multiplication table in 'a disorderly old billiard-room, with all manner of maps in it'. Had he been privileged to read Christiana's diary he would scarcely have been reassured. The children had no stockings, but no matter: 'Babes' room with sweet elaborately vaulted ceiling painted with yellow stars, yellow satin hangings . . . exquisite Italian combination of sunshine, campanile, cypress, hill, and palazzo . . . Went to take down an art in the blessed moonlight near the ruined tower.'

Christiana's 'arts', as she called her pictures, played a great part in her life; she sang also and played the piano, and wrote her ingenuous diary, while her adoring children trailed after her, rootless, but much loved and certainly not unhappy. It was fortunate for them that their father, a man of culture, scholarship, and extreme sensibility, should have lavished upon their education all the trouble he would have accorded to a son. Dickens might be right in thinking it unorthodox: it was undoubtedly enriching. The younger daughter, in her essay *A Remembrance*, has left a delicately drawn portrait of this un-usual being, who, 'loving literature, never lifted a pen except to write a letter', and asks where she herself shall find a pen fastidious enough to define so many significant negatives? 'The things he refrained from were all exquisite.' A contrast indeed he must have presented to his over-flowing wife, whose 'arts', one may be allowed to suspect, were scarcely of a nature to stimulate any creative activity of his own. It is easy to trace the influence of his austerity upon the spirit that later informed every gesture of Alice Meynell.

By the time their daughters were aged respectively nineteen

and eighteen, it had occurred to their parents to offer them a more conventional life in their native country. The ruinous palaces and disorderly billiard-rooms were replaced by a solid house in the Isle of Wight, where the Babes, the sweet Babes, the Angels, of their mother's diary, learnt to discard their Genoese dialect and to converse in the approved Victorian manner with the young men they met at croquet parties, concerts, and dances. During this brief period, Alice achieved the frivolity of the normal light-hearted young woman. 'I wore a ravishing yellow tarlatan of the palest possible tint . . . with a plaid *écharpe* over one shoulder, a red rose with its leaves in my hair and one at my waist . . . Glorious fun . . . I had no particular flirtation, and no particular compliments, save . . . that the men quarrelled to dance with me.'

Glorious fun! But this was an untrue, a superimposed mood for the Thompson sisters. They were both intensely serious. The diary that records pleasure in the yellow tarlatan records also that 'the sorrow in my soul is beyond words, beyond all expression, beyond the comprehension of happy spirits'. True it is that this may refer to an abortive love-affair, but the violence of the expression reflects the sensibility of the victim. Not yet having found her vocation, Alice at eighteen was restless and incomplete. She had realized the satisfaction which lies in intellectual work, but she had realized also the disadvantages of being a woman — the date, remember, is 1864. 'Shall I confess that I have nothing to do? . . . I must try to cultivate that rhyming faculty which I used to have, if it is not quite gone from me. But whatever I write will be melancholy and self-conscious, as are all women's poems.' Matters were perhaps not made any easier by the happier example of her sister Elizabeth who, with her definite and more recognizable gifts as a painter, had been studying diligently at the South Kensington School of Art, in the company as it happened of Kate Greenaway, and subsequently in Florence and Rome, a prelude to the staggering success which attended a battle-piece she exhibited at the Royal Academy. This picture, quietly commissioned by a Manchester industrialist for £100, aroused such emotions in the breasts of the public that a policeman had to be specially detailed to control the crowds surging round it; Queen Victoria borrowed it from the exhibition for a few hours that she might contemplate it privately and at leisure; Elizabeth's name was proposed as the first woman R.A. and Mr. Punch came out with a cartoon of the President suggesting to the annual banquet 'Shall we join the lady?'; the astonished merchant in Manchester, having refused the Prince of Wales, was induced to give up his purchase to the Queen; and Elizabeth received £1200 copyright fee from the engravers. The title of the picture was 'The Roll Call'.

Alice, meanwhile, worked underground like a mole. She must have been greatly preoccupied with her conversion to Catholicism, of which she characteristically says little, but she was also writing poems, receiving much encouragement from a priest whose intelligent perception of her gifts created so close a bond between them that, as Viola Meynell discreetly puts it — and God forbid that I should inquire further into this hint of a private grief — 'in keeping with the strict precautionary rules of his priesthood it was considered best that this friendship should end and that they should see each other no more'. Not all the poems written at this time were included in her first published volume, *Preludes* (1875). A sonnet inspired by that enforced separation was omitted. I do not know whether she omitted it because in her own severe judgment 'whatever I write will be melancholy and self-conscious', or because it was too painfully secret. The absent sonnet was entitled 'Renouncement'. It will be found on page 366 of this book.

'The Roll Call', once having to be guarded from popular enthusiasm by the police, now hangs neglected in some corridor of a royal palace. 'Renouncement', concealed, and not allowed to creep into publication out of its author's notebook, now keeps its place in many anthologies and in even more hearts.

Thus did the sisters make their way into active life, Elizabeth with a blare of trumpets, Alice so quietly that even

the string of a violin would have jarred on that proud and
sensitive organism. I must cut short these few pages of
biography, recording now only the few and simple facts
that controlled Mrs. Meynell's outward life. Friends came
to her — Sir Henry Taylor, Aubrey de Vere, John Ruskin,
Tennyson, and finally Wilfrid Meynell to whom she was
married in the autumn of 1877. Her sister had already
married Major Butler (later Sir William Butler) in the summer
of that year.

The young Meynells settled in London, their hands more
than full. Innumerable friends, two periodicals to edit, articles
and paragraphs to write for both, contributions to write for
other papers, eight children to bear, seven to bring up, one
having died in infancy — one can imagine that Mrs. Meynell
found little leisure for poetry. 'You know what it is when I am
mending frocks and everyone is calling me', she writes to
Coventry Patmore; 'these are all sweet duties but sometimes I
am on the verge of crying'. The usual disasters happened, as
always happen when many children are concerned: two of
them get pneumonia; a third falls thirty feet over the well of
the staircase; and in the midst of it all the demands of journal-
ism have to be met and new trimmings sewn on to juvenile
hats — trimmings which invariably fell off the first time they
were worn. Mrs. Meynell was no needlewoman. A little
salutary vagueness enhanced the mysterious charm of this
unusual mother and father, of whom their daughter relates
that they were commonly so absorbed that the children tem-
porarily lost their names and were all indiscriminately called
'Child'. In point of fact, true offspring of literary parents, they
contrived to make themselves so little of a nuisance that they
were seldom relegated to the nursery. 'It was not because our
parents were willing or able to adapt their conditions to us',
writes Viola Meynell, 'but because we just managed to be
sufficiently adaptable ourselves.' Seven little editors like a lot
of puppies crowded under the table, compiling a newspaper of
their own amongst the swirling skirts of their mother busy
writing on the table above them. This newspaper sometimes

included literary criticism: 'There are few real writers alive now. Mrs. Meynell is certainly one of these few that are in existence. Her thought is a thought which very few writers got. It is mystical but excucite. She is a little obscure to readers who are not up in litruture . . .' And sometimes personal notes of a more astringent temper were handed to her: 'My dear Mother, it really takes off a little my liking for you when you write such unconventionan wash as that article if it is worthy of being called an article.'

Not all the editors were always so well behaved as to restrict themselves to a tart remonstrance in writing. One of them, endowed with a passionate and violent character, shared his siblings' worship of their mother to such a degree that, when she locked herself into the bathroom as she was frequently compelled to do in the attempt to write for a few hours undisturbed, he would kick for a whole hour on the bathroom door roaring for his mother to come out; and when she did finally emerge, would pursue her even down the London street until, driven by the need to escape him, she would hail the hansom cab she could ill afford to take. Yet this very child, as a grown man, could affirm that he had never seen his mother 'flustered'. What a tribute! How did Victorian womanhood manage it?

Under such conditions did she continue to produce what George Meredith called her princely journalism. There were friends, too, who made many claims on her: Meredith himself, Patmore, and the strange unhappy figure of Francis Thompson, their rescued waif who practically made his home in their house. And she was not strong. She suffered frequently from paralysing headaches; yet one gets the impression of a lovely if somewhat withdrawn serenity. Of this withdrawn quality she was herself sadly aware. 'My failure of love to those who loved me can never be cancelled or undone', she wrote, thinking perhaps of Coventry Patmore, from whose excessive devotion she had shrunk to the extent of ceasing to see him. Was it an echo of her father, whose life had been a succession of 'significant negatives'?

The picture is one of deep home-happiness, work, some travel, an active though not militant sympathy with women's suffrage, fame, lectures in America, increasing fame, a proposal to make her Poet-laureate (which succeeded no better thàn the proposal, forty years earlier, to make her sister an R.A.) and finally, as is the lot of the majority, a diminution of physical strength with its simple conclusion, Death. She herself, with her extreme fastidiousness over physical matters, had always protested against any prolonged description of last illnesses or death-bed scenes; she thought them unseemly. This biographical note may therefore be concluded with the shortest possible statement that she died on November 27th, 1922. But if I may dare to abbreviate the final paragraph of her daughter's memoir, I should put it like this: 'She died at dawn, while asleep. She was able to say towards the end, "This is not tragic. I am happy".'

She was happy. Was she? Is ever a poet happy? She was happy in her personal life; she loved the man she had married; she loved the seven editors with their small heads clustered underneath her busy table. When one of them stood up, his head at table height, she would run her pencil, perhaps absent-mindedly, along his eyebrow, saying 'Feather!' All the same, it is hard to resist wondering if the artist in her, as opposed to the woman, was ever troubled by a sense of frustration? Admiration, even veneration, were accorded to her in plenty, but would she not have exchanged them for the one thing denied her, a quiet time? Was she making the most of her gift from the gods? It is perhaps significant that the idea of 'wildness' and the corrective symbol of the shepherd or shepherdess should occur so often in her prose and poetry. It is as though she desired the one, and then, alarmed, sought refuge in the other. Was she born wild? and did circumstances smother her away from her natural inclinations into the safety of the Victorian fold? Who knows what hidden turbulences may have torn her — outwardly so composed, so ready to give lovingly in response to the demands of love, her 'pretty, kind, quick-hearted ways', as the human duty clashed with the even more imperative duty of the artist's conscience? Severely self-disciplined, no sign of the struggle appeared, but how can we disbelieve in moments of rebellion when the urgency of journalism, mingled with the clamour of family life, wrung a private sigh from this fragile, overworked woman remembering that she was also intended to be a poet?

This is not to suggest that her work ever bore any trace of pressure or hurry. On the contrary, the roughest reader could not disregard its elaborate finish, whether in prose or verse. Reading her essays, one is reminded of old jewellers sometimes perceived seated at a cluttered table in the back room of a little shop, a cylindrical magnifying-glass fixed in one eye, bent over a skeleton framework, and with infinite delicacy dripping rather than dropping the tiny glittering stones into the setting from the tip of a pair of pincers. Such precision was Alice Meynell's in her choice of words. She wrote, one might believe, with an etching pen. Nor does this virtue of detail exhaust the sum of her literary merits; were it so, her achievement would remain but a small though exquisite thing. The framework had to be there first, and it was no fumbling mind that had tackled its design. The outlines, the scrolls, the arabesques, the niceties, were drawn finely before the filling-in began, for if the words were gems the tracery that held them together was contrived from the firmest thought. Such elegance could never be vapid, when the intellect gave it significance; it was never fine writing for the sake of fine writing, but simply the most shapely form she could devise to carry the intricacies of the idea. For the idea was always there, and in spite of the compulsory nature of journalism one is left with the impression that she never wrote unless she had something which very definitely demanded to be said.

The clarity which thus irradiates the pages of this craftsman has indeed something of the quality of light, perhaps the light of Rome, which she loved so much, but in any case a Latin light never veiled by northern mists of vagueness or vacillation. There is sensitivity, but no haze. In such a light she had been brought up, and even while running barefoot over the pale Mediterranean sands had been ever conscious of guidance by a rare spirit 'whose silence seemed better worth interpreting than the speech of many another', a spirit by whose 'reticent graces' the second-best was instantly rejected as not for a moment to be tolerated. That father's influence, I suspect, can hardly be sufficiently emphasized. It was he who created the permanent climate in which his daughter then and for ever after dwelt.

Her strength lay, not in violent onslaughts, but in the flexible tendons of the fencer's wrist. Not mighty, she frequented her own by-ways, and was not of those who by their vigour and indignation rank among the moulders of contemporary opinion. In her more random writings, it is usually by implication that she rebukes all that is gross, uncivilized, and cruel. The very titles of some essays shall prove it: 'The hours of sleep', 'The spirit of place', 'The little language', 'Rushes and reeds', 'Laughter', 'Solitude', 'At monastery gates', 'The horizon', 'Shadows', 'Cloud', and that series entitled 'The darling young', studies of childhood which few other women (and certainly no man) could have written. Her colours are tender — I had come near to writing the ignominious word pastel, but that would be an insult to the light so limpid that it makes them almost strong, and even more of an affront to that controlling and unsentimental mind. It is something of an achievement to write on dangerously sentimental subjects ('the darling young' sounds full of pitfalls) without provoking even one anticipated quiver of embarrassment in the reader; and this may be especially true of a woman, whose reader, aware of the sex, is thereby the more inclined for suspicion. Mrs. Meynell is always to be trusted. It is perhaps indicative that 'The darling young' should not be a phrase of her own making, but a quotation — and from a man at that.

Nevertheless it may not be irrelevant here to quote the opening sentences of her essay entitled 'The colour of life'. 'Red', she writes, 'has been praised as the colour of life. But the true colour of life is not red: Red is the colour of violence, or of life broken open . . . Or if red is indeed the colour of life, it is so only on condition that it is not seen. Once fully visible, red is the colour of life violated, and in the act of betrayal and of waste. Red is the secret of life, and not the manifestation thereof. It is one of the things the value of which is secrecy, one of the talents that are to be hidden in a napkin. The true colour of life is the colour of the body, the colour of the covered red, the implicit and not explicit red of the living heart and the pulses. It is the modest colour of the unpublished blood.'

Those words must stand amongst the most revealing she wrote. The true colour of life, for her, was not red. There was something shocking, almost vulgar, to her, in the idea of life broken open. The value lay in secrecy. The decencies must be preserved. Fortunately for her, most of her years were passed in that serene time when the world seemed set for prosperity and peace, a time we now survey with an incredulity amounting almost to anger. When life did begin to break hideously open, after 1914, she responded as she might be expected to respond, with the cry of a civilized soul mortally hurt:

> And while this rose made round her cup
> The armies died convulsed. And when
> This chaste young silver sun went up
> Softly, a thousand shattered men,
> One wet corruption, heaped the plain. . . .

Not that she had ever kept herself entirely aloof from life and from what passes as its reality. The Meynells' house, with all the coming and going, all the rush of topical journalism, all the hospitality somewhat vaguely dispensed, had never set up to be an ivory tower: the wind of outside existence blew freely through it. Public events were discussed there, and a lively argumentative interest taken. But in spite of this it must still remain true that to Mrs. Meynell the colour of life was not

red. Every now and again she might be greatly stirred, as by
the cause of Women's Suffrage and later by the First War —
in a woman of intellect and feeling it could scarcely be other-
wise — but I suspect that temperamentally the more delicate
movements of the mind held a greater charm for her. Not that
she was ever soft in her judgments. Her children have testified
that her disapprobation, never explicitly expressed but the
more insupportably implied, was the most desolating snub
they could suffer. And when we consider her essays in
literary criticism, we shall find her strictures were equally un-
mistakable, though, by the very nature of the medium she had
to employ, more plainly set forth; plainly, but always with her
unfailing though deadly courtesy. The real strength and
originality of her mind are nowhere better shown than in her
literary severities: it was a brave assessor that could dare to
exclude Gray's 'Elegy' from her anthology compiled by 'a
gatherer intent upon nothing except the quality of poetry'.
The 'Elegy' failed to satisfy this gatherer's standard. 'It is',
she writes, 'so near to the work of genius as to be most directly,
closely and immediately rebuked by genius.' Mediocrity is
the now expected word; and sure enough, a line or two later,
she gently and logically uses it in the further disparagement of
poor Gray. Never mesmerized by reputation, she would hold
everything up to the light and subject it to a fresh, hard
scrutiny. Gibbon will not pass muster: his Latinity has had a
disastrous effect; look how Charlotte Brontë has been con-
taminated by it! Tennyson, her much admired and most
sensitively understood Tennyson, has sometimes 'a little un-
welcome manner' for which he must be reproved. Swinburne
comes in for a sharper castigation, though after pinking him
neatly for his 'little intellect, paltry degree of sincerity, rachitic
passion, and tumid fancy', she turns with her usual generosity
to the happier task of praise. The major explosion of her ire
is reserved for what seems to her the intolerable vulgarity
of Victorian caricature. Douglas Jerrold, John Leech, and
Charles Keene all come under the lash — and what a lash it
was for once, cutting back at her as she cracked it even as it

had cut and curled round her victims. A whole family of words like *obscene, gross, ignominy, the old common jape*, not usually to be found in her vocabulary, are all here, scathing and hurtful, compressed into three pages which wounded her as she wrote. But a crusading spirit was here urgent, for it was not merely the vulgarity of the caricature which offended her, but the fact that 'literary and pictorial alike, it had for its aim the vulgarizing of the married woman'. She might well have omitted the word *married*, since any coarse ridicule of women in general would equally have aroused the championship of her feminism; yet again, one recalls the intimate gentleness and profound compassion of such phrases as 'There is no innocent sleep so innocent as sleep shared between a woman and a child, the little breath hurrying beside the longer, as a child's foot runs'. That was written by a tender, not a ferocious, woman. It was written by a woman who had borne many children, and who had taken some of them, sometimes, in their moments of alarm, into the warmth of her reassuring bed.

This mother, this journalist, this hostess, this poet, held strong views about the position of women in a world controlled by men. It was a subject on which she had early made up her mind. At the age of eighteen she had written: 'Of all the crying evils in this depraved earth, ay, of all the sins of which the cry must come to Heaven, the greatest, judged by all the laws of God and humanity, is the miserable selfishness of man that keeps women from work — work, the salvation of the world . . .' and after making allowance for the exaggeration of adolescence, since it seems probable that in her journey through life Mrs. Meynell had subsequently discovered the existence of even more loudly crying evils, those were the views which she retained in her maturer judgment. Her whole personal life had been womanly; her clothes, her manner, her quiet assumption of her right as a woman towards whom homage was due, all proclaimed her femineity, but over the question of equality in work she was unaffected. She 'held very insistently the belief that in the practice of literature and the arts women and men must . . . be tried by the same tests and ask no indulgence, the one from the other, on the score of sex'; this was written of her by one who should be well qualified to know, Wilfrid Meynell himself. Most logically she abhorred such designations as *poetess*, *authoress*. *Actress* she would accept, since here the differentiation, for obvious reasons, must be recognized as necessary; but in literature and the other arts she held that all creative artists should be regarded as mentally androgynous. It is difficult to find oneself more vehemently in agreement. Yet, with expected common sense, very much in line with the views later expressed by Virginia Woolf in *A room of one's own*, Mrs. Meynell held that women had a particular contribution to make. She could also be sarcastic on the subject of those men who were themselves sarcastic on the subject of women; and when Mrs. Meynell chose to be sarcastic she could carry it off as trenchantly as any Victorian husband. 'The characteristics of men', she wrote; 'that, at least, is the phrase which women will use when they acquire the way, so wonderful in men, in writing of the other half of the race as an accident and a subject of accidental study . . . Ah, do we ever pause and ask ourselves how much of interest, variety, and charm human life owes to men — to their fondness, their faithfulness, their very unreasonableness, their very faults? Humanity could ill spare them — woman's best companions'. The paraphrase is witty and exact. Women's own contribution, however, was a more serious matter than any jokes she might please to make over the old controversy; and even as she had never desired to imitate man in her personal life, so did she recognize that different brands of talent might, without derogation to one or the other, be apportioned between the two sexes. The genus of Humanity, she wrote, was obviously larger than the species, Womanhood; but the species had its own value, keen and intense. With all her balance, and the absence of fanaticism one would expect from so poised and controlled a character, she could put her finger very neatly on some of the fallacies involved in the argument; especially does she note, in her uninsistent way, one point too often overlooked — 'the habit by which some men reproach a silly woman through her sex, whereas a silly man is not reproached through his'.

It seems inevitable, after these allusions to Mrs. Meynell's attitude towards what is tiresomely called the woman question, to consider her own poems in the light of her femineity. Could a reader tell whether the writer was man or woman? I should not presume to decide. Nature produces virile (not necessarily mannish) women, and feminine (not necessarily effeminate) men; and generalizations take small account of the finer degrees on the sex thermometer where the mercury ascends or descends as in Hot and Cold, Maximum and Minimum, sometimes levelly balanced, sometimes disparate. On the whole, I should incline to attribute Mrs. Meynell's poems to a woman; but in any case, to a highly conscious artist.

This is the interesting point about her poems: she knew so exactly what she was about. From the technical point of view, every poet has much to learn from her. The right word has never been righter. It seems as though she must have lingered long over her choice, yet at the same time she contrives to convince us that the inevitable word must have presented itself spontaneously with the thought — it could not be otherwise. Quotations are unsatisfying, taken out of their context; but nevertheless let us consider the perfection of certain lines — these, for instance, concluding two verses addressed to the sea-nymph Thetis:

> I saw — past Wordsworth and the rest —
> Her natural, Greek, and silver feet.

Is that perhaps a little too deliberate? a trifle chilly? At least no such reproach can be brought against 'The Watershed', lines written between Munich and Verona. Here the emotion is by no means swamped by the artistry; they fit each other as the glove the hand; the whole poem is a cry of the excitement we have all experienced on attaining towards the south once more:

> ... O to see
> Of all the southward brooks the first!
> The travelling heart went free
> With endless streams; that strife was stopped;
> And down a thousand vales I dropped,
> I flowed to Italy,

the image perfectly married to the thought, and perfectly resolved in that single, indicated, awaited word, 'I *flowed* to Italy'.

Such examples could be multiplied. The famous sonnet with its bravely monosyllabic, 'I run, I run', as daring in its repetitive simplicity as Lear's 'Never, never, never ...'; little unfamous lines like

> The rooted liberty of flowers in breeze;

and above all, I think, one verse from a poem about rivers, which to my mind exemplifies the whole quality of Alice Meynell as a great craftsman in the difficult art. None but a great craftsman could have compressed so complicated an idea into so few and simple words. None would have used the cliché 'shining eyes' in so novel and bright a sense — all the ripples of a river are in it. None would have expressed, with no qualifying adjective, the immense implications lying behind the ever-renewed waters and the imperial city — the whole of youth and age is there. Much, much is packed into these two lines; a whole historical philosophy with a poet's vision. It must have been very difficult, yet with what apparent ease she achieves it!

> This moment's Tiber with his shining eyes
> Never saw Rome before.

The bulk of Alice Meynell's poetry is not large. The source of inspiration, like those streams which flow once or twice only in a decade, may not have been very strong or very constant; or possibly the pressure of other occupations may have interfered with its uprising. It seems that she herself was sometimes resigned to its disappearance. 'Who looked for thee', she writes in an early poem,

> Who looked for thee, thou little song of mine?
> This winter of a silent poet's heart
> Is suddenly sweet with thee. But what thou art,
> Mid-winter flower, I wish I could divine.
>
> Art thou a last one, orphan of thy line?
> Did the dead summer's last warmth foster thee?
> Or is Spring folded up unguessed in me,
> And stirring out of sight — and thou the sign?

Whatever the reason for its rarity, the source when it founted was always crystalline. A profoundly religious feeling illumined it; a gentle but incurable melancholy; an acute sense of Time and of the passage of years. 'Unambitious, born modest', George Meredith wrote of her poetry; but a poet preoccupied with such subjects cannot be called slight. The poetry of Alice Meynell is an integral expression of a complete personality — authentic, delicate, and fine.

It must remain according to the taste of the reader to decide on the differing value of her contributions to English letters. Shall it lie in her poetry or in her prose? And if in her prose, then which of the essays shall we select for the highest commendation — those that strayed from topic to topic, or those that more specifically concentrated on the subject she knew best, her own craft of literature? It is possible that her reputation may grow increasingly as a critic, independent and fearless, incisive and acute, uninfluenced by fashion. It took, for instance, a bold perceptive spirit to pulverize Swinburne as she did. Undergraduates might swagger arm-in-arm down the Turl chanting 'Dolores', but Mrs. Meynell saw through the wordy fluff. It must have taken some courage to remark of Miss Austen that her art was not of the highest but of 'an admirable secondary quality'. Her appreciation was equally noble when she bestowed it: witness her short note on one aspect of Shakespeare, called 'Superfluous Kings'. She recognized greatness when she saw it, no less than she mercilessly pricked any bubble she might observe floating about in gay but insubstantial colours.

The first part of this book will perpetuate her achievement as a critical essayist. Too penetratingly wise to be called clever, too soberly thoughtful to be called brilliant, as a critic of her own art she yet retains in controlled degree these two stimulating qualities. She is never heavy-handed, never dull; and never, at any moment, does one suffer from the impression of an opinion presented at second-hand.

V. S.-W.

PREFATORY POEMS

HER PORTRAIT

OH, but the heavenly grammar did I hold
Of that high speech which angels' tongues turn gold!
So should her deathless beauty take no wrong,
Praised in her own great kindred's fit and cognate tongue:
Or if that language yet with us abode
Which Adam in the garden talked with God!
But our untempered speech descends —poor heirs!
Grimy and rough-cast still from Babel's bricklayers:
Curse on the brutish jargon we inherit,
Strong but to damn, not memorize, a spirit!
A cheek, a lip, a limb, a bosom, they
Move with light ease in speech of working-day;
And women we do use to praise even so.
But here the gates we burst, and to the temple go.
Their praise were her dispraise: who dare, who dare,
Adulate the seraphim for their burning hair?
How, if with them I dared, here should I dare it?
How praise the woman, who but know the spirit?
How praise the colour of her eyes, uncaught
While they were coloured with her varying thought?
How her mouth's shape, who only use to know
What tender shape her speech will fit it to?
Or her lips' redness when their joinèd veil
Song's fervid hand has parted till it wore them pale?

If I would praise her soul (temerarious if!),
All must be mystery and hieroglyph.
Heaven, which not oft is prodigal of its more
To singers, in their song too great before
(By which the hierarch of large poesy is
Restrained to his one sacred benefice),

27

Only for her the salutary awe
Relaxes and stern canon of its law;
To her alone concedes pluralities,
In her alone to reconcile agrees
The Muse, the Graces, and the Charities;
To her, who can the trust so well conduct
To her it gives the use, to us the usufruct.

What of the dear administress then may
I utter, though I spoke her own carved perfect way?
What of her daily gracious converse known,
Whose heavenly despotism must needs dethrone
And subjugate all sweetness but its own?
Deep in my heart subsides the infrequent word,
And there dies slowly throbbing like a wounded bird.
What of her silence, that outsweetens speech?
What of her thoughts, high marks for mine own thoughts to reach?
Yet, (Chaucer's antique sentence so to turn)
Most gladly will she teach, and gladly learn;
And teaching her, by her enchanting art,
The master threefold learns for all he can impart.
Now all is said, and all being said, —aye me!
There yet remains unsaid the very She.
Nay, to conclude (so to conclude I dare),
If of her virtues you evade the snare,
Then for her faults you'll fall in love with her.

Alas, and I have spoken of her Muse —
Her Muse, that died with her auroral dews!
Learn, the wide cherubim from harps of gold
Seduce a trepidating music manifold;
But the superior seraphim do know
None other music but to flame and glow.
So she first lighted on our frosty earth,
A sad musician, of cherubic birth,
Playing to alien ears —which did not prize
The uncomprehended music of the skies —

The exiled airs of her far Paradise.
But soon, from her own harpings taking fire,
In love and light her melodies expire.
Now Heaven affords her, for her silenced hymn,
A double portion of the seraphim.

At the rich odours from her heart that rise,
My soul remembers its lost Paradise,
And antenatal gales blow from Heaven's shores of spice;
I grow essential all, uncloaking me
From this encumbering virility,
And feel the primal sex of heaven and poetry :
And, parting from her, in me linger on
Vague snatches of Uranian antiphon.

How to the petty prison could she shrink
Of femineity? —Nay, but I think
In a dear courtesy her spirit would
Woman assume, for grace to womanhood.
Or, votaress to the virgin Sanctitude
Of reticent withdrawal's sweet, courted pale,
She took the cloistral flesh, the sexual veil,
Of her sad, aboriginal sisterhood;
The habit of cloistral flesh which founding Eve indued.

Thus do I know her. But for what men call
Beauty —the loveliness corporeal,
Its most just praise a thing unproper were
To singer or to listener, me or her.
She wears that body but as one indues
A robe, half careless, for it is the use;
Although her soul and it so fair agree,
We sure may, unattaint of heresy,
Conceit it might the soul's begetter be.
The immortal could we cease to contemplate,
The mortal part suggests its every trait.
God laid his fingers on the ivories
Of her pure members as on smoothèd keys,

And there out-breathed her spirit's harmonies.
I speak a little proudly: —I disdain
To count the beauty worth my wish or gain,
Which the dull daily fool can covet or obtain.
I do confess the fairness of the spoil,
But from such rivalry it takes a soil.
For her I'll proudlier speak: —how could it be
That I should praise the gilding on the psaltery?
'Tis not for her to hold that prize a prize,
Or praise much praise, though proudest in its wise,
To which even hopes of merely women rise.
Such strife would to the vanquished laurels yield,
Against her suffered to have lost a field.
Herself must with herself be sole compeer,
Unless the people of her distant sphere
Some gold migration send to melodize the year.
But first our hearts must burn in larger guise,
To reformate the uncharitable skies,
And so the deathless plumage to acclimatize:
Since this, their sole congener in our clime,
Droops her sad, ruffled thoughts for half the shivering time.

Yet I have felt what terrors may consort
In women's cheeks, the Graces' soft resort;
My hand hath shook at gentle hands' access,
And trembled at the waving of a tress;
My blood known panic fear, and fled dismayed,
Where ladies' eyes have set their ambuscade;
The rustle of a robe hath been to me
The very rattle of love's musketry;
Although my heart hath beat the loud advance,
I have recoiled before a challenging glance,
Proved gay alarms where warlike ribbons dance.
And from it all, this knowledge have I got, —
The whole that others have, is less than they have not:
All of which makes other women noted fair,
Unnoted would remain and overshone in her.

How should I gauge what beauty is her dole,
Who cannot see her countenance for her soul,
As birds see not the casement for the sky?
And, as 'tis check they prove its presence by,
I know not of her body till I find
My flight debarred the heaven of her mind.
Hers is the face whence all should copied be,
Did God make replicas of such as she;
Its presence felt by what it does abate,
Because the soul shines through tempered and mitigate:
Where —as a figure labouring at night
Beside the body of a splendid light —
Dark Time works hidden by its luminousness;
And every line he labours to impress
Turns added beauty, like the veins that run
Athwart a leaf which hangs against the sun.

There regent Melancholy wide controls;
There Earth —and Heaven-love play for aureoles;
There Sweetness out of Sadness breaks at fits,
Like bubbles on dark water, or as flits
A sudden silver fin through its deep infinities;
There amorous Thought has sucked pale Fancy's breath,
And Tenderness sits looking toward the lands of Death:
There Feeling stills her breathing with her hand,
And Dream from Melancholy part wrests the wand;
And on this lady's heart, looked you so deep,
Poor Poetry has rocked himself to sleep:
Upon the heavy blossom of her lips
Hangs the bee Musing; nigh her lids eclipse
Each half-occulted star beneath that lies;
And, in the contemplation of those eyes,
Passionless passion, wild tranquillities.

FRANCIS THOMPSON

First published in 1823

ALICIA

AH, sole essential good of earth,
And sweetest accident of Heaven,
Their best rays, on her lucky birth,
    Beamed from the planets seven.

Her body, too, is so like her —
    Sharp honey assuaged with milk,
Straight as a stalk of lavender,
    Soft as a rope of silk.

COVENTRY PATMORE

Written in 1894
First printed in 1922

TO A. M.

A STATELY flower in my garden grows,
Whose colour is the dawn-sky's maiden blue;
The loveliest to my Lady's thinking too.
And when the Lord of June bids her disclose
Her very heart, all bashfully she throws
An inner petal o'er the orange hue,
As one last plea; submitting to his view,
Yet virginally majestic while he glows.
For reasons known to us we give the name
'Alicia Coerulea' to that flower,
Sweet as the Sea-born borne on the sea-wave:
That innocent in shame where is no shame;
That proud Reluctant; that fair slave of power,
Who conquers most when she is most the slave.

GEORGE MEREDITH

Written in 1896
First published in 1923

PREFATORY POEMS

ALICE MEYNELL

HER *Thought was stone: O frugal poet, hard*
Cut the spare chisel on each separate gem —
Jaspar and onyx, emerald and sard:
　Craft and integrity have fashioned them.

V. SACKVILLE-WEST

First printed in 1922

IN MEMORIAM: ALICE MEYNELL

WHEN *none recall*
　Upon her lips the accents heard,
And the last memory dies of all,
Then shall another silence fall
　　Than this, of her remembered word.

　When none rejoice
　Alive, in her remembered voice,
And not an echo lives of all, —
Another silence than she left
　　To us bereft
　Shall, envious, on our silence fall.

WINIFRED LUCAS

First printed in 1923

THE LIBRARY, GREATHAM

(A Memory of Alice Meynell)

THERE *on the hearth a wink of wood-fire glows,*
　But through the door a breath of wildwood Spring
Along the litter of the table flows
　Silverly to the wall, illumining
Those bookshelves where, no less serene and cool,
Wisdom and song still keep their quiet school.

There would her spirit exquisitely take,
  On such a wayward breath, the scent and hue
And stir of wildings everywhere that wake
  On lawn and woodland, by their certain clue
Tracing to far horizons the unrest
Of young desire on Earth's maternal breast.

And still her presence is familiar there
  And still remote; coming and going feet
And voices bringing in the garden air
  Make with her other world a world complete;
While, tender with compassion, her dark eyes
Cease not from intercourse with distant skies.

G. ROSTREVOR HAMILTON

First printed in 1941

FOR A. M.'s ANNIVERSARY

TIME is not mocked. Did you when you were five
  Play ring-a-roses round the slow-foot second?
Go distant journeys twixt the tick and tock?
Perceive your mother, between beck and beckoned,
Age, sicken, die — and come again alive
(O wonderful!) with the rustle of her frock?
If I slipped sideways, breath-bound, swift and supple,
I could pass between the clock-beats to the closet
Not scraping either second of its bloom;
Then from their pegs, like clothes, new lives uncouple,
And try them on, 'gainst my own shape's deposit.
I was the He, the Hunter. Time was the stay-at-home.

My mother died when I was grown a man.
Time came to look. Time lingered. Time began.

FRANCIS MEYNELL

First published in 1944

34

Alice Meynell
PROSE AND POETRY

ALICE MEYNELL AET:47

A pencil portrait (1894) by John Sargent

LITERATURE AND LANGUAGE

Superfluous Kings

Which had superfluous kings for messengers
Not many moons gone by.

Antony and Cleopatra.

As the kings lag, and then pass away from the stage of the world, many men will ask what there is to regret. Assuredly nothing, if not royalty in the mind of Shakespeare. Mankind will in time probably forget or deny that there was ever anything in the life of the world answering to Shakespeare's royalty in Perdita, or to his princeliness in Arviragus and Guiderius, or to his kingliness in Lear, or to his glory in Cleopatra. It may be so, as to the world; there may have been nothing thus answerable. But there was Shakespeare.

And our regrets in regard to him cover all his regalities — the hidden and hereditary and unconscious, and the conscious and braggart and manifest: Perdita's dignity among the romps, and her sportive disputes as to Art and Nature among the clowns, her unflushed composure amid the junketings, and also Lear's loud and indignant death. The splendour of Shakespeare's veneration for kings is perhaps deeper where the kingliness — the blood of it — is unrevealed, as in the shepherdess of *The Winter's Tale*, for here it is matter of Shakespeare's faith. So with the brothers of Imogen who, by the way — and not merely by the way — like her, discuss flowers — 'Then to arms!' They too have the implicit distinction, unknown to the world of their exile, but known to Shakespeare, who is aware of their blood and lineage. Here, and in *The Winter's Tale*, Shakespeare makes his resolute and implicit act of belief in the blood of kings.

In *Lear* that faith suffers outrage and defies it. Many years ago the great actor, Rossi, who did not gain in England such honour as was rendered to Salvini — I fear because his physical personal dignity was not so obvious as Salvini's — played King Lear in Italian. But there was one cry, one royal proclamation, that could not be removed from the English. So Rossi said 'every inch' in English. It needed Shakespeare's word to vindicate Shakespeare's royalism. (One might make sport of any kind of translation: '*ogni centimetro*', 'every centimetre a king', is good farce.) No Italian will serve; the Latin mind has not this degree of imaginative reverence, nor has the Italian language the faculty of giving sudden greatness to a customary word.

But Shakespeare, conceiving for royalty not only 'the beauteous Majesty of Denmark', and the 'courteous action' of the dead — 'being so majestical' — and the dignity of Hermione's daughter, and the tempest of Lear's elemental tragedy, will not consent to touch us with nothing more than pity and terror. He confronts us with the uttermost of pride of life in the royalty he sings; confronts us — no, rather brings us to our knees before the arrogant splendour he conceives:

> Where souls do couch on flowers, we'll hand in hand,
> And with our sprightly port make the ghosts gaze.

It is the pride of life and the pride of death. Only hand in hand with a queen does Antony venture on the prophecy of that immortal vanity. If to him are given the most surprising lines in any of the tragedies, it is only as the lover of a queen that he has the right to them. To him is assigned that startling word, the incomparable word of amorous and tender ceremony — 'Egypt'.

I am dying, Egypt, dying.

That territorial name, murmured to his love in the hour of death, and in her arms — I know not in the records of all genius any other such august farewell. Lear's word is outdone here. Lear a king in every inch of his aged body, but Cleopatra a queen in every league of her ancient realm. Has not majesty spoken its one unexpected word in the mouth of such a lover?

Superfluous kings — Shakespeare's irony could find no other adjective so overcharged with insolence as this. Kings must be as he conceived them in order to that antithesis:

superfluous kings for messengers.

But an antithesis more complete than that of downfall and of servitude is that of mortality. The humiliation of the beaten monarch leaves the Shakespearian conception of kingliness face to face with the mere fortunes of war; the derision of the word 'superfluous' implies, in reversal, an inalienable dignity; so in the act of dying, the visible act, done in life; so with 'sad stories of the death of kings'. The final contradiction is not here; but in the grave itself, in the hidden burial, out of the sight of the populace: it needs the utmost of Shakespeare's passion of royalty to answer to that depth. And here is poetry, not by him, but wonderfully worthy of him, that tells us of

High-born dust
In vaults, thin courts of poor unflattered kings.

Shakespeare only, besides Young, could have written this.

Literature, then, will lose this glory, and with this glory this humiliation. Who will say which is greater, the thesis or the antithesis? But they cannot be parted to be compared. There they are, in our national literature, and cannot be effaced. But who shall hinder their becoming, for the student, first a matter of mere literary interest, then a matter of mere literary curiosity, next a matter of some new derision? (We need no new derisions: our wits are apt to mockery.) Is it well that any one of Shakespeare's many passions should come under our frigid inspection, to be examined so?

When kings are in fact superfluous, Shakespeare's great word 'superfluous' will be cancelled out; when kings are no longer flattered, Young's great word 'unflattered' will be a futile word; when there are no full assiduous courts, the 'thin courts' will suggest no spectres. Regret is for Shakespeare, as has been said; not for Saul, or Louis the Fourteenth, or Charles the Twelfth. But, short of Shakespeare's devotion, there will be some sentiment damaged. When the mortality of kings is no sharper sarcasm than is the mortality we all inherit, then the lamps and the gold that enshrine the bony heads of Caspar, Melchior, and Balthasar at Cologne may take their place, outside of cathedrals, with the unnamed relics of the shepherds who preceded the kings to the manger.

Shakespeare's greatest splendour, then, that so shines down the splendour of history and the world, is under sentence, and under sentence his greatest compassion, and under sentence his greatest terror, and under sentence his greatest irony. And I have placed at the head of these pages a word of neither terror nor compassion, because the word of irony implies the rest.

Heroines

THOUGHTS about Shakespeare cannot pretend to be new. Therefore it is enough that the thoughts of us all should be practised rather than spoken. It might, for example, be insolent for any man to say that Shakespeare is a magnificent humorist for every age, yet to the thinking of our age a very tedious wit; but the man who would not venture to say this aloud knows his *Second Part of Henry IV*, for its humour, through and through, and has not read *Love's Labour's Lost*, for its wit, more than perhaps once. We all know Shakespeare as it were privately, and thus a demand for words about him touches our autobiography. What we think about Shakespeare is part of the public's privacy as well as of our own. For we are all more than content to be like Poins, to whom Prince Henry says: 'Thou art a blessed fellow to think as every man thinks; never a man's thought keeps in the roadway better than thine.' We are safe in the middle of the roadway in our thoughts of Shakespeare. Very few men have tried to be original in regard to Shakespeare, and their dreary experiment had best be forgotten. It will probably not be imitated. Shakespeare's greater readers have done no more than multiply one affection, one praise. Ruskin and Emerson are only more articulate than the rest of their respective nations. It is true that Ruskin seemed to make a kind of discovery when he showed this fact in the dramas — that Shakespeare has no heroes, but only heroines. The 'discovery' only *seems*; Ruskin states the matter, but every simple reader knows that Juliet was steadfast and wise in stratagem and Romeo rash, Juliet single-hearted and Romeo changeable; that Imogen was true and that Posthumus Leonatus was by her magnanimity awarded a kind of triumph when all he should have hoped from her mercy was pardon; that Hermione forgives her lord his suspicion, and the theft of her child, and sixteen years of innocent exile, without a word of forgiveness. Every reader knows the indomitable will of Helena, who condescends to pursue and win a paltry boy, and sweetly thinks herself rewarded by the possession of that poor quarry; the lovely simplicity of Desdemona, which lies as that of a frightened child lies, to save herself from the violence of the noble savage whom she loves; the inarticulate and modest devotion of Virgilia to a great man not too great for insane self-love;

Cordelia's integrity and self-possession among raving men; Isabella's courage in face of a coward brother; Viola's valour and her single love in search of the *contre-coup* of her Duke's affections; Julia, true to a juggling lover; Queen Katharine betrayed by a hypocrite; nay, the maid called Barbara who was forsaken. Barbara, Desdemona, Juliet, Imogen, Virgilia, Miranda, Viola, Hermione, Perdita, Julia, Helena, the other Helena, Mariana, Rosalind, were all enamoured, all impassioned, and all constant.

Why did Shakespeare make heroines and not heroes? It was assuredly because Shakespeare had a master passion for chastity, and because this quality was most credible, in a world not governed by theology, there where he attributed it, lodged it, and adored it — in this *candidatus exercitus* of women.

There is one thing that additionally and adventitiously proves this passion of Shakespeare's spirit, and that is his abstention from the brilliancy and beauty wherewith he knows how to invest the wanton: his vitality in Cressida, his incomparable splendour in Cleopatra. Yet stay — is not Cressida alone in inconstancy? and is it not a senseless action to name Cressida in Cleopatra's glorious company? Shakespeare, able to make unparalleled Cressidas, made only one. Cleopatra is clean, not by water but by her 'integrity of fire'. She too is constant, she too is 'for the dark', for eternity. She entrusts her passion to another world. Let her stand close to the majestic side of Hermione, even though Hermione might not permit Perdita to kiss her.

Does this recognition of Shakespeare's master passion look like the claim to a discovery? Heaven forbid, for it should not.

Harlequin Mercutio

THE first time that Mercutio fell upon the English stage, there fell with him a gay and hardly human figure; it fell, perhaps finally, for English drama. That manner of man — Arlecchino, or Harlequin — had outlived his playmates, Pantaleone, Brighella, Colombina, and the Clown. A little of Pantaleone survives in old Capulet, a little in the father of the Shrew, but the life of Mercutio in the one play, and of the subordinate Tranio in the other — both Harlequins — is less quickly spent, less easily put out, than the smouldering of the old man. Arlecchino frolics in and out of the tragedy and comedy of Shakespeare, until he thus dies in his lightest, his brightest, his most vital shape, Mercutio.

Arlecchino, the tricksy and shifty spirit, the contriver, the busybody, the trusty rogue, the wonder-worker, the man in disguise, the mercurial one, lives on buoyantly in France to the age of Molière. He is officious and efficacious in the skin of Mascarille and Ergaste and Scapin; but he tends to be a lackey, with a reference rather to Antiquity and the Latin comedy than to the Middle Ages, as on the English stage his mere memory survives differently to a later age in the person of 'Charles, his friend'. What convinces me that he virtually died with Mercutio is chiefly this — that this comrade of Romeo's lives so keenly as to be fully capable of the death that he takes at Tybalt's sword-point; he lived indeed, he dies indeed. Another thing that marks a close of a career of ages is his loss of his long customary good luck. Who ever heard of Arlecchino unfortunate before, at fault with his sword-play, overtaken by tragedy? His time had surely come. The gay companion was to bleed; Tybalt's sword had made a way. 'Twas not so deep as a well nor so wide as a church-door, but it served.

Some confusion comes to pass among the typical figures of the primitive Italian play, because Harlequin, on that conventional little stage of the past, has a hero's place, whereas when he interferes in human affairs he is only the auxiliary. He might be lover and bridegroom on the primitive stage, in the comedy of these few and unaltered types; but when Pantaloon, Clown, and Harlequin play with really human beings, then Harlequin can be no more than a friend of the hero, the friend of the bridegroom. The five figures of the old stage dance attendance; they play around the business of those who have the dignity of mortality; they, poor immortals — a clown who does not die, a pantaloon never far from death, who yet does not die, a Columbine who never attains Desdemona's death of innocence, or Juliet's death of rectitude and passion — flit in the backward places of the stage.

Ariel fulfils his office, and is not of one kind with those he serves. Is there a memory of Harlequin in that delicate figure? Something of the subservient immortality, of the light indignity, proper to Pantaleone, Brighella, Arlecchino, Colombina, and the Clown, hovers away from the stage when Ariel is released from the trouble of human things.

Immortality, did I say? It was immortality until Mercutio fell. And if some claim be made to it still because Harlequin has transformed so many scenes for the pleasure of so many thousand children, since Mercutio died, I must reply that our modern Harlequin is no more than a *marionnette*; he has returned whence he came. A man may play him, but he is — as he was first of all — a doll. From doll-hood Arlecchino took life, and, so promoted, flitted through a thousand comedies, only to be again what he first was; save that, as once a doll played the man, so now a man plays the doll. It is but a memory of Arlecchino that our children see, a poor statue or image endowed with mobility rather than with life.

With Mercutio vanished the light heart that had given to the serious ages of the world an hour's refuge from the unforgotten burden of responsible conscience; the light heart assumed, borrowed, made dramatically the spectator's own. We are not serious now, and no heart now is quite light, even for an hour.

An Elizabethan Lyrist

ENGLAND has little primitive poetry, because the Reformers not only broke graven images but destroyed libraries, and gave some centuries of minor literature to the flames. We have much ado in raking together a few stones of their hacking and scattering, but fire has saved their posterity the trouble of trying to restore an annihilated national poetry. Our writers, then (with the obvious exceptions), begin soon after the invention of movable type, and so modern are they that the Elizabethans must serve us for comparative antiquity. The language was mobile between Elizabeth and James, tuned by the hands of the masters whose lives lasted from one developing time into another, and who were themselves England, having history in common with their country.

But Robert Greene was absolutely an Elizabethan — man and boy. He was born in the year of the Queen's accession, and died while she was dancing, an old man of thirty-four, dropsical and horrible, full of repentance, as were then all of his manner of life when they had an illness sufficiently long to give them time. Greene died from too much banqueting, apparently upon the crudest luxuries, but his sorry death-bed gave him room for ample self-reproach, and doubtless Christopher Marlowe also would have left a record of his repentance had the manner of his departure, at even an earlier age than his friend's, been less violent. In later years Carew asked pardon, with many cries, for the greater number of his verses; and, indeed, during these two bright centuries you may hear, if you turn your ear that way, the loud lamentation of poet after dying poet, a single outcry at intervals; not a death-bed without the clamour that closed the song. It is a parting cry, so poignant and sudden, that the air rings with it even while the succeeding singer is heard to be preluding, undaunted for the present. Greene had not a little to repent of in his actions, but nothing to retract in his songs; therefore, the reader who had not beheld his life — his wife was left at 'six and seven', as

45

he phrases it, and certainly very forlorn — has little to do with the grief, pain, and fear of the closing scene, and may well be content with the sweetness of the songs. They were sweet and single, like tunes unharmonized. Without following the fashion of using the terms of one art to describe another, we may permit ourselves this mere imagery: the single note of music to represent the sixteenth-century lyric, harmonics for the seventeenth, counterpoint for the nineteenth. Greene's famous 'Sephestia's Song to Her Child' (by far his best) is the only lyric in which so much as two notes are to be heard; and the double string makes the sound more human.

It is not human to be single as the songs of Greene are single; the fading of pleasure, the cruelty of beauty, the inconstancy of love, the happy lot of the shepherd, and the cares of kings — each thing, one at a time, is so unaccompanied that you wonder how a primitive poet should have had time to reject all checking, mingling, and qualifying thoughts together. For it is hardly youth, hardly inexperience that this simplicity suggests, but rather a mind made up, a mind bent on creating other conditions than those which govern an actual world of which the poet has somewhat grown tired.

'Sephestia's Song', however, has the thrill of sweetly jarring notes in the lines that tell the parting of father and mother over their laughing child — lines that seem to have haunted the ear, if not the mind, of Blake in his own song of birth. Blake's verse has a tempestuous and threatening spiritual wildness of which Greene did not know the language; and it is only in the leaping metre, the clamour of the rhymes that seem striving to be heard above a deafening childish noise, that the two songs have so much likeness.

> The wanton smiled, father wept,
> Mother cried, baby leapt;
> More he crowed, more we cried.

There is a vociferation, a distraction, and a dandling of the child, and you hear also the crying that the mother is seeking to still with her recital of that late scene of sorrow — 'Weep not, my wanton'.

Next in beauty to 'Sephestia's Song' comes, perhaps, 'The Praise of Faunia':

> Ah, were she pitiful as she is fair,
> Or but as mild as she is seeming so,

is a beginning that sounds like a less grave, less strong, and less masculine Shakespeare sonnet. There is sweet line after line in this poem, and many such a phrase as 'the morning-singer's swelling throat' and 'When she sings, all singers else be still!' But the poem is famous chiefly, it may be guessed, for the sake of the final couplet, which has a far more modern kind of ample and intelligible beauty:

> O glorious sun, imagine me the west!
> Shine in my arms, and set thou in my breast!

Next comes that pretty song 'Radagon in Dianam', which is to be praised not as a whole, but for some stanzas in which the cypresses keep a golden sun away from a 'valley gaudy green', and from nymphs in white. There never was any scene at once warmer and more fresh. The fountain is cool in a shade that the sun never shot an arrow through, but the sense of outer sunshine is intense and clear, and the dark trees seem to flame blackly, as they do on such a sky. 'Outer darkness', by the way, is a familiar phrase, but 'outer sunshine' is a presence hardly removed in the southern summer.

This vivid impression from Greene's poem is caused by the most careless of verses. As a lyrist, he never leant hard upon anything; he has the lightest foot, and seems rather to whistle than to sing his tunes upon the way. So lightly is the verse given to the wind that you are apt to read it as carelessly, and so to lose something. This Song of the Fountain, for instance, should be read with more leisure than at a glance it seems to merit.

Greene is dull to any reader who does not take the pains to cancel all the conventions of the times that followed his Elizabethan day. The pure fountains, the nymphs, and the other valleys, gaudy green, must be simply forgotten; and the task is not difficult. Greene has all the good luck by his Elizabethanism — inalienable good luck, which was neither to be repeated by others, nor to be taken from his own head upon whom it alighted first. We, who have been wearied by succeeding nymphs, need not be wearied by those nymphs that were his — and this not because his were best, but because his were first.

But it is hardly possible not to find him somewhat dull, especially when he is not at his best, because he has so little to say. There never was a poet who said less. These poems of his, after all, were, in his own estimation, not important enough to be written for their own sake; they were but snatches of songs in his prose writings — novels and what not; and poems so set flying at any other time and in any other English could not have kept their motion and their spirit so long. They never cost him a thought; and the only sign of attention is in the versification. This is by no means always good, but in 'Radagon in Dianam' it is very good indeed; the foot is elastic and moves with a rebound.

But as to thoughts, he is at no expense. Take his charming description of 'A Shepherd and His Wife'. As though in the idleness of an empty mind, he lets his eyes note what is really hardly matter for verse — the way, for example, in which the flaps of the shepherd's coat were turned over. It is grotesque to produce a rhyme for such a detail as that. But in the same poem are some lively verses about the wife which seem not only to set her up for admiration and delight, but to dance about her in a round when that is done.

Nor is there more in 'The Shepherd Wife's Song', in which the happiest shepherdess in Thessaly compares her love and state with those of queens, and makes her boast sweetly and with a pretty and apt refrain. But 'Fair Samela' — oftener quoted — has a weakness and listlessness that spoil its grace;

and, after this, what is left? Robert Greene was a small poet among the minor poets; but his hour struck in the cool of the morning, and whatever kind of simplicity was in his mind, the authentic simplicity was in his English.

The Lady of the Lyrics

SHE is eclipsed, or gone, or in hiding. But the sixteenth century took her for granted as the object of song; she was a class, a state, a sex. It was scarcely necessary to waste the lyrist's time — time that went so gaily to metre as not to brook delays — in making her out too clearly. She had no more of what later times call individuality than has the rose, her rival, her foil when she was kinder, her superior when she was cruel, her ever fresh and ever conventional paragon. She needed not to be devised or divined; she was ready. A merry heart goes all the day; the lyrist's never grew weary. Honest men never grow tired of bread or of any other daily things whereof the sweetness is in their own simplicity.

This chief lady of the lyrics was not loved in mortal earnest, and her punishment now and then for her ingratitude was to be told that she was loved in jest. She did not love; her fancy was fickle; she was not moved by long service, which, by the way, was evidently to be taken for granted precisely like the whole long past of a dream. She had not a good temper. When the poet groans it seems that she has laughed at him; when he flouts her we may understand that she has chidden her lyrist in no temperate terms. In doing this she has sinned not so much against him as against Love. With that she is perpetually reproved. The lyrist complains to Love, pities Love for her scorning, and threatens to go away with Love, who is on his side.

There is no record of success for this policy. She goes on

dancing or scolding, as the case may be, and the lyrist goes on boasting of his constancy, or suddenly renounces it for a day. The situation has variants, but no surprise or ending. The lover's convention is explicit enough, but it might puzzle a reader to account for the lady's. Pride in her beauty, at any rate, is hers — pride so great that she cannot bring herself to perceive the shortness of her day. She is so unobservant as to need to be told that life is brief, and youth briefer than life.

Now we need not assume that the lady of the lyrics ever lived. But taking her as the almost unanimous conception of the lyrist, how is it she did not discover these things unaided? Why does he imagine her with a mind intensely irritable under his own praise and poetry? Obviously we cannot have her explanation of any of these matters. Why do the poets so much lament the absence of truth in one whose truth would be of little moment? And why was the convention so pleasant, among all others, as to occupy a whole age — nay, two great ages — of literature?

Music seems to be principally answerable. For the lyrics of the lady are 'words for music' by a great majority. There is rarely a poem in the Elizabethan song-books, properly so named, that has what would in our day be called a tone of sentiment. Music had not then the tone herself; she was ingenious, and so must the words be. She had the air of epigram, and an accurately definite limit. So, too, the lady of the lyrics, who might be called the lady of the stanzas, so strictly does she go by measure. When she is quarrelsome it is but fuguishness; when she dances she does it by a canon. She could not but be perverse, merrily sung to such grave notes.

Fair as a lily, hard to please, easily angry, ungrateful for innumerable verses, uncertain with the regularity of the madrigal, and inconstant with the punctuality of a stanza, she has gone with the arts of that day; and neither verse nor music will ever make such another lady. She refused to observe the transiency of roses; she never really intended — much as she was urged — to be a shepherdess; she was never persuaded to mitigate her dress. In return, the world has let her disappear. She scorned the poets until they turned upon her in the epigram of many a final couplet; and of these the last has been long written. Her 'No' was set to counterpoint in the part-song, and she frightened Love out of her sight in a ballet. Those occupations are gone, and the lovely Elizabethan has slipped away.

A Northern Fancy

'I REMEMBER,' said Dryden, writing to Dennis, 'I remember poor Nat Lee, who was then upon the verge of madness, yet made a sober and witty answer to a bad poet who told him, "It was an easy thing to write like a madman." "No," said he, " 'tis a very difficult thing to write like a madman, but 'tis a very easy thing to write like a fool." ' Nevertheless, the difficult song of distraction is to be heard, a light high note, in English poetry throughout two centuries at least, and one English poet lately set that untethered lyric, the mad maid's song, flying again.

A revolt against the oppression of the late sixteenth and early seventeenth centuries — the age of the rediscovery of death; against the crime of tragedies; against the tyranny of Italian example that had made the poets walk in one way of love, scorn, constancy, inconstancy — such a revolt may have caused this trolling of unconsciousness, this tune of innocence, and this carol of liberty, to be held so dear. 'I heard a maid in Bedlam', runs the old song. High and low the poets tried for that note, and the singer was nearly always to be a maid and crazed for love. Except for the temporary insanity so indifferently worn by the soprano of the now deceased kind of Italian opera, and except that a recent French story plays with the flitting figure of a village girl robbed of her wits by woe (and this, too, is a Russian villager, and the Southern author may have found his story on the spot, as he seems to aver) I have not met elsewhere than in England this solitary and detached poetry of the treble note astray.

At least, it is principally a northern fancy. Would the steadfast Cordelia, if she had not died, have lifted the low voice to that high note, so delicately untuned? She who would not be prodigal of words might yet, indeed, have sung in the cage, and told old tales, and laughed at gilded butterflies of the court of crimes, and lived so long in the strange health of an emancipated brain as to wear out

> Packs and sects of great ones
> That ebb and flow by the moon.

She, if King Lear had had his last desire, might have sung the merry and strange tune of Bedlam, like the slighter Ophelia and the maid called Barbara.

It was surely the name of the maid who died singing, as Desdemona remembers, that lingered in the ear of Words-worth. Of all the songs of the distracted, written in the sanity of high imagination, there is nothing more passionate than that beginning ' 'Tis said that some have died for love'. To one who has always recognized the greatness of this poem and who possibly had known and forgotten how much Ruskin prized it, it was a pleasure to find the judgment afresh in *Modern Painters*, where this grave lyric is cited for an example of great imagination. It is the mourning and restless song of the lover ('the pretty Barbara died') who has not yet broken free from memory into the alien world of the insane.

Barbara's lover dwelt in the scene of his love, as Dryden's Adam entreats the expelling angel that he might do, protesting that he could endure to lose 'the bliss, but not the place'. (And although this dramatic 'Paradise Lost' of Dryden's is hardly named by critics except to be scorned, this is assuredly a fine and imaginative thought.) It is nevertheless as a wanderer that the crazed creature visits the fancy of English poets with such a wild recurrence. The Englishman of the far past, barred by climate, bad roads, ill-lighted winters, and the intricate life and customs of the little town, must have been generally a home-keeper. No adventure, no setting forth, and small liberty, for him. But Tom-a-Bedlam, the wild man in patches or in ribbons, with his wallet and his horn for alms of food or drink, came and went as fitfully as the storm, free to suffer all the cold — an unsheltered creature; and the chill fancy of the villager followed him out to the heath on a journey that had no law. Was it he in person, or a poet for him, that made the swinging song: 'From the hag and the hungry goblin'? If a poet, it was one who wrote like a madman and not like a fool.

Not a town, not a village, not a solitary cottage during the English Middle Ages was unvisited by him who frightened the children; they had a name for him as for the wild birds — Robin Redbreast, Dicky Swallow, Philip Sparrow, Tom Tit, Tom-a-Bedlam. And after him came the 'Abram men', who were sane parodies of the crazed, and went to the fairs and wakes in motley. Evelyn says of a fop: 'All his body was dressed like a maypole, or a Tom-a-Bedlam's cap.' But after the Civil Wars they vanished, and no man knew how. In time old men remembered them only to remember that they had not seen any such companies or solitary wanderers of late years.

The mad maid of the poets is a vagrant too, when she is free, and not singing within Bedlam early in the morning, 'in the spring'. Wordsworth, who dealt with the legendary fancy in his 'Ruth', makes the crazed one a wanderer in the hills whom a traveller might see by chance, rare as an Oread, and nearly as wild as Echo herself:

> I too have passed her in the hills
> Setting her little water-mills.

His heart misgives him to think of the rheumatism that must befall in such a way of living; and his grave sense of civilization, *bourgeois* in the humane and noble way that is his own, restores her after death to the company of man, to the 'holy bell', which Shakespeare's Duke remembered in banishment, and to the congregation and their 'Christian psalm'.

The older poets were less responsible, less serious and more sad, than Wordsworth, when they in turn were touched by the fancy of the maid crazed by love. They left her to her light immortality; and she might be drenched in dews; they would not desire to reconcile nor bury her. She might have her hair torn by the bramble, but her heart was light after trouble. 'Many light hearts and wings' — she had at least the bird's heart, and the poet lent to her voice the wings of his verses.

There is nothing in our poetry less modern than she. The vagrant woman of later feeling was rather the sane creature of Ebenezer Elliott's fine lines in 'The Excursion' —

> Bone-weary, many-childed, trouble-tried!
> Wife of my bosom, wedded to my soul!

Trouble did not 'try' the Elizabethan wild one, it undid her. She had no child, or if there had ever been a child of hers, she had long forgotten how it died. She hailed the wayfarer, who was more weary than she, with a song; she haunted the cheerful dawn; her 'good-morrow' rings from Herrick's poem, fresh as cock-crow. She knows that her love is dead, and her perplexity has regard rather to the many kinds of flowers than to the old story of his death; they distract her in the splendid meadows.

All the tragic world paused to hear that lightest of songs, as the tragedy of *Hamlet* pauses for the fitful voice of Ophelia. Strange was the charm of this perpetual alien, and unknown to us now. The world has become once again as it was in the mad maid's heyday, less serious and more sad than Wordsworth; but it has not recovered, and perhaps will never recover, that sweetness. Blake's was a more starry madness. Crabbe, writing of village sorrows, thought himself bound to recur to the legend of the mad maid, but his 'crazed maiden' is sane enough, sorrowful but dull, and sings of her own 'burning brow', as Herrick's wild one never sang; nor is there any smile in her story, though she talks of flowers, or, rather, 'the herbs I loved to rear'; and perhaps she is the surest of all signs that the strange inspiration of the past centuries was lost, vanished like Tom-a-Bedlam himself. It had been wholly English, whereas the English eighteenth century was not wholly English.

It is not to be imagined that the hard Southern mind could ever have played in poetry with such a fancy; or that Petrarch, for example, could so have forgone the manifestation of intelligence and intelligible sentiment. And as to Dante, who put the two eternities into the momentary balance of the human will, cold would be his disregard of this northern dream of innocence. If the mad maid was an alien upon earth, what were she in the Inferno? What word can express her strangeness there, her vagrancy there? And with what eyes would they see this dewy face glancing in at the windows of that City?

The Century of Moderation

AFTER a long literary revolt — one of the recurrences of imperishable Romance — against the eighteenth-century authors, a reaction was due, and it has come about roundly. We are guided back to admiration of the measure and moderation and shapeliness of the Augustan age. And indeed it is well enough that we should compare — not necessarily check — some of our habits of thought and verse by the mediocrity of thought and perfect propriety of diction of Pope's best contemporaries. If this were all! But the eighteenth century was not content with its sure and certain genius. Suddenly and repeatedly it aspired to a 'noble rage'. It is not to the wild light hearts of the seventeenth century that we must look for extreme conceits and for extravagance, but to the later age, to the faultless, to the frigid, dissatisfied with their own propriety. There were straws, I confess, in the hair of the older poets; the eighteenth century stuck straws in its periwig.

That time — surpassing and correcting the century then just past in 'taste' — was resolved to make a low leg to no age, antique or modern, in the chapter of the passions — nay, to show the way, to fire the nations. Addison taught himself, as his hero 'taught the doubtful battle', 'where to rage'. And in the later years of the same literary century Johnson himself summoned the lapsed and alien and reluctant fury. Take such a word as 'madded' — 'the madded land'; there indeed is a word created for the noble rage, as the eighteenth century understood it. Look you, Johnson himself could lodge the fury in his responsible breast:

> And dubious title shakes the madded land.

There is no author of that time of moderation and good sense who does not thus more or less eat a crocodile. It is not necessary to go to the bad poets; we need go no lower than the good.

> And gasping Furies thirst for blood in vain,

says Pope seriously (but the sense of burlesque never leaves the reader). Also

> There purple vengeance bath'd in gore retires.

In the only passage of the *Dunciad* meant to be poetic and not ironic and spiteful, he has 'the panting gales' of a garden he describes. Match me such an absurdity among the 'conceits' of the age preceding!

A noble and ingenious author, so called by high authority but left anonymous, pretends (it is always pretending with these people, never fine fiction or a frank lie) that on the tomb of Virgil he had had a vision of that deceased poet:

> Crowned with eternal bays my ravished eyes
> Beheld the poet's awful form arise.

Virgil tells the noble and ingenious one that if Pope will but write upon some graver themes,

> Envy to black Cocytus shall retire
> And howl with furies in tormenting fire.

'Genius', says another authoritative writer in prose, 'is caused by a furious joy and pride of soul.'

If, leaving the great names, we pass in review the worse poets we find, in Pope's essay 'On the Art of Sinking in Poetry', things like these, gathered from the grave writings of his contemporaries:

> In flaming heaps the raging ocean rolls,
> Whose livid waves involve despairing souls;
> The liquid burnings dreadful colours shew,
> Some deeply red, and others faintly blue.

And a war-horse!

> His eye-balls burn, he wounds the smoking plain,
> And knots of scarlet ribbon deck his mane.

And a demon!

> Provoking demons all restraint remove.

Here is more eighteenth-century 'propriety':

> The hills forget they're fixed, and in their fright
> Cast off their weight, and ease themselves for flight.
> The woods, with terror winged, out-fly the wind,
> And leave the heavy, panting hills behind.

Again, from Nat Lee's *Alexander the Great*:

> When Glory, like the dazzling eagle, stood
> Perched on my beaver in the Granic flood;
> When Fortune's self my standard trembling bore,
> And the pale Fates stood 'frighted on the shore.

Of these lines, with another couplet, Dr. Warburton said that they 'contain not only the most sublime but the most judicious imagery that poetry could conceive or paint'. And here are lines from a tragedy, for me anonymous:

> Should the fierce North, upon his frozen wings,
> Bear him aloft above the wondering clouds,
> And seat him in the Pleiads' golden chariot,
> Thence should my fury drag him down to tortures.

Again:

> Kiss, while I watch thy swimming eye-balls roll,
> Watch thy last gasp, and catch thy springing soul.

It was the age of common sense, we are told, and truly; but of common sense now and then dissatisfied, common sense here and there ambitious, common sense of a distinctively adult kind taking on an innocent tone. I find this little affectation in Pope's word 'sky' where a simpler poet would have 'skies' or 'heavens'. Pope has 'sky' more than once, and always with a little false air of simplicity. And one instance occurs in that masterly and most beautiful poem, the 'Elegy on an Unfortunate Lady':

> Is there no bright reversion in the sky?

'Yes, my boy, we may hope so', is the reader's implicit mental aside, if the reader be a man of humour. Let me, however, suggest no disrespect towards this lovely elegy, of which the eight last lines have an inimitable greatness, a tenderness and passion which the 'Epistle of Eloisa' makes convulsive movements to attain but never attains. And yet how could one, by an example, place the splendid seventeenth century in closer — in slighter yet more significant — comparison with the eighteenth than thus? Here is Ben Jonson:

> What beckoning ghost, besprent with April dew,
> Hails me so solemnly to yonder yew?

And this is Pope's improvement:

> What beckoning ghost along the moonlight shade
> Invites my steps, and points to yonder glade?

But Pope follows this insipid couplet with two lines as exquisitely and nobly modulated as anything I know in that national metre:

> 'Tis she! but why that bleeding bosom gored,
> Why dimly gleams the visionary sword?

That indeed is 'music' in English verse — the counterpart of a great melody, not of a tune.

The eighteenth century matched its desire for wildness in poetry with a like craving in gardens. The symmetrical and architectural garden, so magnificent in Italy, and stately though more rigid and less glorious in France, was scorned by the eighteenth-century poet-gardeners. Why? Because it was 'artificial', and the eighteenth century must have 'nature' — nay passion. There seems to be some passion in Pope's grotto, stuck with spar and little shells.

Truly the age of the 'Rape of the Lock' and the 'Elegy' was an age of great wit and great poetry. Yet it was untrue to itself. I think no other century has cherished so persistent a self-conscious incongruity. As the century of good sense and good couplets it might have kept uncompromised the dignity we honour. But such inappropriate pranks have come to pass in history now and again. The Bishop of Hereford, in merry Barnsdale, 'danced in his boots'; but he was coerced by Robin Hood.

The Swan of Lichfield

Miss Anna Seward should not be made answerable for the poetry of the late eighteenth century but that no office or responsibility could be conferred upon a more willing recipient; the honour is hardly more than she demanded from the respect of the age to come; and when she bequeathed her works to this great man for editing, her letters to that, and her name to posterity, she would have heard with the satisfaction of her conscious hopes, rather than with elation or surprise, that another century would charge her with all the accumulated opinions of 1799.

It is Mr. Lucas's witty commentary[1] that recalls the name

[1] *A Swan and her Friends.*

of Anna Seward and her claim to speak for those days — the time between two ages. I have no intention whatever to write of her with irony. Neither has Mr. Lucas yielded to the obvious temptation. There is something worthy of no slight respect in the justified security of her representative attitude. To deride her would be to deride that age, almost the latest that had full confidence, that took its historic place absolutely, without reluctance, suffered no misgiving, and did not disturb the order and course of history.

The centuries before our own have resembled a river whereof the direction is known, for it is still far from the tidal regions of its journey; so was the course of things in 1799; but in another fifty years the stream of the modern age had, as it were, begun to feel the tides. Waves have set in towards the head of the waters, or they double the current of the ebb. Waters breast waters, and travel against the journey of the stream, making brief excursions foot to foot with Time. Or there is a swing that sends the river turning with the tide, outstripping the pace of the natural pilgrimage.

So was the mind of the nineteenth century lifted and cradled, in suspense like the pause of a vehement heart; so did it tend to the past and set to the future, a tidal flux and influx that flew from the end, flowed from the goal, filled and brimmed upper reaches, revisited pastures of yesterday with eager waves, or ebbed with a run and made haste to leave them twice.

If this, then, was the tidal surge of the stream of letters and the arts, the end of the eighteenth century was almost the last date before the tides began to be perceptible. Almost — for perhaps the days when Walter Savage Landor was seriously discussing the merits of a poem by Miss Chose upon the Queen were really the last of the stream above tides. It may be that the perturbing shock first interrupted the onward flowing just after him. Smooth days, those — there were no doubts as to the way of the wave, and no need to watch the hour in order to know whether backward or forward its course was shaped. A stream is a stately stream above the tidal influence. And in Miss Anna Seward's years the historic river of the mind was unchecked: it glided.

I think there never was a day of more orderly confidence. The 'taste', the laws, that had come to pass were the only laws and the only taste that were timely or possible. From the later Milton to Dryden, from Dryden to Addison, Pope, Johnson, Gray, Cowper, Crabbe — the way is a way that has no turning. We mark it with some mingled feelings, but surprise is not one of them. It is much the same in the matter of town architecture. The brick box that came to pass in the building of London streets, in the course of the same age, followed the time of dignity, beauty, and fancy which was Wren's, and all the degrees thereto were in a kind of order. Doubtless, this is why we have learnt, in the fluttering centre of a renewed architectural town, to look with some degree of esteem upon the black brick box, if only it be truly of that time. And this not because it has a quiet civic majesty of approach to its door *à deux battants*, and passages and rooms proportionate within, but because that very exterior, which was the negation of architecture, was the last truly punctual style of building. And before its day they might be classical, but they were classical in a manner that was of the seventeenth and eighteenth centuries, with an intense spirit of the time. Perhaps the clearest sign of the times before the beating tides is this — their secure self-confidence; for they never doubted that their taste was the best and their criticism the result of accumulated judgment. Nay, in the dregs of times — in 1840 — they had faith in their romances, Italian landscape, steel engraving, portraits with large eyes, in a word, in their 'finish' (the word is ominous); and because of their good faith we may deride even these with good humour.

Now, Miss Seward has an incontestable right to speak in the name of her contemporaries. There is hardly any one else who had all her good faith and solemnity. But first let me pause upon the title given to her with so much dullness and elegance — the Swan of Lichfield. The Swan of Avon had at least a river; he was never the Swan of Stratford-on-Avon. But with all respect to the poet who devised the name for Shakespeare, we may hold that it was not well inspired to suit a poet who sang in his middle days and was silent some time before he died. Let this, however, pass as the perversity of a phrase not without charm. It is the perversity, perhaps, that has made the name so dear and a household word. But at any rate a Swan of Avon could swim, he was not placed on a high road, or in a street, or within the precincts of a cathedral close. The Swan of Lichfield must have been named with an agreeable intention to confer a sweet dignity, and something of that faded dignity remains. The episcopal palace was her home, and she was called a Swan when she was in full career; they did not wait for a swan-song.

So close was she to the first beginnings of the tides that she blundered when she left much of her poetry to Sir Walter Scott, not doubting his willingness to serve her as editor. He did the work, with some considerable excisions, and gave the volumes to the world, but in an 'aside' he has called her poems execrable. So that she was all too confident of the immediate future. Dying early in the nineteenth century, she continued a little too long the assurance of the eighteenth; that was her sole fault. In regard to her own day she had none.

It seems even that 'execrable' is an unjust word. Miss Seward did not attempt to describe a moonlight night without forgoing her bed to match it with a phrase. Her sincerity is not without its literary value, for it succeeds in a measure; if not fully communicated, it is suggested, and this is no small thing. Moreover, there is a poetic thought — an implicit thought, an inclusion — in her sonnet on 'December Morning':

> ... Then to decree
> The grateful thoughts to God, ere they unfold
> To friendship or the Muse.

This surely is not without subtlety; nor is the final line, in which the reader and student is said to fill his days so full that though he be not old he 'outlives the old'. A poet capable of this sense of present time (for here is no mere commonplace as to future influence or literary immortality; she means that the outliving is present) — a poet who had this thought might have been a fine poet; she used her intellect, and that action is the vitality of all poetry that is not song only, but poetry and song.

This is so high a specimen that I will quote no more. Over Miss Seward's criticism it would be but too easy to make merry. 'For the magnificent', she says of her century, 'we have Akenside, Thomson, Collins, Dr. Johnson, Mason, Gray, Chatterton, Darwin, and the sublime Joanna Baillie; in the *simpler* style, Shenstone, Beattie, Cowper, Crowe, Bowles, Burns, Bloomfield, Walter Scott and his school; Coleridge, Southey, and *their* school. Poetry can have no nobler models than these supply to her various styles.' She must have read the 'Ancient Mariner'; she names Coleridge with Southey!

She had the eighteenth-century love for something that was *not* purity of style. I think that the critics of our own day have hardly perceived the violence of an age that wrote 'taught the doubtful battle where to rage'; 'red Arbela'; 'gory horrors crowned each dreadful day'; 'the madding crowd'; 'maddened o'er the land'; and a thousand other things in tatters. Miss Seward rebuked a writer for stealing 'gulphy' from Pope. 'Gulphy', she thought, was too good to steal. 'He stole the picturesque epithet "gulphy" from Pope':

And gulphy Xanthus foams along the field.

'Than which a more poetic line', she decides, 'was *never* written.'

Mary Wollstonecraft's Letters

THAT Mary Wollstonecraft's public writings remain fresh and instructive, while Godwin's offer to our wearied minds a curious combination of truisms and mares'-nests, is, in part, due to this fact — that in social ethics, which were her province, the world slowly changes its mind, while in political science, which was her husband's field, general thought in England developed apace. Another striking difference between the two is that Godwin had a man's power and privilege of impersonal generalization; professional at thinking, he was an amateur at living; but all that Mary Wollstonecraft wrote, however large and general in its sympathies and speculations, is quick with the feelings of the personal and intense woman, who took her life so greatly to heart. If this be so in her public works, how vital are the letters to Imlay in which she shows herself; making a disclosure too intimate for good taste, perhaps too intimate for good feeling, to accept.

Mary, Eliza, and Everina Wollstonecraft were three girls whose home was laid waste by the ill-conduct of a father, and who were thrown on the world without means of livelihood, except their own labours; one brother was selfish and grudging, the other was a ne'er-do-weel and a burden; one of the girls had the additional misfortune of being married to a savage, who ill-treated her to the verge of madness. From his clutches her sister Mary rescued her, harbouring her and working for her afterwards; this was the first revolt against society attempted by the future author of *A Vindication of the Rights of Woman*. With the three sisters was associated a fourth girl, a poor little artist, who lived by her brush, and whom the large-hearted Mary tenderly loved — Fanny Blood, the daughter of a drunken spendthrift. Mark how it chanced that in Mary Wollstone-craft's experience and observation of life virtuous and indus-trious women suffered by the idleness of dissolute men; for the claim which she afterwards made on behalf of her sex for equal intellectual and political rights is thus the more easily under-stood. During this time of early struggles with poverty we find her an independent and energetic, a most self-sacrificing and loving, and distinctively a pious woman. If her piety be less observable as her life advanced, we yet see no reason for believ-ing that it suffered any great diminution. After her rescue of her sister the most marked incident of her laborious youth is a very characteristic one. Her friend, Fanny Blood, had married, and gone to live in Portugal with her husband. Her confinement approaching, she begged Mary to go over and nurse her; and Mary immediately set sail, leaving the school which the sisters were toiling to keep up, and which fell to pieces in her absence. Fanny Blood died in childbirth, and when Mary returned to England the Wollstonecrafts' sorrowful little home was divided, and she took a governess's place, working the while for the first time with her pen, and doing all in the hope of providing for her two sisters, whose sorrows and necessities caused her a constant, keen, and almost morbid agony of mind. Then for five years she lived alone in lodgings in London, writing for a publisher, helping her sisters to governesses' places, and sheltering them when unemployed.

During this period her *Vindication of the Rights of Woman* was written and published. It brought her immediate fame — an admiration which was almost worship from one section of society, suspicion and dislike from another. Her sisters being at the moment in comfort, she for the first time indulged herself, gratifying her desire for culture and accomplishments, and at the same time her large and generous interest in the destinies of the world, by a residence in Paris in time of revolution. Here at the age of thirty-four, when her mind, ripening late like her beautiful person, was, in spite of past sorrows, fresh and keen, and deep in its capacity for happiness, she met Gilbert Imlay, an American of talent, and in course of time contracted with him what she intended to be a lifelong union. Love had never before entered into her tender and maidenly heart. Her life had been as clean of thought as a nun's life; and now her offence, though a great and grave one, was, in part at least, an intellectual offence; she set aside the divine institution of marriage, presuming to think it unnecessary to a real and permanent tie. Taking the following sentences, gathered almost at random from her book, it is difficult to think that the hand which wrote them was yielded except in dignity and honour and faith in the cleanness of its bond:

'A Christian has still nobler motives to incite her to preserve chastity . . . for her body has been called the Temple of the living God; of that God who requires more than modesty of mien. His eye searcheth the heart; and let her remember that if she hope to find favour in the sight of purity itself, her chastity must be founded on modesty, and not on worldly prudence; or verily, a good reputation will be her only reward.'

'My sisters . . . when love, even innocent love, is the whole employ of your lives, your hearts will be too soft to afford modesty that tranquil retreat where she delights to dwell, in close union with humanity.'

Still more strikingly she says, in one of the letters to Imlay, that she prefers the word 'affection' to 'love', because the former implies temperance and habit. The man whose wife Mary Wollstonecraft considered herself (and any Scotchwoman would be virtuously married with less form than passed between them) seems, from glimpses in her letters, to have been a free-thinker, who had reduced immorality to a principle of conduct. Although she knew his love of change Mary watched the calming of his passion for her with a noble equanimity, trusting to her own worth to attach her lover for ever to her. 'You *must* esteem me!' she exclaims with dignity. The story of her desertion need scarcely be told here; it is told with pathos and power in her letters to Imlay. Her scorn of wealth ('Nothing worth having is to be purchased', she says), her sweet playfulness, her serene and womanly affectionateness, her anguish in the betrayal, combine in a self-painted, unconscious portrait, almost unequalled in beauty. There is a rising tone of pain throughout the letters: 'My friend, my friend, I am not well! a deadly weight of sorrow lies heavily on my heart. I am again tossed on the billows of life . . . I long every night to go to bed, to hide my melancholy face in my pillow; but there is a canker-worm in my bosom that never sleeps.' 'Writing to you, whenever an affectionate epithet occurs, my eyes fill with tears, and my trembling hand stops . . . If I am doomed to be unhappy, I will confine my anguish to my own bosom . . . God bless you!' When her courage gave way she attempted to drown herself, with so much resolution that she was insensible when some passing watermen saw and rescued her. She was reconciled to life only by the duty of working for the little girl Imlay had left her — the little girl who was afterwards that 'Fanny Godwin' whose tragical death by her own hand has never been explained.

Clinging to her theories with a culpable infatuation, Mary's marriage with Godwin did not take place until five months before the birth of her daughter Mary, afterwards Mary Shelley. She seems to have loved Godwin tenderly, though with less than the fervour of her first union; but these few months of peace were cut short by her death in childbirth, at the age of thirty-eight. It is difficult to believe that she was more than negatively happy as Godwin's wife; there was little in common between her genius and his 'large head full of cold brains', to use Ticknor's word. Mr. Kegan Paul relates a characteristic incident of her last hours. At the sudden cessation of great pain she cried to her husband, 'Oh, Godwin, I am in heaven!' and he replied, 'You mean, my dear, that your physical sensations are somewhat easier.'

Her style, in the letters to Imlay, as in her public works, is peculiarly direct, sincere, and strong; we are always conscious of a certain reserve of power. The few living persons who have read her *Rights of Woman* must have been struck with the force of reasoning exerted and husbanded throughout a long argumentative work. Her originality of mind is so great that she dispenses with all such eccentricities of style as simulate originality. Every action of her reason is quick with charity toward the individual, with philanthropy toward the race.

Elizabeth Inchbald

The portrait of Mrs. Inchbald by Romney is something of a disappointment to those who had hitherto known only the portrait written by her own delighted hand, so full of spirit and sweetness that one might wish literature to be exclusively entrusted with all records of human beauty — the beauty that cannot, or should not, be proved. Painting tries to prove it to demonstration. But the written portrait is not importunate. It is not motionless. It bids you hail and farewell, and eludes you and is away. It confesses its flatteries all the more gaily as it defies you to refute them; and happily persuades you, to make amends, that you can be trusted to imagine a charming person. In the painting, Elizabeth Inchbald, though slight and slender, has none of the quickness of life in her eyes. She has the negative look that is the least attractive in any face. And to be painted she evidently clad herself in her best. One had hoped to see her in the gentle and adaptable garments which were 'always becoming, and very seldom worth so much as eightpence'. What portrait-painter could tell us that, by the way? And then, too, what painter could inform us of his sitter's regrets for the freckles, and for the slight 'coarsening' of the skin upon her cheeks and arms? The painter simply refuses to see the red, and he ignores the freckles; and if he did not he would be doing an injury and injustice to the integrity of the effect of fairness and fineness. No, the painter is at a disadvantage. He cannot add to the charm of the delicate hair by confiding to you the lady's misgiving that it was a little too straight as well as thin; nor can he entrust you with the distress wherewith, year by year, she saw the marks of age upon her beauty. During some years, Mrs. Inchbald confesses, she had no other trouble. Nor can he assure you that she was, in her own happy eyes, 'excessively interesting'.

She who wrote her own portrait so much more gaily than Romney, painted it gives us the previous moment and the moment to come — nay, the previous years of youth regretted, and the years of reluctant but beautiful fading. She is majestic, but just away on a frolic. Romney's Elizabeth Inchbald never woke the echoes of a quiet street on Sunday with runaway knocks. Mrs. Inchbald's Elizabeth Inchbald did that among other things.

She was not capable of vulgarity. Her merry memoirs are

throughout fragrant with propriety, her fiction (more careful)
is stiff with quite beautiful prudery. For she was on her very
best behaviour in her novels. We hear of her owning, in her
own person, to a candid susceptibility, and of her telling an ad-
mirer, too eagerly for her little stammer, that she would not
only have accepted him, she would have 'j-j-jumped at him'.
But not so bear themselves her heroines. Miss Milner, in *A
Simple Story*, finds it necessary to lie down whenever the deli-
cacy of her emotions seems in danger. Someone always leads
her to a sofa and at once yields her with scrupulous haste into
the hands of her maid. A fairly careful research has not made
us acquainted with the maidenly secret of her Christian name.
No one calls her by it — not her *fiancé*, not her guardian, not
the old, old lady of thirty-five who receives her confidence and
has to shed so many tears on her behalf, not her girl contem-
porary of eighteen. She is Miss Milner until she becomes Lady
Elmwood, and in her last letter to her husband she reminds
him of the time when she was his dear Miss Milner. Her
daughter, Lady Matilda, is allowed to confess a Christian
name, only, it is evident, on account of the exigencies and
safeguards of her title.

Poor Miss Milner behaves very badly, but her sins are
narrated with the more exquisite propriety as they grow the
graver. She goes to a masquerade against the wishes of her
Dorriforth. The character she has chosen for her costume is
that of the 'goddess of chastity', but the petticoat was festooned.
'It had at the first glance,' says Mrs. Inchbald, 'the appearance
of a female much less virtuous'; for, in fact, Miss Milner wore
boots. Upon hearing of the boots Dorriforth, in spite of the
warmth of his devotion, breaks off the engagement. 'They
were not boots,' says her maid in tears; 'they were only half-
boots.' 'My girl,' replies Dorriforth's clerical friend, 'your
own evidence convicts your mistress; for what has a woman to
do with *any* boots?'

Dorriforth is, in the phrase of the time, 'very much the
gentleman'. Miss Milner plays him false, but he never swerves
from the highest dignity and decorum possible to man. He is

never mastered by any passion except that of a lofty anger, and
for this he makes amends on the field of honour, as well as by
a prayer, in which he approaches his Creator, as he says, 'en-
couraged by that long intercourse which religion has effected'.
Altogether he is the best figure in the book — woman's hero
though he may be. For Miss Milner is somewhat too perverse
for patient reading; her friend of thirty-five has no character-
istic except the fidelity and indulgent sympathy proper to
declining years, and the crabbed friend of the hero is not often
amusing in his animosities. But dear Dorriforth is always equal
to the occasion. He is never ridiculous. He has so hard a life,
and suffers misfortunes so unmerited, that the reader is thank-
ful to leave him with a daughter who inherits his own sense of
decorum in a highly 'female' form. The Lady Matilda grows
up at the close of the novel, and is surprised into a confession
of attachment. She is greatly distressed to have been thus taken
unawares. 'Could Lord Elmwood,' she asks her suitor, 'know
for what he sent me?' 'He did,' replies Rushbrook; 'I boldly
told him of my presumptuous love, and he has given you alone
the power over my happiness or misery. Oh, do not doom me
to the latter.' Lady Matilda does not doom him to the latter.
But Mrs. Inchbald can hardly bring herself to say so.

A Simple Story can hardly be admired as a fine novel. The
division into two very unequal parts is too abrupt. The parts
are unequal, not so much in length as in interest. After follow-
ing Miss Milner, in much detail, through the errors of her
youth, witnessing her many tears, and attending her to many
sofas, the reader finds the close of her career rather summary,
when she is 'no longer beautiful, no longer beloved, no longer —
tremble while you read it! — no longer virtuous'. And after the
close of that tragedy no one has much goodwill to begin afresh
with a Lady Matilda. Besides, Mrs. Inchbald should not have
had the heart to turn her Dorriforth into a tyrant. Above all
she should not, after interesting us so well in his sensibility,
make him, in after life, the object of something like irony.
When he learns the death of his disgraced wife — his 'once-
adored Miss Milner' — he leaves his chocolate untasted. If

this were a little more clever it would be Miss Austenish. Mrs. Inchbald should have nothing to do with irony.

Although she describes herself so charmingly she does not describe her heroines, giving only a general assurance of their surpassing beauty. The three who are young in *A Simple Story* are lovely. And Miss Milner, of course, is an heiress. The literature of that day centred about heiresses. Finally, before closing this column, we were struck by a sudden thought. Dorriforth's Christian name! We turned back to look. No, the Christian name of Dorriforth is not granted us.

Joanna Baillie

WOULD Joanna Baillie's *Plays on the Passions* have been so shunned by later generations and then so forgotten, if the writers of Literary Histories had remembered to mention the 'Comedies on the Passions' as well as the 'Tragedies'? For every tragedy Joanna Baillie, whose plan of dramatic labours was drawn up with a singular completeness, wrote also a comedy; and one at least of these sprightlier plays is so buoyant, so busy, so apt in speech, and so pleasant, within the limits of eighteenth-century wit, that a modern manager might surely do worse than try his luck with it.

If any man should desire to possess the full intention of Joanna Baillie in her undertaking, in her dealing with the Passions, he may have it in a great many pages of most explicit introduction, with her own decisions on all such controversies as those touching the individual and the type, in tragedy. Joanna Baillie had thought out all such matters. But her few readers are, perhaps, content to take as read this treatise, with its good sense and its very small charm. She knows well what she is about, this at any rate is certain: and when she addresses herself with a most simple sense of responsibility to the tragic presentation of Hatred, Remorse, Jealousy, and Fear, her good faith and gravity, and the admirable manner in which she puts the murderer to school, nearly quiet the reader's natural resentment and inclination to revolt.

With average goodwill and a fair readerly spirit, you may take these resolute tragedies, with their enormous *parti pris*, as works of no despicable art. Joanna Baillie would by no means permit you to slight her art. She has a passage in which she disclaims the crude intention of setting up the image of a single passion as the whole nature of a man. If there were no conflict, she says, there would be no force, for the passion would have nothing to compel, to break or bend, within the passionate heart. But neither will she allow the units of humankind to puzzle us on the tragic stage with their asymmetry of nature. Her jealous man has other impulses for jealousy to grapple with, but they serve his jealousy so. She will not endure, as she tells us, eccentricity.

Add to this manner of planning an eighteenth-century blank verse of the second order, and you have the drama which seemed Shakespearian to many.

It is not too much to say that any other drama — Antiquity and Shakespeare apart — would have had grave reason to be proud of Joanna Baillie. Her plays seem to be built up and locked together soundly; they close with a conventional but not obtrusive dignity. Knowing the Passion that has been the theme, you are apt to turn to the final speech over the hero's long-vexed body, the comment that proclaims an impartial sentence in tragic peace, and you find no weaknesses; the silence follows upon no manifest failure. Vivacity among the smaller characters, and some of the strength of the ages (being the strength of tradition) in the greater, leave her tragedies in no mean place; leave them there too literally, for few are the readers to put them to any test or question. In their day they and the 'metaphysical preface', as Mrs. Thrale calls it, were the occasion of some sayings hard to our ears. 'A masculine performance' is the expected opinion, duly expressed, but we are not so well prepared for Sir Walter Scott's reply to Lockhart:

'If you wish to speak of a real poet, Joanna Baillie is now the highest genius of our country.'

It is the comedy following the tragedy of 'Basil' that takes my fancy. Love seems to be the passion in hand, and Joanna Baillie makes such pretty eighteenth-century sport of her theme (her hero keeping the fine sensibilities, expressed with impassioned elegance, of Steele's *Conscious Lovers*) that it is not easy to realize that she passed the middle of the nineteenth century, albeit in extreme old age. Of the preceding tragedy I will say merely that one may detect in it a fancy of Antiquity, as the eighteenth century dressed it, which is wonderfully pleasing: a little boy, Mirando, vexes the capricious heroine by naming her lovers; he creeps into her arms and begins to trouble her free heart, making guesses for sugar-plums. The reader likes to think that by a candid allegory, fit for Sir Joshua Reynolds's painting of a gold-headed boy and a brown-eyed maid, Miss Joanna Baillie had given the name of Mirando to none other than Love himself, Cupid the bee.

But to the comedy. It is called 'The Trial', and turns upon the device, since repeated, perhaps, more than once, of shuffling a couple of heroines, so that she who is the heiress may disguise herself in the dresses of her penniless cousin, and receive impertinences, suffer neglect, and also test the true heart proffered in intention to her as a girl without wealth. It is the exceeding sweetness of the two good girls bent upon their frolic (which is also a romp) that makes the charm of this happy play. They exchange names upon the wildest impulse consistent with their Georgian manners. They are audacious and decorous; confess their quest, which is for a 'sensible lover'; busy themselves therein, make inquiries, hide behind screens, plot together the exposure of the fortune-hunter, acknowledge the full value of their own beauty, and this with a propriety all of its own time.

Agnes has the better wit as well as the gold, but the lesser beauty. She it is who lays the plot, and persuades the uncle, when he would fall out with her and her cousin, to second their game. He would not, he avers, make a holiday mummery for their pleasure, and his wig is too old for a ball. 'Nay, don't lay the fault upon the wig, good sir, for it is as youthful and as sly, and as saucy-looking as the best head of hair in the county. As for your old wig, indeed, there was so much curmudgeon-like austerity about it that young people fled before it, as, I daresay, the birds do now.' As for the unlucky 'fops' — the fops whom Joanna Baillie brings forward and overthrows in incredible effigy, after the fashion of the other satirists — Agnes, or, rather, her cousin Mariane, is troubled by many. Each one is mimicked in the dressing-room dialogues of these two enterprising rogues, and the appropriate humiliation is prepared for each with all precision. 'Such a man must be laughed at, not scorned; contempt must be his portion.' Mariane falls in: 'He shall have it then. And as for his admirer and imitator . . . any kind of bad treatment, I suppose, that happens to come into my head will be good enough for him.' This last is pretty wit. So is this gipsy's reply to her uncle's reproof in regard to her dealings with yet another: 'He would not let me have time to give a civil denial, but ran on planning settlements . . . I could just get in my word with a flat refusal as he was about to provide for our descendants to the third generation . . . He is only angry that he can't take the law of me for laughing at him.'

Even when you hear of the 'genteel young man, with dark grey eyes, and a sensible countenance', and are at once aware that it is indeed *he*, this charming Agnes is hard to capture. As he walks backwards before her with a play of homage (for he too can be light) she mocks him with her dance, and dances him up the stage and out at the door. And if there were any living actress who had the eighteenth-century propriety it would be pretty to see her do it. The eighteenth-century baggages! They called their admirers by their surnames *tout court*, and their breeding was admirable.

Hardly less pleasant is the comedy on 'Hatred', in which a candidate for a parliamentary election hears good news about his detested rival: 'Art thou sure that they laughed at him? In his own inn and over his own liquor? Ha, ha! ungrateful merry varlets!'

74

She, who had this humour, to be called 'the highest genius in our country', and to be so taken up with 'the passions of human kind'! One of the eulogists of her tragic power calls her 'undeviating'; yet she deviated delightfully.

A Vanquished Man

HAYDON died by his own act in 1846, and it was not, in the event, until 1853 that his journal was edited, not by Elizabeth Barrett Browning, as he wished, but by Tom Taylor. Turning over these familiar and famous volumes, often read, I wonder once more how any editor was bold to 'take upon himself the mystery of things' in the case of Haydon, and to assign to that venial moral fault or this the ill-fortune and defeat that beset him, with hardly a pause for the renewal of the resistance of his admirable courage.

That he made a mere intellectual mistake, gave thanks with a lowly and lofty heart for a genius denied him, that he prepared himself to answer to Heaven and earth for the gift he had not, to suffer its reproach, to bear its burden, and that he looked for its reward, is all his history. There was no fault of the intellect in his apprehension of the thing he thought to stand possessed of. He conceived it aright, and he was just in his rebuke of a world so dull and trivial before the art for which he died. He esteemed it aright, except when he deemed it his.

His editor, thinking himself to be summoned to justify the chastisement, the destruction, the whole retribution of such a career, looks here and there for the sins of Haydon; the search is rewarded with the discovery of faults such as every man and woman entrusts to the common generosity, the general consciousness. It is a pity to see any man conning such offences by heart, and setting them clear in an editorial judgment because he thinks himself to hold a trust, by virtue of his biographical office, to explain the sufferings and the failure of a conquered man.

What, in the end, are the sins which are to lead the reader, sad but satisfied, to conclude with 'See the result of ——', or 'So it ever must be with him who yields to ——', or whatever else may be the manner of ratifying the sentence on the condemned and dead? Haydon, we hear, omitted to ask advice, or, if he asked it, did not shape his course thereby unless it pleased him. Haydon was self-willed; he had a wild vanity, and he hoped he could persuade all the powers that include the powers of man to prosper the work of which he himself was sure. He did not wait upon the judgment of the world, but thought to compel it.

Should he, then, have waited upon the judgment of such a world? He was foremost in the task of instructing, nay, of compelling it when there was a question of the value of the Elgin Marbles, and when the possession — which was the preservation — of these was at stake. There he was not wrong; his judgment, that dealt him, in his own cause, the first, the fatal, the final injury — the initial subtle blow that sent him on his career so wronged, so cleft through and through, that the mere course and action of life must ruin him — this judgment, in art, directed him in the decision of the most momentous of all public questions. Haydon admired, wrote, protested, declaimed, and fought; and in great part, it seems, we owe our perpetual instruction by those Judges of the Arts which are the fragments of the Elgin sculptures, to the fact that Haydon trusted himself with the trust that worked his own destruction. Into the presence especially of those seated figures commonly called the Fates, we habitually bring our arts for sentence. He lent an effectual hand to the setting-up of that Tribunal of headless stones.

The thing we should lament is rather that the world which refused, neglected, forgot him — and by chance-medley was right, was right! — had no possible authority for anything that it did against him, and that he might have sent it to school, for all his defect of genius; moreover, that he was mortally wounded in the last of his forty years of battle by this ironic wound: among the bad painters chosen to adorn the Houses of Parliament with fresco, he was not one. This affront he took at the hands of men who had no real distinctions in their gift. He might well have had, by mere chance, some great companion with whom to share that rejection. The unfortunate man had no such fortuitous fellowship at hand. How strange, the solitude of the bad painter outcast by the worst, and capable of making common cause indomitably with the good, had there been any such to take heart from his high courage!

There was none. There were ranged the unjust judges with their blunders all in good order, and their ignorance new dressed, and there was no artist to destroy except only this one, somewhat better than their favoured, their appointed painters in fresco; one uncompanioned, and a man besides through whose heart the public reproach was able to cut keenly.

Is this sensibility to be made a reproach to Haydon? It has always seemed to me that he was not without greatness — yet he was always without dignity — in those most cruel passages of his life, such as that of his defeat, towards the close of his war, by the show of a dwarf, to which all London thronged, led by Royal example, while the exhibition of his picture was deserted. He was not betrayed by anger at this end of hopes and labours in which all that a man lives for had been pledged. Nay, he succeeded in bearing what a more inward man would have taken more hardly. He was able to say in his loud voice, in reproach to the world, what another would have barred within: one of his great pictures was in a cellar, another in an attic, another at the pawnbroker's, another in a grocer's shop, another unfinished in his studio; the bills for frames and colours and the rent were unpaid. Some solace he even found in stating a few of these facts, in French, to a French official or diplomatic visitor to London, interested in the condition of the arts. Well, who shall live without support? A man finds it where he can.

After these offences of self-will and vanity Tom Taylor finds

us some other little thing — I think it is inaccuracy. Poor
Haydon says in one phrase that he paid all his friends on such
a day, and in another soon following that the money given or
lent to him had been insufficient to pay them completely; and
assuredly there are many revisions, after-thoughts, or other
accidents to account for such a slip. His editor says the dis-
crepancy is 'characteristic', but I protest I cannot find another
like it among those melancholy pages. If something graver
could but be sifted out from all these journals and letters of
frank confession, by the explainer! Here, then, is the last and
least: Haydon was servile in his address to 'men of rank'. But
his servility seems to be very much in the fashion of his day—
nothing grosser; and the men who set the fashion had not to
shape their style to Haydon's perpetual purpose, which was to
ask for commissions or for money.

Not the forsaken man only but also the fallen city evokes
this exercise of historical morality, until a man in flourishing
London is not afraid to assign the causes of the decay of Venice;
and there is not a watering place upon our coasts but is securely
aware of merited misfortune on the Adriatic.

Haydon was grateful, and he helped men in trouble; he had
pupils, and never a shilling in pay for teaching them. He
painted a good thing — the head of his Lazarus. He had no
fault of theory: what fault of theory can a man commit who
stands, as he did, by 'Nature and the Greeks'? In theory he
soon outgrew the Italians then most admired; he had an honest
mind.

But nothing was able to gain for him the pardon that is never
to be gained, the impossible pardon — pardon for that first and
last mistake — the mistake as to his own powers. If to pardon
means to dispense from consequence, how should this be
pardoned? Art would cease to be itself, by such an amnesty.

Tennyson

FIFTY years after Tennyson's birth he was saluted a great poet by that unanimous acclamation which includes mere clamour. Fifty further years, and his centenary was marked by a new detraction. It is sometimes difficult to distinguish the obscure but not unmajestic law of change from the sorry custom of reaction. Change hastes not and rests not, reaction beats to and fro, flickering about the moving mind of the world. Reaction — the paltry precipitancy of the multitude — rather than the novelty of change, has brought about a ferment and corruption of opinion on Tennyson's poetry. It may be said that opinion is the same now as it was in the middle of the nineteenth century — the same, but turned. All that was not worth having of admiration then has soured into detraction now. It is of no more significance, acrid, than it was, sweet. What the herding of opinion gave yesterday it is able to take away to-day, that and no more.

But besides the common favour-disfavour of the day, there is the tendency of educated opinion, once disposed to accept the whole of Tennyson's poetry as though he could not be 'parted from himself', and now disposed to reject the whole, on the same plea. But if ever there was a poet who needed to be thus 'parted' — the word is his own — it is he who wrote both narrowly for his time and liberally for all time, and who — this is the more important character of his poetry — had both a style and a manner: a masterly style, a magical style, a too dainty manner, nearly a trick; a noble landscape and in it figures something ready-made. He is a subject for our alternatives of feeling, nay, our conflicts, as is hardly another poet. We may deeply admire and wonder, and, in another line or hemistich, grow indifferent or slightly averse. He sheds the luminous suns of dreams upon men and women who would do well with footlights; waters their way with rushing streams of Paradise and cataracts from visionary hills; laps them in divine darkness; leads them into those touching landscapes, 'the lovely that are not beloved', long grey fields, cool sombre summers, and meadows thronged with unnoticeable flowers; speeds his carpet knight — or is that hardly a just name for one whose sword 'smites' so well? — upon a carpet of authentic wild flowers; pushes his rovers, in costume, from off blossoming shores, on the keels of old romance. The style and the manner, I have said, run side by side. If we may take one poet's too violent phrase, and consider poets to be 'damned to poetry', why, then, Tennyson is condemned by a couple of sentences, 'to run concurrently'. We have the style and the manner locked together at times in a single stanza, locked and yet not mingled. There should be no danger for the more judicious reader lest impatience at the peculiar Tennyson trick should involve the great Tennyson style in a sweep of protest. Yet the danger has in fact proved real within the present and recent years, and seems about to threaten still more among the less judicious. But it will not long prevail. The vigorous little nation of lovers of poetry, alive one by one within the vague multitude of the nation of England, cannot remain finally insensible to what is at once majestic and magical in Tennyson. For those are not qualities they neglect in their other masters. How, valuing singleness of heart in the sixteenth century, splendour in the seventeenth, composure in the eighteenth; how, with a spiritual ear for the note — commonly called Celtic, albeit it is the most English thing in the world — the wild wood note of the remoter song; how, with the educated sense of style, the liberal sense of ease; how, in a word, fostering Letters and loving Nature, shall that choice nation within England long disregard these virtues in the nineteenth-century master? How disregard him, for more than the few years of reaction, for the insignificant reasons of his bygone taste, his insipid courtliness, his prettiness, or what not? It is no dishonour to Tennyson, for it is a dishonour to our education, to disparage a poet who wrote but the two — had he written no more of their kind — lines of 'The Passing of Arthur', of which, before I quote them, I will permit myself the personal remembrance of a great contemporary author's opinion. Meredith, speaking to me of the high-water mark of English style in poetry and prose, cited those lines as topmost in poetry:

> On one side lay the ocean, and on one
> Lay a great water, and the moon was full.

Here is no taint of manner, no pretty posture or habit, but the simplicity of poetry and the simplicity of Nature, something on the yonder side of imagery. It is to be noted that this noble passage is from Tennyson's generally weakest kind of work — blank verse; and should thus be a sign that the laxity of so many parts of the 'Idylls' and other blank verse poems was a kind of unnecessary fault. Lax this form of poetry undoubtedly is with Tennyson. His blank verse is often too easy; it cannot be said to fly, for the paradoxical reason that it has no weight; it slips by, without halting or tripping indeed, but also without the friction of the movement of vitality. This quality, which is so near to a fault, this quality of ease, has come to be disregarded in our day. That Horace Walpole overpraised this virtue is not good reason that we should hold it for a vice. Yet we do more than undervalue it; and several of our authors, in prose and poetry, seem to find much merit in the manifest difficulty; they will not have a key to turn, though closely and tightly, in oiled wards; let the reluctant iron catch and grind, or they would even prefer to pick you the lock.

But though we may think it time that the quality once overprized should be restored to a more proportionate honour, our great poet Tennyson shows us that of all merits ease is, unexpectedly enough, the most dangerous. It is not only, with him, that the wards are oiled, it is also that the key turns loosely. This is true of much of the beautiful 'Idylls', but not of their best passages, nor of such magnificent blank verse as that of the close of 'A Vision of Sin', or of 'Lucretius'. As to the question of ease, we cannot have a better maxim than Coventry Patmore's saying that poetry 'should confess, but not suffer from, its difficulties'. Tennyson is always an artist, and the finish of his work is one of the principal notes of his versification. How this finish comports with the excessive ease of his prosody remains his own peculiar secret. Ease, in him, does not mean that he has any unhandsome slovenly ways. On the contrary, he resembles rather the warrior with the pouncet box. Tennyson certainly *worked*, and the exceeding ease of his blank verse comes perhaps of this little paradox — that he makes somewhat too much show of the hiding of his art.

In the first place the poet with the great welcome style and the little unwelcome manner, Tennyson is, in the second place, the modern poet who withstood France. (That is, of course, modern France — France since the Renaissance. From medieval Provence there is not an English poet who does not own inheritance.) It was some time about the date of the Restoration that modern France began to be modish in England. A ruffle at the Court of Charles, a couplet in the ear of Pope, a *tour de phrase* from Mme de Sévigné much to the taste of Walpole, later the good example of French painting — rich interest paid for the loan of our Constable's initiative — later still a scattering of French taste, French critical business, over all the shallow places of our literature — these have all been phases of a national vanity of ours, an eager and anxious fluttering or jostling to be foremost and French. Matthew Arnold's essay on criticism fostered this anxiety, and yet I find in this work of his a lack of easy French knowledge, such as his misunderstanding of the word *brutalité*, which means no more, or little more, than roughness. Matthew Arnold, by the way, knew so little of the French character as to be altogether ignorant of French provincialism, French practical sense, and French 'convenience'. 'Convenience' is his dearest word of contempt, 'practical sense' his next dearest, and he throws them a score of times in the teeth of the English. Strange is the irony of the truth. For he bestows those withering words on the nation that has the fifty religions, and attributes 'ideas' — as the antithesis of 'convenience' and 'practical sense' — to the nation that has the fifty sauces. And not for a moment does he suspect himself of this blunder, so manifest as to be disconcerting to his reader. One seems to hear an incurably

English accent in all this, which indeed is reported, by his acquaintance, of Matthew Arnold's actual speaking of French. It is certain that he has not the interest of familiarity with the language, but only the interest of strangeness. Now, while we meet the effect of the French coat in our seventeenth century, of the French light verse in our earlier eighteenth century, and of French philosophy in our later, of the French revolution in our Wordsworth, of the French painting in our nineteenth-century studios, of French fiction — and the dregs are still running — in our libraries, of French poetry in our Swinburne, of French criticism in our Arnold, Tennyson shows the effect of nothing French whatever. Not the Elizabethans, not Shakespeare, not Jeremy Taylor, not Milton, not Shelley were (in their art, not in their matter) more insular in their time. France, by the way, has more than appreciated the homage of Tennyson's contemporaries; Victor Hugo avers, in *Les Misérables*, that our people imitate his people in all things, and in particular he rouses in us a delighted laughter of surprise by asserting that the London street-boy imitates the Parisian street-boy. There is, in fact, something of a street-boy in some of our late more literary mimicries.

We are apt to judge a poet too exclusively by his imagery. Tennyson is hardly a great master of imagery. He has more imagination than imagery. He sees the thing, with so luminous a mind's eye, that it is sufficient to him; he needs not to see it more beautifully by a similitude. 'A clear-walled city' is enough; 'meadows' are enough — indeed Tennyson reigns for ever over all meadows; 'the happy birds that change their sky'; 'Bright Phosphor, fresher for the night'; 'Twilight and evening bell'; 'the stillness of the central sea'; 'that friend of mine who lives in God'; 'the solitary morning'; 'Four grey walls and four grey towers'; 'Watched by weeping queens'; these are enough, illustrious, and needing not illustration.

If we do not see Tennyson to be the lonely, the first, the *one* that he is, this is because of the throng of his following, though a number that are of that throng hardly know, or else would deny, their flocking. But he added to our literature not only in the way of cumulation, but by the advent of his single genius. He is one of the few fountain-head poets of the world. The new landscape which was his — the lovely unbeloved — is, it need hardly be said, the matter of his poetry and not its inspiration. It may have seemed to some readers that it is the novelty, in poetry, of this homely unscenic scenery — this Lincolnshire quality — that accounts for Tennyson's freshness of vision. But it is not so. Tennyson is fresh also in scenic scenery; he is fresh with the things that others have outworn; mountains, desert islands, castles, elves, what you will that is conventional. Where are there more divinely poetic lines than those, which will never be wearied with quotation, beginning, 'A splendour falls'? What castle walls have stood in such a light of old romance, where in all poetry is there a sound wilder than that of those faint 'horns of elfland'? Here is the remoteness, the beyond, the light delirium, not of disease but of more rapturous and delicate health, the closer secret of poetry. This most English of modern poets has been taunted with his mere gardens. He loved, indeed, the 'lazy lilies', of the exquisite garden of 'The Gardener's Daughter', but he betook his ecstatic English spirit also far afield and overseas; to the winter places of his familiar nightingale:

> When first the liquid note beloved of men
> Comes flying over many a windy wave;

to the lotus-eaters' shore; to the outland landscapes of 'The Palace of Art' — the 'clear-walled city by the sea', the 'pillared town', the 'full-fed river'; to the 'pencilled valleys' of Monte Rosa; to the 'vale in Ida', to that tremendous upland in the 'Vision of Sin':

> At last I heard a voice upon the slope
> Cry to the summit, Is there any hope?
> To which an answer pealed from that high land,
> But in a tongue no man could understand.

The Cleopatra of 'The Dream of Fair Women' is but a ready-made Cleopatra, but when in the shades of her forest she remembers the sun of the world, she leaves the page of Tennyson's poorest manner and becomes one with Shakespeare's queen:

We drank the Libyan sun to sleep.

Nay, there is never a passage of manner but a great passage of style rebukes our dislike and recalls our heart again. The dramas, less than the lyrics, and even less than the 'Idylls', are matter for the true Tennysonian. Their action is, at its liveliest, rather vivacious than vital, and the sentiment, whether in 'Becket' or in 'Harold', is not only modern, it is fixed within Tennyson's own peculiar score or so of years. But that he might have answered, in drama, to a stronger stimulus, a sharper spur, than his time administered, may be guessed from a few passages of 'Queen Mary', and from the dramatic terror of the arrow in 'Harold'. The line has appeared in prophetic fragments in earlier scenes, and at the moment of doom it is the outcry of unquestionable tragedy:

Sanguelac — Sanguelac — the arrow — the arrow! — Away!

Tennyson is also an eminently all-intelligible poet. Those whom he puzzles or confounds must be a flock with an incalculable liability to go wide of any road — 'down all manner of streets', as the desperate drover cries in the anecdote. But what are streets, however various, to the ways of error that a great flock will take in open country — minutely, individually wrong, making mistakes upon hardly perceptible occasions, or none — 'minute fortuitous variations in any possible direction', as used to be said in exposition of the Darwinian theory? A vast outlying public, like that of Tennyson, may make you as many blunders as it has heads; but the accurate clear poet proved his meaning to all accurate perceptions. Where he hesitates, his is the sincere pause of process and uncertainty. It has been said that Tennyson, midway between the student of material science and the mystic, wrote and thought according to an age that wavered, with him, between the two minds, and that men have now taken one way or the other. Is this indeed true, and are men so divided and so sure? Or have they not rather already turned, in numbers, back to the parting, or meeting, of eternal roads? The religious question that arises upon experience of death has never been asked with more sincerity and attention than by him. If 'In Memoriam' represents the mind of yesterday it represents no less the mind of to-morrow. It is true that pessimism and insurrection in their ignobler forms — nay, in the ignoblest form of a fashion — have, or had but yesterday, the control of the popular pen. Trivial pessimism or trivial optimism, it matters little which prevails. For those who follow the one habit to-day would have followed the other in a past generation. Fleeting as they are, it cannot be within their competence to neglect or reject the philosophy of 'In Memoriam'. To the dainty stanzas of that poem, it is true, no great struggle of reasoning was to be committed, nor would any such dispute be judiciously entrusted to the rhymes of a song of sorrow. Tennyson here proposes, rather than closes with, the ultimate question of our destiny. The conflict, for which he proves himself strong enough, is in that magnificent poem of a thinker, 'Lucretius'. But so far as 'In Memoriam' attempts, weighs, falters, and confides, it is true to the experience of human anguish and intellect.

I say intellect advisedly. Not for him such blunders of thought as Coleridge's in 'The Ancient Mariner' or Wordsworth's in 'Hartleap Well'. Coleridge names the sun, moon, and stars as when, in a dream, the sleeping imagination is threatened with some significant illness. We see them in his great poem as apparitions. Coleridge's senses are infinitely and transcendently spiritual. But a candid reader must be permitted to think the mere story silly. The wedding-guest might rise the morrow morn a sadder but he assuredly did not rise a wiser man.

As for Wordsworth, the most beautiful stanzas of 'Hartleap Well' are fatally rebuked by the truths of Nature. He shows us the ruins of an aspen wood, a blighted hollow, a dreary place, forlorn because an innocent stag, hunted, had there broken his heart in a leap from the rocks above; grass would not grow there.

> This beast not unobserved by Nature fell,
> His death was mourned by sympathy divine.

And the signs of that sympathy are cruelly asserted by the poet to be these woodland ruins — cruelly, because the daily sight of the world blossoming over the agonies of beast and bird is made less tolerable to us by such a fiction.

> The Being that is in the clouds and air
>
> .   .   .   .   .   .
>
> Maintains a deep and reverential care
> For the unoffending creature whom He loves.

The poet offers us as a proof of that 'reverential care', the visible alteration of Nature at the scene of suffering — an alteration we have to dispense with every day we pass in the woods. We are tempted to ask whether Wordsworth himself believed in a sympathy he asks us — on such grounds! — to believe in? Did he think his faith to be worthy of no more than a fictitious sign and a false proof?

Nowhere in the whole of Tennyson's thought is there such an attack upon our reason and our heart. He is more serious than the solemn Wordsworth.

And this poem, with all else that Tennyson wrote, tutors, with here and there a subtle word, this nature-loving nation to perceive land, light, sky, and ocean, as he perceived. To this we return, upon this we dwell. He has been to us, firstly, the poet of two geniuses — a small and an immense; secondly, the modern poet who answered in the negative that most significant modern question, French or not French? But he was, before the outset of all our study of him, of all our love of him, the poet of landscape, and this he is more dearly than pen can describe him. This eternal character of his is keen in the verse that is winged to meet a homeward ship with her 'dewy decks', and in the sudden island landscape,

> The clover sod,
> That takes the sunshine and the rains,
> Or where the kneeling hamlet drains
> The chalice of the grapes of God.

It is poignant in the garden-night:

> A breeze began to tremble o'er
> The large leaves of the sycamore,
>
> .   .   .   .   .   .
>
> And gathering freshlier overhead,
> Rocked the full-foliaged elm, and swung
> The heavy-folded rose, and flung
> The lilies to and fro, and said
> 'The dawn, the dawn', and died away.

His are the exalted senses that sensual poets know nothing of. I think the sense of hearing as well as the sense of sight, has never been more greatly exalted than by Tennyson:

> As from beyond the limit of the world,
> Like the last echo born of a great cry.

As to this garden-character so much decried I confess that the 'lawn' does not generally delight me, the word nor the thing. But in Tennyson's page the word is wonderful, as though it had never been dull: 'The mountain lawn was dewy-dark.' It is not that he brings the mountains too near or ranks them in his own peculiar garden-plot, but that the word withdraws, withdraws to summits, withdraws into dreams; the lawn is aloft, alone, and as wild as ancient snow. It is the same with many another word or phrase changed, by passing into his vocabulary, into something rich and strange. His own especially is the March month — his 'roaring moon'. His is the spirit of the dawning month of flowers and storms; the golden, soft names of daffodil and crocus are caught by the gale as you speak them in his verse, in a fine disproportion with the energy and gloom. His was a new apprehension of nature, an increase in the number, and not only in the sum, of our national apprehensions of poetry in nature. Unaware of a separate angel of modern poetry is he who is insensible to the Tennyson note — the new note that we reaffirm even with the notes of Vaughan, Traherne, Wordsworth, Coleridge, Blake well in our ears — the Tennyson note of splendour, all-distinct. He showed the perpetually transfigured landscape in transfiguring words. He is the captain of our dreams. Others have lighted a candle in England, he lit a sun. Through him our daily suns, and also the backward and historic suns long since set, which he did not sing, are magnified; and he bestows upon us an exalted retrospection. Through him Napoleon's sun of Austerlitz rises, for us, with a more brilliant menace upon arms and the plain; through him Fielding's 'most melancholy sun' lights the dying man to the setting-forth on that last voyage of his with such an immortal gleam, denying hope, as would not have lighted, for us, the memory of that seaward morning, had our poetry not undergone the illumination, the transcendent sunrise, of Tennyson's genius.

Emerson knew that the poet speaks adequately then only when he speaks 'a little wildly, or with the flower of the mind'. Tennyson, the clearest-headed of poets, is our wild poet; wild, notwithstanding that little foppery we know of in him — that walking delicately, like Agag; wild, notwithstanding the work, the ease, the neatness, the finish; notwithstanding the assertion of manliness which, in asserting, somewhat misses that mark; a wilder poet than the rough, than the sensual, than the defiant, than the accuser, than the denouncer. Wild flowers are his — great poet — wild winds, wild lights, wild heart, wild eyes!

The Roaring Moon

'WHAT moon ever roared?' asks an able writer upon poetic words. For, in a literary paper appears an article built of appreciations of 'schismatic' words, those vanward phrases, as one might name them, whereby the poets (some poets) have broken through the order of language in quest of stronger manifestations of their liberal moods. 'Language,' says this critic, '. . . is an imperfect vehicle for thought. It expresses the half but not the demi-semi tones . . . To convey some shadowy sense of the inexpressible, we can only essay the use of what the laws of harmony pronounce to be discords — marriages, or combinations of sounds hitherto kept apart; the significance of which we *feel*, though we cannot analyse our motives in applying them. Great men — popular writers — have been moved to the schism before now, though it was not the schism that made them popular. Take a single illustration — from Tennyson:

> . . . with a common will
> Here in *this roaring moon of daffodil*
> *And crocus*, to put forth and brave the blast.

The writer in question goes on to provoke the wonder of his reader by making a picture of the brilliant moon 'anchored up there in the flood — stemming it — rocking on it . . . An *im*pression has been given *ex*pression, in fact, by means of a discord.' He hopes to move his readers to something like a reverent dismay. See, he seems to say, what a poet will do if he has a mind to astonish you; how he defies your customary interpretations, and takes the language into his own hands, and how well it is that there should be someone to justify and to explain these brave conquests of fresh speech. 'What moon was ever built up' (says this eulogist) 'of daffodil and crocus? What moon ever roared? Yet the daring phrase (Who shall have the daring to deny it?) makes real in two words what descriptive classicism could not have compassed in fifty.'

And lo! all this is because the critic, apparently unaccustomed to an older poetic fashion, did not know that Tennyson had put the word 'moon' in place of the word 'month' as a mere equivalent! No more daring than this is the redoubtable phrase, no more impression than this is here, no more discord; no more schism, or sense of the inexpressible; and no blow is struck at descriptive classicism. Tennyson, in truth, is by no means the man to strike such blows, but precisely the man to take a somewhat older form of a word as the more romantic: such is moon for month. To call the windy month of March 'the roaring moon' is so exceedingly Tennysonian that no sound of voice or trick of manner could be more personal. The habit and action of your friend, the custom of his hands, the inflexion of his tones, are not more charged with the associations of his name than is this phrase for March burdened with the whole legend of Tennyson. It breathes his breath, which is his spirit.

No poet was ever more readily contented than he with the language as he found it; provided only he might rediscover these little bygone fashions — such as to say parcel for part, and traveller's joy for clematis. He took a pleasure in restoring these as a kind of decoration; not because he intended 'to convey some shadowy sense of the inexpressible', but because it was a pity that pretty and favourable phrases should be lost, and because these in particular seemed proper to the polished antiquity, the dainty Middle Ages, of which he makes a show that is so bright and so decorous, and, being called manly, does, like other things that are definitely called manly, perhaps vaguely miss that mark. Tennyson loved the picturesque word, and if his readers take less delight than he in moon for month, they make amends by confessing the new poetry wherewith he was able to transfigure a modern word.

The less need had he of breaking through the bonds of language, he who was pleased with a very little measure of quaint English, as though he had found a treasure, and he, moreover, who could make a drawing-room word spiritual. He needed no such acts of violence, and they are alien to him. Moon for month is right Tennyson, and 'roaring' — if it has its own violence, somewhat less than strong — is splendid, for it is the very March. Who is not filled by this verse with the spirit of the dawning month of flowers and storms? In that verse the golden soft names of daffodil and crocus are caught by the gale as you speak them, in a fine disproportion with that energy and gloom.

No other has sung March with so early and magical a voice. Birds on the swinging grey branch singing in cloudy daybreak are not newer, nor the shattered lights of windy morning wilder, nor the fires of a scattered sunset broken upon the flying east. March is Tennyson's. A reader might well give many pages of the delicate Idylls for one March passage in the 'May Queen': 'All in the wild March morning', or —

The trees began to whisper and the wind began to roll.

. . . . . .

It was when the moon was setting, and the dark was over all.

Like to this wild and new poetry in the verses of Tennyson's youth is the poetry, new and wild after fifty years, of the sonnet on the Roaring Moon. It was the new spirit of the apprehension of nature, an increase in the number of the possessions of poetry, and it is this to-day when other things, such as the shores that are 'smitten' and even the 'dim rich city', no longer seem to us so fine. If other boasts of Tennyson's poetry also should pass out of the true treasury, and if perhaps the most ordinarily conspicuous of its qualities should be among those that pass, there is always the Vision of nature abiding as he knew it first; a sun, a dazzling darkness, a night, a breeze. Who does not know the moments when Tennyson turns his face to that apparition? Not at all in certain pages; fully and with the peace and perception of exalted sense, with their splendour and peace, in the poetry of 'The Passing of Arthur', and again in passages of 'In Memoriam' and 'The Vision of Sin'. Was he, indeed, the first? Blake, with the more exalted senses of night and dreams, seems to be there before him. It is difficult to say of any man that he was the first. But it is certain that Tennyson gave these visions to the world and transfigured the words.

In short, what he did was precisely *not* the compelling of English poetry to make a roaring moon out of daffodils. All his greatness, all his character, all his vision, all his (comparative) limitation of intellect were against such adventures. He never set out upon those ways. He never found, as the critic who praises him for the roaring daffodil moon says he found, 'that the conservative and the classical are not necessarily adequate to the expression of intricate modern moods'. His modern moods were never too intricate for himself. But he had his foppery, whereby 'month' seemed to him too prosaic a word for that sonnet. By the way, there is a passage in the 'Idylls' which speaks of twelve months as 'twelve sweet moons'. Would our critic have praised him for the schism, the style, the audacity of lighting the night of his romance with twelve satellites where the conservative and the classical had seen but one since the beginning of letters?

And Tennyson — Tennyson did but mean to name a twelve-month!

Robert Browning

It says much for the power of Browning that he was able to leaven the mass of cultivated people by means of a comparatively little knot of readers. That he should be popular in any literal sense of the word had always been an impossibility which Browning very frankly accepted. Too obscure to be understood without unusual power of thought and especially without unusual mobility of mind, on the part of his reader, his work is also seldom musical enough to haunt the memory; and these two defects, if defects they be, have become proverbial with regard to him, and inseparable from his name. Yet he has, now and then, written verse in which a difficult thought has been expressed pellucidly, and verse ringing with true significant music, and occasionally even with a too obvious and insistent tune; but these exceptions are very naturally lost sight of in his prevailing practice. Now, in our opinion no author should be blamed for obscurity, nor should any pains be grudged in the effort to understand him, provided that he has done his best to be intelligible. Difficult thoughts are quite distinct from difficult words. Difficulty of thought is the very heart of poetry. Those who complain of it would restrict poetry to literal narrative for its epics, to unanalysed — and therefore ultimately to unrealized and conventional — passion for its drama, and to songs for its lyrics. Doubtless narrative, dramas of primary passion, and singable songs are all excellent things; masterpieces have been done in these ways — but in the past — in a fresher, broader, and simpler time than ours. Those masterpieces bring their own age with them, as it were, into our hearts; we ourselves assume a singleness of mind as we read them; they are neither too obvious nor too unthoughtful to interest us; but it is far otherwise with modern work which is laid upon the same lines.

Our age is not simple — we inherit so much from other ages; and our language has lost the freshness of its early literature — reasons why the poetry of our time should be complex in thought and should depend upon something more mental than the charm of form sufficient in the lyrics of the Elizabethans. The English language was once so beautiful, so fresh and free, that any well-composed group of English words would make a poem. But some of the vitality has been written out of the language since then; it is richer now than ever, but it has lost that youthfulness of form; and though the poems of those other times cannot themselves cease to be fresh to us, nothing can now be written of exactly their character. Beauty of manner must therefore be secondary in modern poetry to importance of thought; and no true thinking is altogether easy. Granted that modern poetry must be thoughtful or nothing, and that thought is difficult, we shall here have a sufficient apology for more than half Browning's obscurity. The rest must, as usual, be ascribed to the mere construction of his phrases; he has his own way of dropping out articles and other little words, which leads to grammatical ambiguities never, perhaps, suspected by the author himself and greatly to be lamented; grammatical obscurity is, perhaps, the one obscurity of which a reader has a right to complain. The same habit of contraction adds greatly to the tenseness of the verse, and it is this tenseness which we might wish to see relaxed. Even when his thought is closest, the words might fit it a little less tightly, we think; but Browning's mannerisms are not, as mannerisms, displeasing, for they are full of himself — of one of the most original personalities of contemporary literature. He, like Tennyson, is essential, not accidental, in English poetry.

Browning is, as a poet, distinctively a man of the world; we use the term in the sense in which it is employed by men when they intend praise; he is keenly interested in things as they are; he is impartial and has a masculine tolerance and patience which belong essentially to the dramatic genius; he prefers to be shrewd rather than profound in the mental analysis which delights him; there are heights in the human soul that tempt this explorer less than level ways — provided these are intricate enough. Browning is distinctively human, but not in the sense which the word generally bears; he is not exactly gentle or sympathetic, or penetrated with the pathos of the human tragedy; he is curious in human things, interested, experimental, and he preserves a sane cheerfulness altogether characteristic of himself. This last, which supports him through pages upon pages of inquiries and experiments as to the mental processes of a spirit-rapping cheat also inspires him with poems on death, now heroically grotesque, now ecstatic.

I would hate that death bandaged my eyes, and forebore,
    And bade me creep past.
No! Let me taste the whole of it, fare like my peers,
    The heroes of old,
Bear the brunt, in a minute pay glad life's arrears
    Of pain, darkness, and cold.
      .   .   The fiend-voices that rave
    Shall dwindle, shall blend,
Shall change, shall become first a peace out of pain,
    Then a light, then thy breast,
O thou soul of my soul! I shall clasp thee again,
    And with God be the rest!

In the following the 'little minute's sleep' is past:

'What! and is it you again?' quoth I.
'I again; whom else did you expect?' quoth she.

Then he tells her how much relieved he is to be rid of life and he sketches his own epitaph:

'Afflictions sore long time be bore; do end,' quoth I.
I end with 'Love is all and death is nought,' quoth she.

He carries this same temper of mind through his study of Bishop Blougram's sophistries, and through the resignation of *Any Wife to Any Husband*. And surely Browning's work loses something by this equanimity, this large tolerance of his. A mind less serene, whole, scientific, and independent might oftener be touched, or hurt, or discouraged into seeking a lofty and lovely ideal which is rare in his poetry. Not that Browning cannot conceive it, but that he is too closely and intently at work with things as they are to attend to it.

But no one who has not followed him through his labours of analysis, can understand the pleasure of the more studious reader at hearing Browning's cool, strong, argumentative voice break in the rare note of emotion, caused by his own sudden rise to a higher moral and mental beauty than lies in the path of a man of the world. When this happens, not the feeling only, but the verse softens and relaxes; for his style, like his thought, is knotted — is as knotty, indeed, as a fugue. But when that higher, fresher thought comes, it brings with it its own inevitable music. No poet has written fuller, more important, and more significant music than Browning at these rare moments. For instance, in that fine drama, *The Return of the Druses*, there is some difficulty in the character of Anael with her double love and her half-deliberate delusion, so that much of the verse allotted to her is intricate enough; but where strong single feeling rises in the heart of this exiled Druse girl, what exquisite music sweeps out indeliberately! —

Dost thou snow-swathe thee kinglier, Lebanon,
Than in my dreams?

English poetry might in vain be searched for a nobler cadence. In *Pippa Passes* (to our mind the most beautiful, though not therefore necessarily the most intellectual, of all Browning's works) such music is too frequent to allow us to choose examples; it occurs in *Balaustion's Adventure*, now and then, and less frequently elsewhere. Far more strongly accented musical pieces occur now and then in his work; *Evelyn Hope* and *A Lover's Quarrel* are as melodious — except for an occasional jerk — as the warmest admirers of insistently rhythmic verse could possibly require; but these bear the same relation to the higher music of which we have just spoken, as is borne by a tune of Rossini's to one of Schumann's significant sentences of notes.

The Brontës

CHARLOTTE BRONTË's history, her work, her sorrows, take the imagination of man, woman, and child; and with the ambition, the day-dream, the self-consciousness, and the anger of women born to obscurity her great example wrought. To the un-numbered ranks of girls in the generation following her own, destined, most unjustly, to one inevitable career of teaching, the fame of the governess, poor, born in mediocrity, perhaps ill-favoured, but with a fiery heart, was a single message of hope and suggestion of glory. Many a woman out of reach of envy towards the fortunate and the brilliant was touched to the quick by the renown of the unfortunate author of *Jane Eyre*. It seemed a possible, a not improbable, an accessible splendour; something golden lurking in the dullest of all dull worlds, and discoverable haply yet once again.

Charlotte Brontë, throughout her career, altered greatly. She did, in fact, inherit a manner of English that had been strained beyond restoration, fatigued beyond recovery, by the 'corrupt following' of Gibbon; and there was within her a sense of propriety that caused her to conform to it. Straitened and serious elder daughter of her time, she kept the house of literature. She practised those verbs 'to evince', 'to reside', 'to intimate', 'to peruse'. She wrote 'communicating instruction' for 'teaching'; 'an extensive and eligible connection'; 'a small competency'; 'an establishment on the Continent'; 'It operated as a barrier to further intercourse'; and of a child (with a singular unfitness with childhood) 'For the toys he possesses he seems to have contracted a partiality amounting to affection'. Encumbered by this drift and refuse of English, Charlotte Brontë yet achieved the miracle of her vocabulary. It is less wonderful that she should have appeared out of such a parsonage than that she should have arisen out of such a language.

A re-reading of her works is always a new amazing of her reader who turns back to review the harvest of her English. It must have been with rapture that she claimed her own simplicity. And with what a moderation, how temperately, and how seldom she used her mastery! To the last she has an occasional attachment to her bonds; for she was not only fire and air. In one passage of her life she may remind us of the little colourless and thrifty hen-bird that Lowell watched nest-building with her mate, and cutting short the flutterings and billings wherewith he would joyously interrupt the business; Charlotte's nesting bird was a clergyman. He came, lately affianced, for a week's visit to her parsonage, and she wrote to her friend before his arrival: 'My little plans have been dis-arranged by an intimation that Mr. —— is coming on Monday'; and afterwards, in reference to her sewing, 'he hindered me for a full week'.

Those were days when the domestic English banished their children out of sight in a manner not considered quite affectionate by other nations. If the Brontës were evidently hard and unsympathetic governesses, probably that was because nobody had taken much delight in their own childhood. 'Mr. Brontë', says Mrs. Gaskell, in perfect good faith, 'was not naturally fond of children, and felt their frequent appearance on the scene both as a drag on his wife's strength and as an interruption to the comfort of the household.' Nor was the mother, in her long, last illness, 'anxious to see much of her children'. This wonderful view of the gravest of all human responsibilities — for what have we to answer for to that which has made us, compared with what we have to answer for to that which we have made? — was common enough in the most correct, the severest, and, in a dull sense, the most conscientious homes in the world. A contempt for the signs and shows of love must make existence ugly enough in the eyes of that vigilant looker-on, the child. When Charlotte Brontë had been surprised into writing 'darling' to a friend, she added, 'Strike that out, it's humbug'. And her biographer names as 'gush' the little affectionate demonstration of a child.

In alternate pages *Villette* is a book of spirit and fire, and a novel of illiberal rancour, ungentle, ignoble. In order to forgive its offences we have to remember in its author's favour not her pure style set free, not her splendour in literature, but rather the immeasurable sorrow of her life. To read of that sorrow again is to open once more a wound which most men perhaps, certainly most women, received into their hearts in childhood, when they first heard in what narrow beds 'the three are laid' — the two sisters and the brother — and in what a bed of living insufferable memories the one left lay alone, reviewing the hours of their death — alone in the sealed house that was only less narrow than their graves. The rich may set apart and dedicate a room, the poor change their street, but Charlotte Brontë, in the close captivity of the fortunes of mediocrity, rested in the chair that had been her dying sister's, and held her melancholy bridals in the dining-room that had been the scene of terrible and reluctant death.

But closer than the conscious house was the conscious mind. Locked with intricate wards within the unrelaxing and unlapsing thoughts of this lonely sister, dwelt a sorrow inconsolable. It is well for the perpetual fellowship of mankind that no child should read this life and not take therefrom a perdurable scar, albeit her heart was somewhat frigid towards childhood, and she died before her motherhood could be born.

Mistress of some of the best prose of her century, Charlotte Brontë was subject to a Lewes, a Chorley, a Miss Martineau: that is, she suffered what in Italian is called *soggezione* in their presence. When she had met six minor contemporary writers — by-products of literature — at dinner, she had a headache and a sleepless night. She writes to her friend that these contributors to the quarterly Press are greatly feared in literary London, and there is in her letter a sense of tremor and exhaustion. And what nights did the heads of the critics undergo after the meeting? Lewes, whose own romances are all condoned, all forgiven by time and oblivion, who gave her lessons, who told her to study Jane Austen? The others, whose reviews doubtless did their proportionate part in still further hunting and harrying the tired English of their day? And before Harriet Martineau she bore herself reverently. Harriet Martineau, albeit a woman of masculine understanding (we may imagine we hear her contemporaries give her the title), could not thread her way safely in and out of two or three negatives, but wrote — about this very Charlotte Brontë: 'I did not consider the book a coarse one, though I could not answer for it that there were no traits which, on a second leisurely reading, I might not dislike.' Mrs. Gaskell quotes the passage with no consciousness of anything amiss.

As for Lewes's vanished lesson upon the methods of Jane Austen, it served one only sufficient purpose. Itself is not quoted by anyone alive, but Charlotte Brontë's rejoinder adds one to our little treasury of her incomparable pages. If they were twenty, they are twenty-one by the addition of this, written in a long-neglected letter and saved for us by Mr. Shorter's research, for I believe his is the only record: 'What sees keenly, speaks aptly, moves flexibly, it suits her to study; but what throbs fast and full, though hidden, what blood rushes through, what is the unseen seat of life and the sentient target of death — that Miss Austen ignores.'

When the author of *Jane Eyre* faltered before six authors,

more or less, at dinner in London, was it the writer of her
second-class English who was shy, or was it the author of the
passages here to follow — and therefore one for whom the
national tongue was much the better? There can be little
doubt. The Charlotte Brontë who used the English of a
world long corrupted by 'one good custom' — the good custom
of Gibbon's Latinity grown fatally popular — could at any
time hold up her head amongst her reviewers; for her there
was no sensitive interior solitude in that society. She who
cowered was the Charlotte who made Rochester recall 'the
simple yet sagacious grace' of Jane's first smile; she who
wrote: 'I looked at my love; it shivered in my heart like a
suffering child in a cold cradle'; who wrote: 'To see what a
heavy lid day slowly lifted, what a wan glance she flung upon
the hills, you would have thought the sun's fire quenched in
last night's floods.' This new genius was solitary and afraid,
and touched to the quick by the eyes and voice of judges.
In her worse style there was no 'quick'. Latin-English,
whether scholarly or unscholarly, is the mediate tongue. An
unscholarly Latin-English is proof against the world. The
scholarly Latin-English wherefrom it is disastrously derived
is, in its own nobler measure, a defence against more august
assaults than those of criticism. In the strength of it did
Johnson hold parley with his profounder sorrows — hold par-
ley (by his phrase), make terms (by his definition), give them
at last lodging and entertainment after sentence and treaty.

But those vain phrases fall from before Charlotte Brontë's
face and her bared heart. To the heart, to the heart she took
the shafts of her griefs. She tells them therefore as she suffered
them, vitally and mortally: 'A great change approached.
Affliction came in that shape which to anticipate is dread; to
look back on, grief. My sister Emily first declined. Never in
all her life had she lingered over any task that lay before her,
and she did not linger now. She made haste to leave us.' 'I
remembered where the three were laid — in what narrow, dark
dwellings.' 'Do you know this place? No, you never saw it;
but you recognize the nature of these trees, this foliage — the

cypress, the willow, the yew. Stone crosses like these are not unfamiliar to you, nor are these dim garlands of everlasting flowers. Here is the place.' 'Then the watcher approaches the patient's pillow, and sees a new and strange moulding of the familiar features, feels at once that the insufferable moment draws nigh.' In the same passage comes another single word of genius, 'the sound that so wastes our strength'. And, fine as 'wastes', is the 'wronged' of another sentence — 'some wronged and fettered wild beast or bird'. It is easy to gather such words, more difficult to separate the best from such a mingled page as that on 'Imagination': 'A spirit, softer and better than human reason, had descended with quiet flight to the waste'; and 'My hunger has this good angel appeased with food sweet and strange'; and 'This daughter of Heaven remembered me to-night; she saw me weep, and she came with comfort; "Sleep," she said, "sleep sweetly — I gild thy dreams." ' 'Was this feeling dead? I do not know, but it was buried. Sometimes I thought the tomb unquiet.'

Perhaps the most 'eloquent' pages are unluckily those wherein we miss the friction — friction that sensibly proves the use, the buoyancy, the act of language. Sometimes an easy eloquence resembles the easy labours of the daughters of Danaus. To draw water in a sieve is an easy art, rapid and relaxed. But no laxity is ever, I think, to be found in her brief passages of landscape: 'The keen, still cold of the morning was succeeded, later in the day, by a sharp breathing from the Russian wastes; the cold zone sighed over the temperate zone and froze it fast.' 'Not till the destroying angel of tempest had achieved his perfect work would he fold the wings whose waft was thunder, the tremor of whose plumes was storm.' 'The night is not calm: the equinox still struggles in its storms. The wild rains of the day are abated: the great single cloud disappears and rolls away from Heaven, not passing and leaving a sea all sapphire, but tossed buoyant before a continued, long-sounding, high-rushing moonlight tempest ... No Endymion will watch for his goddess to-night: there are no flocks on the mountains.' See, too, this ocean: 'The sway of the whole Great Deep above a herd of whales rushing through the livid and liquid thunder down from the frozen zone.' And this promise of the visionary Shirley: 'I am to be walking by myself on deck, rather late of an August evening, watching and being watched by a full harvest moon: something is to rise white on the surface of the sea, over which that moon mounts silent, and hangs glorious...I think I hear it cry with an articulate voice...I show you an image fair as alabaster emerging from the dim wave.'

Charlotte Brontë knew well the experience of dreams. She seems to have undergone the inevitable dream of mourners — the human dream of the Labyrinth, shall I call it? the uncertain spiritual journey in search of the waiting and sequestered dead, which is the obscure subject of the 'Eurydice' of Coventry Patmore's Odes. There is the lately dead, in exile, remote, betrayed, foreign, indifferent, sad, forsaken by some vague malice or neglect, sought by troubled love astray.

In Charlotte Brontë's page there is an autumnal and tempestuous dream: 'A nameless experience that had the hue, the mien, the terror, the very tone of a visitation from eternity...Suffering brewed in temporal or calculable measure tastes not as this suffering tasted.' Finally, is there any need to cite the passage of *Jane Eyre* that contains the avowal, the vigil in the garden? Those are not words to be forgotten. Some tell you that a fine style will give you the memory of a scene and not of the recording words that are the author's means. And others again would have the phrase to be remembered foremost. Here, then, in *Jane Eyre*, are both memories equal. The night is perceived, the phrase is an experience; both have their place in the reader's irrevocable past. 'Custom intervened between me and what I naturally and inevitably loved.' 'Jane, do you hear that nightingale singing in the wood?' 'A waft of wind came sweeping down the laurel walk, and trembled through the boughs of the chestnut; it wandered away to an indefinite distance...The nightingale's voice was then the only voice of the hour; in listening I again wept.'

Whereas Charlotte Brontë walked, with exultation and enterprise, upon the road of symbols, under the guidance of her own visiting genius, Emily seldom went out upon those far avenues. She was one who practised imagery sparingly. Her style had the key of an inner prose which seems to leave imagery behind in the way of approaches — the apparelled and arrayed approaches and ritual of literature — and so to go further and to be admitted among simple realities and antitypes.

Charlotte Brontë also knew that simple goal, but she loved her imagery. In the passage of *Jane Eyre* that tells of the return to Thornfield Hall, in ruins by fire, she bespeaks her reader's romantic attention to an image which in truth is not all golden. She has moments, on the other hand, of pure narrative, whereof each word is such a key as I spoke of but now, and unlocks an inner and yet an inner door of spiritual realities. There is, perhaps, no author who, simply telling what happened, tells it with so great a significance: 'Jane, did you hear that nightingale singing in the wood?' and 'She made haste to leave us'. But her characteristic calling is to images, those avenues and temples oracular, and to the vision of symbols.

You may hear the poet of great imagery praised as a great mystic. Nevertheless, although a great mystical poet makes images he does not do so in his greatest moments. He is a great mystic because he has a full vision of the mystery of realities, not because he has a clear invention of similitudes.

> Of many thousand kisses the poor last,

and

> Now with his love, now in the coldë grave

are lines on the yonder side of imagery. So is this line also:

> Sad with the promise of a different sun,

and

> Piteous passion keen at having found,
> After exceeding ill, a little good.

Shakespeare, Chaucer, and Patmore yield us these great examples. Imagery is for the time when, as in these lines, the shock of feeling (which must needs pass, as the heart beats and pauses) is gone by:

> Thy heart with dead winged Innocencies filled,
> Even as a nest with birds,
> After the old ones by the hawk are killed.

I cite these lines of Patmore's because of their imagery in a poem that without them would be insupportably close to spiritual facts; and because it seems to prove with what a yielding hand at play the poet of realities holds his symbols for a while. A great writer is both a major and a minor mystic, in the self-same poem; now suddenly close to his mystery (which is his greater moment), and anon making it mysterious with imagery (which is the moment of his most beautiful lines).

The student passes delighted through the several courts of poetry, from the outer to the inner, from riches to more imaginative riches, and from decoration to more complex decoration; and prepares himself for the greater opulence of the innermost chamber. But when he crosses the last threshold he finds this midmost sanctuary to be a hypaethral temple, and in its custody and care a simple earth and a space of sky.

Emily Brontë seems to have a nearly unparalleled unconsciousness of the delays, the charms, the pauses and preparations, of imagery. Her strength does not dally with the parenthesis, and her simplicity is ignorant of those rites. Her lesser work, therefore, is plain narrative, and her greater work is no more. On the hither side — the daily side — of imagery she is still a strong and solitary writer; on the yonder side she has written some of the most mysterious passages in all plain prose. And with what direct and incommunicable art! ' "Let me alone, let me alone," said Catherine. "If I've done wrong, I'm dying for it. You left me too . . . I forgive you. Forgive me!" "It is hard to forgive, and to look at those eyes and feel those wasted hands," he answered. "Kiss me again, and don't let me see your eyes: I forgive what you have done to me.

I love my murderer — but *yours*! How can I?" They were
silent, their faces hid against each other, and washed by each
other's tears.' 'So much the worse for me that I am strong,'
cries Heathcliff in the same scene. 'Do I want to live? What
kind of living will it be when you —— Oh, God, would you
like to live with your soul in the grave?'

Charlotte Brontë's noblest passages are her own speech or
the speech of one like herself acting the central part in the
dreams and dramas of emotion that she had kept from her
girlhood — the unavowed custom of the ordinary girl by her
so splendidly avowed in a confidence that surprised the world.
Emily had no such confessions to publish. She contrived —
but the word does not befit her singular spirit of liberty, that
knew nothing of stealth — to remove herself from the world;
as her person left no pen-portrait, so her 'I' is not heard here.
She lends her voice in disguise to her men and women; the
first narrator of her great romance is a young man, the second
a servant-woman; this one or that among the actors takes up
the story, and her great words sound at times in paltry mouths.
It is then that for a moment her reader seems about to come
into her immediate presence, but by a fiction she denies herself
to him. To a somewhat trivial girl (or a girl who would be
trivial in any other book, but Emily Brontë seems unable to
create anything consistently meagre) — to Isabella Linton she
commits one of her most memorable passages, and one which
has the rare image, one of a set of a terrifying little company
of visions amid terrifying facts: 'His attention was roused, I
saw, for his eyes rained down tears among the ashes . . . The
clouded windows of hell flashed for a moment towards me; the
fiend which usually looked out was so dimmed and drowned.'
But in Heathcliff's own speech there is no veil or circumstance:
'I'm too happy; and yet I'm not happy enough. My soul's bliss
kills my body, but does not satisfy itself.' 'I have to remind
myself to breathe, and almost to remind my heart to beat.'
'Being alone, and conscious two yards of loose earth was the
sole barrier between us, I said to myself: "I'll have her in my
arms again." If she be cold, I'll think it is this north wind that

chills me; and if she be motionless, it is sleep.' What art, more-
over, what knowledge, what a fresh ear for the clash of repeti-
tion; what a chime in that phrase: 'I dreamt I was sleeping the
last sleep by that sleeper, with my heart stopped, and my cheek
frozen against hers.'

Emily Brontë was no student of books. It was not from
among the fruits of any other author's labour that she gathered
these eminent words. But I think I have found the suggestion
of this action of Heathcliff's — the disinterment. Not in any
inspiring ancient Irish legend, as has been suggested, did
Emily Brontë find her incident; she found it (but she made,
and did not find, its beauty) in a mere costume romance of
Bulwer Lytton, whom Charlotte Brontë, as we know, did not
admire. And Emily showed no sign at all of admiration when
she did him so much honour as to borrow the action of his
studio-bravo.

Heathcliff's love for Catherine's past childhood is one of the
profound surprises of this unparalleled book; it is to call her
childish ghost — the ghost of the little girl — when she has
been a dead adult woman twenty years that the inhuman lover
opens the window of the house on the Heights. Something is
this that the reader knew not how to look for. Another thing
known to genius and beyond a reader's hope is the tempestuous
purity of those passions. This wild quality of purity has a
counterpart in the brief passages of nature that make the
summers, the waters, the woods, and the windy heights of that
murderous story seem so sweet. The 'beck' that was audible
beyond the hills after rain, the 'heath on the top of Wuthering
Heights' whereon, in her dream of Heaven, Catherine, flung
out by angry angels, awoke sobbing for joy; the bird whose
feathers she — delirious creature — plucks from the pillow of
her deathbed ('This — I should know it among a thousand —
it's a lapwing's. Bonny bird; wheeling over our heads in the
middle of the moor. It wanted to get to its nest, for the clouds
had touched the swells and it felt rain coming'); the only two
white spots of snow left on all the moors, and the brooks brim-
full; the old apple trees, the smell of stocks and wallflowers in

the brief summer, the few fir trees by Catherine's window-bars, the early moon — I know not where are landscapes more exquisite and natural. And among the signs of death where is any fresher than the window seen from the garden to be swinging open in the morning, when Heathcliff lay within, dead and drenched with rain?

None of these things are presented by images. Nor is that signal passage wherewith the book comes to a close. Be it permitted to cite it here again. It has taken its place, it is among the paragons of our literature. Our language will not lapse or derogate while this prose stands for appeal: 'I lingered . . . under that benign sky; watched the moths fluttering among the heath and harebells, listened to the soft wind breathing through the grass, and wondered how anyone could ever imagine unquiet slumbers for the sleepers in that quiet earth.'

Finally, of Emily Brontë's face the world holds only an obviously unskilled reflection, and of her aspect no record worth having. Wild fugitive, she vanished, she escaped, she broke away, exiled by the neglect of her contemporaries, banished by their disrespect, outlawed by their contempt, dismissed by their indifference. And such an one was she as might rather have pronounced upon these the sentence passed by Coriolanus under sentence of expulsion; she might have driven the world from before her face and cast it out from her presence as he condemned his Romans: '*I* banish you.'

Dickens

It was said for many years, until the reversal that now befalls the sayings of many years had happened to this also, that Thackeray was the unkind satirist and Dickens the kind humorist. The truth seems to be that Dickens imagined more evil people than did Thackeray, but that he had an eager faith in good ones. Nothing places him so entirely out of date as his trust in human sanctity, his love of it, his hope for it, his leap at it. He saw it in a woman's face first met, and drew it to himself in a man's hand first grasped. He looked keenly for it. And if he associated minor degrees of goodness with any kind of folly or mental ineptitude, he did not so relate sanctity; though he gave it, for companion, ignorance; and joined the two, in Joe Gargery, most tenderly. We might paraphrase, in regard to these two great authors, Dr. Johnson's famous sentence: 'Marriage has many pains, but celibacy has no joys.' Dickens has many scoundrels, but Thackeray has no saints. Helen Pendennis is not holy, for she is unjust and cruel; Amelia is not holy, for she is an egoist in love; Lady Castlewood is not holy, for she too is cruel; and even Lady Jane is not holy, for she is jealous; nor is Colonel Newcome holy, for he is haughty; nor Dobbin, for he turns with a taunt upon a plain sister; nor Esmond, for he squanders his best years in love for a material beauty; and these are the best of his good people. And readers have been taught to praise the work of him who makes none perfect; one does not meet perfect people in trains or at dinner, and this seemed good cause that the novelist should be praised for his moderation; it seemed to imitate the usual measure and moderation of nature.

But Charles Dickens closed with a divine purpose divinely different. He consented to the counsels of perfection. And thus he made Joe Gargery, not a man one might easily find in a forge; and Esther Summerson, not a girl one may easily meet at a dance; and Little Dorrit, who does not come to do a day's sewing; not that the man and the women are inconceivable, but that they are unfortunately improbable. They are creatures created through a creating mind that worked its six days for the love of good, and never rested until the seventh, the final Sabbath. But granting that they are the counterpart, the heavenly side, of caricature, this is not to condemn them. Since when has caricature ceased to be an art good for man — an honest game between him and nature? It is a tenable opinion that frank caricature is a better incident of art than the mere exaggeration which is the more modern practice. The words mean the same thing in their origin — an overloading. But as we now generally delimit the words they differ. Caricature, when it has the grotesque inspiration, makes for laughter, and when it has the celestial, makes for admiration; in either case there is a good understanding between the author and the reader, or between the draughtsman and the spectator. We need not, for example, suppose that Ibsen sat in a room surrounded by a repeating pattern of his hair and whiskers on the wallpaper, but it makes us most exceedingly mirthful and joyous to see him thus seated in Mr. Max Beerbohm's drawing; and perhaps no girl ever went through life without harbouring a thought of self, but it is very good for us all to know that such a girl was thought of by Dickens, that he loved his thought, and that she is ultimately to be traced, through Dickens, to God.

But exaggeration establishes no good understanding between the reader and the author. It is a solemn appeal to our credulity, and we are right to resent it. It is the violence of a weakling hand — the worst manner of violence.

It takes for granted some degree of imbecility in the reader, whereas caricature takes for granted a high degree of intelligence. Dickens appeals to our intelligence in all his caricature, whether heavenly, as in Joe Gargery, or impish, as in Mrs. Micawber. The word 'caricature' that is used a thousand times to reproach him is the word that does him singular honour.

If I may define my own devotion to Dickens, it may be stated as chiefly, though not wholly, admiration of his humour, his dramatic tragedy, and his watchfulness over inanimate things and landscape. Passages of his books that are ranged otherwise than under those characters often leave me out of the range of their appeal or else definitely offend me. And this is not for the customary reason — that Dickens could not draw a gentleman, that Dickens could not draw a lady. It matters little whether he could or not. But as a fact he did draw a gentleman, and drew him excellently well, in Cousin Feenix, as Mr. Chesterton has decided. The question of the lady we may waive; if it is difficult to prove a negative, it is difficult also to present one; and to the making, or producing, or liberating, or detaching, or exalting, of the character of a lady there enter many negatives; and Dickens was an obvious and a positive man. Esther Summerson is a lady, but she is so much besides that her ladyhood does not detach itself from her sainthood and her angelhood, so as to be conspicuous — if, indeed, conspicuousness may be properly predicated of the quality of a lady. It is a conventional saying that sainthood and angelhood include the quality of a lady, but that saying is not true; a lady has a great number of negatives all her own, and also some things positive that are not at all included in goodness. However this may be — and it is not important — Dickens, the genial Dickens, makes savage sport of women. Such a company of envious dames and damsels cannot be found among the persons of the satirist Thackeray. Kate Nickleby's beauty brings upon her at first sight the enmity of her workshop companions; in the innocent pages of *Pickwick* the aunt is jealous of the niece, and the niece retorts by wounding the vanity of the aunt as keenly as she may; and so forth through early books and late. He takes for granted that the women, old and young, who are not his heroines, wage this war within the sex, being disappointed by defect of nature and fortune. Dickens is master of wit, humour, and derision; and it must be confessed that his derision is abundant, and is cast upon an artificially exposed and helpless people; that is, he, a man, derides the women who miss what a man declared to be their 'whole existence'.

The advice which M. Rodin received in his youth from Constant — 'Learn to see the other side; never look at forms only in extent; learn to see them always in relief' — is the contrary of the counsel proper for a reader of Dickens. That counsel should be: 'Do not insist upon seeing the immortal figures of comedy "in the round". You are to be satisfied with their face value, the face of two dimensions. It is not necessary that you should seize Mr. Pecksniff from beyond, and grasp the whole man and his destinies.' The hypocrite is a figure dreadful and tragic, a shape of horror; and Mr. Pecksniff is a hypocrite, and a bright image of heart-easing comedy. For comic fiction cannot exist without some such paradox. Without it, where would our laugh be in response to the generous genius which gives us Mr. Pecksniff's parenthesis to the mention of sirens ('Pagan, I regret to say'); and the scene in which Mr. Pecksniff, after a stormy domestic scene within, goes as it were accidentally to the door to admit the rich kinsman he wishes to propitiate? 'Then Mr. Pecksniff, gently warbling a rustic stave, put on his garden hat, seized a spade, and opened the street door, as if he thought he had, from his vineyard, heard a modest rap, but was not quite certain.' The visitor had thundered at the door while outcries of family strife had been rising in the house. ' "It is an ancient pursuit, gardening. Primitive, my dear sir; for, if I am not mistaken, Adam was the first of the calling. My Eve, I grieve to say, is no more, sir; but" (and here he pointed to his spade, and shook his head, as if he were not cheerful without an effort) "but I do a little bit of Adam still." He had by this time got them into the best parlour, where the portrait by Spiller and the bust by Spoker were.' And again, Mr. Pecksniff, hospitable at the supper table: ' "This," he said, in allusion to the party, not the wine, "is a Mingling that repays one for much disappointment and vexation. Let us be merry." Here he took a captain's biscuit. "It is a poor heart that never rejoices; and our hearts are not poor. No!" With such stimulants to merriment did he beguile the time and do the honours of the table.' Moreover it is a mournful thing and an inexplicable, that a man should be as mad as Mr. Dick. None the less is it a happy thing for any reader to watch Mr. Dick while David explains his difficulty to Traddles. Mr. Dick was to be employed in copying, but King Charles the First could not be kept out of the manuscripts; 'Mr. Dick in the meantime looking very deferentially and seriously at Traddles, and sucking his thumb'. And the amours of the gentleman in gaiters who threw the vegetable marrows over the garden wall. Mr. F.'s aunt, again! And Augustus Moddle, our own Moddle, whom a great French critic most justly and accurately brooded over. 'Augustus, the gloomy maniac,' says Taine, 'makes us shudder.' A good medical diagnosis. Long live the logical French intellect!

Truly, Humour talks in his own language, nay, his own dialect, whereas Passion and Pity speak the universal tongue.

It is strange — it seems to me deplorable — that Dickens himself was not content to leave his wonderful hypocrite — one who should stand imperishable in comedy — in the two dimensions of his own admirable art. After he had enjoyed his own Pecksniff, tasting him with the 'strenuous tongue' of Keats's voluptuary bursting 'joy's grapes against his palate fine', Dickens most unfairly gives himself the other and incompatible joy of grasping his Pecksniff in the third dimension, seizes him 'in the round', horsewhips him out of all keeping, and finally kicks him out of a splendid art of fiction into a sorry art of 'poetical justice', a Pecksniff not only defeated but undone.

And yet Dickens's retribution upon sinners is a less fault than his reforming them. It is truly an act denoting excessive simplicity of mind in him. He never veritably allows his responsibility as a man to lapse. Men ought to be good, or else to become good, and he does violence to his own excellent art, and yields it up to his sense of morality. Ah, can we measure by years the time between that day and this? Is the fastidious, the impartial, the non-moral novelist only the grandchild, and not the remote posterity, of Dickens, who would not leave Scrooge to his egoism, or Gradgrind to his facts, or Mercy Pecksniff to her absurdity, or Dombey to his pride? Nay, who makes Micawber finally to prosper? Truly, the most unpardonable thing Dickens did in those deplorable last chapters of his was the prosperity of Mr. Micawber. 'Of a son, in difficulties' — the perfect Micawber nature is respected as to his origin, and then perverted as to his end. It is a pity that Mr. Peggotty ever came back to England with such tidings. And our last glimpse of the emigrants had been made joyous by the sight of the young Micawbers on the eve of emigration; 'every child had its own wooden spoon attached to its body by a strong line', in preparation for Colonial life. And then Dickens must needs go behind the gay scenes, and tell us that the long and untiring delight of the book was over. Mr. Micawber, in the Colonies, was never again to make punch with lemons, in a crisis of his fortunes, and 'resume his peeling with a desperate air'; nor to observe the expression of his friends' faces during Mrs. Micawber's masterly exposition of the financial situation or of the possibilities of the coal trade; nor to eat walnuts out of a paper bag what time the die was cast and all was over. Alas! nothing was over until Mr. Micawber's pecuniary liabilities were over, and the perfect comedy turned into dulness, the joyous impossibility of a figure of immortal fun into cold improbability.

There are several such late or last chapters that one would gladly cut away: that of Mercy Pecksniff's pathos, for example; that of Mr. Dombey's installation in his daughter's home; that which undeceives us as to Mr. Boffin's antic disposition. But how true and how whole a heart it was that urged these unlucky conclusions! How shall we venture to complain? The hand that made its Pecksniff in pure wit, has it not the right to belabour him in earnest — albeit a kind of earnest that disappoints us? And Mr. Dombey is Dickens's own Dombey, and he must do what he will with that finely wrought figure of pride. But there is a little irony in the fact that Dickens leaves more than one villain to his orderly fate for whom we care little either way; it is nothing to us, whom Carker never convinced, that the train should catch him, nor that the man with the moustache and the nose, who did but weary us, should be crushed by the falling house. Here the end holds good in art, but the art was not good from the first. But then, again, neither does Bill Sikes experience a change of heart, nor Jonas Chuzzlewit; and the end of each is most excellently told.

George Meredith said that the most difficult thing to write in fiction was dialogue. But there is surely one thing at least as difficult — a thing so rarely well done that a mere reader might think it to be more difficult than dialogue; and that is the telling *what happened*. Something of the fatal languor and preoccupation that persist beneath all the violence of our stage — our national undramatic character — is perceptible in the narrative of our literature. The things the usual modern author says are proportionately more energetically produced than those he tells. But Dickens, being simple and dramatic and capable of one thing at a time, and that thing whole, tells us what happened with a perfect speed which has neither hurry nor delays. Those who saw him act found him a fine actor, and this we might know by reading the murder in *Oliver Twist*, the murder in *Martin Chuzzlewit*, the coming of the train upon Carker, the long moment of recognition when Pip sees his guest, the convict, reveal himself in his chambers at night. The swift spirit, the hammering blow of his narrative, drive the great storm in *David Copperfield* through the poorest part of the book — Steerforth's story. There is surely no greater gale to be read of than this: from the first words, ' "Don't you think that," I said to the coachman, "a very remarkable sky?" ' to the end of a magnificent chapter. 'Flying clouds tossed up into most remarkable heaps, suggesting greater heights in the clouds than there were depths below them ... There had been a wind all day; and it was rising then with an extraordinary great sound ... Long before we saw the sea, its spray was on our lips ... The water was out over the flat country, and every sheet and puddle lashed its banks, and had its stress of little breakers. When we came within sight of the sea, the waves on the horizon, caught at intervals above the boiling abyss, were like glimpses of another shore, with towers and buildings ... The people came to their doors all aslant, and with streaming hair.' David dreams of a cannonade, when at last he 'fell — off a tower and down a precipice — into the depths of sleep'. In the morning, 'the wind might have lulled a little, though not more sensibly than if the cannonading I had dreamed of had been diminished by the silencing of half a dozen guns out of hundreds'. 'It went from me with a shock, like a ball from a rifle,' says David in another place, after the visit of a delirious impulse; here is the volley of departure, the shock of passion vanishing more perceptibly than it came.

The tempest in *David Copperfield* combines Dickens's
dramatic tragedy of narrative with his wonderful sense of sea
and land. But here are landscapes in quietness: 'There has
been rain this afternoon, and a wintry shudder goes among the
little pools in the cracked, uneven flag-stones . . . Some of the
leaves, in a timid rush, seek sanctuary within the low-arched
cathedral door; but two men coming out resist them, and cast
them out with their feet.' The autumn leaves fall thick, 'but
never fast, for they come circling down with a dead lightness'.
Again: 'Now the woods settle into great masses as if they were
one profound tree.' And yet again: 'I held my mother in my
embrace, and she held me in hers; and among the still woods in
the silence of the summer day there seemed to be nothing but
our two troubled minds that was not at peace.' Yet, with
a thousand great felicities of diction, Dickens had no *body*
of style.

Dickens, having the single and simple heart of a moralist,
had also the simple eyes of a free intelligence, and the light
heart. He gave his senses their way, and well did they serve
him. Thus his eyes — and no more modern man in anxious
search of 'impressions' was ever so simple and so masterly:
'Mr. Vholes gauntly stalked to the fire, and warmed his funereal
gloves.' ' "I thank you," said Mr. Vholes, putting out his long
black sleeve, to check the ringing of the bell, "not any." ' Mr.
and Mrs. Tope 'are daintily sticking sprigs of holly into the
carvings and sconces of the cathedral stalls, as if they were
sticking them into the button-holes of the Dean & Chapter'.
The two young Eurasians, brother and sister, 'had a certain
air upon them of hunter and huntress; yet withal a certain air
of being the objects of the chase rather than the followers'.
This phrase lacks elegance — and Dickens is not often inele-
gant, as those who do not read him may be surprised to learn —
but the impression is admirable; so is that which follows: 'An
indefinable kind of pause coming and going on their whole
expression, both of face and form.' Here is pure, mere impres-
sion again: 'Miss Murdstone, who was busy at her writing-
desk, gave me her cold finger-nails.' Lady Tippins's hand is

'rich in knuckles'. And here is vision with great dignity: 'All beyond his figure was a vast dark curtain, in solemn movement towards one quarter of the heavens.'

With that singleness of sight — and his whole body was full of the light of it — he had also the single hearing; the scene is in the Court of Chancery on a London November day: 'Leaving this address ringing in the rafters of the roof, the very little counsel drops, and the fog knows him no more.' 'Mr. Vholes emerged into the silence he could scarcely be said to have broken, so stifled was his tone.' 'Within the grill-gate of the chancel, up the steps surmounted loomingly by the fast-darkening organ, white robes could be dimly seen, and one feeble voice, rising and falling in a cracked monotonous mutter, could at intervals be faintly heard ... until the organ and the choir burst forth and drowned it in a sea of music. Then the sea fell, and the dying voice made another feeble effort; and then the sea rose high and beat its life out, and lashed the roof, and surged among the arches, and pierced the heights of the great tower; and then the sea was dry and all was still.' And this is how a listener overheard men talking in the cathedral hollows: 'The word "confidence", shattered by the echoes, but still capable of being pieced together, is uttered.'

Wit, humour, derision — to each of these words we assign by custom a part in the comedy of literature; and (again) those who do not read Dickens — perhaps even those who read him a little — may acclaim him as a humorist and not know him as a wit. But that writer is a wit, whatever his humour, who tells us of a member of the Tite Barnacle family who had held a sinecure office against all protest, that 'he died with his drawn salary in his hand'. But let it be granted that Dickens the humorist is foremost and most precious. For we might well spare the phrase of wit just quoted rather than the one describing Traddles (whose hair stood up), as one who looked 'as though he had seen a cheerful ghost'. Or rather than this:

'He was so wooden a man that he seemed to have taken his wooden leg naturally, and rather suggested to the fanciful observer that he might be expected — if his development received no untimely check — to be completely set up with a pair of wooden legs in about six months.'

Or rather than the incident of the butcher and the beef-steak. He gently presses it, in a cabbage leaf, into Tom Pinch's pocket. ' "For meat," he said with some emotion, "must be humoured, not drove." '

A generation, between his own and the present, thought Dickens to be vulgar; if the cause of that judgment was that he wrote about people in shops, the cause is discredited now that shops are the scenes of the novelist's research. 'High life' and most wretched life have now given place to the little shop and its parlour, during a year or two. But Dr. Brown, the author of *Rab and His Friends*, thought that Dickens committed vulgarities in his diction. 'A good man was Robin' is right enough; but 'He was a good man, was Robin' is not so well, and we must own that it is Dickensian; but assuredly Dickens writes such phrases as it were dramatically, playing the cockney. I know of but two words that Dickens habitually misuses, and Charles Lamb misuses one of them precisely in Dickens's manner; it is not worth while to quote them. But for these his English is admirable; he chooses what is good and knows what is not. A little representative collection of the bad or foolish English of his day might be made by gathering up what Dickens forbore and what he derided; for instance, Mr. Micawber's portly phrase, 'gratifying emotions of no common description', and Littimer's report that 'the young woman was partial to the sea'. This was the polite language of that time, as we conclude when we find it to be the language that Charlotte Brontë shook off; but before she shook it off she used it. Dickens, too, had something to throw off; in his earlier books there is an inflation — rounded words fill the inappropriate mouth of Bill Sikes himself — but he discarded them with a splendid laugh. They are charged upon Mr. Micawber in his own character as author. See him as he sits by to hear Captain Hopkins read the petition in the debtors' prison 'from His Most Gracious Majesty's unfortunate subjects'. Mr. Micawber listened, we read, 'with a little of an author's vanity, con-

templating (not severely) the spikes upon the opposite wall'·
It should be remembered that when Dickens shook himself free
of everything that hampered his genius he was not so much
beloved or so much applauded as when he gave to his cordial
readers matter for facile sentiment and for humour of the
second order. His public were eager to be moved and to laugh,
and he gave them Little Nell and Sam Weller; he loved to
please them, and it is evident that he pleased himself also. Mr.
Micawber, Mr. Pecksniff, Mrs. Nickleby, Mrs. Chick, Mrs.
Pipchin, Mr. Augustus Moddle, Mrs. Jellyby, Mrs. Plornish,
are not so famous as Sam Weller and Little Nell; nor is
Traddles, whose hair looked as though he had seen a cheerful
ghost.

We are told of the delight of the Japanese man in a chance
finding of something strange-shaped, an asymmetry that has
an accidental felicity, an interest. If he finds such a grace or
disproportion — whatever the interest may be — in a stone or
a twig that has caught his ambiguous eye at the roadside, he
carries it to his home to place it in its irregularly happy place.
Dickens seems to have had a like joy in things mis-shapen or
strangely shapen, uncommon or grotesque. He saddled even
his heroes — those heroes are, perhaps, his worst work, young
men at once conventional and improbable — with whimsically
ugly names; while his invented names are whimsically perfect:
that of Vholes for the predatory silent man in black, and that
of Tope for the cathedral verger. A suggestion of dark and
vague flight in Vholes; something of old floors, something
respectably furtive and musty, in Tope. In Dickens, the love
of lurking, unusual things, human and inanimate — he wrote
of his discoveries delightedly in his letters — was hyper-
trophied; and it has its part in the simplest and the most fan-
tastic of his humours, especially those that are due to his
child-like eyesight; let us read, for example, of the rooks that
seemed to attend upon Dr. Strong (late of Canterbury) in his
Highgate garden, 'as if they had been written to about him by
the Canterbury rooks and were observing him closely in conse-
quence'; and of Master Micawber, who had a remarkable head

voice — 'On looking at Master Micawber again I saw that he had a certain expression of face as if his voice were behind his eyebrows'; and of Joe in his Sunday clothes, 'a scarecrow in good circumstances'; and of the cook's cousin in the Life Guards, with such long legs that 'he looked like the afternoon shadow of somebody else'; and of Mrs. Markleham, 'who stared more like a figurehead intended for a ship to be called the Astonishment, than anything else I can think of'. But there is no reader who has not a thousand such exhilarating little sights in his memory of these pages. From the gently grotesque to the fantastic run Dickens's enchanted eyes, and in Quilp and Miss Mowcher he takes his joy in the extreme of deformity; and a spontaneous combustion was an accident much to his mind.

Dickens wrote for a world that either was exceedingly excitable and sentimental, or had the convention or tradition of great sentimental excitability. All his people, suddenly surprised, lose their presence of mind. Even when the surprise is not extraordinary their actions are wild. When Tom Pinch calls upon John Westlock in London, after no very long separation, John, welcoming him at breakfast, puts the rolls into his boots, and so forth. And this kind of distraction comes upon men and women everywhere in his books — distractions of laughter as well. All this seems artificial to-day, whereas Dickens in his best moments is the simplest, as he is the most vigilant, of men. But his public was as present to him as an actor's audience is to the actor, and I cannot think that this immediate response was good for his art. Assuredly he is not solitary. We should not wish him to be solitary as a poet is, but we may wish that now and again, even while standing applauded and acclaimed, he had appraised the applause more coolly and more justly, and within his inner mind.

Those critics who find what they call vulgarisms think they may safely go on to accuse Dickens of bad grammar. The truth is that his grammar is not only good but strong; it is far better in construction than Thackeray's, the ease of whose phrase sometimes exceeds and is slack. Lately, during the recent centenary time, a writer averred that Dickens 'might not always be parsed', but that we loved him for his, etc. etc. Dickens's page is to be parsed as strictly as any man's. It is, apart from the matter of grammar, a wonderful thing that he, with his little education, should have so excellent a diction. In a letter that records his reluctance to work during a holiday, the word 'wave' seems to me perfect: 'Imaginary butchers and bakers wave me to my desk.' In his exquisite use of the word 'establishment' in the following phrase, we find his own perfect sense of the use of words in his own day; but in the second quotation given there is a most beautiful sign of education. 'Under the weight of my wicked secret' (the little boy Pip had succoured his convict with his brother-in-law's provisions) 'I pondered whether the Church would be powerful enough to shield me . . . if I divulged to that establishment.' And this is the phrase that may remind us of the eighteenth-century writers of prose, and among those writers of none so readily as of Bolingbroke: it occurs in that passage of Esther's life in which, having lost her beauty, she resolves to forgo a love unavowed. 'There was nothing to be undone; no chain for him to drag or for me to break.'

If Dickens had had the education which he had not, his English could not have been better; but if he had had the *usage du monde* which as a young man he had not, there would have been a difference. He would not, for instance, have given us the preposterous scenes in *Nicholas Nickleby* in which parts are played by Lord Frederick Verisopht, Sir Mulberry Hawk, and their friends; the scene of the hero's luncheon at a restaurant and the dreadful description of the mirrors and other splendours would not have been written. It is a very little thing to forgive to him whom we have to thank for — well, not perhaps for the 'housefull of friends' for the gift of whom a stranger, often quoted, once blessed him in the street; we may not wish for Mr. Feeder, or Major Bagstock, or Mrs. Chick, or Mrs. Pipchin, or Mr. Augustus Moddle, or Mr. F.'s aunt, or Mr. Wopsle, or Mr. Pumblechook, as an inmate of our homes. Lack of knowledge of the polite world is, I say, a very little

thing to forgive to him whom we thank most chiefly for show-
ing us these interesting people just named as inmates of the
comedy homes that are not ours. We thank him because they
are comedy homes, and could not be ours or any man's; that
is, we thank him for his admirable art.

A Hundred Years Ago

An old book called *The Mirror of the Months*, published
anonymously in 1826, seemed, at a glance, to a random
reader, to contain little thin springs of thoughts that walked
the world in volume and dignity fifty years later. There was
nothing else to hint that the book was the work of the father
of a poet, but the father of one among all poets was manifestly
the author. Soon after, the same reader found it attributed, in
a bookseller's catalogue, to P. G. Patmore.

The earliest or the directest spring is called the source of a
river; but we know not how far apart and on what scattered
watersheds rose the tributary waters, early and late, that filled
a splendid summoning and gathering stream, and charged it
with rains of the four courts of heaven. It need not dismay us
to find the one discoverable source to be something so slight
as — for example — a passage on the month of February in *The
Mirror of the Months* (it is hardly worth quoting) whereof the
ode on 'St. Valentine's Day' of Coventry Patmore was the
ultimate fulfilment. Yet a reader may be reluctant to find a
small thought, lying cold in a minor mind, to be the certain
beginning of a great thought in an illustrious mind; the per-
fectly recognizable yet insignificant origin of what we love is
more surprising than would be a stranger beginning. Perhaps
we feel this unwelcome surprise because we had been too ready
to believe that what is original is strong, and what is original is
warm. It was easier to think of a first impulse tiring or becom-

ing more composed, of a passion gradually losing light and flame, than of this increase, kindling, and quickening. It is because the small source of 'St. Valentine's Day' is really authentic that its inadequacy does little less than startle us. At any rate the incident is one that may instruct us in the history of that second step which is momentous in intellectual things.

Furthermore, the ambiguous questions of heredity seem thereby to gain in mystery; and some things must needs gain in mystery before we can at all undertake to think upon them. Without mystery they are all obscure. Who can think, for instance, of the infinity of space without adding inconceivable things to his meditation? And, in like manner, the bond of fathers and sons seems to become somewhat more intelligible if we add to the comparatively easy thought of the responsibility of a father for the mind of a child some confession of the retrospective answer to be exacted from the child, inasmuch as in the child is the fulfilment of what was but prophesied in the father, whom the son at last justifies.

In 1826 Leigh Hunt must have dominated unduly. *The Mirror of the Months* would evidently have been graver, fresher, and more frank, in thought and in English alike, but for the example of the excessive amiability that makes Leigh Hunt's poem of *Rimini*, among others, ridiculous. It was a mere fashion, apparently, and it is not difficult to imagine that even Leigh Hunt could talk with a better simplicity than the simplicity of the universal literary smile he practised in his books. There is something that does but ape the humane, the liberal, the gracious. It is an early nineteenth-century attempt at the favour and prettiness of the Elizabethans, with an absolute rejection of the Elizabethan 'horrors'.

Yet without 'horrors', without a real murder among the dances, without royal madness embowered, and noble distraction wearing flowers, without the wild convention, without the noble spirit, wilder than nature — a barbaric artifice outfacing nature — what were the Elizabethan favour and prettiness worth? Nay, they would never have been there but to adorn frightful deeds. The men of a hundred years ago took one part and left the other, and were delighted in the civilized choice they had the grace — as they held it — to make, in a tolerant rebuke, in a liberal approval, of the great past. And see the fruit of that choice. Not being fond of Leigh Hunt, I had not read *Rimini* until a year or two ago, and now already the most conspicuous memory I have of the story of that poem is the memory of an incidental picnic.

It is possible, of course, that my angry fancy may have exaggerated the cause of its own derision — and that the event sung in the canto in question may have been some modification of a picnic; as it were a mitigated picnic; I have not the poem for reference. Nevertheless, there stands a picnic of some sort — a contribution of the English man of letters to the story of the Adriatic cities and of the antecedents of Dante's Hell.

A picnic, I maintain it, a drive, a cloth under the trees, are there. I am quite certain, at any rate, that the place chosen therefor is called by Leigh Hunt, in so many words, 'a rural spot'.

A far greater man than Leigh Hunt — nay, there is no common measure of comparison — has, by some ill luck, at nearly the same moment of our literary history, also made the same Francesca da Rimini the subject of some entirely nineteenth-century feeling. I speak of Walter Savage Landor, and of the exquisite passage of the *Imaginary Conversations* (the *Pentameron*). What he does he does, unlike Leigh Hunt, with genius; but — one must have the courage to say so — in error as complete as the little writer's. The reader may be reminded of that tender page about Francesca: 'She stops: she would avert the eyes of Dante from her: he looks for the sequel: she thinks he looks severely: she says, "Galeotto is the name of the book", fancying by this timorous little flight she has drawn him far enough from the nest of her young loves. No, the eagle beak of Dante and his piercing eyes are yet over her. "Galeotto is the name of the book." "What matters that?" "And of the writer." "Or that either?" At last she disarms him; but how? "*That* day we read no more." Such a depth of intuitive judgment, such a delicacy of perception, exists not in any other

work of human genius.' And this judgment, for greater mis-
fortune, he puts into the mouth of Boccaccio, because he loved
him, and intended that he should speak from Landor's heart;
and so, indeed, he does. But the day of Boccaccio was not ours,
and there is no possible exchange of hearts. Are we candid if
we persuade ourselves to find these pauses in the speech of
Francesca? I protest that I read the line in one cold breath of
almost indifferent anger. 'The name of the book', as Landor
has it, is not in Dante at all. 'A pander was that book, and
the writer thereof', is simply what the Francesca of Dante
says.[1]

To come back to *The Mirror of the Months*. This is a volume
so full of charm that it is something less than just to reproach
it so hastily with Leigh Hunt's universal literary smile. Some-
thing of that it has, indeed, but it has also the smile of spirit
and that of sweetness. Of two wits of yesterday two phrases,
for example, are familiar in admiring quotation: 'The age of
indiscretion', and 'Yes, nature is creeping up', or, in another
form, 'Not like his portrait? He *will* be like it.' Every one
recognizes the phrases so well that there is perhaps not a
reader in England who needs to be more than reminded of
them. Now 'the age of indiscretion' is in *The Mirror of the
Months*, where it got no fame, or little; and 'Nature is creeping
up' is fairly anticipated in the passage: 'Cattle wade into the
shallow pools of warm water, and stand half a day there stock
still, in exact imitation of Cuyp's pictures.' Take this descrip-
tion of the parent birds' business of bringing out their young
broods and dismissing them, 'while they (the parents) proceed
in their periodical duty of providing new flocks of the same
kind of "fugitive pieces", as regularly as the editors of a

---

[1] Francesca calls the book a Galeotto and him who wrote it a Galeotto,
because 'Galeotto' was then the synonym for 'pander'. Galeotto (Gallehault)
was he who brought Lancilotto and Ginevra to their first sin, according to the
Tavola Rotonda, a romance popular in Francesca's time. Dante had none of the
pretty and complex meanings imputed to him by Landor. Dante, the insistent
moralist, simply intended a simple warning against dangerous reading; he was
in this obedient to a Bull (in 1313) whereby the Pope condemned *La Tavola
Rotonda* — one of the earliest books to be thus banned.

magazine'. And this for a mere laugh: 'The only specific reason why I object to March is that she drives hares mad; which is a great fault.'

Moreover, the procession and recession of the year is here noted in the garden and in the open field of England by senses full of spirit. The separate and atmospheric effect of an oat-field among all other grain is well expressed in the phrase where the oats are said to hang 'like raindrops in the air'. And the author has eyes for the scarcely perceptible and most slender growth that in July pricks through the short and level turf and makes the grassy downs live in the winds, as poplars make the woods. 'April', says this forgotten writer, 'is worth two Mays, because it tells of May' — a subtlety somewhat like that of his son's minor fancies.

And finally another small spring of the poetry to come in the following generation is in the mere phrase 'The pomp of health and the lustre of loveliness'. Coventry Patmore, with the poet's finer verbal art, had afterwards

> So much simplicity of mind
> In such a pomp of loveliness.

Coventry Patmore

To prophesy that the odes of Coventry Patmore shall be confessed, a hundred years hence, high classic poetry, is assuredly to promise the critics of a hundred years hence high classic quality in their judgment. It is to look for a definite intelligence and for an explicit code of literary law, inasmuch as a mind trained in the less obvious measures and restraints both of thought and of verse is needed to recognize the law of *The Unknown Eros*. It is to look, not only for such precision, but for its rare companions — liberty, flight, height, courage, a sense of space and a sense of closeness, readiness for spiritual experience, and all the gravity, all the resolution, of the lonely reader of a lonely poet. Whatever criticism may learn in time to come, *The Unknown Eros* will hardly then have many readers, and will no doubt still keep the accidental loneliness that surrounds it now by reason of the indifference of the majority; but its essential loneliness is its own quality, conferred by no world's neglect; not an effect of conspicuousness or difference; not a mere contrast, for it is relative to nothing.

The reader undertakes at least to know and to watch that solitude. It was assuredly a sense of the gravity of this enterprise that inspired the phrase, 'lonely watcher of the skies'; a star is lonely, and its student, whatever his conditions, lonely as he watches. Pausing upon that significant phrase, we ask for a moment whose it is. Not Keats's, evidently; and it proves at last to be a word of Patmore's own; and the lonely watcher is his rapt and vigilant reader. In a now cancelled passage of Coventry Patmore's ode, *Tired Memory*, occurs the 'lonely' astronomer. Who can complain that there are not many prepared for such a vigil? Moreover, *The Unknown Eros*, although we may attempt images of sidereal distance to express its profound flight, has the more dreadful solitude of an experience, and goes far in an inverse flight, through the essentially single human heart — intimately into time and space, remotely into the heart of hearts.

Of many words of praise, the word 'classic' is chosen here because it suggests no exclusions of schools or kinds, nor even any preferences for poetry of one kind of perfection, to the slighting of poetry of another. None the less is it the most sharp and severe of all words of criticism, or it shall here have that character, if the reader will agree to understand as 'classic' all poetry that is *one* — thought and word. The fusion of thought and word is unmistakable, whether the fire of an impassioned thought bring it to pass, or the close coldness of fancy made perfect; for since we hear that metals pass into one another, *in vacuo*, by pressure in the cold, this latter image is possible; but even if, with Thomas à Kempis, we contemplate the metal that is one with fire and is changed into fire, it is less by the fusion of fire that a greatly classic poem is to be figured, than by a more vital union; mind and body, where tidal thought and feeling are quick with the blood and various with the breath of life, give a juster, as well as a simpler and a human, image of a vital poem. Besides, the fire of life is made sensible to us by warmth and not by flame, and there are in literature a far greater number of humanly warm poems that are classic and vital, than of poems that are classic and vital with apparent and uncovered flame. Some of these last, indeed, there are, but few. The image of warm life is the general measure of poetry. Then is poetry proved classic and alive when a reader, struck to the heart, moved and shaken like Leontes looking on the figure of Hermione, having seen her colour, her height, her light, her age, knows her indeed, and confesses her at last by another sign: 'Oh, she's warm!'

In *The Unknown Eros* the poet's intention, single, separate, strikes unique strokes against which the reader's human heart is all unarmed by custom. It is mastery, and not violence, that so comes home, dividing soul and spirit. There is not a violence in the world that does not seem a dissipation and an essential weakness when reproached by such a majestic energy, able to curb its hand.

Not without profoundly conscious art did Coventry Patmore achieve the ultimate, the mortal, pathos of such an ode as *Eurydice*. He was ready to tell the secret which no others could use as he used it, however it might be guessed; and the secret of *Eurydice* was: 'After exceeding ill, a little good.' The slenderness of the good and the poignancy of the ill are mingled, in this ode on dreams, with such closeness of fear as no other poet has ever endured. *Eurydice* is the dream of the mourner, who night by night follows some dreary clue through labyrinths without hope, to find the dear dead living the thin, remote, neglected life that the dead do live in these intolerable dreams. But Coventry Patmore does not always capture terror for such purposes of eternal sadness; he is able to marry terror to joy in the magnificent ode of reunion, *The Day after To-morrow*:

O, heaving sea,
That heav'st as if for bliss of her and me,
And separatest not dear heart from heart,
Though each 'gainst other beats too far apart.

. . . . . .

O, weary Love, O folded to her breast,
Love in each moment years and years of rest.

. . . . . .

O Life, too liberal, when to take her hand
Is more of hope than heart can understand.

. . . . . .

One day's controllèd hope, and one again,
And then the third, and ye shall have the rein,
O Life, Death, Terror, Love!

Ultima dolcezza was once exquisitely said of the skylark;
ultima amarezza should be the words for the lines:

Thou whom ev'n more than Heaven lov'd I have,
And yet have not been true, even to thee;

and the extremity of grief without bitterness, the grief that
kisses and says a conscious 'farewell, farewell', is in *Departure*,
and in this passage of too significant allusion, with years of
tears lightly implied by a negative:

When the one darling of our widowhead,
The nurseling Grief, is dead,
And no dews blur our eyes
To see the peach-bloom come in evening skies.

Nor does a public sorrow utter less life and death. The ode
entitled *Proem* foretells with a singular peace of grief the day
when England, 'a dim heroic nation, long since dead', shall be
benignly remembered no otherwise than by 'the bird-voice
and the blast of her omniloquent tongue' — by the poets of her
then dead language.

As to the 'natural description' for which the reader is apt to
look — it might not unfairly be said that Patmore never

described. He claimed the truths of science, to which in youth he had devoted his attention, to serve his poem with images; and thus he used them in his speech, as when the perception he gained of Divine truths by the act of contemplation and the holding his spirit still, ready, and free, was likened by him to the photographic picture of stars invisible even to the camera but made visible by a long accumulation of continuous imperceptible impressions. And nature, evasive to the mere describer, yielded imagery to him with an indescribable freshness. There is an instance in the ode, *Wind and Wave*, with its final flash of sea and sea-margins, and waves that

> Traverse wildly, like delighted hands,
> The fair and fleckless sands

> .   .   .   .   .   .

> And burst in wind-kissed splendours on the deafening beach.

The smile of Psyche is

> Like sunny eve in some forgotten place;

love shows in the dark eyes of the dying woman,

> As when a south wind sombres a March grove.

In *Amelia* we receive the candid, simple shock of the line in which every meeting with her beauty is likened to a first beholding of the ocean. In this ode, also, stands the 'little bright, surf-breathing town', and the westering sun fills with shade 'the dimples of our homeward hills'. Whenever Coventry Patmore touches nature it is with a sudden sight, often it is also with a sudden insight. The blackbird at dawn, a lonely thrush at evening, singing notes few and fine, and 'sad with promise of a different sun', brought him in full the message of the wild suggestion that never left poet's heart at rest. When he wrote the *Odes*, and used thus a free metre because he knew himself to be set at liberty by his very knowledge and love of law, that heart beat in the sensitive line, and he caught rapturous breath, or sighed, as a spirit blowing whither it will.

The quality of poetry is not strained. It has not to abide our repeated question. It tests and is not tested. Every true lover of poetry knows that when he cites great lines it is not the poetry but the hearer that is to be judged. This true lover may well have outlived the desire to give to others a convincing or converting reason for his own certainties as to the most poetic things in poetry, but he still desires to know whose mind's ear is fine, and how many have the ear, as time goes on. To the treasure of these most beautiful things, to which the dramatic and the epic poets have given passages or phrases, the lyric poets stanzas or lines, it is a wonder to find how much Coventry Patmore has added. The slender volume of his odes furnishes them out of all measure. Even those readers who will not hold the author of that small volume to have answered all the conditions on which a poet is acknowledged great, will confess this extraordinary disproportion. The mental apprehension of poetry can be put to the proof by Patmore's odes — and indeed by not a few passages of the contemned *Angel in the House* — much oftener than by honoured classical poems from which we gather those testing lines by precious threes and twos. *The Unknown Eros* yields them to us in overwhelming beauty and in strong numbers. Some have that poetry of imagery — so enkindling, so exalting that we say of imagery that it is poetry itself, until we find the poetry of the yonder side, for some again are of the simplicity, the further simplicity, that is beyond imagery. One of the testing lines of our literature has this latter character — Chaucer's, chosen by Matthew Arnold, on the lot of man:

Now with his love, now in the coldë grave.

From Coventry Patmore's odes we gather them with both hands, exalted, subdued, and greatly moved by our riches.

Why *The Unknown Eros* should have found so few readers it might be hard to say. We should have expected something different from the literary liberty and literary variety of England. Ignorance of Patmore's odes might have been looked for, that is, from readers fairly of one mind in the admiration of Byron and Scott, but it is not easily to be explained in readers of various minds admiring Byron, Scott, Wordsworth, Crashaw, Campion, Blake, Milton, and Shakespeare the lyrist. Probably a doubt as to the whole meaning of many among the odes has discouraged even Patmore's willing readers. The beauty was there, but it was to them an uncertain magnificence, a glow from a doubtful fire, a pealing call of an uncertain word, remote as thunder, the heart-piercing utterance of an obscure grief — obscure as waters are obscure because they are profound, not because they are turbid. Some of our esteemed poets have left us meanings troubled by the lowest of difficulties — the grammatical. Their waters have matter in mechanical suspension rather than in chemical solution. It is often impossible to decide to what nouns some of the pronouns in *Sordello* refer. But Patmore's pure diction, uttered in the composure that gives high dignity to his most poignant poems, permits no such baffling of inquiry. Nevertheless some of the odes of *The Unknown Eros* are difficult. Some, we say, and are again puzzled at finding them so few. *The Day after To-morrow* is not readily understood to refer to reunion after death; the Psyche odes sing of a spiritual experience alien to the history, to the aspirations, and even the desires, of the greater number of deeply spiritual men; the matter of the mystical ode called *The Unknown Eros* itself is all but hidden; *Deliciae Sapientiae de Amore* darkly sings the triumph of virginity and its sacrifice at once; few or no readers will guess the *Arbor Vitae* of a very fine ode to be the Catholic Church, and the 'nests of the hoarse bird, who talks and understands not his own word' to be (a most unjust image) the clusters of her clergy; and a few other necessities for explanation there may be. But, on the other hand, there can be no doubt, to all initiate in the world of poetry, as to the full significance — the furthest significance, to every inner alley and retreat of meaning, to every ultimate pang of sensitiveness — expressed in that terrible record of a mourner's dreams, *Eurydice*; in *Departure*; in *If I were Dead*; in *Saint Valentine's Day*; or in the ode on the decline of England, already named, which contains the memorable description of her literature. Why, of these all-intelligible poems, is only one generally known, even with the relative generalness possible among the little minority that cares for poetry? That one is, needless to say, *The Toys*, a very beautiful and tender poem, but one containing less essential poetry than any other page of the odes.

It must be owned that some of the accessory persons and conditions of the story of *The Angel in the House* are unwelcome to poetry as we have learnt to hold it. But this is an avowal that we are either content, or very weakly, very ineffectually, ill content to live in a social world that we confess to be unworthy of poetry. Coventry Patmore, as we understand his attitude, refused to be content with such a world, and refused, moreover, to be impotently discontent. If the world was unfit for his poem, he would reject the world — and he at least knew how to reject and did not play at rejection. He did not believe that there was such unfitness, because love and immortality were there, as elsewhere, with humanity. The modern age chose to be ashamed of the manner in which it chose to live, to be associated, to prosper, to order its affairs; no other age had condescended to that kind of shame. But Coventry Patmore was not modern in this matter. He thought the daily civilized ways of a Cathedral town, granted that they were delicate and gay, and not dull, no more unfit for 'realistic' art than other contemporary ways, neither delicate nor gay, have been held to be before, and notably since, the writing of *The Angel in the House*. Coventry Patmore wrote of conventions in the manner of a realist, and he had for this precedents older than his critics stopped to remember. If so much of explanation is to be offered in answer to still current criticisms, how does it befall that any reader should pause upon the mere intervals in poetry so profound and penetrating as, in a hundred passages, shakes the metre with a hand of control?

Among such passages are these records of beauty:

> Her eyes incredulously bright,
>   And all her happy beauty blown
> Beneath the beams of my delight.

> So much simplicity of mind
> In such a pomp of loveliness!

> Eyes that softly lodge the light.

And elsewhere are words that touch the heart so close as these:

> His only Love, and she is wed!
> His fondness comes about his heart
> As milk comes when the babe is dead.

And again:

> Alone, alone with sky and sea
> And her, the third simplicity.

Here is a quatrain winged, not weighted, with meaning:

> Far round each blade of harvest bare
> Its little load of bread;
> Each furlong of that journey fair
> With separate sweetness sped.

Again:

> Blest in her place, blissful is she;
> And I, departing, seem to be
> Like the strange waif that comes to run
> A few days flaming near the sun,
> And carries back, through boundless night,
> Its lessening memory of light.

It is possible that this early poem is contemned because the reader takes the 'Angel' to be the woman, and an angel obviously feminine is a kind of sentimentality. But I prefer to take the 'Angel' to be Love. Patmore's masculine mind probably referred the name rather to such an angel as he who in the Old Testament took up a prophet by the hair of his head and carried him across country. Together with Love, Patmore's subject was the Child in the House, before ever Pater had so varied Patmore's title. Together with the revelation of youthful love he has coupled all the sweet revelations made to a child:

This and the Child's unheeded Dream
Was all the light of all his day.

We find that there are two master-emotions in modern poetry — in that Romance literature which has been the complementary life of Europe now for many centuries; one dates from Dante's day, and one chiefly from the day of Henry Vaughan (Wordsworth's virtually immediate precursor). Love, and the love of Nature, mystically passionate, are what they are with us, not because all men, but because two boys, conceived them. It needs the childish dream to raise these emotions into the regions of mystery, sweetness, tenderness, and terror which they have gained because Dante was a child in love with a girl, and Vaughan a child in love with Nature. Other lovers have loved in childhood, or else they have profited by Dante's childhood; other poets have conceived the passion for Nature in their childhood, or have profited by the childhood of Wordsworth, of Vaughan, and of Traherne. The wilder and the more real, the more delirious and the more innocent these remote experiences, the more has the lover's love the quality of Romance, and the poet's imaginative verse the quality of the poetry of Nature. Men could never have done for mankind what these boys have done; literature owes her two ideal adult passions to the dreams of childhood.

Coventry Patmore's ardour and mystery acknowledged that dear and ignorant origin. He did more than remember that incomparable antiquity; with him childhood hardly needed remembering, for it remained, the companion of his complete intellect, the rapture of his profoundly experienced heart, the strange and delicate witness of manly sorrows.

The most beautiful of all gardens is assuredly not that which is rather forest or field than garden, the 'landscape garden' of a false taste; nor, on the other hand, the shaven and trimmed and weeded parterre with an unstarred lawn; but rather the garden long ago strictly planned, rigidly ordered, architecturally piled, smooth and definite, but later set free, given over to time and the sun; not a wilderness, but having an enclosed wildness, a directed liberty, a designed magnificence and excess. Comparable to such a garden is Coventry Patmore's mind, obedient to an ancient law, but wildly natural under an inspiration of visiting winds and a splendid sun of genius.

No poet ever had a greater value for poetry or attributed to it a greater dignity than the value and the dignity that consecrated it in Patmore's heart. As he very literally and actually held the members of the body to be divine, so may it be said that he saw in poetry also the incarnate word; the metre, the diction, the pause, the rhyme, the phrase were not accidental but essential. Hence his extraordinary mastery of style. And as to his sense of the greatness of poetry as a power and domination we have but to compare it with the sense of one who spared no words in praise of poetry, and who speculated boldly as to its work and mission — Matthew Arnold.[1] Failing the religious sanction, failing the fundamental law with its code, poetry, Arnold thought, might take its place, whether as temporary regent or regent without a térm. It would, he said, console and soothe mankind. As though a race in need of the spur and the curb, the example, the threat, and the canon, were sufficiently to be served by those unmanly ministrations! As though to be soothed in an ill-temper and comforted in an ill-humour were the chief necessities of men, a race worthy of the dignities of chastisement! In raising poetry to what he thought this eminence, assuredly Matthew Arnold did it no honour. Never was poetry more conscious than Patmore's. Nor, perhaps, if we seek among the homages of the poets to their art shall we find graver or profounder veneration than Patmore's, hardly even excepting Wordsworth's, explicit and implicit.

He valued his country chiefly for her poets. So must we learn to do, and to value her for him.

[1] He thought the value of the religions to be their 'unconscious poetry'. 'It is part of the man's unconscious poetry', says Harold Skimpole — he is alluding to the family butcher (unpaid) — 'that he always calls it "his little bill".'

Poetry and Childhood

WHICH is the language of poetry? For each, perhaps, the language that first named for him a flock of sheep, a hill, a mountain river, or whatever thing touched a child's mind with a remote and yet familiar love. The poets who have for him a lifelong advantage over all others are the poets who write that tongue. No other word than theirs will be to him the very name of what he finds so fresh. Thus, for my own part, reading again the *Chants du Crépuscule*, the *Feuilles d'Automne*, *Contemplations*, and *Les Voix Intérieures*, I own the power of the poet who knows the true name of an orchard, and so calls it 'le verger'. 'Le verger' is purely yonder steep field of fruit trees round and soft above their separate shadows. In another tongue the name is translated, and therefore removed by one step; it has no longer the shape and figure and spirit which the name first known has for the child learning the thing and the word in one.

Besides, Victor Hugo falls in with the mood of one who has profound childish memories connected with his common words, by writing so closely of infantine things as though to secure the charm for all a reader's lifetime to come, and to establish the authority of his French precisely upon those names of childish import that are most subject to such an early spell.

A reader who, when he had learnt that there are birds, had learnt their English name, and had, moreover, received his father, his mother, his bed, his sleep, his nurse's song, his little breakfast, in English, has not, I think, an equal poet to rehearse for him those words, those things rather, in his later years. For there seems to be no poet in our master-poetry to do for him that singular office, and to sing the language of his first nurse to a great and authentic lyre. He may learn all nature with our poets, and he hears the Gospel first in an incomparable tongue; and his first sense of Greece doubtless comes with an adequate word. But he has no august poet to resume his ancient lullabies, heard once in ancient regions between sleeping and waking, the immemorial night-light, the homely language of antiquity and old romance as children have the sense of them in their little words at play upon the floor, at play upon the moss. He has not had Victor Hugo's French.

Furthermore still, an English reader whose childish life was uttered in French has half forgotten, amid later English, some of the daily words of that time, unused by grown men and women. These Victor Hugo sings to him. They return to him out of the past and out of his poetic page at once. They had but dropped to sleep in imperishable memory; they wake again, and they are more fresh to his heart than swallows, and than torrents from the Alps.

Here, then, is the tongue of poetry for him. The child and the poet know it together. They meet, they understand, they have the way of it together. And if they meet again across age and change and disuse, how close, how light, how natural is this encounter, how sudden and how old the intimacy! Poet and child have their traffic, no doubt, in every life; but what incomparable traffic is this of Victor Hugo and an English reader who had a French childhood! How ingenious is fortune to bring their communion to pass! Many are the things, small and all-important, known fully, and more than known — recognized, known after estrangement — between these two only of all the pairs of poet and child, in the world. Where else can there be just such a commerce? In the first place that poet is unique. He, too, breathes the breath of the moss closely; he has not only the child's sense of it, but also the child's inexpert and invaluable word. And the reader, on his part, has, as I have said, a peculiar experience both of memory and of oblivion. For him, then, the French language has that grace of election which makes it wholly, invincibly successful — the grace of each man's first tongue; and in overplus it has the powers of the tongue in which Victor Hugo was wont to write of children, and, again, the powers of the tongue of a great romance. Of a word in that language, therefore, it may be said, as of the elect lady in a violent world —

> Her gentle step to go or come
> Gains her more merit than a martyrdom.

The word of poetry in after-life is sublime and tragic by will, by force and conquest; the word, in the French of Hugo, has for me but to be uttered. 'Le verger' possesses not only a young child's sight of trees under the sun and moon, a young child's touch of the grass, but also the genius of the South of France, of ancient agriculture and of early song.

Assuredly those to whom the word first learnt was 'the orchard' must be content with something less than this.

A reading of later French persuades one easily that Victor Hugo was alone, and is alone, the speaker of what has become so mysterious and so intelligible, so surcharged and so buoyant a language:

> Oh, 'tis not Spanish, but 'tis Heaven she speaks!

cries Crashaw. Victor Hugo speaks not so much French as childhood, and a peculiar childhood; Romance, and a unique Romance; nature, too, as no eyes of Latin race had seen it until then, with insight as well as with perception — in Emerson's phrase, 'a little wildly, or with the flower of the mind'.

Apart from all this which makes the lyrics of this great poet so dear, for exclusive and accidental reasons, to one reader among many, I have no praise for the French poetic tongue. It is true that the word 'souffle' is for my ear all a summer wind at night — it has more merit than a martyrdom of description; that is by chance. It is by genius, however, that Victor Hugo makes this word so fresh and dark.

What I have to suggest is that the poets, since he ceased to write (ceased as a lyrist, not as a rhetorician), have done little more for the enlargement of their language than he did in the distant days when his work was a very revolution; and this in spite of their metrical liberty, which seems to have no bounds. The freedom he claimed from the bonds of the preceding century or so was precisely no more than his art needed. Nothing was done for the sake of liberty, for the sake of others, for the

sake of pioneership, or for any other of the causes that medio-
crity is fond of. All was purely for his own poetry, and because,
being Victor Hugo, he could not write within the laws that
held Boileau content. Where he found no need of change he
obeyed Boileau or another, or La Harpe or another, with a
cheerful docility that has left his verse to-day far behind the
reforms of modern French prosody, 'reforms' that seem to
have been inspired by the revolt of a Walt Whitman, and make
easy havoc of the whole order, the whole law. Even in the
enlarged liberty made for French poetry by Victor Hugo's
advance, the wave of verse met salutary bars and measures as
strong as rocks. But his successors have spilt their art thinly
over all boundaries, and the flat country is already under
shallow water.

I have under my hand the volume of a little recent symbolist,
side by side with *Les Voix Intérieures*, and the comparison
persuades me that not all this new licence is able to make the
French language a really liberal instrument. What has been
written here must be the proof that if I have a prejudice it is
for French, and that for me magic and the caprice of destiny
are on that side. But there are disabilities; and it is not
metrical liberty, or the chance medley of masculine and
feminine endings, or the ignoring of the *e* mute, or rhymes
that are but the suggestion of a jingle, or any other of these
later liberties that can make this language sufficient. It lacks
the second part, the other side, the splendour of alternative.
It has the strangest blanks. It cannot so much as call an
author shallow, nor a teacup, nor a sea.

As it has no alternative of derivation, French has none of
time; no place apart for poems and prayers, but the whole
language is at the disposal of the daily grocer and the trade-
circular. The French of commerce, merely exaggerated, has
tempted poets to make that ready eloquence resound, when
the lyric could do no more, for lack of strings.

A word as to syllables — those great units of verse — and
their motions. The Italian syllables dance, springing from
their double consonants and long vowels; the English walk,

with all variety of gait, and fly with all variety of wing; the French trot. 'Égalisez les syllabes.' The Frenchman who speaks right Parisian equalizes the syllables not only of his own language but of every other. Hear him speak Italian thus; hear him, as a good pastor in England, read the English Testament.

The New Helena

NEVER was a more impassioned claim made for poetry by the heart of a great romance writer than the all-instant claim of Meredith in *The Amazing Marriage*. All is sinned and suffered for despair of poetry. Lord Fleetwood himself is the seeker after poetry, the avenger of the honour of poetry upon the cold and worldly ignorance — so he thinks — of his unhappy bride.

Poetry is the conspicuous secret of the book. Poetry is the simple and apparent Carinthia. Her husband looks further, looks aside, looks wide, and though he sees her, does not see it. As in this great book, so in life, poetry is not hidden. It is unrevealed. And there are mystics who aver that all the now unrevealed secrets of this human life are obvious things that we daily and ignorantly use — things that we know, yet do not recognize.

Carinthia is mistaken and misunderstood through her own simplicity, her accessibility, as it were, her very presence. Besides this, Meredith causes her to be belied by a kind of accident. It might have been an even higher act of art to avoid this mere misunderstanding — the misunderstanding from without — whereby Lord Fleetwood is misled. If Meredith had devised no such incident as that of the suppression of the message from Fleetwood to his betrothed, he would have concealed Carinthia in nothing but her own unconcealment and its accompaniment — her own credulity. Then Carinthia would not have been slandered, but only misjudged, and hidden from the fastidious eyes of her lord not by any accidental darkness, but by essential light.

Not, certainly, that the chances of events and the trivial effects of the minor passions — nay, the blunders — of smaller persons are not to be used by an author for grave issues. Some nonsense has been written, in a certain school of criticism, as to the unlawfulness of such incidents in tragedy. But none the less have the masters of great drama broken heroic hearts by a servant's delay, an overheard whisper misunderstood, or a handkerchief snatched away. Not so is the dignity of human sorrow compromised.

It is not, therefore, for any unheroic fear of unheroic things — such a fear as English masters have never owned, the very English language being too grave and homely to be afraid, as the French is afraid, of derogating by familiarity — it is not for any such timorousness that we could wish the integrity of Carinthia to have stood alone, unbelied, and merely unbelieved. The wish, if indeed we form the wish, is only for the sake of doing more honour to the sufficiency of candour — the sufficiency of candour alone, alone, to ensure contempt in such a world as the world of Fleetwood's destiny.

It may be said that obviously this difference — the absence of any definite deception in the bridegroom's opinion of the bride — would have left him more inexcusable in the reader's mind. Not so. It is not for his misconception that he is inexcusable; it would even be possible to take from him some part of his excuse and yet to leave him as much forgiven as the intricate meditations readers of Meredith can take upon themselves to forgive — as much as life forgives, and that is after an half-hearted manner. In truth, Fleetwood might be, even at a greater stress, partly pardonable for so believing the mountain maid as to refuse her. One thing is finally unpardonable, and one thing only — the return to the inn which was incredibly to be the prologue to the last abandonment. And this outrage is none the less an outrage because Fleetwood had been deceived by the plots of others as to the nature of Carinthia. It is indeed the more squalid for that deception. He would have been the more nearly pardonable if he had believed in her, for an hour, for love's sake, before he left her for ever for the sake of his resolve.

But for this return of Lord Fleetwood to the sign of the 'Royal Sovereign' it might be said of him that all he did he did for the honour of poetry, even to the avenging of poetry upon a girl.

'The nature of Carinthia' are words that bring the fancy back from this rather too curious criticism to the heart of the book, which is nature, poetry, and Carinthia, all misbelieved, all sought for amiss, all refused to their faces, and known too late. Always secret, always present, nature is the simplest thing in the most intricate book of the world.

It is curious to turn from *The Amazing Marriage*, in which nothing ends well, to the play of the earlier and ruder Carinthia — *All's Well that Ends Well*. 'A rude Carinthian boor' Helena seems indeed, in certain of her ways, beside the upright creature of Meredith. But there is a certain kinship between these two daughters of dear and remembered fathers, rejected by their lords, women of will. When Carinthia says, 'I hate sleep; I hate anything that robs me of my will', she seems to be speaking with Helena's voice. They have the same unalterable courage. They have the same traducers:

> There is a gentleman that serves the Count
> Reports but coarsely of her.

And when the Countess says of Helena, 'She derives her honesty and achieves her goodness', the phrase might be spoken in honour of the Old Buccaneer's daughter.

Each has her 'miraculous child'. Shakespeare keeps so secret his heroine's poetry, about the middle of the play, that it must be said to disappear. No matter; he has all the more confidence in nature, because he passes her poetry by under an absolute silence. And Carinthia and Helena alike win a world out of the world to love them:

> He lost a wife
> Whose beauty did astonish the survey
> Of richest eyes, whose words all ears took captive,
> Whose dear perfection hearts that scorned to serve
> Humbly called mistress.

There is no hero in *All's Well that Ends Well*, only an angry and dishonest boy, and Helena gets from him the promise of a heart changed and a spirit renewed by the very conventions of a happy comedy. Lord Fleetwood is manifestly something more than the 'weak young man' that Carinthia is slowly constrained — and here, again, accident bears its bitter part — to find him. But there is no hero in the book except Carinthia.

Such and so great a hero even Meredith has not created before. The vitality which is the value of virtue, and of which beauty is but a suggestion, is hers, as it were fifty-fold. When she is not speaking, all the story is significant with her silence. Her heart beats in the one most silent passage of the book. Her longest speech is her most innocent talk on the box seat of the coach on her cruel wedding-day. The anguish of the twenty days and nights of her first abandonment is not told.

It was a Shakespearean act to give her life. The exceeding dignity of the women who are greater than Helena is hers. She is filial and sisterly and maternal. She humbles her heart. It would seem as though Meredith had put more landscape and sky, more climate and wind, into this book than into most of his books, in honour of Carinthia. The west wind and the north-east wind freshen the story of that undaunted spirit. The clouds fly with it.

If Bertram is altered and renewed for Helena in cheerful comedy, so is Fleetwood for Carinthia in heavy tragedy. For in his story 'the better pays for the worse', and his changed heart condemns him.

The reader's retort to Meredith's title is 'An amazing book'. But it should be 'a wonderful book', not an amazing book. Let the world of Lord Fleetwood's London be amazed when it is surprised. The readers of this novel are to be struck to something very different from stupidity. They are awakened and compelled to another rate and way of thinking than their own. 'Run faster than you can', said a brilliant and ardent child to his playmate. That is how he runs who has a grasp of George Meredith's mighty hand. He runs further and faster than he can. There is no amazement, but a stress of quickening surprise, and a liberation from the disabilities of everyday — the timidities.

For Meredith writes of a courageous soul with the courage of his imagination. There is nothing in literature more fearless than his phrase. What is there wilder than a wild image? It is like the forms of the flying cloud. But Meredith compels the wild image to serve him.

Christina Rossetti

IF it is true that in many of Christina Rossetti's lighter poems the fine quality is thin, you do not call the thinnest beaten gold a cheap thing. What she was when she did not scatter, but gathered up, is to be seen in such poems as *The Convent Threshold*, *The Three Enemies*, *Advent*, *Uphill*, and *Amor Mundi*. To the name of poet her right is so sure that proof of it is to be found everywhere in her 'unconsidered ways'. How does a poet approach the best beauties of his poem? From the side of poetry or from the side of commonplace? His manner of approaching these — his direction — gives us the pleasure of giving him a long welcome. It is the daily life of his muse: an approach so important, so significant of origin, so marked with character, so charged with memories, so indicative of sequestered life. It is the day by day, the waking and sleeping, the temper and the nature. In love it is all the justification; for, without a whole approach, love is profanity. Christina

Rossetti is not often on the heights; but all her access is by poetry.

In *The Convent Threshold* there is, I think, more passion than in any other poem written by a woman. It seems as though the lines were shaken by the force of a feeling that never breaks into the relief of violence. The penitent, who sends back to her lover from her convent threshold this call to leave the easy way and seek the narrow, says of her own sharpest conflict:

> My words were slow, my tears were few;
> But through the dark my silence spoke
> Like thunder.

The speaker looks up, above her bitter life. She sees the saints:

> They bore the Cross, they drained the cup,
> Racked, roasted, crushed, wrenched limb from limb,
> They the offscouring of the world:
> The heaven of starry heavens unfurled,
> The sun before their face is dim.

In *Amor Mundi* there is terror, though the terror that is not instant, but that flies and sings, as ominous as a bird of warning — terror suggested but not suffered. In *The Three Enemies*, again, fear is uttered, not sharply, but with a constant sense of

> the sadness of all sin
> When looked at in the light of love.

The exquisiteness with which she chose the beautiful word is illustrated even in the slight quatrain written to teach a child how to know the waxing from the waning moon:

> O lady moon, your horns point to the east —
> Shine, be increased!
> O lady moon, your horns point to the west,
> Wane, be at rest!

An easy world is hers, and not only easy, but beautiful. She has no unhandsome secrets of composition, or difficulties of attainment. She keeps the intimate court of a queen. The country of poetry is her home, and she is 'manifest house-keeper'. Nevertheless, we are not surprised to hear that she generally did not work. Her poems show this, when they lack friction and weight — friction of water and the oar, of air and the pinion. In *Goblin Market*, for instance, the story, for all its freshness and freedom, has not the reasonableness we have the right to expect even from a fairy-tale — or especially from a fairy-tale. The moral is hardly intelligible — we miss any perceptible reason why the goblin fruits should be deadly at one time and restorative at another.

She lived sequestered by her own solemn choice, serving her mother, from whom, during fifty-six years, she was hardly a night absent — a service she called 'her chief dignity'. To religious service and to the succour of the poor — in a word, to duty — she dedicated herself informally. Her diversion was to make up scrap-books for children and hospitals — 'to an extent one would hardly credit', says her brother William. She refused to be tempted out of that solitude so full for her of spirituality; nevertheless, she did not deny herself to those who sought her. She was simply and frankly kind, rather talkative than silent, so as to make her visitor happier. In the most beautiful of her portraits there is too much of the habit of the hand that drew it — a brother's — too much of the curled lips and the long chin for a real likeness. One of her photographs shows her to have had more than a little likeness to himself, as had her art to his. And a look of her face is in the head of Christ in *The Light of the World*: it was in her that Mr. Holman Hunt found something that he wanted. She died in the act of prayer in 1894, aged sixty-four years, bequeathing a ring from her dead hand to the offertory of the church of her worship.

The sadness of Christina Rossetti's song was the one all-human sadness, its fear the one true fear. Acquainted with grief, she yet found in grief no cause of offence. She left revolt to the emotion of mere spectators and strangers. When one of the many widows of the monarchs of France heard of the murder of her son she whispered, 'I will not say, my God, that it is too much, but it is much'. Christina Rossetti lived a life of sacrifice, suffered many partings — twice voluntarily from those she loved; unreluctantly endured the pains of her spirituality. But she kept in their quickness her simple and natural love of love and hope of joy. Such sufferings as hers do indeed refuse, but they have not denied, delight. Delight is all their faith.

Swinburne

THE makers of epigrams, of phrases, of pages — of all more or less brief judgments — assuredly waste their time when they sum up any one of all mankind; and how do they squander it when their matter is a poet! They may hardly describe him; nor shall any student's care, or psychologist's formula, or man-of-letters' summary, or wit's sentence define him. Definitions, because they must not be inexact or incomprehensive, sweep too wide, and the poet is not held within them; and out of the mere describer's range and capture he may escape by as many doors as there are outlets from a forest. But much ready-made platitude brings about the world's guesses at a poet, and false and flat thought lies behind its epigrams. It is not long since the general guess-work assigned melancholy, without authority, to a poet lately deceased. Real poets, it was said, are unhappy, and this was one exceptionally real. How unhappy must he, then, certainly have been! And the blessed Blake himself was incidentally cited as one of the company of depression and despair! It is, perhaps, a liking for symmetry that prompts these futile syllogisms; perhaps, also, it is the fear of human mystery. The biographer used to see 'the finger of God' pat in the history of a man; he insists now that he shall at any rate see the finger of a law, or rather of a rule, a custom, a generality. Law I will not call it; there is no intelligible law that, for example, a true poet should be an unhappy man; but the observer thinks he has noticed a custom or habit to that effect, and Blake, who lived and died in bliss, is named at ignorant random, rather than that an example of the custom should be lost.

But it is not only such a platitude of observation, such a cheap generality, that is silenced in the presence of the poet whose name is at the head of these pages. For if ever Nature showed us a poet in whom our phrases, and the judgments they record, should be denied, defeated, and confused, Swinburne is he. We predicate of a poet a great sincerity, a great imagination, a great passion, a great intellect; these are the master qualities, and yet we are compelled to see here — if we would not wilfully be blind or blindfold — a poet, yes, a true poet, with a perfervid fancy rather than an imagination, a poet with puny passions, a poet with no more than the momentary and impulsive sincerity of an infirm soul, a poet with small intellect — and thrice a poet.

And, assuredly, if the creative arts are duly humbled in the universal contemplation of Nature, if they are accused, if they are weighed, if they are found wanting; if they are excused by nothing but our intimate human sympathy with dear and interesting imperfection; if poetry stands outdone by the passion and experience of an inarticulate soul, and painting by the splendour of the day, and building by the forest and the cloud, there is another art also that has to be humiliated, and this is the art and science of criticism, confounded by its contemplation of such a poet. Poor little art of examination and formula! The miracle of day and night and immortality are needed to rebuke the nobler arts; but our art, the critic's, mine to-day, is brought to book, and its heart is broken, and its sincerity disgraced, by the paradoxes of the truth. Not in the heavens nor in the sub-celestial landscape does this minor art find its refutation, but in the puzzle between a man and his gift; and in part the man is ignoble and leads us by distasteful paths, and compels us to a reluctant work of literary detection. Useful is the critical spirit, but it loses heart when (to take a very definite instance) it has to ask what literary sincerity — what value for art and letters — lived in Swinburne, who hailed a certain old friend, in a dedication, as 'poet and painter' when he was pleased with him, and declared him 'poetaster and dauber' when something in that dead man's posthumous autobiography offended his own self-love; when, I say, criticism finds itself called upon, amid its admiration, to do such scavenger work, it loses heart as well as the clue, and would gladly go out into the free air of greater arts, and, with them, take exterior Nature's nobler reprobation.

I have to cite this instance of a change of mind, or of terms and titles, in Swinburne's estimate of art and letters, because it is all-important to my argument. It is a change he makes in published print, and, therefore, no private matter. And I cite it, not as a sign of moral fault, with which I have no business, but as a sign of a most significant literary insensibility — insensibility, whether to the quality of a poetaster when he wrote 'poet', or to that of a poet when he wrote 'poetaster', is of no matter.

Rather than justify the things I have ventured to affirm as to Swinburne's little intellect, and paltry degree of sincerity, and rachitic passion, and tumid fancy — judgment-confounding things to predicate of a poet — I turn to the happier task of praise. A vivid writer of English was he, and would have been one of the recurring renewers of our often-renewed and incomparable language, had his words not become habitual to himself, so that they quickly lost the light, the breeze, the breath; one whose fondness for beauty deserved the serious name of love; one whom beauty at times favoured and filled so visibly, by such obvious visits and possessions, favours so manifest, that inevitably we forget we are speaking fictions and allegories, and imagine her a visiting power exterior to her poet; a man, moreover, of a less, not more, than manly receptiveness and appreciation, so that he was entirely and easily possessed by admirations. Less than manly we must call his extraordinary recklessness of appreciation; it is, as it were, ideally feminine; it is possible, however, that no woman has yet been capable of so entire an emotional impulse and impetus; more than manly it might have been but for the lack of a responsible intellect in that impulse; had it possessed such an intellectual sanction, Swinburne's admiration of Victor Hugo, Mazzini, Dickens, Baudelaire, and Théophile Gautier might have added one to the great generosities of the world.

We are inclined to complain of such an objection to Swinburne's poetry as was prevalent at his earlier appearance and may be found in criticisms of the time, before the later fashion of praise set in — the obvious objection that it was as indigent in thought as affluent in words; for, though a truth, it is an inadequate truth. It might be affirmed of many a verse-writer of not unusual talent and insignificance, whose affluence of words was inselective and merely abundant, and whose poverty of thought was something less than a national disaster. Swinburne's failure of intellect was, in the fullest and most serious sense, a national disaster, and his instinct for words was a national surprise. It is in their beauty that Swinburne's art finds its absolution from the obligations of meaning, according to the vulgar judgment; and we can hardly wonder.

I wish it were not customary to write of one art in the terms of another, and I use the words 'music' and 'musical' under protest, because the world has been so delighted to call any verse pleasant to the ear 'musical', that it has not supplied us with another and more specialized and appropriate word. Swinburne is a complete master of the rhythm and rhyme, the time and accent, the pause, the balance, the flow of vowel and clash of consonant, that make the 'music' for which verse is popular and prized. We need not complain that it is for the tune rather than for the melody — if we must use those alien terms — that he is chiefly admired, and even for the jingle rather than for the tune: he gave his readers all three, and all three in perfection. Nineteen out of twenty who take pleasure in this art of his will quote you first

When the hounds of Spring are on winter's traces
The Mother of months, in meadow and plain,

and the rest of the buoyant familiar lines. I confess there is something too obvious, insistent, emphatic, too dapper, to give me more than a slight pleasure; but it is possible that I am prejudiced by a dislike of English anapaests (I am aware that the classic terms are not really applicable to our English metres, but the reader will understand that I mean the metre of the lines just quoted). I do not find these anapaests in the Elizabethan or in the seventeenth-century poets, or most rarely. They were dear to the eighteenth century, and, much more than the heroic couplet, are the distinctive metre of that age. They swagger — or, worse, they strut — in its lighter verse, from its first year to its last. Swinburne's anapaests are far too delicate for swagger or strut; but for all their dance, all their spring, all their flight, all their flutter, we are compelled to perceive that, as it were, they *perform*. I love to see English poetry move to many measures, to many numbers, but chiefly with the simple iambic and the simple trochaic foot. Those two are enough for the infinite variety, the epic, the drama, the lyric, of our poetry. It is, accordingly, in these old traditional and proved metres that Swinburne's music seems to me most worthy, most controlled, and most lovely. *There* is his best dignity, and therefore his best beauty. For even beauty is not to be thrust upon us; she is not to solicit us or offer herself thus to the first comer; and in the most admired of those flying lyrics she is thus immoderately lavish of herself. 'He lays himself out', wrote Francis Thompson in an anonymous criticism, 'to delight and seduce. The great poets entice by a glorious accident . . . but allurement, in Mr. Swinburne's poetry, is the alpha and omega.' This is true of all that he has written, but it is true, in a more fatal sense, of these famous tunes of his 'music'. Nay, delicate as they are, we are convinced that it is the less delicate ear that most surely takes much pleasure in them, the dull ear that chiefly they delight.

Compare with such luxurious canterings the graver movement of this 'Vision of Spring in Winter':

Sunrise it sees not, neither set of star,
  Large nightfall, nor imperial plenilune,
  Nor strong sweet shape of the full-breasted noon;
But where the silver-sandalled shadows are,
Too soft for arrows of the sun to mar,
  Moves with the mild gait of an ungrown moon.

Even more valuable than this exquisite rhymed stanza is the
blank verse which Swinburne released into new energies, new
liberties, and new movements. Milton, it need hardly be said,
is the master of those who know how to place and displace the
stress and accent of the English heroic line in epic poetry.
His most majestic hand undid the mechanical bonds of the
national line and made it obey the unwritten laws of his genius.
His blank verse marches, pauses, lingers, and charges. It feels
the strain, it yields, it resists; it is all-expressive. But if the
practice of some of the poets succeeding him had tended to
make it rigid and tame again, Swinburne was a new liberator.
He writes, when he ought, with a finely appropriate regularity,
as in the lovely line on the forest glades

  That fear the faun's and know the dryad's foot,

in which the rule is completely kept, every step of the five
stepping from the unaccented place to the accented without
a tremor. (I must again protest that I use the word 'accent' in
a sense that has come to be adapted to English prosody,
because it is so used by all writers on English metre, and is
therefore understood by the reader, but I think 'stress' the
better word.) But having written this perfect English-iambic
line so wonderfully fit for the sensitive quiet of the woods, he
turns the page to the onslaught of such lines — heroic lines
with a difference — as report the short-breathed messenger's
reply to Althea's question by whose hands the boar of Calydon
had died:

  A maiden's and a prophet's and thy son's.

It is lamentable that in his latest blank verse Swinburne
should have made a trick and a manner of that most energetic

device of his by which he leads the line at a rush from the first syllable to the tenth, and on to the first of the line succeeding, with a great recoil to follow, as though a rider brought a horse to his haunches. It is in the same boar hunt:

> And fiery with invasive eyes,
> And bristling with intolerable hair,
> Plunged; —

Sometimes we may be troubled with a misgiving that Swinburne's fine narrative, as well as his descriptive writing of other kinds, has a counterpart in the programme-music of some now by-gone composers. It is even too descriptive, too imitative of things, and seems to outrun the province of words, somewhat as that did the province of notes. But, though this hunting, and checking, and floating, and flying in metre may be to strain the arts of prosody and diction, with how masterly a hand is the straining accomplished! The spear, the arrow, the attack, the charge, the footfall, the pinion, nay, the very stepping of the moon, the walk of the wind, are mimicked in this enchanting verse. Like to programme-music we must call it, but I wish the concert-platform had ever justified this slight perversion of aim, this excess — almost corruption — of one kind of skill, thus miraculously well.

Now, if Swinburne's exceptional faculty of diction led him to immoderate expressiveness, to immodest sweetness, to a jugglery, and prestidigitation, and conjuring of words, to transformations and transmutations of sound — if, I say, his extraordinary gift of diction brought him to this exaggeration of the manner, what a part does it not play in the matter of his poetry! So overweening a place does it take in this man's art that I believe the words to hold and use his meaning, rather than the meaning to compass and grasp and use the word. I believe that Swinburne's thoughts have their source, their home, their origin, their authority and mission in those two places — his own vocabulary and the passion of other men. This is a grave charge.

First, then, in regard to the passion of other men. I have

given to his own emotion the puniest name I could find for it;
I have no nobler name for his intellect. But other men had
thoughts, other men had passions; political, sexual, natural,
noble, vile, ideal, gross, rebellious, agonizing, imperial,
republican, cruel, compassionate; and with these he fed his
verses. Upon these and their life he sustained, he fattened, he
enriched his poetry. Mazzini in Italy, Gautier and Baudelaire
in France, Shelley in England, made for him a base of passion-
ate and intellectual supplies. With them he kept the all-
necessary line of communication. We cease, as we see their
active hearts possess his active art, to think a question as to
his sincerity seriously worth asking; what sincerity he has is
so absorbed in the one excited act of receptivity. That, indeed,
he performs with all the will, all the precipitation, all the rush,
all the surrender, all the whole-hearted weakness of his sub-
servient and impetuous nature. I have not named the Greeks,
nor the English Bible, nor Milton, as his inspirers. These he
would claim; they are not his. He received too partial, too
fragmentary, too arbitrary an inheritance of the Greek spirit,
too illusory an idea of Milton, of the English Bible little more
than a tone; — this poet of eager, open capacity, this poet who
is little more, intellectually, than a too-ready, too-vacant
capacity, for those three august severities has not room
enough.

Charged, then, with other men's purposes — this man's
Italian patriotism; this man's love of sin (by that name, for sin
has been denied, as a fiction, but Swinburne, following Baude-
laire, acknowledges it to love it); this man's despite against the
Third Empire or what not; this man's cry for a political
liberty granted or gained long ago — a cry grown vain; this
man's contempt for the Boers — nay, was it so much as a man,
with a man's evil to answer for, that furnished him here; was
it not rather that less guilty judge, the crowd? — this man's —
nay, this boy's — erotic sickness, or his cruelty — charged with
all these, Swinburne's poetry is primed; it explodes with
thunder and fire. But such sharing is somewhat too familiar
for dignity; such community of goods parodies the Francis-

cans. As one friar goes darned for another's rending, having no property in cassock or cowl, so does many a poet, not in humility, but in a paradox of pride, boast of the past of others. And yet one might rather choose to make use of one's fellow-men's old shoes than to put their old secrets to usufruct, and dress poetry in a motley of shed passions, twice corrupt. Promiscuity of love we have heard of; Pope was accused, by Lord Hervey's indignation and wit, of promiscuity of hatred, and of scattering his disfavours in the stews of an indiscriminate malignity; and here is another promiscuity — that of memories, and of a licence partaken.

But by the unanimous poets' splendid love of the landscape and the skies, by this also was Swinburne possessed, and in this he triumphed. By this, indeed, he profited; here he joined an innumerable company of that heavenly host of earth. Let us acknowledge then his honourable alacrity here, his quick fellowship, his agile adoption, and his filial tenderness — nay, his fraternal union with his poets. No tourist's admiration for all things French, no tourist's politics in Italy — and Swinburne's French and Italian admirations have the tourist manner of enthusiasm — prompts him here. Here he aspires to brotherhood with the supreme poets of supreme England, with the sixteenth century, the seventeenth, and the nineteenth, the impassioned centuries of song. Happy is he to be admitted among these, happy is he to merit by his wonderful voice to sing their raptures. Here is no humiliation in ready-made lendings; their ecstasy becomes him. He is glorious with them, and we can imagine this benign and indulgent Nature confounding together the sons she embraces, and making her poets — the primary and the secondary, the greater and the lesser — all equals in her arms. Let us see him in that company where he looks noble amongst the noble; let us not look upon him in the company of the ignoble, where he looks ignobler still, being servile to them; let us look upon him with the lyrical Shakespeare, with Vaughan, Blake, Wordsworth, Patmore, Meredith; not with Baudelaire and Gautier; with the poets of the forest and the sun, and not with those of the alcove. We can make peace with him for love of them; we can imagine them thankful to him who, poor and perverse in thought in so many pages, could yet join them in such a song as this:

> And her heart sprang in Iseult, and she drew
> With all her spirit and life the sunrise through,
> And through her lips the keen triumphant air
> Sea-scented, sweeter than land-roses were,
> And through her eyes the whole rejoicing east
> Sun-satisfied, and all the heaven at feast
> Spread for the morning; and the imperious mirth
> Of wind and light that moved upon the earth,
> Making the spring, and all the fruitful might
> And strong regeneration of delight
> That swells the seedling leaf and sapling man.

He, nevertheless, who was able, in high company, to hail the sea with such fine verse, was not ashamed, in low company, to sing the famous absurdities about 'the lilies and languors of virtue and the roses and raptures of vice', with many and many a passage of like character. I think it more generous, seeing I have differed so much from the Nineteenth Century's chorus of excessive praise, to quote little from the vacant, the paltry, the silly — no word is so fit as that last little word — among his pages. Therefore, I have justified my praise, but not my blame. It is for the reader to turn to the justifying pages: to 'A Song of Italy', 'Les Noyades', 'Hermaphroditus', 'Satia te Sanguine', 'Kissing her Hair', 'An Interlude', 'In a Garden', or such a stanza as the one beginning

> O thought illimitable and infinite heart
>   Whose blood is life in limbs indissolute
> That all keep heartless thine invisible part
>   And inextirpable thy viewless root
> Whence all sweet shafts of green and each thy dart
>   Of sharpening leaf and bud resundering shoot.

It is for the reader who has preserved rectitude of intellect, sincerity of heart, dignity of nerves, unhurried thoughts, an unexcited heart, and an ardour for poetry, to judge between such poems and an authentic passion, between such poems and truth, I will add between such poems and beauty.

Imagery is a great part of poetry; but out, alas! vocabulary has here too the upper hand. For in what is still sometimes called the magnificent chorus in 'Atalanta' the words have swallowed not the thought only but the imagery. The poet's grievance is that the pleasant streams flow into the sea. What would he have? The streams turned loose all over the unfortunate country? There is, it is true, the river Mole in Surrey. But I am not sure that some foolish imagery against the peace of the burrowing river might not be due from a poet of facility. I am not censuring any insincerity of thought; I am complaining of the insincerity of a paltry, shaky, and unvisionary image.

Having had recourse to the passion of stronger minds for his provision of emotions, Swinburne had direct recourse to his own vocabulary as a kind of 'safe' wherein he stored what he needed for a song. Claudius stole the precious diadem of the kingdom from a shelf and put it in his pocket; Swinburne took from the shelf of literature — took with what art, what touch, what cunning, what complete skill! — the treasure of the language, and put it in his pocket.

He is urgent with his booty of words, for he has no other treasure. Into his pocket he thrusts a hand groping for hatred, and draws forth 'blood' or 'Hell' — generally 'Hell', for I have counted many 'Hells' in a quite short poem. In search of wrath he takes hold of 'fire'; anxious for wildness he takes 'foam', for sweetness he brings out 'flower', much linked, so that 'flower-soft' has almost become his, and not Shakespeare's. For in that compound he labours to exaggerate Shakespeare, and by his insistence and iteration goes about to spoil for us the 'flower-soft hands' of Cleopatra's rudder-maiden; but he shall not spoil Shakespeare's phrase for us. And behold, in all this fundamental fumbling Swinburne's critics saw only a 'mannerism', if they saw even thus much offence.

One of the chief pocket-words was. 'Liberty'. O Liberty! what verse is committed in thy name! Or, to cite Madame Roland more accurately, O Liberty, how have they 'run' thee!

Who, it has been well asked by a citizen of a modern free country, is thoroughly free except a fish? *Et encore* — even the 'silent and footless herds' may have more inter-accommodation than we are aware. But in the pocket of the secondary poet how easy and how ready a word is this, a word implying old and true heroisms, but significant here of an excitable poet's economies. Yes, economies of thought and passion. This poet, who is conspicuously the poet of excess, is in deeper truth the poet of penury and defect.

And here is a pocket-word which might have astonished us had we not known how little anyway it signified. It occurs in something customary about Italy:

> Hearest thou,
> Italia? Tho' deaf sloth hath sealed thine ears,
> The world has heard thy children — and God hears.

Was ever word so pouched, so produced, so surely a handful of loot, as the penultimate word of this verse?

What, finally, is his influence upon the language he has ransacked? A temporary laying-waste, undoubtedly. That is, the contemporary use of his vocabulary is spoilt, his beautiful words are wasted, spent, squandered, *gaspillés*. The contemporary use — I will not say the future use, for no critic should prophesy. But the past he has not been able to violate. He has had no power to rob of their freshness the sixteenth-century flower, the seventeenth-century fruit, or by his violence to shake from either a drop of their dews.

At the outset I warned the judges and the pronouncers of sentences how this poet, with other poets of quite different character, would escape their summaries, and he has indeed refuted that maxim which I had learned at illustrious knees: 'You may not dissociate the matter and manner of any of the greatest poets; the two are so fused by integrity of fire, whether

in tragedy or epic or in the simplest song, that the sundering
is the vainest task of criticism.' But I cannot read Swinburne
and not be compelled to divide his secondhand and enfeebled
and excited matter from the successful art of his word. Of that
word Francis Thompson has said again, 'It imposes a law on
the sense'. Therefore, he too perceived that fatal division. Is,
then, the wisdom of the maxim confounded? Or is Swinburne's
a 'single and excepted case'? Excepted by a thousand degrees
of talent from any generality fitting the obviously lesser poets,
but, possibly, also excepted by an essential inferiority from this
great maxim fitting only the greatest?

Anima Pellegrina!

EVERY language in the world has its own phrase, fresh for the
stranger's fresh and alien sense of its signal significance; a
phrase that is its own essential possession, and yet is dearer to
the speaker of other tongues. Easily — shall I say cheaply? —
spiritual, for example, was the nation that devised the name
anima pellegrina, wherewith to crown a creature admired. 'Pil-
grim soul' is a phrase for any language, but 'pilgrim soul!'
addressed, singly and sweetly, to one who cannot be over-
praised, 'pilgrim-soul!' is a phrase of fondness, the high
homage of a lover, of one watching, of one who has no more
need of common flatteries, but has admired and gazed while
the object of his praises visibly surpassed them — this is the
facile Italian ecstasy, and it rises into an Italian heaven.

It was by chance, and in an old play, that I came upon this
impetuous, sudden, and single sentence of admiration, as it
were a sentence of life passed upon one charged with
inestimable deeds; and the modern editor had thought it
necessary to explain the exclamation by a note. It was, he
said, poetical.

Anima pellegrina seems to be Italian of no later date than Pergolese's airs, and suits the time as the familiar phrase of the more modern love-song suited the day of Bellini. But it is only Italian, bygone Italian, and not a part of the sweet past of any other European nation, but only of this.

To the same local boundaries and enclosed skies belongs the charm of those buoyant words:

> Felice chi vi mira,
> Ma più felice chi per voi sospira!

And it is not only a charm of elastic sound or of grace; that would be but a property of the turn of speech. It is rather the profounder advantage whereby the rhymes are freighted with such feeling as the very language keeps in store. In another tongue you may sing, 'happy who looks, happier who sighs'; but in what other tongue shall the little meaning be so sufficient, and in what other shall you get from so weak an antithesis the illusion of a lovely intellectual epigram? Yet it is not worthy of an English reader to call it an illusion; he should rather be glad to travel into the place of a language where the phrase *is* intellectual, impassioned, and an epigram; and should thankfully for the occasion translate himself, and not the poetry.

I have been delighted to use a present current phrase whereof the charm may still be unknown to Englishmen — '*piuttosto bruttini*'. See what an all-Italian spirit is here, and what contempt, not reluctant, but tolerant and familiar. You may hear it said of pictures, or works of art of several kinds, and you confess at once that not otherwise should they be condemned. *Brutto* — ugly — is the word of justice, the word for any language, everywhere translatable, a circular note, to be exchanged internationally with a general meaning, wholesale, in the course of the European concert. But *bruttino* is a soothing diminutive, a diminutive that forbears to express contempt, a diminutive that implies innocence, and is, moreover, guarded by a hesitating adverb, shrugging in the rear — 'rather than not'. 'Rather ugly than not, and ugly in a little way that we need say few words about — the fewer the better'; nay, this paraphrase cannot achieve the homely Italian quality whereby the printed and condemnatory criticism is made a family affair that shall go no further. After the sound of it, the European concert seems to be composed of brass instruments.

How unlike is the house of English language and the enclosure into which a traveller hither has to enter! Do we possess anything here more essentially ours (though we share it with our sister Germany) than our particle 'un'? Poor are those living languages that have not our use of so rich a negative. The French equivalent in adjectives reaches no further than the adjective itself — or hardly; it does not attain the participle; so that no French or Italian poet has the words 'unloved', 'unforgiven'. None such, therefore, has the opportunity of the gravest and the most majestic of all ironies. In our English, the words that are denied are still there — 'loved', 'forgiven': excluded angels, who stand erect, attesting what is not done, what is undone, what shall not be done.

No merely opposite words could have so much denial, or so much pain of loss, or so much outer darkness, or so much barred beatitude in sight. All-present, all-significant, all-remembering, all-foretelling is the word, and it has a plenitude of knowledge.

We have many more conspicuous possessions that are, like this, proper to character and thought, and by no means only an accident of untransferable speech. And it is impossible for a reader, who is a lover of languages for their spirit, to pass the words of untravelled excellence, proper to their own garden enclosed, without recognition. Never may they be disregarded or confounded with the universal stock. If I would not so neglect *piuttosto bruttini*, how much less a word dominating literature! And of such words of ascendancy and race there is no great English author but has abundant possession. No need to recall them. But even writers who are not great have, here and there, proved their full consciousness of their birthright. Thus does a man who was hardly an author, Haydon the painter, put out his hand to take his rights. He has incomparable language when he is at a certain page of his life; at that time he sate down to sketch his child, dying in its babyhood, and the head he studied was, he says, full of 'power and grief'.

This is a phrase of different discovery from that which reveals a local rhyme-balanced epigram, a gracious antithesis, taking an intellectual place — *Felice chi vi mira* — or the art-critic's phrase — *piuttosto bruttini* — of easy, companionable, and equal contempt.

As for French, if it had no other sacred words — and it has many — who would not treasure the language that has given us — no, not that has given us, but that has kept for its own — *ensoleillé*? Nowhere else is the sun served with such a word. It is not to be said or written without a convincing sense of sunshine, and from the very word come light and radiation. The unaccustomed North could not have made it, nor the accustomed South, but only a nation part-north and part-south; therefore neither England nor Italy can rival it. But there needed also the senses of the French — those senses of which they say far too much in every second-class book of their enormous, their general second-class, but which they have matched in their time with some inimitable words. Perhaps that matching was done at the moment of the full literary consciousness of the senses, somewhere about the famous 1830. For I do not think *ensoleillé* to be a much older word — I make no assertion. Whatever its origin, may it have no end! They cannot weary us with it; for it seems as new as the sun, as remote as old Provence; village, hill-side, vineyard, and chestnut wood shine in the splendour of the word, the air is light, and white things passing blind the eyes — a woman's linen, white cattle, shining on the way from shadow to shadow. A word of the sense of sight, and a summer word, in short, compared with which the paraphrase is but a picture. For *ensoleillé* I would claim the consent of all readers — that they shall all acknowledge the spirit of that French. But perhaps it is a mere personal preference that makes *le jour s'annonce* also sacred.

If the hymn 'Stabat Mater dolorosa' was written in Latin, this could be only that it might in time find its true language and incomparable phrase at last — that it might await the day of life in its proper German. I found it there (and knew at once the authentic verse, and knew at once for what tongue it had been really destined) in the pages of the prayer-book of an apple-woman at an Innsbruck church, and in the accents of her voice.

The Little Language

DIALECT is the elf rather than the genius of place, and a dwarfish master of the magic of local things.

In England we hardly know what a concentrated homeliness it nourishes; inasmuch as, with us, the castes and classes for whom Goldoni and Gallina and Fogazzaro have written in the patois of the Veneto, use no dialect at all.

Neither Goldoni nor Gallina has charged the Venetian language with so much literature as to take from the people the shelter of their almost unwritten tongue. Signor Fogazzaro, bringing tragedy into the homes of dialect, does but show us how the language staggers under such a stress, how it breaks down, and resigns that office. One of the finest of the characters in the ranks of his admirable fiction is that old manageress of the narrow things of the house whose daughter is dying insane. I have called the dialect a shelter. This it is; but the poor lady does not cower within; her resigned head erect, she is shut out from that homely refuge, suffering and inarticulate. The two dramatists in their several centuries also recognized the inability of the dialect. They laid none but light loads upon it. They caused it to carry no more in their homely plays than it carries in homely life. Their work leaves it what it was — the talk of a people talking much about few things; a people like our own and any other in their lack of literature, but local and all Italian in their lack of silence.

Common speech is surely a greater part of life to such a people than to one less pleased with chatter or more pleased with books. I am writing of men, women, and children (and children are not forgotten, since we share a patois with children on terms of more than common equality) who possess, for all occasions of ceremony and opportunities of dignity, a general, national, liberal, able, and illustrious tongue, charged with all its history and all its achievements; for the speakers of dialect, of a certain rank, speak Italian, too. But to tamper with their dialect, or to take it from them, would be to leave them houseless and exposed in their daily business. So much does their patois seem to be their refuge from the heavy and multitudinous experiences of a literary tongue, that the stopping of a fox's earth might be taken as the image of any act that should spoil or stop the talk of the associated seclusion of their town, and leave them in the bleakness of a larger patriotism.

The Venetian people, the Genoese, and the other speakers of languages that might all have proved right 'Italian' had not Dante, Petrarch, and Boccaccio written in Tuscan, can neither write nor be taught hard things in their dialect, although they can live, whether easy lives or hard, and evidently can die, therein. The hands and feet that have served the villager and the citizen at homely tasks have all the lowliness of his patois, to his mind; and when he must perforce yield up their employment, we may believe that it is a simple thing to die in so simple and so narrow a language, one so comfortable, neighbourly, tolerant, and compassionate; so confidential; so incapable, ignorant, unappalling, inapt to wing any wearied thought upon difficult flight or to spur it upon hard travelling.

Not without words is mental pain, or even physical pain, to be undergone; but the words that have done no more than order the things of the narrow street are not words to put a fine edge or a piercing point to any human pang. It may even well be that to die in dialect is easier than to die in the eloquence of Manfred, though that declaimed language, too, is doubtless a defence, if one of a different manner.

These writers in Venetian — they are named because in no other Italian dialect has work so popular as Goldoni's been done, nor so excellent as Signor Fogazzaro's — have left the unlettered

local language in which they loved to deal, to its proper limita-
tions. They have not given weighty things into its charge, nor
made it heavily responsible. They have added nothing to it
nay, by writing it they might even be said to have made it
duller, had it not been for the reader and the actor. Insomuch
as the intense expressiveness of a dialect — of a small vocabu-
lary in the mouth of a dramatic people — lies in the various
accent wherewith a southern citizen knows how to enrich his
talk, it remains for the actor to restore its life to the written
phrase. In dialect the author is forbidden to search for the
word, for there is none lurking for his choice; but of tones, of
allusions, and of references and inferences of the voice, the
speaker of dialect is a master. No range of phrases can be his
but he has the more or the less confidential inflexion, until at
times the close communication of the narrow street becomes a
very conspiracy.

Let it be borne in mind that dialect properly so called is
something all unlike, for instance, the mere jargon of London
streets. The difference may be measured by the fact that
Italian dialects have a highly organized and orderly grammar
The Londoner cannot keep the small and loose order of the
grammar of good English; the Genoese conjugates his patois
verbs, with subjunctives and all things of that handsome kind
lacked by the English of Universities.

The middle class — the *piccolo mondo* — that shares Italian
dialect with the poor are more strictly local in their manners
than either the opulent or the indigent of the same city. They
have moreover the busy intelligence (which is the intellect of
patois) at its keenest. Their speech keeps them a sequestered
place which is Italian, Italian beyond the ken of the traveller
and beyond the reach of alteration. And — what is pretty to
observe — the speakers are well conscious of the characters of
this intimate language. An Italian countryman who has known
no other climate will vaunt, in fervent platitudes, his Italian
sun; in like manner he is conscious of the local character of his
language, and tucks himself within it at home, whatever Tus-
can he may speak abroad. A properly spelt letter, Swift said

would seem to expose him and Mrs. Dingley and Stella to the eyes of the world; but their little language, ill-written, was 'snug'.

Lovers have made a little language in all times; finding the greater language insufficient, do they ensconce themselves in the smaller? discard noble and literary speech as not noble enough, and in despair thus prattle and gibber and stammer? Rather perhaps this departure from English is but an excursion after gaiety. The ideal lovers, no doubt, would be so simple as to be grave; that is a tenable opinion. Nevertheless, age by age they have been gay; and age by age they have exchanged language imitated from the children they doubtless never studied, and perhaps never loved. Why so? They might have chosen broken English of other sorts — that, for example, which was once thought amusing in farce, as spoken by the Frenchman conceived by the Englishman — a complication of humour fictitious enough, one might think, to please anyone; or else a fragment of negro dialect; or the style of telegrams; or the masterly adaptation of the simple savage's English devised by Mrs. Plornish in her intercourse with the Italian. But none of these found favour. The choice has always been of the language of children. Let us suppose that the flock of winged Loves worshipping Venus in the Titian picture, and the noble child that rides his lion erect with a background of Venetian gloomy dusk, may be the inspirers of those prattlings. 'See then thy selfe likewise art lyttle made', says Spenser's Venus to her child.

Swift was the best prattler. He had caught the language, surprised it in Stella when she was veritably a child. He did not push her clumsily back into a childhood he had not known; he simply prolonged in her a childhood he had loved. He is 'seepy'. 'Nite, dealest dea, nite dealest logue.' It is a real good-night. It breathes tenderness from that moody and uneasy bed of projects.

The Second Person Singular

THE cause of the modern monotony of 'you' might be sought
in the mere slovenliness of our civilization in the practice of
the inflexions of grammar. All things tend to become special-
ized, except only words. Though in the house of life itself the
organs, as life grows more perfect, begin to draw apart to their
own separate functions; though the labourer, in the later
association of mankind, finds his task by degrees to dwindle in
range and to be enforced within closer and closer repetitions
and though only a small division of any of the sciences that
have come towards adult and responsible age falls to the share
of a single specialist, the word alone grows not expert and
special, but general and inexpert.

It is obliged to do more various things, and to do them with
less directness and, as it were, a less sequestered intention. It
is engaged upon enterprises of unskilled labour. The industrial
word has less and less craft, less dignity, less leisure, less rest
and more mere utility.

Moreover, it loses, in the work-a-day life, its own varieties
amid the varieties of the casual task. It changes not its vesture
and the inflexion is lost.

Why it is that some, at least, of the civilized peoples, in the
inevitable evolution of things, should tend to become poor
careless, and inexact grammarians it is hard to understand. The
fact is, needless to say, well enough known. Some of the French
missionaries, students of American-Indian languages, have
astonished us with reports of the enormous vocabularies and
the scientific order of those tongues. The people are in the
nomadic stage of society, their languages in the finished, the
special, the sub-divided condition; intricate in system, organic
arranged, logical, full of expressive differences, cases that pre-
cisely assign action, and tenses that deal finely with time, turn-
ing the future to look upon the past, and anticipating that turn
and making a shifting perspective of the past; distinguishing
persons not merely by pointing the rude forefinger of a pro-

noun, but by the allusion of all the inflexions of a verb. All that the antique grammars did, and more, is done, we hear, by those doomed languages of an unaltering people, a people with neither literature nor history, a people whose antiquities have no interest nor value, nor date, because their centuries resembled each other.

Not only the tactics of grammar, but an innumerable variety of words is theirs, so that a speaker might hardly name a common thing without a conscious play of choice, according as the syllables of a sentence were to fold and close. Rhythmic prose is hardly possible, when it has the charge of thought, without some degree of a like liberty of choice, and modern prose in all languages has, obviously, for the lack of this liberty — for lack of rich alternatives — somewhat forgone the practice of rhythm; forgone it altogether in the explanations of science, for instance, or the processes of reasoning. A Red-Indian speech, translated even into sentimental English, as used formerly to be done, must have undergone a sorry process, and a yet sorrier change when it was done into sentimental French.

It is, however, among English races chiefly that an unwillingness to be troubled with the distinctions of grammar has had this effect of making a word run errands and serve the first purpose at hand; and it is among English races that inflexions (never very numerous or subtle) have been neglected and let fall. That most orderly of grammars, the Spanish, is still in full use; the Italians keep all their inflexions nominally, use them all in Tuscany, use a certain number in Rome, retain as few as possible in Liguria — making shift with auxiliary verbs rather than conjugate properly, everywhere except in the Tuscan districts. The French go about to avoid certain of their own subjunctives, even in literature, and in speech the perfect tenses are passed askance, for fear of pedantry. None but ourselves has been so roughly impatient as to put an end to the second person singular. 'You' was manifestly a trick of politeness in all languages, until it became depreciated by general use, when Germans, Spaniards, and Italians sought for a yet more distant pronoun of courtesy.

The literary Genius was kind to its wayward, chosen people and kept for us a plot of the language apart for the phrase o piety and poetry. As things are, we need not envy the French for example, their second person singular. It has but two kee significances — the first use in love and the disuse in the reproo of children. The second is, perhaps, the more important; it i renewed, and loses nothing of its pain by recurrence. To sa 'vous' to a naughty child is to enforce insatiate retribution; fev children deserve so much justice, for this is a rebuke tha touches the personality, and alters the relations of life.

As to that other occasion, first-mentioned, it is by no mean certain that the second person singular, with its single delight – the first — never to be renewed, has not to answer for the vulga regrets of the world for the flights of its joys. 'Toi', the firs 'toi', is an arbitrary, a conventional happiness, a happiness be cause it is single — it has no quality but that. The 'many thou sand' of 'toi' are insignificant, and therefore it has no 'poo last'; it sets a paltry example, therefore.

And then, while the second person singular plays this am biguous part in love, see how primly it is eschewed in prayer 'May your name be sanctified' is a second phrase of the *oraiso* *dominicale* (*oraison dominicale!* the name says everything) whicl we should be loth to have in place of our own. With us ther is not only the poetic 'thy', but the obsolete valuing of the las syllable of the past participle — hallowed — and the unworn the still fresh word itself to make the sentence beautiful Decidedly, if we took such words into familiar use we shoulc gain much, but we should lose a most distinctive characteristic bestowed upon us by the literary Genius, as though in rewarc of our very sins — our unique plot of disregarded language tha the traffic of the world passes by. For though the Italian have a poetic Italian, the differences of this with their dail prose are rather in the form of the words than in the word themselves. Now the French have the Psalms of David ir the language of the trade circular charged with a littl rhetoric.

As to our civilized sloth in neglecting rules, and its effectua influence in effacing them, it could not be more distinctly proved than by the Quaker speech. Restoring the second person singular to the language (by way of denying the primitive hyperbole of courtesy from which the general second person plural took its use), the followers of Penn restored none of the inflexions. Or if for a generation or so they were in practice, yet the increase of carelessness and the generalizing habit of speech in a world more and more intent upon special tasks in all things else, quickly made an end of them. So that Quakerism began to talk a horrible grammar unknown to the Gentiles. If Mrs. Beecher Stowe makes Quakers speak according to their use, they suppressed 'thou' more or less, and would neither decline or conjugate. Nothing but the slovenly indifference that has made all our verbs so dull could be the cause of this perversion of a reform.

Like to the Quaker grammarians are certain of our own poets, who seem to find a difficulty in carrying the second person singular safely through a stanza. If one verb agrees in order, ten to one there is another, a little more out of sight, that does not. As Shelley wrote —

Thou lovest, but ne'er knew love's sad satiety,

so write others of the moderns.

Nevertheless, it is not excusable. It was not done in the other centuries. Must we needs, as we go on, grow so lax, and do these unhandsome things? If we do by some obscure process grow so lax, why should there not be, in a time of revisions, a revision of these customs? A little of the subjunctive was restored many years ago by Mr. Henley in the *National Observer*; that this little soon fell aside again is not encouraging; nevertheless, 'it were' worth while for some author, unencouraged, to recall, responsibly, the second person singular, and with it certain tenses long out of use.

There might be such a literary restoration — a literary and a familiar restoration — as would make our language again more various and more charming, and yet would not turn the speech poetic to vulgar use, nor decrease the dignity of what Jeremy

Taylor at his prayers called 'the essential and ornamental measures of address'.

Whatever our slovenly ways with ordinary grammar, we have the treasure of the sequestered poetic and religious language in good order and perfect syntax, And our advantage of the two derivations may well be dwelt upon afresh, now when so many of our writers are obsequious to the French language. (How is it, by the way, that Ireland is so ungrateful to us for the gift of English?) French cannot be the great poetic language, in spite of the opinion of Louis Blanc, delivered from a grand-fatherly hearth-rug: 'L'anglais et le français; ce sont les deux langues qui resteront: l'anglais pour le commerce, le français pour la littérature.' The blood of a silent listener was only ten years old, but it boiled. And here is a less arrogant but quite characteristic French judgment upon Browning: 'What a singular man! his middle is not in the centre.' That French-man discovered a racial fact. The middle of an English poet is not in the centre; it is one focus of an ellipse, like the sun. Our national imagination takes wide adventures and unequal velocities. It was once thought (before Kepler) that the earth's orbit must be circular, because a circle is 'perfect'. And this is the kind of perfection, in another region of thoughts, that the French mind has long cherished.

French lacks much besides those alien powers, our Latin and Teutonic inheritances, forbidden as it is to thunder from oppo-site heavens, with the Danube between, or the Alps between.

It lacks also negatives worth having; making shift with half-hearted particles or the grotesquely insufficient *peu*. *Peu* is at any rate detachable, and it is the only negative for some of the most energetic adjectives. Meanwhile we have our profound and powerful particle, the 'un' that summons in order that it may banish, and keeps the word present to hear sentence and denial, showing the word 'unloved' to be no less than archangel ruined.

Composure

Tribulation, Immortality, the Multitude: what remedy of composure do these words bring for their own great disquiet! Without the remoteness of the Latinity the thought would come too close and shake too cruelly. In order to the sane endurance of the intimate trouble of the soul an aloofness of language is needful. Johnson feared death. Did his noble English control and postpone the terror? Did it keep the fear at some courteous, deferent distance from the centre of that human heart, in the very act of the leap and lapse of mortality? Doubtless there is in language such an educative power. Speech is a school. ,Every language is a persuasion, an induced habit, an instrument which receives the note indeed but gives the tone. Every language imposes a quality, teaches a temper, proposes a way, bestows a tradition: this is the tone — the voice — of the instrument. Every language, by counter-change, returns to the writer's touch or breath his own intention, articulate: this is his note. Much has always been said, many things to the purpose have been thought, of the power and the responsibility of the note. Of the legislation and influence of the tone I have been led to think by comparing the tranquillity of Johnson and the composure of Canning with the stimulated and close emotion, the interior trouble, of those writers who have entered as disciples in the school of the more Teutonic English.

For if every language be a school, more significantly and more educatively is a part of a language a school to him who chooses that part. Few languages offer the choice. The fact that a choice is made implies the results and fruits of a decision. The French author is without these. They are of all the heritages of the English writer the most important. He receives a language of dual derivation. He may submit himself to either University, whither he will take his impulse and his character, where he will leave their influence, and whence he will accept their re-education. The Frenchman has certainly a style to develop within definite limits; but he does not subject himself to suggestions tending mainly hitherwards or thitherwards, to currents of various race within one literature. Such a choice of subjection is the singular opportunity of the Englishman. I do not mean to ignore the necessary mingling. Happily that mingling has been done once for all for us all. Nay, one of the most charming things that a master of English can achieve is the repayment of the united teaching by linking their results so exquisitely in his own practice, that words of the two schools are made to meet each other with a surprise and delight that shall prove them at once gayer strangers, and sweeter companions, than the world knew they were. Nevertheless there remains the liberty of choice as to which school of words shall have the place of honour in the great and sensitive moments of an author's style: which school shall be used for conspicuousness, and which for multitudinous service. And the choice being open, the perturbation of the pulses and impulses of so many hearts quickened in thought and feeling in this day suggests to me a deliberate return to the recollectedness of the more tranquil language. 'Doubtless there is a place of peace.'

A place of peace, not of indifference. It is impossible not to charge some of the moralists of the eighteenth century with an indifference into which they educated their platitudes and into which their platitudes educated them. Addison thus gave and took, until he was almost incapable of coming within arm's-length of a real or spiritual emotion. There is no knowing to what distance the removal of the 'appropriate sentiment' from the central soul might have attained but for the change and renewal in language, which came when it was needed. Addison had assuredly removed eternity far from the apprehension of the soul when his Cato hailed the 'pleasing hope', the 'fond desire'; and the touch of war was distant from him who conceived his 'repulsed battalions' and his 'doubtful battle'. What came afterwards, when simplicity and nearness were restored once more, was doubtless journeyman's work at times. Men were too eager to go into the workshop of language. There were unreasonable raptures over the mere making of common words. 'A hand-shoe! a finger-hat! a foreword! Beautiful!' they cried; and for the love of German the youngest daughter of Chrysale herself might have consented to be kissed by a grammarian. It seemed to be forgotten that a language with all its construction visible is a language little fitted for the more advanced mental processes; that its images are material; and that, on the other hand, a certain spiritualizing and subtilizing effect of alien derivations is a privilege and an advantage incalculable — that to possess that half of the language within which Latin heredities lurk and Romanesque allusions are at play is to possess the state and security of a dead tongue, without the death.

But now I spoke of words encountering as gay strangers, various in origin, divided in race, within a master's phrase. The most beautiful and the most sudden of such meetings are of course in Shakespeare. 'Superfluous kings', 'A lass unparalleled', 'Multitudinous seas': we needed not to wait for the eighteenth century or for the nineteenth or for the twentieth to learn the splendour of such encounters, of such differences, of such nuptial unlikeness and union. But it is well that we should learn them afresh. And it is well, too, that we should not resist the rhythmic reaction bearing us now somewhat to the side of the Latin. Such a reaction is in some sort an ethical need for our day. We want to quell the exaggerated decision of monosyllables. We want the poise and the pause that imply vitality at times better than headstrong movement expresses it. And not the phrase only but the form of verse might render us timely service. The controlling couplet might stay with a touch a modern grief, as it ranged in order the sorrows of Canning for his son. But it should not be attempted without a distinct intention of submission on the part of the writer. The couplet transgressed against, trespassed upon, used loosely is like a law outstripped, defied — to the dignity neither of the rebel nor of the rule.

To Letters do we look now for the guidance and direction which the very closeness of the emotion taking us by the heart makes necessary. Shall not the Thing more and more, as we compose ourselves to literature, assume the honour, the hesitation, the leisure, the reconciliation of the Word?

A Corrupt Following

DURING the whole nineteenth century our language underwent a certain derogation, notorious, different in kind from the corruptions of all other ages, and as familiar as brick and slate, gas, and the architecture of stations — and apparently, of yesterday, and to-day and of a morrow seen in rather dull and discouraging prospect. But the truth is that this common speech is due to the enormous influence of a great author who was born in 1737, was for forty-seven years the contemporary of Dr. Johnson, and died well within the eighteenth century.

Whose, for instance, is the use of 'I expect' for a conjecture referring to the past? It is Gibbon's: 'I should expect that the eunuchs were not expelled from the palace.' What is the 'and which' and 'who' of the slovenly? and what the 'whose' applied to inanimate things by authors too fine and too modern to write 'whereof'? Gear of Gibbon's style, both: 'Below the citadel stood a palace of gold, decorated with precious stones, and whose value might be esteemed', etc.; and 'A Menapian of the meanest origin, but who had long signalized his skill as a pilot'. There is the inanimate 'whose' of a more illustrious and older author, but this claims the excuse of metre.

Whence have we that peculiarly harsh vulgarism, 'so much per month', instead of 'so much a month', or 'per mensem'? From Gibbon. And whose is the confusion of speech that cannot give the word 'same' its proper completion, but saddles it with a relative pronoun? Gibbon's 'The Western countries were civilized by the same hands which subdued them'. 'The hands which subdued them' would be correct, and certainly more majestic.

Gibbon set the example of this common lax grammar: 'Instead of receiving with manly resolution the inevitable stroke, his unavailing cries and entreaties disgraced the last moments of his life'; and 'The election of Carus was decided without expecting the approval of the Senate'; and 'A peasant and a soldier, his nerves yielded not easily to the impressions of sympathy'. And there is nothing that (Gibbon always says which) illiterate politeness is so fond of as this unconstructed and decorated phrase. Gibbon's literature was scholarly, and these errors of his alter little or nothing of the honour due to his eminent elegance of style. But it was these laxities that took the public taste mightily, and it was the 'corrupt following' of this apostle that set the fashion of an animated strut of style — a strut that was animated in its day and soon grew inanimate, as the original authentic Gibbon never does. His own narrative never fails to reply to a perpetual stimulation.

But to deal with the rest of the grammatical ill-example, left to unlucky generations from the very middle of the century of propriety, and made so much our own. It is very modern to have 'either' or 'neither' followed by more than two things, and it is pure Gibbon; all the more conspicuous as Gibbon dearly loves the sound of three: 'The policy of the senate, the active emulation of the consuls, and the martial enthusiasm of the people'; 'The undertaking became more difficult, the event more doubtful, and the possession more precarious'. But the three go ill with 'either': 'either food, plunder, or glory'; 'either salt, or oil, or wood'. 'The generals were either respected by their troops, or admired for valour, or beloved for frankness and generosity.'

Finally, for a very little and silly blunder, what is more modern and current and popular than this: 'Magnus, with four thousand of his supposed accomplices, were put to death'? And even this is Gibbon.

To have done with mere grammar, there is surely no author in the history of our literature who has so imposed a new manner of writing upon an admiring people   He changed a hundred years of English prose. The dregs of his style have encumbered the nation. Changes that have been ascribed to Johnson were his doing and not Johnson's.

He belonged to the eighteenth century; but the nineteenth century belonged to him, because he possessed it. That is why he and his English are thus modern; the times became conformed to him; and he was himself not his own age, but that which succeeded and admired him.

It was to the broad face of astonishment and with the self-conscious face of novelty, that Gibbon addressed his prose. That shortened sentence (for it was he who shortened the sentence, and Macaulay did but imitate his full stops for the pauses of historical surprise) was to strike and to demonstrate, and this with a gesture constantly renewed. 'Suspicion was equivalent to proof. Trial to condemnation.' 'The strict economy of Vespasian was the source of his magnificence. The works of Trajan bear the stamp of his genius.' His, too, is the full ceremony of the ushering phrase: 'It is easier to deplore the fate, than to describe the actual condition, of Corsica.' His too, the 'latter and the former', which became a favourite fashion. 'Oh, do not condemn me to the latter!' exclaims a lover in one of Mrs. Inchbald's stories, after a statement of his hopes and fears; and this phrase of emotion was a debt to Gibbon. The reader finds that the lady does not condemn him to the latter; she permits some prospect of the former. 'Peruse' is his verb, and 'extensive' a most favourite adjective. To him we owe 'the mask of hypocrisy' and 'the voice of flattery'. It is not his fault that posterity divided that property so lavishly among themselves.

And yet is there no fault in his own frigid prodigality? Take this sentence in all its splendour: 'The Tyber rolled at the foot of the seven hills of Rome, and the country of the Sabines, the Latins, and the Volsci, from that river to the frontiers of Naples, was the theatre of her infant victories.' And this: 'A distant hope, the child of a flattering prophecy.' This all-inhuman image reminds us, by contrast, of Shelley, who often has this figure of a child, and never, however remote the thought, without a sense of childhood. So cold is Gibbon that when the incessant stimulation of his rhetorical intention spurs him to describe a murder thus: 'A thousand swords were plunged at once into the bosom of the unfortunate Probus', we are moved to tell him trivially that he exaggerates. When Burke said 'A thousand swords' he meant a thousand, and had a right to mean them, but Gibbon did not, obviously, mean a thousand.

'The unfortunate Probus' is the model of a sentence that sometimes becomes monotonous even with the carefully various Gibbon: 'The prudent Atticus' begins a phrase, and 'the equitable Nerva' passes it on to 'the cautious Athenian', and then again to 'the generous Atticus'. His is a frigidity that deals broadly with massacre and the sack of cities. And from amid these generalities, as it were invisible unless viewed from afar, he suddenly plucks us this man's 'smile', or that man's 'blush'. Whatever Gibbon's race, there never was a writer so exceedingly Latin in spirit.

'To view', by the way is one of his favourite verbs: 'Viewing with a smile of pity and indulgence the various errors of the vulgar . . . and sometimes condescending to act a part on the theatre of superstition, they concealed the sentiments of an atheist under the sacerdotal robes.' Readers with a sense of humour may remember under what conditions Zenobia 'reiterated the experiment'; and the fatal manner in which the tradesman's circular of to-day has 'diffused' (as Gibbon would say) the last ruins of his prose by post, is rather curiously illustrated thus: a little while ago some infamous face-wash was described in advertisements as a mixture of drugs brought across the desert by fleet dromedaries. And here is Gibbon's Zenobia 'mounting her fleetest dromedary'.

How great, nevertheless, how sombre are the nobler habits of his language: 'The veteran legions of the Rhine and the Danube.' What armies! what time, space! what war! 'Give back my legions, Varus!' Give back our legions, Gibbon! We may count our regiments, but thou hast named, not counted, multitudes.

And when Gibbon 'gratifies' these legionaries, the polite

word does but make them more remote: 'After suppressing a competitor who had assumed the purple at Mentz, he refused to gratify his troops with the plunder of the rebellious city.' So that we do not forgive the corrupters who so scattered the word that burlesque was necessary for sweeping it out of the way. When Mr. Micawber confesses his 'gratifying emotions of no common description', he rallies a lofty and a distant Gibbon.

Ruskin, student of Hooker in the further, and of Johnson in the nearer, past, was the first writer of pure prose — the first by a long tale of years — to reject the whole encumbrance of the vain spoils of Gibbon; yet even he has one little patch of them: 'A steep bank of earth that has been at all exposed to the weather contains in it . . . features capable of giving high gratification to a careful observer.' It is solitary in *Modern Painters*; it is the nether Gibbon, a waste product of Gibbon.

But now I spoke of burlesque; and Dickens's burlesque of style is admirable; there is also a burlesque of another and more innocent kind: When the author of a recent English work on the *Divine Comedy*, says that Paolo and Francesca were to receive from Dante 'such alleviation as circumstances would allow', that also is a distant, a shattered Gibbon, a drift of Gibbon.

WOMEN

Arabella Stuart

THE cruel places of history are for ever emptied of their suffering tenants, and it is only to our inappeasable sympathies that the lifelong prisoners seem to be recaptured, sent back to their intolerable hours and places, long after they have once for all, unchallenged, passed the guard. Every martyrdom of the past has ceased to be; it concerns no one how sharp, how insupportable it was in its day. There is no living pain now in all the universe to continue it, to answer it, to rehearse it, or perhaps to regret it. And if we complain that the past is not to be revoked or undone, we might rather confess the complete consolation of the passing of time, the undoing, the effacement, and the more than death. It is only by moments that we apprehend what it is to be past, or that we perceive how clean is natural oblivion; the uneasy human retrospection stirs nothing but itself, and wounds the now living heart with a present pity for that which is not. Nothing else on earth remembers.

The popular phrase is expressive: 'I know the thing is over and done; but it afflicts me to think of it.' So we acknowledge that there is no trouble but in the present, and that though our minds seem to travel into the past, in truth they do not budge; and we, prisoners of our own moment, are fluttered with the present sympathy, and not with the vanished sorrow, for it is not.

By far the greater number of human sufferings have been forgotten by man as purely and freshly as by nature. Of a few, that fictitious memory which is history and tradition renews the report with so much attention as to preserve something like the dramatic unity of time. To read of them and to think of them is nearly as long as it was to endure them. But of others again we have the brief record that shows long hollow spaces of time, perfectly dark and indescribed. Among these is the bitter life and death of Arabella Stuart, told by our popular historians in a short paragraph that ends with her death of a 'broken heart' — the extravagant phrase interrupting the historical style and making the page conspicuous to childish learners.

Evelyn has her in his list of learned women, although she is not in the catalogue of those whom he sacrificed at one blow to the glory of the Duchess of Newcastle. 'Hilpylas, the mother-in-law of the young Plinie, Cornelia so neere the greate Scipio', and Lucretia Marinella, who is not mentioned as anyone's mother-in-law, but as the author of a work *Dell' excellenzia delle Donne, con difetti e mancamenti degli Huomini* — with the inferiority of these and such as these does he flatter the surpassing Duchess. The sorrows of Arabella Stuart would have made her name too sad a sacrifice for such a train. The other ladies are presented gaily and as it were in garlands: 'They possesse but that divided which your Grace retaines in one.'

Nevertheless, Arabella was, even for an age when women of station were well taught, notable for her education. Her Latin letters are still there to attest it. She was named a 'modern poetess' by Mr. Philips, who was Milton's nephew. These secondary, second-hand, relative distinctions are in touching disproportion with her original, immediate and authentic sufferings. The delicately sharp edging that a more or less literary training gives to the natural human mind, making it aware, had been given to hers; and she was so prepared by delicate erudition that the loss of all she loved was complete to her, the suspense of imprisonment inconsolable, and its idleness more than mortal. She lost better than her life, for the prison ruined her reason before it released her body, twice rifled and destitute, and dismissed it to Westminster Abbey and the grave.

It is in her letters to her husband, and only in these, that Arabella Stuart is perceptible as she lived. The letters of entreaty to King James are the letters of those abject times. They declare her to be in despair, not because of the separation from her husband and only friend, and not because of her solitude in perpetual prison, but on account of the King's disfavour, of her exile from his presence, and by reason of the remorse and contrition of one who had disobeyed him, even unwittingly. By these forms of ignominy did men and women rule, not their phrases only, but, apparently, their very thoughts. Such declarations were much more than a courtesy due to kings or the decorum of a style in letter-writing. Hearts beat hard to that most grotesque tune; those were real self-reproaches; they banished real sleep, human sleep, afflicted real consciences, set the tears of men running, and squandered and scattered to waste that human treasure, humility.

Lady Arabella's remorse, as she took leave to remind the King, was poignant for her offence in having bestowed herself in marriage *upon the King's permission*. He seems to have either forgotten or silently rescinded his consent, and for this she overwhelmed herself in professions of regret and promises of obedience. She sent to the Queen some little pieces of needlework, the sewing of which, she said, had beguiled the time 'for her whose serious mind must invent some relaxation'. 'Womanish toys', she called them, conscious of her education, and she thanked the gentleman who was her gaoler for consenting to present them. Her way of submission was even approved by the tyrant. One of her letters to the King, said Dr. Montford, 'was penned by her in the best terms, as she can do right well. It was often read without offence; nay, it was even commended by his Highness, with the applause of Prince and Council'. The best terms are of course the most reverent. The clergy exhorted her with one voice. The stricter keeping, to which she so dreaded to be consigned as to fall ill of fear, was that of the Bishop of Durham.

She had the heart to deny her commended letters so far as to practise some secret disobedience, heaping up self-reproach for the vigils of her solitude. The letters to her husband, from whom she had been parted after but a few months of marriage, were contraband. Even in these, her allusions to the King were most dutiful, but her husband was her theme. 'Rachel wept', she wrote, 'and would not be comforted, because her children were no more. And that, indeed, is the remedyless sorrow, and none else! And, therefore, God bless us from that, and I will hope well for the rest, though I see no apparent hope.' Seymour had been ill, as she heard from others. 'Sir,' she wrote, 'I am exceeding sorry to hear that you have not been well. I am not satisfied with the reason Smith gives for it; but, if it be a cold, I will impute it to some sympathy betwixt us, having myself gotten a swollen cheek at the same time with a cold. For God's sake, let not your grief of mind work upon your body. You may see by me what inconvenience it will bring one to; and no fortune, I assure you, daunts me so much as that weakness of body I find in myself; for "si nous vivons l'âge d'un veau", as Marot says, we may, by God's grace, be happier than we look for, in being suffered to enjoy ourself with his Majesty's favour. But if we be not able to live it, I, for my part, shall think myself a pattern of misfortune, in enjoying so great a blessing as you so little while.'

Again, she reminded him that he had not written to her 'this good while'. 'You see when I am troubled, I trouble you with tedious kindness, for so I think you will account so long a letter. But, sweet Sir, I speak not this to trouble you with writing but when you please. Be well, and I shall account myself happy in being your faithful and loving wife.'

As soon as these letters were discovered the writing was stopped. Enough was written, and enough even remains, to show the spirit, generous, worthy of liberty, capable of gaiety, forced to grief, of this unfortunate. A graver revolt against her tyrants was her escape to join her husband in flight from the Tower. Ill fortune set all the times, tides, and winds wrong on that unhappy adventure. She would not save herself without him. She was brought back, and from the new imprisonment there was no escape. The indignant King satisfied justice by refusing another little offering of her needlework. In her appeal to the Queen she had entreated that the gloves she had made might be accepted 'in remembrance of the poor prisoner that wrought them, in hopes her royal hands will vouchsafe to wear them, which, till I have the honour to kiss, I shall live in a great deal of sorrow'.

'In all humility, the most wretched and unfortunate creature that ever lived prostrates itselfe at the feet of the most merciful King that ever was.' These are among the last 'best terms' that Arabella Stuart penned.

Her King and Queen and country sent her civilization into solitude, gagged her classics, disproved her poetry, and thrust her 'expanded mind' into the inner darkness.

Mrs. Dingley

WE cannot do her honour by her Christian name.[1] All we have to call her by more tenderly is the mere D, the D that ties her to Stella, with whom she made the two-in-one whom Swift loved 'better a thousand times than life, as hope saved'. MD, without full stops, Swift writes it eight times in a line for the pleasure of writing it. 'MD sometimes means Stella alone', says one of many editors. 'The letters were written nominally to Stella and Mrs. Dingley,' says another, 'but it does not require to be said that it was really for Stella's sake alone that they were penned.' Not so. 'MD' never stands for Stella alone. And the editor does not yet live who shall persuade one honest reader, against the word of Swift, that Swift loved Stella only, with an ordinary love, and not, by a most delicate exception, Stella and Dingley, so joined that they make the 'she' and 'her' of the letters. And this shall be a paper of reparation to Mrs. Dingley.

[1] I found it afterwards; it was Rebecca.

No one else in literary history has been so defrauded of her honours. In love 'to divide is not to take away', as Shelley says; and Dingley's half of the tender things said to MD is equal to any whole, and takes nothing from the whole of Stella's half. But the sentimentalist has fought against Mrs. Dingley from the outset. He has disliked her, shirked her, misconceived her, and effaced her. Sly sentimentalist — he finds her irksome. Through one of his most modern representatives he has but lately called her a 'chaperon'. A chaperon!

MD was not a sentimentalist. Stella was not so, though she has been pressed into that character; D certainly was not, and has in this respect been spared by the chronicler; and MD together were 'saucy charming MD', 'saucy little, pretty, dear rogues', 'little monkeys mine', 'little mischievous girls', 'nautinautinautidear girls', 'brats', 'huzzies both', 'impudence and saucy-face', 'saucy noses', 'my dearest lives and delights', 'dear little young women', 'good dallars, not crying dallars' (which means 'girls'), 'ten thousand times dearest MD', and so forth in a hundred repetitions. They are, every now and then, 'poor MD', but obviously not because of their own complaining. Swift called them so because they were mortal; and he, like all great souls, lived and loved, conscious every day of the price, which is death.

The two were joined by love, not without solemnity, though man, with his summary and wholesale ready-made sentiment, has thus obstinately put them asunder. No wholesale sentiment can do otherwise than foolishly play havoc with such a relation. To Swift it was the most secluded thing in the world. 'I am weary of friends, and friendships are all monsters, except MD's'; 'I ought to read these letters I write after I have done. But I hope it does not puzzle little Dingley to read, for I think I mend: but methinks', he adds, 'when I write plain, I do not know how, but we are not alone, all the world can see us. A bad scrawl is so snug; it looks like PMD'. Again: 'I do not like women so much as I did. MD, you must know, are not women.' 'God Almighty preserve you both and make us happy together.' 'I say Amen with all my heart and vitals, that we may never be asunder ten days together while poor Presto lives.' 'Farewell, dearest beloved MD, and love poor, poor Presto, who has not had one happy day since he left you, as hope saved.'

With them — with her — he hid himself in the world, at Court, at the bar of St. James's coffee-house, whither he went on the Irish mail-day, and was 'in pain except he saw MD's little handwriting'. He hid with them in the long labours of these exquisite letters every night and morning. If no letter came, he comforted himself with thinking that 'he had it yet to be happy with'. And the world has agreed to hide under its own manifold and lachrymose blunders the grace and singularity — the distinction — of this sweet romance. 'Little, sequestered pleasure-house' — it seemed as though 'the many could not miss it', but not even the few have found it.

It is part of the scheme of the sympathetic historian that Stella should be the victim of hope deferred, watching for letters from Swift. But day and night Presto complains of the scantiness of MD's little letters; he waits upon 'her' will: 'I shall make a sort of journal, and when it is full I will send it whether MD writes or not; and so that will be pretty.' 'Naughty girls that will not write to a body!' 'I wish you were whipped for forgetting to send. Go, be far enough, negligent baggages.' 'You, Mistress Stella, shall write your share, and then comes Dingley altogether, and then Stella a little crumb at the end; and then conclude with something handsome and genteel, as "your most humble cumdumble".' But Scott and Macaulay and Thackeray are all exceedingly sorry for a pining Stella. Thackeray represents her wearing out her life in wait for Swift's 'cold heart'.

Swift is most charming when he is feigning to complain of his task: 'Here is such a stir and bustle with this little MD of ours; I must be writing every night; O Lord, O Lord!' 'I must go write idle things, and twittle twattle.' 'These saucy jades take up so much of my time with writing to them in the morning.' Is it not a stealthy wrong done upon Mrs. Dingley that she should be stripped of all these ornaments to her name

and memory? When Swift tells a woman in a letter that there
he is 'writing in bed, like a tiger', she should go gay in the
eyes of all generations.

They will not let Stella go gay, because of sentiment; and
they will not let Mrs. Dingley go gay, because of sentiment
for Stella. Marry come up! Why did not the historians assign
all the tender passages (taken very tearfully) to Stella, and let
Dingley have the jokes, then? That would have been no ill
share for Dingley. But no, forsooth, Dingley is allowed
nothing.

There are passages, nevertheless, which can hardly be
taken from her. For now and then Swift parts his dear MD.
When he does so he invariably drops those initials and writes
'Stella' or 'Ppt' for the one, and 'D' or 'Dingley' for the other.
There is no exception to this anywhere. He is anxious about
Stella's 'little eyes', and about her health generally; whereas
Dingley is strong. Poor Ppt, he thinks, will not catch the
'new fever', because she is not well; 'but why should D escape
it, pray?' And Mrs. Dingley is rebuked for her tale of a
journey from Dublin to Wexford. 'I doubt, Madam Dingley,
you are apt to lie in your travels, though not so bad as Stella;
she tells thumpers.' Stella is often reproved for her spelling,
and Mrs. Dingley writes much the better hand. But she is
a puzzle-headed woman, like another. 'What do you mean by
my fourth letter, Madam Dinglibus? Does not Stella say you
had my fifth, goody Blunder?' 'Now, Mistress Dingley, are
you not an impudent slut to expect a letter next packet? Un-
reasonable baggage! No, little Dingley, I am always in bed
by twelve, and I take great care of myself.' 'You are a pretend-
ing slut, indeed, with your "fourth" and "fifth" in the margin,
and your "journal" and everything. O Lord, never saw the
like, we shall never have done.' 'I never saw such a letter, so
saucy, so journalish, so everything.' Swift is insistently grate-
ful for their inquiries for his health. He pauses seriously to
thank them in the midst of his prattle. Both women — MD —
are rallied on their politics: 'I have a fancy that Ppt is a Tory,
I fancy she looks like one, and D a sort of trimmer.'

But it is for Dingley separately that Swift endured a wild bird in his lodgings. His man Patrick had got one to take over to her in Ireland. 'He keeps it in a closet, where it makes a terrible litter; but I say nothing; I am as tame as a clout.'

Forgotten Dingley, happy in this, has not had to endure the ignominy, in a hundred modern essays, to be retrospectively offered to Swift as an unclaimed wife; so far so good. But two hundred years is long for her to have gone stripped of so radiant a glory as is hers by right. 'Better, thanks to MD's prayers', wrote the immortal man who loved her, in a private fragment of a journal, never meant for Dingley's eyes, nor for Ppt's, nor for any human eyes; and the rogue Stella has for two centuries been made to steal all the credit of those prayers, and all the thanks of that pious benediction.

Steele's Prue

THROUGH the long history of human relations, which is the history of the life of our race, there sounds at intervals the clamour of a single voice which has not the tone of oratory, but asks, answers, interrupts itself, interrupts — what else? Whatever else it interrupts is silence; there are pauses, but no answers. There is the jest without the laugh, and again the laugh without the jest. And this is because the letters written by Madame de Sévigné were all saved, and not many written to her; because Swift burnt the letters that were the dearest things in life to him, while 'MD' both made a treasury of his; and because Prue kept all the letters which Steele wrote to her from their marriage-day onwards, and Steele kept none of hers.

In Swift's case the silence is full of echoes; that is to say, his letters repeat the phrases of Stella's and Dingley's, to play with them, flout them, and toss them back against the two silenced voices. He never lets the word of these two women fall to the ground; and when they have but blundered with it, and aimed it wide, and sent it weakly, he will catch it, and play you twenty delicate and expert juggling pranks with it as he sends it back into their innocent faces. So we have something of MD's letters in the 'Journal', and this in the only form in which we desire them, to tell the truth; for when Swift gravely saves us some specimens of Stella's wit, after her death, as she spoke them, and not as he mimicked them, they make a sorry show.

In many correspondences, where one voice remains and the other is gone, the retort is enough for two. It is as when, the other day, the half of a pretty quarrel between nurse and child came down from an upper floor to the ears of a mother who decided that she need not interfere. The voice of the un-daunted child it was that was audible alone, and it replied, 'I'm not; *you* are'; and anon, 'I'll tell *yours*'. Nothing was really missing there.

But Steele's letters to Prue, his wife, are no such simple matter. The turn we shall give them depends upon the un-heard tone whereto they reply. And there is room for conjec-ture. It has pleased the more modern of the many spirits of banter to supply Prue's eternal silence with the voice of a scold. It is painful to me to complain of Thackeray; but see what a figure he makes of Prue in 'Esmond'. It is, says the nine-teenth-century humorist, in defence against the pursuit of a jealous, exacting, neglected, or evaded wife that poor Dick Steele sends those little notes of excuse: 'Dearest Being on earth, pardon me if you do not see me till eleven o'clock, having met a schoolfellow from India'; 'My dear, dear wife, I write to let you know I do not come home to dinner, being obliged to attend some business abroad, of which I shall give you an account (when I see you in the evening), as becomes your dutiful and obedient husband'; 'Dear Prue, I cannot come home to dinner. I languish for your welfare'; 'I stay here in order to get Tonson to discount a bill for me, and shall dine with him to that end'; and so forth. Once only does Steele really afford the recent humorist the suggestion that is apparently always so welcome. It is when he writes that he is invited to supper to Mr. Boyle's, and adds: 'Dear Prue, do not send after me, for I shall be ridiculous.' But even this is to be read not ungracefully by a well-graced reader. Prue was young and unused to the world. Her husband, by the way, had been already married; and his greater age makes his constant deference all the more charming.

But with this one exception, Steele's little notes, kept by his wife while she lived, and treasured after her death by her daughter and his, are no record of the watchings and dodgings of a London farce. It is worth while to remember that Steele's dinner, which it was so often difficult to eat at home, was a thing of midday, and therefore of mid-business. But that is a detail. What is desirable is that a reasonable degree of sweetness should be attributed to Prue; for it is no more than just. To her Steele wrote in a dedication: 'How often has your tenderness removed pain from my aching head, how often anguish from my afflicted heart. If there are such beings as guardian angels, they are thus employed. I cannot believe one of them to be more good in inclination, or more charming in form, than my wife.'

True, this was for the public; but not so were these daily notes; and these carry to her his assurance that she is 'the beautifullest object in the world. I know no happiness in this life in any degree comparable to the pleasure I have in your person and society'. 'But indeed, though you have every perfection, you have an extravagant fault, which almost frustrates the good in you to me; and that is, that you do not love to dress, to appear, to shine out, even at my request, and to make me proud of you, or rather to indulge the pride I have that you are mine.' The correction of the phrase is finely considerate.

Prue cannot have been a dull wife, for this last compliment is a reply, full of polite alacrity, to a letter from her asking for a little flattery. How assiduously, and with what a civilized absence of uncouthness, of shamefacedness, and of slang of the mind, with what simplicity, alertness, and finish, does he step out at her invitation, and perform! She wanted a compliment, though they had been long married then, and he immediately turned it. This was no dowdy Prue.

Her request, by the way, which he repeats in obeying it, is one of the few instances of the other side of the correspondence — one of the few direct echoes of that one of the two voices which is silent.

The ceremony of the letters and the deferent method of address and signature are never dropped in this most intimate of letter-writing. It is not a little depressing to think that in this very form and state is supposed, by the modern reader, to lurk the stealthiness of the husband of farce, the 'rogue'. One does not like the word. Is it not clownish to apply it with intention to the husband of Prue? He did not pay, he was always in difficulties, he hid from bailiffs, he did many other things that tarnish honour, more or less, and things for which he had to beg Prue's special pardon; but yet he is not a fit subject for the unhandsome incredulity which is proud to be always at hand with an ironic commentary on such letters as his.

I have no wish to bowdlerize Sir Richard Steele, his ways and words. He wrote to Prue at night when the burgundy had been too much for him, and in the morning after. He announces that he is coming to her 'within a pint of wine'. One of his gayest letters — a love-letter before the marriage, addressed to 'dear lovely Mrs. Scurlock' — confesses candidly that he had been pledging her too well: 'I have been in very good company, where your health, under the character of the woman I loved best, has been often drunk; so that I may say that I am dead drunk for your sake, which is more than *I die for you.*'

Steele obviously drank burgundy wildly, as did his 'good company'; as did also the admirable Addison, who was so solitary in character and so serene in temperament. But no one has, for this fault, the right to put a railing accusation into the mouth of Prue. Every woman has a right to her own silence, whether her silence be hers of set purpose or by accident. And every creature has a right to security from the banterings peculiar to the humorists of a succeeding age. To every century its own ironies, to every century its own vulgarities. In Steele's time they had theirs. They might have rallied Prue more coarsely, but it would have been with a different rallying. Writers of the nineteenth century went about to rob her of her grace.

She kept some four hundred of these little letters of her lord's. It was a loyal keeping. But what does Thackeray call it? His word is 'thrifty'. He says: 'There are four hundred letters of Dick Steele's to his wife, which that thrifty woman preserved accurately.'

'Thrifty' is a hard word to apply to her whom Steele styled, in the year before her death, his 'charming little insolent'. She was ill in Wales, and he, at home, wept upon her pillow, and 'took it to be a sin to go to sleep'. Thrifty they may call her, and accurate if they will; but she lies in Westminster Abbey, and Steele called her 'your Prueship'.

Mrs. Johnson

THIS paper shall not be headed 'Tetty'. What may be a graceful enough freedom with the wives of other men shall be prohibited in the case of Johnson's, she with whose name no writer until now has scrupled to take freedoms whereto all graces were lacking. 'Tetty' it should not be, if for no other reason, for this — that the chance of writing 'Tetty' as a title is a kind of facile literary opportunity; it shall be denied. The Essay owes thus much amends of deliberate care to Dr. Johnson's wife. But, indeed, the reason is graver. What wish would he have had but that the language in the making whereof he took no ignoble part should somewhere, at some time, treat his only friend with ordinary honour?

Men who would trust Dr. Johnson with their orthodoxy, with their vocabulary, and with the most intimate vanity of their human wishes, refuse, with every mark of insolence, to trust him in regard to his wife. On that one point no reverence is paid to him, no deference, no respect, not so much as the credit due to our common sanity. Yet he is not reviled on account of his Thrale — nor, indeed, is his Thrale now seriously reproached for her Piozzi. It is true that Macaulay, preparing himself and his reader 'in his well-known way' (as a rustic of Mr. Hardy's might have it) for the recital of her second marriage, says that it would have been well if she had been laid beside the kind and generous Thrale when, in the prime of her life, he died. But Macaulay has not left us heirs to his indignation. His well-known way was to exhaust those possibilities of effect in which the commonplace is so rich. And he was permitted to point his paragraphs as he would, not only by calling Mrs. Thrale's attachment to her second husband 'a degrading passion', but by summoning a chorus of 'all London' to the same purpose. She fled, he tells us, from the laughter and hisses of her countrymen and countrywomen to a land where she was unknown. Thus when Macaulay chastises Mrs. Elizabeth Porter for marrying Johnson, he is not inconsistent, for he pursues Mrs. Thrale with equal rigour for her audacity in keeping gaiety and grace in her mind and manners longer than Macaulay liked to see such ornaments added to the charm of twice 'married brows'.

It is not so with succeeding essayists. One of these minor biographers is so gentle as to call the attachment of Mrs. Thrale and Piozzi 'a mutual affection'. He adds, 'No one who has had some experience of life will be inclined to condemn Mrs. Thrale'. But there is no such courtesy, even from him, for Mrs. Johnson. Neither to him nor to any other writer has it yet occurred that if England loves her great Englishman's memory, she owes not only courtesy, but gratitude, to the only woman who loved him while there was yet time.

Not a thought of that debt has stayed the alacrity with which a caricature has been acclaimed as the only possible portrait of Mrs. Johnson. Garrick's school reminiscences would probably have made a much more charming woman grotesque. Garrick is welcome to his remembrances; we may even reserve for ourselves the liberty of envying those who heard him. But honest laughter should not fall into that tone of common antithesis which seems to say, 'See what are the absurdities of the great! Such is life! On this one point we, even we, are wiser than Dr. Johnson — we know how grotesque was his wife. We know something of the privacies of her toilet-table. We are able to compare her figure with the figures we, unlike him in his youth, have had the opportunity of admiring — the figures of the well-bred and well-dressed'. It is a sorry success to be able to say so much.

But in fact such a triumph belongs to no man. When Samuel Johnson, at twenty-six, married his wife, he gave the dull an advantage over himself which none but the dullest will take. He chose, for love, a woman who had the wit to admire him at first meeting, and in spite of first sight. 'That,' she said to her daughter, 'is the most sensible man I ever met.' He was penniless. She had what was no mean portion for those times and those conditions; and, granted that she was affected, and provincial, and short, and all the rest with which she is charged, she was probably not without suitors; nor do her defects or faults seem to have been those of an unadmired or neglected woman. Next, let us remember what was the aspect of Johnson's form and face, even in his twenties, and how little he could have touched the senses of a widow fond of externals. This one loved him, accepted him, made him happy, gave to one of the noblest of all English hearts the one love of its sombre life. And English literature has had no better phrase for her than Macaulay's — 'She accepted, with a readiness which did her little honour, the addresses of a suitor who might have been her son'.

Her readiness did her incalculable honour. But it is at last worth remembering that Johnson had first done her incalculable honour. No one has given to man or woman the right to judge as to the worthiness of her who received it. The meanest man is generally allowed his own counsel as to his own wife; one of the greatest of men has been denied it. 'The lover', says Macaulay, 'continued to be under the illusions of the wedding day till the lady died.' What is so graciously said is not enough. He was under those 'illusions' until he too died, when he had long passed her latest age, and was therefore able to set right that balance of years which has so much irritated the impertinent. Johnson passed from this life twelve years older than she, and so for twelve years his constant eyes had to turn backwards to dwell upon her. Time gave him a younger wife.

And here I will put into Mrs. Johnson's mouth, that mouth to which no one else has ever attributed any beautiful sayings, the words of Marceline Desbordes-Valmore to the young husband she loved: 'Older than thou! Let me never see thou knowest it. Forget it! I will remember it, to die before thy death.'

Macaulay, in his unerring effectiveness, uses Johnson's short sight for an added affront to Mrs. Johnson. The bridegroom was too weak of eyesight 'to distinguish ceruse from natural bloom'. Nevertheless, he saw well enough, when he was old, to distinguish Mrs. Thrale's dresses. He reproved her for wearing a dark dress; it was unsuitable, he said, for her size; a little creature should show gay colours 'like an insect'. We are not called upon to admire his wife; why, then, our taste being thus uncompromised, do we not suffer him to admire her? It is the most gratuitous kind of intrusion. Moreover, the biographers are eager to permit that touch of romance and grace in his relations to Mrs. Thrale, which they officially deny in the case of Mrs. Johnson. But the difference is all on the other side. He would not have bidden his wife dress like an insect. Mrs. Thrale was to him 'the first of womankind' only because his wife was dead.

Beauclerc, we learn, was wont to cap Garrick's mimicry of Johnson's love-making by repeating the words of Johnson himself in after-years — 'It was a love-match on both sides'. And obviously he was as strange a lover as they said. Who doubted it? Was there any other woman in England to give such a suitor the opportunity of an eternal love? 'A life radically wretched', was the life of this master of Letters; but she, who has received nothing in return except ignominy from these unthankful Letters, had been alone to make it otherwise. Well for him that he married so young as to earn the ridicule of all the biographers in England; for by doing so he, most happily, possessed his wife for nearly twenty years. I have called her his only friend. So indeed she was, though he had followers, disciples, rivals, competitors, and companions, many degrees of admirers, a biographer, a patron, and a public. He had also the houseful of sad old women who quarrelled under his beneficent protection. But what friend had he? He was 'solitary' from the day she died.

Let us consider under what solemn conditions and in what immortal phrase the word 'solitary' stands. He wrote it, all Englishmen know where. He wrote it in the hour of that melancholy triumph when he had been at last set free from the dependence upon hope. He hoped no more, and he needed not to hope. The 'notice' of Lord Chesterfield had been too long deferred; it was granted at last, when it was a flattery which Johnson's court of friends would applaud. But not for their sake was it welcome. To no living ear would he bring it and report it with delight.

He was indifferent, he was known. The sensitiveness to pleasure was gone, and the sensitiveness to pain, slights, and neglect would thenceforth be suffered to rest; no man in England would put that to proof again. No man in England, did I say? But, indeed, that is not so. No slight to him, to his person, or to his fame could have had power to cause him pain more sensibly than the customary, habitual, ready-made ridicule that has been cast by posterity upon her whom he loved for twenty years, prayed for during thirty-two years more, who satisfied one of the saddest human hearts, but to whom the world, assiduous to admire him, hardly accords human dignity. He wrote praises of her manners and of her person for her tomb. But her epitaph, that does not name her, is in the greatest of English prose. What was favour to him? 'I am indifferent ... I am known ... I am solitary, and cannot impart it.'

Hester

Too much contemporary literature tampered with the history
of Mrs. Thrale. She was the victim of end-of-the-century
styles. It was not only her Fanny Burney that made her the
subject of a first manner, a second manner, and a third manner.
She was the object of Dr. Johnson, in letters that were to be
preserved; but she was also his topic, in talk that would have
been better forgotten. It was reported to her by the hostile
Boswell, when it seemed more or less to belie the letters of the
past. And all the world knows by heart how Mrs. Thrale's
story became Macaulay's opportunity.

Fanny Burney's literary style was in training, and had
almost reached its final point of absurdity when she recorded
her drive away from Streatham with the discarded Dr. Johnson.
It is hardly possible to write such a style as hers was at the
time, and to keep a narrative in the right condition of actual
facts. She could not so drive away with Johnson from the
house of the friend whom he loved, and who was forming a
dearer tie, and not so drive away 'for ever'. Dr. Johnson
lived in much content in Mrs. Thrale's house for six weeks
at a time after this parting, and later dined, and dined, and
dined, as of old. But Miss Burney's narrative was bound to be
symmetrical. For how could she be true to the turns and
returns of life, the resumptions, the renewals — or, rather, the
recommencements that are not new but withered — the hopes
that are disguised remembrances, the indecision, the inaction,
the change, the unsaying, and the undoing that shatter the
design of an actual human life — how could she record these
in the accomplished manner of the author of *Cecilia*? Miss
Burney respected her own manner too much to compromise it
by transactions with nature. Her dates were ranged and ranked
in arbitrary order. And not the least of her losses was,
therefore, the loss of the human significance of dates. She
told a futile, complete, insignificant, intelligible story, un-

touched with the delicate variations between to-day and yester-
day, unaffectedly the perpetual difference and difficulty. In
this one life the present year's heartache is not last year's,
though the cause have the same name.

See, too, how Macaulay lavished his talents upon Mrs.
Thrale. Here, indeed, there was not the symmetry necessary
to Miss Burney. But there was something more tyrannous
still, necessary to Macaulay. There was the necessary incon-
gruity, suddenly stated, in order to make the reader catch his
breath — the necessary crash. To these also the story of
Streatham was hewn and shaped.

But those who will take the trouble to know something
more of Mrs. Thrale than Boswell and Miss Burney have told
us as witnesses, or than Macaulay has told us as historian, to
those who think her autobiography worth attention, she has
all the interest belonging of right to a woman altogether of her
time. To be a man or woman of your time is not, it should be
needless to say, so paltry a thing as to be in a 'movement'. It
is to accept, not to snatch, a place and a share in the inheritance
of the age. It is to be historical, and not restless and dis-
composed.

She has all the eighteenth-century good sense. Her
reasoning is always admirable. They called her flighty, but
her flights were captive flights, tethered flights. Imagination
was not of her world. In one thing she had her will, but at no
cost of principle. Indeed, accepted and inherited principle,
with all its secure dignities, ruled her soul better than the more
intimate pressure of conscience has ruled souls greater than
hers.

The one thing in which she had her will against the will of
her world was her second marriage. It needs no excuse nor
even apology now. The thing to be wondered at is rather her
long-suffering under the oppression that forbade it. When
Johnson, with research, found the most frigidly indignant
word for it, and told her it was ignominious, he might have
remembered the marriage of his youth, and how well that word
would have served the angry sons of the woman he married —

had they been masters of words. The wife he loved had braved much more ready, easy and obvious laughter when she had made his life happy than Mrs. Thrale defied when she broke his heart by marrying Piozzi.

And Fanny Burney, too, who disapproved with so much security and severity? It might possibly be less ignominious to marry a Frenchman than an Italian; that was for the islanders of 1780 to determine. But as for the two things the two men were about, we will not be sure that the difference was not on the other side. Piozzi was a musician, and honoured his work consistently. Miss Burney's Frenchman, when she made his acquaintance, was engaged in transcribing Mme de Staël's essay on 'The Influence of the Passions'. One might prefer the fiddles.

Miss Burney, at about forty-two, married M. d'Arblay in the midst of his transcribing. Transcribing — the word has a dignity all its own. Mr. Thrale's widow was no older when she married her Italian, who was of her own age — a man with two coats and everything handsome about him; a man who saved rather than spent, and who, in his own country, was held to have derogated by marrying the brewer's widow.

Hester loved him; let us restore to the little creature her Christian name, by which nobody seemed to call her. She always called her first husband, whom she married to obey her mother, 'My dear master', and her second husband 'Piozzi' — 'My dear, my lovely Piozzi'. Johnson called her 'My Mistress', 'Madam', or 'My dear Angel', and she called him 'Sir'. She spoke of her oppressive eldest daughter as 'Miss Thrale'. Can we not make some amends now to her, who suffered derision for no disgrace, by giving her the grace of a woman's name? Dr. Johnson rebuked her for spending on her household what might make several poor families happy, and she was wont to take the chiding as she sat with him while he, having risen towards dinner-time, breakfasted. Her daughters reproved her coldly, so that the tender creature sacrificed her romance — and nearly died of it — for a year, to please them. To Miss Thrale, who devoted herself (while her mother was on her honeymoon) to the study of mathematics and fortification, Hester's ardours no doubt seemed foolish enough.

Admirable was the English this friend of Johnson habitually wrote. Not *she* gave him back his literature as from a cheap looking-glass. But once she overbalances herself in a too customary antithesis. She says of her daughters: 'When the anguish I suffered on their account nearly took away my life and reason, the younger ridiculed *as a jest* those agonies which the elder despised *as a philosopher.*' The italics are used here to point her rather puzzle-headed little error.

These great words, by the way, are not usual with her. As a rule she takes her troubles more temperately, and as she turns her weather-beaten little head from the blast, turns a phrase as well. 'Oh, 'tis a pleasant situation! and whoever would wish, as the Greek lady phrased it, to tease himself and repent of his sins, let him borrow his children's money, be in love against their interest and prejudice, forbear to marry by their advice, and then shut himself up to live with them.'

If vanity is cruelty, as M. Bourget says, Hester had no vanity. She was a generous friend: 'I do not observe with any pleasure, I fear, that my husband [Thrale] prefers Miss Streatfield to me, though I must acknowledge her younger, handsomer, and a better scholar . . . Mr. Thrale loves her better by a thousand degrees than he does me or any one else, and even now desires nothing on earth half so much as the sight of his Sophia.' Once, it must be confessed, she made a 'scene'. Mr. Thrale asked his wife to give her place at table to Sophy Streatfield, who had a sore throat and must be out of the draught; and Hester left the table and made a demonstration. None the less did she trust Sophy perfectly: 'She was bred by Dr. Collier in the strictest principles of piety and virtue.'

Equally loyal was she to all the other pretty friends who filled the Streatham house and frolicked in the Streatham park. They were but half-loyal to her, and more than one of the men who dined at the table which her wit, her sweet temper, her

gay and careless tongue made the most delightful in England,
repaid her ill, derided and decried her — and for what? For
fulfilling a man's idea of a woman's destiny, and living for
love. ' 'Tis woman's whole existence', was never said by a
woman. A certain man said it, and perhaps, being vain to
fatuity, believed it. And he who is given over to believe it
has two kinds of derision at the service of women — one kind
for her who fails to get her 'whole existence', and another kind
for her who is resolute to get her 'whole existence', and gets it.

II

'More in anger, than in sorrow', said Mrs. Thrale in her
old age, had been her countenance towards those of her guests
who, in memoirs, diaries, and biographies, had censured and
slighted her, had confused friendship, and had worked the
final wrong of spoiling the past. She would not spend grief
upon them, and her anger was mingled not only with good
spirits, but with sweet humour. She did many a kindness in
after years to the men who derided her for her second marriage.
She had obviously little of the more obvious kind of dignity,
except when she borrowed Johnson's own noble style to bid
him her admirable farewell! but the wilder dignity of her
own freedom, the dignity of nature, was always hers.

Of all her adversaries, those over whom she seems never to
have had any kind of victory were her own daughters — 'the
ladies', as she generally calls them. One is reminded by that
title of the two aunts in *One of our Conquerors* — the more that
there is also something Meredithian in passages of Mrs.
Thrale's own career; but 'the ladies' in the novel were delicate
and old, and our English habits of speech have no ordinary
title grave enough for such unmarried old age; whereas the
'ladies' of Mrs. Thrale were of the age of schoolgirls —
beautiful young creatures who appear in her noisy little story
implacable, unmoved, and all but absolutely silent.

It is their silence, indeed, that gives them this solitary
advantage. All the other adversaries speak at least as much as

Mrs. Thrale herself. We have all heard them. Some speak many words against her, others weighty words, and others, again, explosive words, like Macaulay's. But Miss Thrale and her sisters hold their peace. They have all the unuttered replies. Theirs is the incalculable benefit of the cause unpleaded. And their mother was plainly aware that her protests were but sorry efforts in face of their displeasure.

Mrs. Thrale is perhaps the most conspicuous of all hostesses. She had not merely the authority of a mistress of a house according to the English idea; she did not entertain only as the wife of her husband. Her birth, her education, and her wit gave her a distinct place. Her marriage had, besides, the more French character of a partnership of fortune. The men who dined at her husband's table were her guests as well as the pensioners of her smile.

But she was, in her own estimation, as in theirs, an author of more importance than any hostess. And all she wrote had an established consciousness of wit, except only the very impulsive marginal notes to Boswell's life of her greatest (not her dearest) friend. If Mrs. Thrale needs excuse for her parting from Johnson, it ought not to be forgotten that she never loved him as she had loved the Dr. Collier of her youth; so that she had an enormous insult to forgive from a man who had never had much of her heart. To have gained 'attention and friendship' from Dr. Collier when he was four times her age was one of her happiest memories when she had long passed the years he had when his quadrupled hers. 'The sentiment with which dear Dr. Collier inspired me in 1757 remains unaltered now in the year 1815.' Her mother, as she records with a sweet and filial patience, thought fit to part her from him, for fear that her friend should foster her dislike to the marriage with Mr. Thrale — a man who never took the trouble to make himself acceptable to the bride, paying all his visits, his compliments, and his homage to her mother.

She confesses, in one of the few passages of her long confidences to her friends and the world that have the slight vibration of an intimate feeling, very candidly the whole history of her loyal affections: 'Never have I failed remembering *him* [Dr. Collier] with a preference as completely distinct from the venerating solicitude which hung heavily over my whole soul whilst connected with Dr. Johnson, as it was from the strong connubial duty that tied my every thought to Mr. Thrale's interest, or from one fervid and attractive passion which made twenty years passed in Piozzi's enchanting society seem like a happy dream of twenty hours.'

'Mrs. Thrale loves you', said Johnson to Boswell in the *Life*. 'Not I. I never loved him', says Mrs. Thrale in the margin. Nor will she ever allow a like remark to pass. 'She has a great regard for you.' 'Not I — never had. I thought him a clever and a comical fellow.' Again: 'You continue to stand high with Mrs. Thrale.' 'Poor Mrs. Thrale', she writes, 'was obliged to say so in order to keep well with Johnson.' And when Johnson rebukes the all-candid Boswell, 'Have you no better manners? That is your want', Mrs. Thrale's note is underlined, '*So it was*'.

Of her wit these notes have some of the best examples. This, for instance, is hers. 'Who would believe Goldy when he told of a ghost? A man whom one could not believe when he told of a brother. It is questionable now whether he had a brother or not.' She very keenly appreciates the charm that Beauclerc had for Johnson — the charm of entering unprepared upon conversation. Who does not own this as a charm now? Who does not feel it after meeting a Frenchman? It is a rather negative quality, no doubt, but it is great, it is national. No one seems to have had it at the Streatham dinner-table except Beauclerc. Mr. Thrale might have had it, but he evaded the matter by his silence. 'Dr. Johnson,' says Mrs. Thrale, 'who was all emphasis himself, felt *épris* of such a character.'

She had Johnson's praise for her versification. She loved to translate Latin or French epigrams into eighteenth-century English verse, and he told her that he could not have done it more closely himself. She had the honour to teach Johnson something about pauses.

Upon a phrase in the *Lives of the Poets* to the effect that 'Milton had left the University alienated by the injudicious severity of his governors', Mrs. Thrale adds: 'They have never whipt a lad since, for fear of driving away a second Milton! There was no danger.' She has her comment also upon the fact that Swift never saw Mrs. Dingley or Stella without a witness; she names this third person a *'sunk fence* between Swift and his ladies'.

Of the scientific experiments of her days she says: 'Never was poor Nature so put to the torture, and never, of course, was she made to tell so many lies.' She tells a significant story with reticence even when her own life is concerned, as in the gentle passage that describes how she saw in after years, at an exhibition in Pall Mall, 'The Lady's Last Stake', for which she had sat to Hogarth in her youth, and which had been one of the pictures of the famous collection at Streatham Park. Mrs. Thrale was very old. 'I asked Mrs. Hoare, who was admiring it, if she ever saw any person it resembled. She said no, unless it might once have been like me, and we turned away to look at something else.' She was still older when she wrote 'General Donkin is married and Mrs. Wroghton dead. They were nearly of an age, but the lady's is the more prudent step, sure, after ninety.'

She gave a ball when she was eighty, and inspired verses then, and later. To the latest of these her answer might almost — it lacks the poetry but has the closeness — be one of the slighter verses of the 'Angel in the House':

> Praises are pretty things, 'tis true.
>   Yet, to a well-turned mind, the pain
> Of making them indeed our due,
>   Is the best pleasure we can gain.

Little is remembered now, except perhaps her allegories. Of these it must be owned that their fancy is ordinary, their vivacity somewhat insignificant. It is not for her authorship that we keep her memory fresh, but for her goodness, her dutifulness, and her invincible courage in life and love.

Marceline Valmore

'PRENDS garde a moi, ma fille, et couvre moi bien!' Marceline Desbordes-Valmore, writing from France to her daughter Ondine, who was delicate and chilly in London in 1841, has the same solicitous, journeying fancy as was expressed by two other women, both also Frenchwomen, and both articulate in tenderness. Eugénie de Guérin, that queen of sisters, had preceded her with her own complaint, 'I have a pain in my brother's side'; and in another age Mme de Sévigné had suffered, in the course of long posts and through infrequent letters — a protraction of conjectured pain — within the frame of her absent daughter. She phrased her plight in much the same words, confessing the uncancelled union with her child that had effaced for her the boundaries of her personal life.

Is not what we call a life — the personal life — a separation from the universal life, a seclusion, a division, a cleft, a wound? For these women, such a severance was in part healed, made whole, closed up, and cured. Life was restored between two at a time of human-kind. Did these three women guess that their sufferings of sympathy with their children were indeed the signs of a new and universal health — the prophecy of human unity?

The sign might have been a more manifest and a happier prophecy had this union of tenderness taken the gay occasion as often as the sad. Except at times, in the single case of Mme de Sévigné, all three — far more sensitive than the rest of the world — were yet not sensitive enough to feel equally the less sharp communication of joy. They claimed, owned, and felt sensibly the pangs and not the pleasures of the absent. Or if not only the pangs, at least they were apprehensive chiefly in that sense which human anxiety and foreboding have lent to the word; they were apprehensive of what they feared. 'Are you warm?' writes Marceline Valmore to her child. 'You have so little to wear — are you really warm? Oh, take care of me — cover me well.' Elsewhere she says, 'You are an insolent child to think of work. Nurse your health, and mine. Let us live like fools'; whereby she meant that she should work with her own fervent brain for both, and take the while her rest in ·Ondine. If this living and unshortened love was sad, it must be owned that so, too, was the story. Eugénie and Maurice de Guérin were both to die soon, and Marceline was to lose this daughter and another.

But set free from the condition and occasion of pain and sorrow, this life without boundaries which mothers have undergone seems to suggest and to portend what the progressive charity of generations may be — and is, in fact, though the continuity does not always appear — in the course of the world. If a love and life without boundaries go down from a mother into her child, and from that child into her children again, then incalculable, intricate, universal, and eternal are the unions that seem — and only seem — so to transcend the usual experience. The love of such a mother passes unchanged out of her own sight. It drops down ages, but why should it alter? What in her daughter should she make so much her own as that daughter's love for her daughter in turn? There are no lapses.

Marceline Valmore, married to an actor who seems to have 'created the classic genre' in vain, found the sons and daughters of other women in want. Some of her rich friends, she avers, seem to think that the sadness of her poems is a habit — a matter of metre and rhyme, or, at most, that it is 'temperament'. But others take up the cause of those whose woes, as she says, turned her long hair white too soon. Sainte-Beuve gave her his time and influence, succoured twenty political offenders at her instance, and gave perpetually to her poor. 'He never has any socks', said his mother; 'he gives them all away, like Béranger.' 'He gives them with a different accent', added the literary Marceline.

Even when the stroller's life took her to towns she did not hate, but loved — her own Douai, where the names of the streets made her heart leap, and where her statue stands, and Bordeaux, which was, in her eyes, 'rosy with the reflected colour of its animating wine' — she was taken away from the country of her verse. The field and the village had been dear to her, and her poems no longer trail and droop, but take wing, when they come among winds, birds, bells, and waves. They fly with the whole volley of a summer morning. She loved the sun and her liberty, and the liberty of others. It was apparently a horror of prisons that chiefly inspired her public efforts after certain riots at Lyons had been reduced to peace. The dead were free, but for the prisoners she worked, wrote, and petitioned. She looked at the sentinels at the gates of the Lyons gaols with such eyes as might have provoked a shot, she thinks.

During her lifetime she very modestly took correction from her contemporaries, for her study had hardly been enough for the whole art of French verse. But Sainte-Beuve, Baudelaire, and Verlaine have praised her as one of the poets of France. The later critics — from Verlaine onwards — will hold that she needs no pardon for certain slight irregularities in the grouping of masculine and feminine rhymes, for upon this liberty they themselves have largely improved. The old rules in their completeness seemed too much like a prison to her. She was set about with importunate conditions — a caesura, a rhyme, narrow lodgings in strange towns, bankruptcies, salaries astray — and she took only a little gentle liberty.

A Woman in Grey

THE mothers of Professors were indulged in the practice of jumping at conclusions, and were praised for their impatience of the slow process of reason.

Professors have written of the mental habits of women as though they accumulated generation by generation upon women, and passed over their sons. Professors take it for granted, obviously by some process other than the slow process of reason, that women derive from their mothers and grandmothers, and men from their fathers and grandfathers. This, for instance, was written lately: 'This power [it matters not what] would be about equal in the two sexes but for the influence of heredity, which turns the scale in favour of the woman, as for long generations the surroundings and conditions of life of the female sex have developed in her a greater degree of the power in question than circumstances have required from men.' 'Long generations' of subjection are, strangely enough, held to excuse the timorousness and the shifts of women to-day. But the world, unknowing, tampers with the courage of its sons by such a slovenly indulgence. It tampers with their intelligence by fostering the ignorance of women.

And yet Shakespeare confessed the participation of man and woman in their common heritage. It is Cassius who speaks:

> Have you not love enough to bear with me
> When that rash humour which my mother gave me
> Makes me forgetful?

And Brutus who replies:

> Yes, Cassius, and from henceforth
> When you are over-earnest with your Brutus
> He'll think your mother chides, and leave you so.

Dryden confessed it also in his praises of Anne Killigrew:

> If by traduction came thy mind,
> Our wonder is the less to find
> A soul so charming from a stock so good.
> Thy father was transfused into thy blood.

The winning of Waterloo upon the Eton playgrounds is very well; but there have been some other, and happily minor, fields that were not won — that were more or less lost. Where

did this loss take place, if the gains were secured at football?
This inquiry is not quite so cheerful as the other. But while
the victories were once going forward in the playground, the
defeats or disasters were once going forward in some other
place, presumably. And this was surely the place that was not
a playground, the place where the future wives of the football
players were sitting still while their future husbands were
playing football.

This is the train of thought that followed the grey figure of
a woman on a bicycle in Oxford Street. She had an enormous
and top-heavy omnibus at her back. All the things on the near
side of the street — the things going her way — were going at
different paces, in two streams, overtaking and being overtaken.
The tributary streets shot omnibuses and carriages, cabs and
carts — some to go her own way, some with an impetus that
carried them curving into the other current, and other some
making a straight line right across Oxford Street into the street
opposite. Besides all the unequal movement, there were the
stoppings. It was a delicate tangle to keep from knotting. The
nerves of the mouths of horses bore the whole charge and
answered it, as they do every day.

The woman in grey, quite alone, was immediately dependent
on no nerves but her own, which almost made her machine
sensitive. But this alertness was joined to such perfect com-
posure as no flutter of a moment disturbed. There was the
steadiness of sleep, and a vigilance more than that of an
ordinary waking.

At the same time, the woman was doing what nothing in her
youth could well have prepared her for. She must have passed
a childhood unlike the ordinary girl's childhood, if her steadi-
ness or her alertness had ever been educated, if she had been
rebuked for cowardice, for the egoistic distrust of general rules,
or for claims of exceptional chances. Yet here she was, trusting
not only herself but a multitude of other people; taking her
equal risk; giving a watchful confidence to averages — that last,
perhaps, her strangest and greatest success.

No exceptions were hers, no appeals, and no forewarnings.

She evidently had not in her mind a single phrase, familiar to women, made to express no confidence except in accidents, and to proclaim a prudent foresight of the less probable event. No woman could ride a bicycle along Oxford Street with any such baggage as that about her.

The woman in grey had a watchful confidence not only in a multitude of men but in a multitude of things. And it is very hard for any untrained human being to practise confidence in things in motion — things full of force, and, what is worse, of forces. Moreover, there is a supreme difficulty for a mind accustomed to search timorously for some little place of insignificant rest on any accessible point of stable equilibrium; and that is the difficulty of holding itself nimbly secure in an equilibrium that is unstable. Who can deny that women are generally used to look about for the little stationary repose just described? Whether in intellectual or in spiritual things, they do not often live without it.

She, none the less, fled upon unstable equilibrium, escaped upon it, depended upon it, trusted it, was 'ware of it, was on guard against it, as she sped amid her crowd: her own unstable equilibrium, her machine's, that of the judgment, the temper, the skill, the perception, the strength of men and horses.

She had learnt the difficult peace of suspense. She had learnt also the lowly and self-denying faith in common chances. She had learnt to be content with her share — no more — in common security, and to be pleased with her part in common hope. For all this, it may be repeated, she could have had but small preparation. Yet no anxiety was hers, no uneasy distrust and disbelief of that human thing — an average of life and death.

To this courage the woman in grey had attained with a spring, and she had seated herself suddenly upon a place of detachment between earth and air, freed from the principal detentions, weights, and embarrassments of the usual life of fear. She had made herself, as it were, light, so as not to dwell either in security or danger, but to pass between them. She confessed difficulty and peril by her delicate evasions, and con-

sented to rest in neither. She would not owe safety to the mere
motionlessness of a seat on the solid earth, but she used gravita-
tion to balance the slight burdens of her wariness and her con-
fidence. She put aside all the pride and vanity of terror, and
leapt into an unsure condition of liberty and content.

She leapt, too, into a life of moments. No pause was possible
to her as she went, except the vibrating pause of a perpetual
change and of an unflagging flight. A woman, long educated
to sit still, does not suddenly learn to live a momentary life
without strong momentary resolution. She has no light
achievement in limiting not only her foresight, which must
become brief, but her memory, which must do more; for it
must rather cease than become brief. Idle memory wastes times
and other things. The moments of the woman in grey as they
dropped by must needs disappear, and be simply forgotten, as
a child forgets. Idle memory, by the way, shortens life, or
shortens the sense of time, by linking the immediate past
clingingly to the present. Here may possibly be found one of
the reasons for the length of a child's time, and for the brevity
of the time that succeeds. The child lets his moments pass by
and quickly become remote through a thousand little successive
oblivions. He has not yet the languid habit of recall.

'Thou art my warrior,' said Volumnia. 'I holp to frame
thee.'

Shall a man inherit his mother's trick of speaking, or her
habit and attitude, and not suffer something, against his will,
from her bequest of weakness, and something, against his
heart, from her bequest of folly? From the legacies of an un-
lessoned mind, a woman's heirs-male are not cut off in the
Common Law of the generations of mankind. Brutus knew
that the valour of Portia was settled upon his sons.

The Mother

from 'Mary, the Mother of Jesus'

THE mothers of all ages are those who have suffered because others suffered; for each of them, self is less sensitive than the self of her child. Self is not locked up in the maternal heart, there to be cherished, as it is by the egoist, or to be crushed and silenced as it is by the Saint. In the mother, self is not lost, but loses all its evil by the passionate personal love that distributes it among sons and daughters. Perfect self-less love would perhaps be distributed through the multitude, but a mother is not perfect; nature has so much use for her — separate, family use — that she cannot let her go free from irrational, indispensable partialities and limitings, even injustices, all serving the turn of the race. And these very injustices have so delighted mankind that Thackeray, for instance, makes a heroine of her who will not only defame herself by denying her own legal marriage, but will by the same act defraud the lawful heirs to certain possessions so that the foster-child she loves may enjoy them. This is surely the corruption of a fine thing humanly incomplete. For a mother's partial love that merits any of the reverence, or worthily calls up any of the wonder, of the contemplative man or novelist is not so much unjust as merely incomplete. Incomplete in regard to the extent of the world and human kind, not incomplete in time; for it passes to a daughter and to a daughter's daughter, to a son and a son's child, and knows no stop in its bequest, and no stop in its consciousness but that of the separation of the grave. Thus finally are bound together the generations, (to use Abigail's words) the bundle of the living. . . .

Filial love is most simple in French literature; and most reticent (the reticence is a matter of national self-approval) in our own. Our days are humorous days, and a very great English novelist has bantered the conventional Frenchman's appeal to his mother's memory and to the sanction of her honoured head, her knee at which he was taught, and her grave where his wreath hangs. This was done humorously by changing the word 'mother' to 'mama'. Filial piety is various in attitude and utterance; and those who have not uttered it at all after their childhood was over have been known to wish that they had given it some speech while the ears to hear it could still hear.

When John Evelyn wishes to praise a contemporary lady by comparing her (to their disadvantage) with illustrious ladies of the past, and especially, as became a scholar and a gentleman, with those of Antiquity, he gives them their title of honour chiefly as the mothers of the great, and even, in one case, as the mother-in-law. The glory he attributes to these distinguished ladies is a glory reflective and retrospective. In giving them thus a derivative honour he does but rehearse a fact much beyond his present purpose. For the greatest honour ever given to a woman, or indeed to any creature, was absolutely a reflective honour. Of all reflective glory the glory of the Mother of Christ is the supreme example — so perfect an example that it might rather be called the solitary pattern. Have some enthusiasts seemed — whether they were poets writing sonnets in honour of the moon or Christians singing hymns in honour of Mary — to give their more sensible tenderness to the secondary splendour, have they seemed to forget that the moonlight is the sunlight simply returned, and Mary a moon to the sun of Christ, they have only seemed. The consciousness of God, as the giver, the giver of all, lay immovably deep in the heart of the peasant saying ten 'Aves' to one 'Pater Noster'. Nay, the case of Mary is singular in this entire humility and humiliation. For we may all irrationally and nearly unconsciously attribute some glory of genius to the poet, for instance, as though it were his own by origin; but in the case of the Mother of Christ there is no such vague illusion. The little idolatries that are offered to the poet or the soldier are withheld from her who is pre-eminent only for sanctity bestowed, and distinguished only by her office assigned, the preparation therefor, and the reward thereafter. And this similitude of Mary and the moon is so perfect that it is a wonder the simple should need, or the churches erect, images of the Virgin of Nazareth, the virgin of the Annunciation, the Mother of the Seven Sorrows, or Our Lady of Peace, or the Mother of Christ by His Cross, or Mary under any invocation whatever, when, month by month, newly lighted every month, the moon presents her absolute similitude, her image with the superscription of her Lord. And yet there is a nation with a noble language that incredibly makes the moon masculine, facing — with effrontery — a feminine sun.

COMMENTARIES

The Rhythm of Life

IF life is not always poetical, it is at least metrical. Periodicity rules over the mental experience of man, according to the path of the orbit of his thoughts. Distances are not gauged, ellipses not measured, velocities not ascertained, times not known. Nevertheless, the recurrence is sure. What the mind suffered last week, or last year, it does not suffer now; but it will suffer again next week or next year. Happiness is not a matter of events; it depends upon the tides of the mind. Disease is metrical, closing in at shorter and shorter periods towards death, sweeping abroad at longer and longer intervals towards recovery. Sorrow for one cause was intolerable yesterday, and will be intolerable to-morrow; to-day it is easy to bear, but the cause has not passed. Even the burden of a spiritual distress unsolved is bound to leave the heart to a temporary peace; and remorse itself does not remain — it returns. Gaiety takes us by a dear surprise. If we had made a course of notes of its visits, we might have been on the watch, and would have had an expectation instead of a discovery. No one makes such observations; in all the diaries of students of the interior world, there have never come to light the records of the Kepler of such cycles. But Thomas à Kempis knew of the recurrences, if he did not measure them. In his cell alone with the elements — 'What wouldst thou more than these? for out of these were all things made' — he learnt the stay to be found in the depth of the hour of bitterness, and the remembrance that restrains the soul at the coming of the moment of delight, giving it a more conscious welcome, but presaging for it an inexorable flight. And 'rarely, rarely comest thou', sighed Shelley, not to Delight merely, but to the Spirit of Delight. Delight can be compelled beforehand, called, and constrained to our service — Ariel can be bound to a daily task; but such artificial violence throws life out of metre, and it is not the spirit that is thus compelled. *That* flits upon an orbit elliptically or parabolically or hyperbolically curved, keeping no man knows what trysts with Time.

It seems fit that Shelley and the author of the 'Imitation' should both have been keen and simple enough to perceive these flights, and to guess at the order of this periodicity. Both souls were in close touch with the spirits of their several worlds, and no deliberate human rules, no infractions of the liberty and law of the universal movement, kept from them the knowledge of recurrences. *Eppur si muove.* They knew that presence does not exist without absence; they knew that what is just upon its flight of farewell is already on its long path of return. They knew that what is approaching to the very touch is hastening towards departure. 'O wind', cried Shelley, in autumn,

> O wind,
> If winter comes can spring be far behind?

They knew that the flux is equal to the reflux; that to interrupt with unlawful recurrences, out of time, is to weaken the impulse of onset and retreat; the sweep and impetus of movement. To live in constant efforts after an equal life, whether the equality be sought in mental production, or in spiritual sweetness, or in the joy of the senses, is to live without either rest or full activity. The souls of certain of the saints, being singularly simple and single, have been in the most complete subjection to the law of periodicity. Ecstasy and desolation visited them by seasons. They endured, during spaces of vacant time, the interior loss of all for which they had sacrificed the world. They rejoiced in the uncovenanted beatitude of sweetness alighting in their hearts. Like them are the poets whom, three times or ten times in the course of a long life, the Muse has approached, touched, and forsaken. And yet hardly like them; not always so docile, nor so wholly prepared for the departure, the brevity, of the golden and irrevocable hour. Few poets have fully recognized the metrical absence of their Muse. For full recognition is expressed in one only way — silence.

It has been found that several tribes in Africa and in America worship the moon, and not the sun; a great number worship both; but no tribes are known to adore the sun, and not the moon. On her depend the tides; and she is Selene, mother of Herse, bringer of the dews that recurrently irrigate lands where rain is rare. More than any other companion of earth is she the Measurer. Early Indo-Germanic languages knew her by that name. Her metrical phases are the symbol of the order of recurrence. Constancy in approach and in departure is the reason of her inconstancies. Juliet will not receive a vow spoken in invocation of the moon; but Juliet did not live to know that love itself has tidal times — lapses and ebbs which are due to the metrical rule of the interior heart, but which the lover vainly and unkindly attributes to some outward alteration in the beloved. For man — except those elect already named — is hardly aware of periodicity. The individual man either never learns it fully, or learns it late. And he learns it so late, because it is a matter of cumulative experience upon which cumulative evidence is long lacking. It is in the after-part of each life that the law is learnt so definitely as to do away with the hope or fear of continuance. That young sorrow comes so near to despair is a result of this young ignorance. So is the early hope of great achievement. Life seems so long, and its capacity so great, to one who knows nothing of all the intervals it needs must hold — intervals between aspirations, between actions, pauses as inevitable as the pauses of sleep. And life looks impossible to the young unfortunate, unaware of the inevitable and unfailing refreshment. It would be for their peace to learn that there is a tide in the affairs of men, in a sense more subtle— if it is not too audacious to add a meaning to Shakespeare — than the phrase was meant to contain. Their joy is flying away from them on its way home; their life will wax and wane; and if they would be wise, they must wake and rest in its phases, knowing that they are ruled by the law that commands all things — a sun's revolutions and the rhythmic pangs of maternity.

———————

The Colour of Life

RED has been praised for its nobility as the colour of life. But the true colour of life is not red. Red is the colour of violence, or of life broken open, edited, and published. Or if red is indeed the colour of life, it is so only on condition that it is not seen. Once fully visible, red is the colour of life violated, and in the act of betrayal and of waste. Red is the secret of life, and not the manifestation thereof. It is one of the things the value of which is secrecy, one of the talents that are to be hidden in a napkin. The true colour of life is the colour of the body, the colour of the covered red, the implicit and not explicit red of the living heart and the pulses. It is the modest colour of the unpublished blood.

So bright, so light, so soft, so mingled, the gentle colour of life is outdone by all the colours of the world. Its very beauty is that it is white, but less white than milk; brown, but less brown than earth; red, but less red than sunset or dawn. It is lucid, but less lucid than the colour of lilies. It has the hint of gold that is in all fine colour; but in our latitudes the hint is almost elusive. Under Sicilian skies, indeed, it is deeper than old ivory; but under the misty blue of the English zenith, and the warm grey of the London horizon, it is as delicately flushed as the paler wild roses, out to their utmost, flat as stars, in the hedges of the end of June.

For months together London does not see the colour of life in any mass. The human face does not give much of it, what

with features and beards, and the shadow of the top-hat and
chapeau melon of man, and of the veils of woman. Besides, the
colour of the face is subject to a thousand injuries and accidents.
The popular face of the Londoner has soon lost its gold, its
white, and the delicacy of its red and brown. We miss little
beauty by the fact that it is never seen freely in great numbers
out-of-doors. You get it in some quantity when all the heads
of a great indoor meeting are turned at once upon a speaker;
but it is only in the open air, needless to say, that the colour of
life is in perfection, in the open air, 'clothed with the sun',
whether the sunshine be golden and direct, or dazzlingly
diffused in grey.

The little figure of the London boy it is that has restored to
the landscape the human colour of life. He is allowed to come
out of all his ignominies, and to take the late colour of the
midsummer north-west evening, on the borders of the Serpen-
tine. At the stroke of eight he sheds the slough of nameless
colours — all allied to the hues of dust, soot, and fog, which
are the colours the world has chosen for the clothing of its
boys — and he makes, in his hundreds, a bright and delicate
flush between the grey-blue water and the grey-blue sky.
Clothed now with the sun, he is crowned by-and-by with twelve
stars as he goes to bathe, and the reflection of an early moon is
under his feet.

So little stands between a gamin and all the dignities of
Nature. They are so quickly restored. There seems to be
nothing to do, but only a little thing to undo. It is like the art
of Eleonora Duse. The last and most finished action of her
intellect, passion, and knowledge was, as it were, the flicking
away of some insignificant thing mistaken for art by other
actors, some little obstacle to the way and liberty of Nature.

All the squalor is gone in a moment, kicked off with the
second boot, and the child goes shouting to complete the land-
scape with the lacking colour of life. You are inclined to
wonder that, even undressed, he still shouts with a Cockney
accent. You half expect pure vowels and elastic syllables from
his restoration, his spring, his slenderness, his brightness, and

his glow. Old ivory and wild rose in the deepening midsummer
sun, he gives his colours to his world again.

It is easy to replace man, and it will take no great time, when
Nature has lapsed, to replace Nature. It is always to do, by the
happily easy way of doing nothing. The grass is always ready
to grow in the streets — and no streets could ask for a more
charming finish than your green grass. The gasometer even
must fall to pieces unless it is renewed; but the grass renews
itself. There is nothing so remediable as the work of modern
man — 'a thought which is also', as Mr. Pecksniff said, 'very
soothing'. And by remediable I mean, of course, destructible.
As the bathing child shuffles off his garments — they are few,
and one brace suffices him — so the land might always, in
reasonable time, shuffle off its yellow brick and purple slate,
and all the things that collect about railway stations. A single
night almost clears the air of London.

But if the colour of life looks so well in the rather sham
scenery of Hyde Park, it looks brilliant and grave indeed on a
real sea-coast. To have once seen it there should be enough to
make a colourist. O memorable little picture! The sun was
gaining colour as it neared setting, and it set not over the sea,
but over the land. The sea had the dark and rather stern, but
not cold, blue of that aspect — the dark and not the opal tints.
The sky was also deep. Everything was very definite, without
mystery, and exceedingly simple. The most luminous thing
was the shining white of an edge of foam, which did not cease
to be white because it was a little golden and a little rosy in the
sunshine. It was still the whitest thing imaginable. And the
next most luminous thing was the little unclad child, also
invested with the sun and the colour of life.

In the case of women, it is of the living and unpublished
blood that the violent world has professed to be delicate and
ashamed. See the curious history of the political rights of
woman under the Revolution. On the scaffold she enjoyed an
ungrudged share in the fortunes of party. Political life might
be denied her, but that seems a trifle when you consider how
generously she was permitted political death. She was to spin

and cook for her citizen in the obscurity of her living hours; but to the hour of her death was granted a part in the largest interests, social, national, international. The blood wherewith she should, according to Robespierre, have blushed to be seen or heard in the tribune, was exposed in the public sight unsheltered by her veins.

Against this there was no modesty. Of all privacies, the last and the innermost — the privacy of death — was never allowed to put obstacles in the way of public action for a public cause. Women might be, and were, duly silenced when, by the mouth of Olympe de Gouges, they claimed a 'right to concur in the choice of representatives for the formation of the laws'; but in her person, too, they were liberally allowed to bear political responsibility to the Republic. Olympe de Gouges was guillotined. Robespierre thus made her public and complete amends.

Eyes

THERE is nothing described with so little attention, with such slovenliness, or so without verification — albeit with so much confidence and word-painting — as the eyes of the men and women whose faces have been made memorable by their works. The describer generally takes the first colour that seems to him probable. The grey eyes of Coleridge are recorded in a proverbial line, and Procter repeats the word, in describing from the life. Then Carlyle, who shows more signs of actual attention, and who caught a trick of Coleridge's pronunciation instantly, proving that with his hearing at least he was not slovenly, says that Coleridge's eyes were brown — 'strange, brown, timid, yet earnest-looking eyes'. A Coleridge with brown eyes is one man, and a Coleridge with grey eyes another — and, as it were, more responsible. As to Rossetti's eyes, the various inattention of his friends has assigned to them, in all the ready-made phrases, nearly all the colours.

So with Charlotte Brontë. Matthew Arnold seems to have thought the most probable thing to be said of her eyes was that they were grey and expressive. Thus, after seeing them, does he describe them in one of his letters. Whereas Mrs. Gaskell, who shows signs of attention, says that Charlotte's eyes were a reddish haze', made up of 'a great variety of tints', to be discovered by close looking. Almost all eyes that are not brown are, in fact, of some such mixed colour, generally spotted in, and the effect is vivacious. All the more if the speckled iris has a dark ring to enclose it.

Nevertheless, the eye of mixed colour has always a definite character, and the mingling that looks green is quite unlike the mingling that looks grey; and among the greys there is endless difference. Brown eyes alone are apart, unlike all others, but having no variety except in the degrees of their darkness.

The colour of eyes seems to be significant of temperament, but as regards beauty there is little or nothing to choose among colours. It is not the eye, but the eyelid, that is important, beautiful, eloquent, full of secrets., The eye has nothing but its colour, and all colours are fine within fine eyelids. The eyelid has all the form, all the drawing, all the breadth and length; the square of great eyes irregularly wide; the long corners of narrow eyes; the pathetic outward droop; the delicate contrary suggestion of an upward turn at the outer corner, which Sir Joshua loved.

It is the blood that is eloquent, and there is no sign of blood in the eye; but in the eyelid the blood hides itself and shows its signs. All along its edges are the little muscles, living, that speak not only the obvious and emphatic things, but what reluctances, what perceptions, what ambiguities, what half-apprehensions, what doubts, what interceptions! The eyelids confess, and reject, and refuse to reject. They have expressed all things ever since man was man.

And they express so much by seeming to hide or to reveal that which indeed expresses nothing. For there is no message from the eye. It has direction, it moves, in the service of the sense of sight; it receives the messages of the world. But expression is outward, and the eye has it not. There are no windows of the soul, there are only curtains; and these show all things by seeming to hide a little more, a little less. They hide nothing but their own secrets.

But, some may say, the eyes have emotion inasmuch as they betray it by the waxing and contracting of the pupils. It is, however, the rarest thing, this opening and narrowing under any influences except those of darkness and light. It does take place exceptionally; but I am doubtful whether those who talk of it have ever really been attentive enough to perceive it. A nervous woman, brown-eyed and young, who stood to tell the news of her own betrothal, and kept her manners exceedingly composed as she spoke, had this waxing and closing of the pupils; it went on all the time like a slow, slow pulse. But such a thing is not to be seen once a year.

Moreover, it is — though so significant — hardly to be called expression. It is not articulate. It implies emotion, but does not define, or describe, or divide it. It is touching, insomuch as we have knowledge of the perturbed tide of the spirit that must cause it, but it is not otherwise eloquent. It does not tell us the quality of the thought, it does not inform and surprise us with intricacies. It speaks no more explicit or delicate things than does the pulse in its quickening. It speaks with less division of meanings than does the taking of the breath, which has impulses and degrees.

No, the eyes do their work, but do it blankly, without communication. Openings into the being they may be, but the closed cheek is more communicative. From them the blood of Perdita never did look out. It ebbed and flowed in her face, her dance, her talk. It was hiding in her paleness, and cloistered in her reserve, but visible in prison. It leapt and looked, at a word. It was conscious in the fingers that reached out flowers. It ran with her. It was silenced when she hushed her answers to the king. Everywhere it was close behind the doors — everywhere but in her eyes.

How near at hand was it, then, in the living eyelids that expressed her in their minute and instant and candid manner! All her withdrawals, every hesitation, fluttered there. A flock of meanings and intelligences alighted on those mobile edges.

Think, then, of all the famous eyes in the world, that said so much, and said it in no other way but only by the little exquisite muscles of their lids. How were these ever strong enough to bear the burden of those eyes of Heathcliff's in *Wuthering Heights?* 'The clouded windows of Hell flashed a moment towards me; the fiend which usually looked out, however was so dimmed and drowned———' That mourning fiend, who had wept all night, had no expression, no proof or sign of himself, except in the edges of the eyelids of the man.

And the eyes of Garrick? Eyelids, again. And the eyes of Charles Dickens, that were said to contain the life of fifty men? On the mechanism of the eyelids hung that fifty-fold vitality. 'Bacon had a delicate, lively, hazel eye', says Aubrey in his *Lives of Eminent Persons.* But nothing of this belongs to the eye except the colour. Mere brightness the eyeball has or has not, but so have many glass beads: the liveliness is the eyelid's. 'Dr. Harvey told me it was like the eie of a viper.' So intent and narrowed must have been the attitude of Bacon's eyelids.

'I never saw such another eye in a human head,' says Scott in describing Burns, 'though I have seen the most distinguished men in my time. It was large, and of a dark cast, and glowed (I say literally *glowed*) when he spoke with feeling or interest. The eye alone, I think, indicated the poetical character and temperament.' No eye literally glows; but some eyes are polished a little more, and reflect. And this is the utmost that can possibly have been true as to the eyes of Burns. But set within the meanings of impetuous eyelids the lucidity of the dark eyes seemed broken, moved, directed into fiery shafts.

See, too, the reproach of little, sharp, grey eyes addressed to Hazlitt. There are neither large nor small eyes, say physiologists, or the difference is so small as to be negligible. But in the eyelids the difference is great between large and small, and also between the varieties of largeness. Some have large openings, and some are in themselves broad and long, serenely covering eyes called small. Some have far more drawing than others, and interesting foreshortenings and sweeping curves.

Where else is spirit so evident? And where else is it so spoilt? There is no vulgarity like the vulgarity of vulgar eyelids. They have a slang all their own, of an intolerable kind. And eyelids have looked all the cruel looks that have ever made wounds in innocent souls meeting them surprised.

But all love and all genius have winged their flight from those slight and unmeasurable movements, have flickered on the margins of lovely eyelids quick with thought. Life, spirit, sweetness are there in a small place; using the finest and the slenderest machinery; expressing meanings a whole world apart, by a difference of material action so fine that the sight which appreciates it cannot detect it; expressing intricacies of intellect; so incarnate in slender and sensitive flesh that nowhere else in the body of man is flesh so spiritual.

A Remembrance

WHEN the memories of two or three persons now upon earth shall be rolled up and sealed with their records within them, there will be no remembrance left open, except this, of a man whose silence seems better worth interpreting than the speech of many another. Of himself he has left no vestiges. It was a common reproach against him that he never acknowledged the obligation to any kind of restlessness. The kingdom of heaven suffereth violence, but as he did none there was nothing for it but that the kingdom of heaven should yield to his leisure. The delicate, the abstinent, the reticent graces were his in the heroic degree. Where shall I find a pen fastidious enough to define and limit and enforce so many significant negatives? Words seem to offend by too much assertion, and to check the suggestions of his reserve. That reserve was life-long. Loving literature, he never lifted a pen except to write a letter. He was not inarticulate, he was only silent. He had an exquisite style from which to refrain. The things he abstained from were all exquisite. They were brought from far to undergo his judgment, if haply he might have selected them. Things ignoble never approached near enough for his refusal; they had not with him so much as that negative connection. If I had to equip an author I should ask no better than to arm him and invest him with precisely the riches that were renounced by the man whose intellect, by integrity, had become a presence-chamber.

It was by holding session among so many implicit safeguards that he taught, rather than by precepts. Few were these in his speech, but his personality made laws for me. It was a subtle education, for it persuaded insensibly to a conception of my own. How, if he would not define, could I know what things were and what were not worthy of his gentle and implacable judgment? I must needs judge them for myself, yet he constrained me in the judging. Within that constraint and under that stimulus, which seemed to touch the ultimate springs of thoughts before they sprang, I began to discern all things in literature and in life — in the chastity of letters and in the honour of life — that I was bound to love. Not the things of one character only, but excellent things of every character. There was no tryanny in such a method. His idleness justified itself by the liberality it permitted to his taste. Never having made his love of letters further a secondary purpose, never having bound the literary genius — that delicate Ariel — to any kind of servitude, never having so much as permitted himself a prejudice whereby some of his delights should be stinted while others were indulged beyond the sanctions of modest reason, he barely tolerated his own preferences, which lay somewhat on the hither side of full effectiveness of style. These the range of his reading confessed by certain exclusions. Nevertheless it was not of deficiencies that he was patient: he did but respect the power of pause, and he disliked violence chiefly because violence is apt to confess its own limits. Perhaps, indeed, his own fine negatives made him only the more sensible of any lack of those literary qualities that are bound in their full complement to hold themselves at the disposal of the consummate author — to stand and wait, if they may do no more.

Men said that he led a *dilettante* life. They reproached him with the selflessness that made him somewhat languid. Others, they seemed to aver, were amateurs at this art or that; he was an amateur at living. So it was, in the sense that he never grasped at happiness, and that many of the things he had held slipped from his disinterested hands. So it was, too, in this unintended sense; he loved life. How should he not have loved a life that his living made honourable? How should he not have loved all arts, in which his choice was delicate, liberal, instructed, studious, docile, austere? An amateur man he might have been called, too, because he was not discomposed by his own experiences, or shaken by the discovery which life brings to us — that the negative quality of which Buddhism seems to accuse all good is partaken by our happiness. He had always prayed temperate prayers and harboured probable wishes. His sensibility was extreme, but his thought was generalized. When he had joy he tempered it not in the common way by meditation upon the general sorrow but by a recollection of the general pleasure. It was his finest distinction to desire no differences, no remembrance, but loss among the innumerable forgotten. And when he suffered, it was with so quick a nerve and yet so wide an apprehension that the race seemed to suffer in him. He pitied not himself so tenderly as mankind, of whose capacity for pain he was then feelingly persuaded. His darkening eyes said in the extreme hour: 'I have compassion on the multitude.'

Charmian

'SHE is not Cleopatra, but she is at least Charmian', wrote Keats, conscious that his damsel was not in the vanward of the pageant of ladies. One may divine that he counted the ways wherein she was not Cleopatra, the touches whereby she fell short of and differed from, nay, in which she mimicked, the Queen.

In like manner many of us have for some years past boasted of our appreciation of the inferior beauty, the substitute, the waiting gentlewoman of corrupt or corruptible heart; Keats confessed, but did not boast. It is a vaunt now, an emulation, who shall discover her beauty, who shall discern her.

She is most conspicuous in the atmosphere in smoke 'effects', in the 'lurid', the 'mystery'; such are the perfervid words. But let us take the natural and authentic light as our symbol of Cleopatra, her sprightly port, her infinite jest, her bluest vein, her variety, her laugh. 'O Eastern star!'

Men in cities look upward not much more than animals, and these — except the dog when he bays the moon — look skyward not at all. The events of the sky do not come and go for the citizens, do not visibly approach and withdraw, threaten and pardon; they merely happen. And even when the sun so condescends as to face them at the level of their own horizon (say from the western end of the Bayswater Road), when he searches out the eyes that have neglected him all day, finds a way between their narrowing lids, looks straight into their unwelcoming pupils, explores the careful wrinkles, singles and numbers the dull hairs, even, I say, to sudden sunset in our dim climate, the Londoner makes no reply; he would rather look into puddles than into the pools of light among clouds.

Yet the light is as characteristic of a country as is its landscape. So that I would travel for the sake of a character of early morning, for a quality of noonday, or a tone of afternoon, or an accident of moonrise, or a colour of dusk, at least as far as for a mountain, a cathedral, rivers, or men. The light is more important than what it illuminates. When Mr. Tomkins — a person of Dickens's earliest invention — calls his fellow-boarders from the breakfast-table to the window, and with emotion shows them the effect of sunshine upon the left side of a neighbouring chimney-pot, he is far from cutting the grotesque figure that the humorist intended to point out to banter. I am not sure that the chimney-pot with the pure light upon it was not more beautiful than a whole black Greek or a whole black Gothic building in the adulterated light of a customary London day. Nor is the pleasure that many writers, and a certain number of painters, tell us they owe to such adulteration anything other than a sign of derogation — in a word, a pleasure in the secondary thing.

Are we the better artists for our preference of the waiting-woman? It is a strange claim. The search for the beauty of the less-beautiful is a modern enterprise, ingenious in its minor pranks, insolent in its greater. And its chief ignobility is the love of marred, defiled, disordered, dulled, and imperfect skies, the skies of cities.

Some will tell us that the unveiled light is too clear or sharp for art. So much the worse for art; but even on that plea the limitations of art are better respected by natural mist, cloudy gloom of natural rain, natural twilight before night, or natural twilight — Corot's — before day, than by the artificial dimness of our unlovely towns. Those, too, who praise the 'mystery' of smoke are praising rather a mystification than a mystery; and must be unaware of the profounder mysteries of light. Light is all mystery when you face the sun, and every particle of the innumerable atmosphere carries its infinitesimal shadow.

Moreover, it is only in some parts of the world that we should ask for even natural veils. In California we may, not because the light is too luminous, but because it is not tender. Clear and not tender in California, tender and not clear in England; light in Italy and in Greece is both tender and clear.

When one complains of the ill-luck of modern utilities, the sympathetic listener is apt to agree, but to agree wrongly by denouncing the electric light as something modern to be deplored. But the electric light is the one success of the last century. It is never out of harmony with natural things — villages, ancient streets of cities, where it makes the most beautiful of all street-lighting, swung from house to opposite house in Genoa or Rome. With no shock, except a shock of pleasure, does the judicious traveller, entering some small sub-alpine hamlet, find the electric light, fairly, sparingly spaced, slung from tree to tree over the little road, and note it again in the frugal wine-shop, and solitary and clear over the church portal.

Yet, forsooth, if yielding to the suggestions of your restless hobby, you denounce, in any company, the spoiling of your Italy, the hearer, calling up a 'mumping visnomy', thinks he echoes your complaint by his sigh, 'Ah, yes — the electric light; you meet it everywhere now; so modern, so disenchanting'. It is, on the contrary, enchanting. It is as natural as lightning. By all means let all the waterfalls in all the Alps be 'harnessed', as the lamentation runs, if their servitude gives us electric light. For thus the power of the waterfall kindles a lovely lamp. All this to be done by the simple force of gravitation — the powerful fall of water. 'Wonderful, all that water coming down!' cried the tourist at Niagara, and the Irishman said, 'Why wouldn't it?' He recognized the simplicity of that power. It is a second-rate passion — that for the waterfall. Yet your cascade is dearer to every sentimentalist than the sky. Standing near the folding-over place of Niagara, at the top of the fall, I looked across the perpetual rainbow of the foam, and saw the whole further sky deflowered by the formless, edgeless, languid, abhorrent murk of smoke from the nearest town. Much rather would I see that water put to use than the sky so outraged. As it is, only by picking one's way between cities can one walk under, or as it were in, a pure sky. The horizon in Venice is thick and ochreous, and no one cares; the sky of Milan is defiled all round. In England I must choose a path alertly; and so does now and then a wary, fortunate, fastidious wind that has so found his exact, uncharted way, between this smoke and that, as to clear me a clean moonrise, and heavenly heavens.

There was an ominous prophecy to Charmian. 'You shall outlive the lady whom you serve.' She has outlived her in every city in Europe; but only for the time of setting straight her crown — the last servility. She could not live but by comparison with the Queen.

IN ITALY

In a South Alpine Castle

THE English proprietor plants out the cottages even though they pay him rent, and likes best the view that shows nothing that is not his own, from the pond to the cloud, from the ground-game to the pilgrim shower. But the Piedmontese castello rises on Roman foundations whereto the village clings, locked into the rock. From the machicolations — the swallow-tail battlements of tower and long enclosing wall — and from the windows with their thick internal shutters of timber, the dwellers in the castle see something else than a little English smoke from low roofs, or a jack-in-the-green cottage with its poverty stifled in ornamental ivy. They look down the steep rock into the climbing streets of stone, into the courtyards netted in and out with vine, down a score of open stairways, and down the course of the falling stream. Terrace under terrace of grey stone they see, roof under roof of dark red tile roughly curved, walled vineyard under vineyard; and not far from the level of the castle gateway, the top of the clamorous belfry tower.

Nothing is hidden except extreme sickness, birth and death by those broad roofs; the villagers live outside their narrow doors, and their illnesses are brief. You cannot persuade them to keep their beds until the eve of death.

Nor are they tenants of the castle's lord, under whose eyes their lives are passed thus visibly; all the people of the village are peasant-proprietors, owners of the small and rich pastures, and strips of maize and of every grain, planted with innumer-

233

able mulberry trees linked by vines. This is not the Italy of
the olive, the silver and blue, grey-roofed coast, fertile but pale
nor is it the Italy of stony hills where the people creep begging,
and one wonders what there can be within reach for money to
buy; it is an emerald country, fostered by Alpine river and
rivulet and rain from the Alpine cloud, deep-charged with the
soil washed from long, profound valleys leading into Switzer-
land, open to an infinite south. Six hay-harvests between spring
and autumn are nothing to boast of, and you hear of twelve.
Not a house scattered abroad over this splendid plain but is, in
early June, whispering within with silkworms feeding on their
leaves. Father to son leaves the ancient house on the rock-side
and the parcel of green country. It might be thought that here,
if not in Liguria, where the farmer pays rent, nor in Tuscany,
where he takes half the gross produce of the land and the use
of house and tools in exchange for all his labour — here in full
ownership the countryman could live. So he can, but, under
the imposts of an ambitious nation and a corrupt executive, at
a price of more than human labour and privation; and hardly
even so, without a year's work, when the seasons are bad, in
factory or mine, for his sons. He eats none of his own meat, or
butter, or bread, or milk, but grows early old for want of food.
It is difficult to discover when he sleeps, so late at night is he
footing, naked sole on silent stones, so early at work clad to
the waist in silken crops.

Three churches are in the village, and one of these — need-
less to say, in late Renaissance taste — large enough for a town,
was built by the unpaid volunteer labour of the villagers
Within these walls they spend half an hour before the hard
work of every day, and the greater part of every Sunday. More-
over, from these belfries the loud bells peal in the middle of
the night or in the dark of the dawn whenever thunder and
lightning and the downpour of Alpine rains threaten the
fields. There is no sleeping through the bells; they are not
swung so as to spare the slumbers of the tired. No one lies far
from the sound of that summons to prayer and to the bitter
vigil of the farmer in the floods.

The June of my visit was a time of floods. The days were Italy's, open to the sun and the luminous plain, but the nights were the mountains'. Few were the fields that lifted themselves again after those loud rains that roared against the bells. The bell-ringer, who led this most courageous army against sleep, against what George Eliot called the anaesthetics, and who roused the men and women of the anxious hamlet to endure awake — this old man was the humorist of that population, a merry man. His annual salary for all the bell-ringing, Sunday, festa, and storm, was sixty francs; in the daytime his work was to spray the vines with sulphur against disease, and whenever he came there was a question ready for him in the field, in the expectation of his fantastic answer.

The mountains rise suddenly to their full height at what looks like a stone's-throw from the steep builded and castled rock. Their feet are in the translucent green, and their heads snowbound in the cloud. Long and even, as though a slanting ruler had drawn it, the great moraine of this range makes in its place the single bridge, as it were, between the abrupt upland and the gentlest of all plains, the brightest, and the farthest. The moraine still bears its burden of prehistoric stones. It is the only barren thing below the mountain side.

The reader familiar with the small wildness of England — a wildness somewhat like that of a little girl-child out of bounds — must not look for English tracts of field-flowers here at the gates of the south. Wild flowers have no place to grow broadcast; they nowhere assemble to make a colour or paint the meadows with delight; they grow only in the narrow margins that the road wastes reluctantly, a thread of soil uncharged with the bearing of bread. But on the rocky hill, between the terraces of vine, the beautiful golden flower of the Indian fig — a kind of cactus — creeps close to the stone.

Now and then a night came in June when there was no storm. Clear of thunder, rain, and bells, those nights were audible under the moon, The ear of man was barely able to catch their thrilling voice. Tree-frogs, it seems, make this subtle and universal trill, softer but nearly as fine as the bats'

cry, sweeter than the crickets', and so slight a sound that th
long song of the nightingales was as clear against the scattere
whisper as a strong star shows distinct upon the Milky Way
the sound shook the night air as though a finger touched
string in tune.

The nightingales pealed by twos and threes from a sma
wood within the castle walls, that has its roots lapped about th
Roman stones. Fireflies do not come so near to the norther
limits of Italy, and therefore the night lacked their shuttle
threads of movement, but its profound brightness was threade
by slender sound as the warmer night of Tuscany by comin
and vanishing fireflies with their slender flashes. The fine a
seemed to be strung for the touches of those finer sounds.

Not a child's voice stirred in the village; and never — albe
even the murmurs of that short sleep seemed to enter at th
castle windows in the night — was there any sound of oppres
sion of women or children, of violence, imprecation, or de
rision. The people love their children throughout this country
The image of a young father, with his young child on hi
shoulder, seems to be the most familiar of all remembrances o
a Piedmontese, or Venetian, or Lombard holiday. The chil
holds on to its father's hair, in church or in the street, an
steers the way of the man, and seems generally to direct th
spending of their day together. Of unkindness or neglect yo
see no sign, for the children of the poorest are delicately kep
and sweetly cherished.

Never was country placed under a more appropriate invoca
tion than that of the cathedral dominating North Italy — th
cathedral that sees Mont Blanc and can be seen from the lengt
of half the populous plain seaward. Base Gothic and imported
unauthorized and late, thin despite its weight and cheap for a
its cost, is the Gothic of the Cathedral of Milan; but it carrie
a title upon its front that dedicates to an infant something mor
than the frigid building — for it devotes the city with its people
the over-driven, harassed, and patient villagers, and the moun
taineers of those valleys of the Alps that have waters flowing t
the south — devotes them not to the 'Nativity of Mary', as the

translate it in the travellers' books, but to the babe, 'Mariae Nascenti'. Never was more unanimous consent to a consecration, or a people more ready daily to obey the helpless.

Here it is Turinese, not Milanese, jurisdiction, but the spirit is unalterable; no young child is struck or sworn at or abandoned in the village of poverty.

For the sake of the creature too young to work, man and woman began to move down the steep streets and on the level road afield, long before sunrise of the midsummer morning.

To Italy with Evelyn

Is anyone so courageous as to wish for a glimpse of the city and the landscape of the future, two centuries and a half hence? Even if so, he can hardly desire it so warmly as the fainter-hearted desires the sight of the past. At any rate, if there be any scene that we would willingly be admitted to see as it is to be, that scene is not in Italy.

Thither would we willingly journey not later than in the day of John Evelyn, when he travelled in his youthful dignity, provided with letters, and spent some seasons in Rome, and studied for a year at the University of Padua. Everyone knows his journal of the English Church under the Commonwealth, of the Plague, of the Fire, of the Court of Charles II. But not the least charming part of one of the most readable of books — a book written in an English prose that had not yet undergone much manipulation, but was still a little rigid, but rigid with vitality — is somewhat neglected; it is the part that records this progress through France to the Coast, and thence into Italy as far as Naples, and home by Venice, the Lakes, the Simplon Pass, and Switzerland. The happy man! When he drew near, after peril of shipwreck, to the port of Genoa, he 'perfectly smelt the joyes of Italy'. This was off the noble village of Sanpierdarena, where now you may smell the odour of factories — soap-boiling and other things — for it has lately come to be stifled with thick smoke, and the mountain gardens are dying with their blackened arbours. Only of late have those ancient, coloured terraces, coloured as a few masterly landscapes are painted, so that a little of the canvas, or a little of the view, might be set in a ring and worn as a jewel — only of late have the gardens, once in rich and fortunate neglect, ceased to breathe their ancient breath.

'We recovered the shore, which we now kept in view within half a league, in sight of those pleasant villas, and within scent of those fragrant orchards which are on this coast, full of princely retirements for the sumptuousnesse of their buildings and noblesse of the plantations, from whence, the wind blowing as it did, might perfectly be smelt the joyes of Italy, in the perfumes of orange, citron, and jasmine flowers for divers leagues seaward.' And Evelyn was so much struck by the aura of this coast as to record it again in the dedication of his 'Fumifugium' to Charles II. What has befallen Sanpierdarena — that one place precisely, of all others — in the years just past makes the whole incident of this welcoming message from the cultivated lands and of the ensuing treatise and its title, sound somewhat cruel in irony.

John Evelyn tried in vain to stay the approaching smoke, as he tried also — by an application to the same monarch — to avert the course of fashion in the then important dress of men. The East he thought better worth following than France, and he proposed a whole revision of the Western mode, and presented the King with a plan whereby the trivial fashions of 'the monsieurs' were to be exchanged for an Oriental 'noblesse'. Charles accepted the pamphlet, and was soon after seen to wear a Persian robe; but he rather shabbily left Evelyn to conjecture in silence, that it was his advice that had been taken. In the end, the King slid back, and 'the monsieurs' had it. If John Evelyn had had that glimpse into the future which few of us desire to-day, how could he have endured those French inventions to which the East has now been partly converted, and the fumes of that ash-strewn piece of coast? 'But a soap-factory!' cries the English reader, seeing all kinds of happy national sarcasm in the industry that, among others, has brought about this special local change. It happens, however, pat to this matter of soap, that Evelyn makes a note to the effect that he bought, in one of the towns of North Italy, certain 'wash-balls' which seemed to be new to him; he speaks of them as a useful invention. Before the factory had taken the place of the fragrant orchards the people of that coast had the constant custom of washing all their clothes. It is much to be feared that the smoke of the soap-factory has already put an end to that habit by making it too difficult, or impossible.

Some consolation is to be found in this — that if a mile of that incomparable coast is spoilt, there remain scores of miles all untouched, differing only in the lesser majesty of the houses and gardens with their great sea-walls. The 'sumptuousnesse' admired by Evelyn will never be restored; but of the mere walls of those rougher houses too, in their place in the landscape, pieces might be set as jewels. It was always in praise of gardens that Evelyn wrote. Otherwise the general modern complaint as to the insensibility of the older writers to the daily splendours of nature is hardly unjust in his case. He, without noting, saw the change of skies that sets alight the world when you have crossed the Alps, and of the further illumination of a southern spring he says nothing; but he makes mention of the 'extraordinary long' tail of a horse, which he saw in a collection of curiosities, nor do two horns of as many unicorns go unrecorded, for he had a grave and simple admiration of such things as petrifactions, flies in amber, and all minor marvels. Nor does he cease to be a learned and most responsible man, in whose adult but innocent style we are to see nothing contrary to the dignities of State and office. The false air of childishness which this kind of English gives to the style of Pepys always makes his public functions and honours seem to us incongruous. In Evelyn's Diary, by the way, we meet Mr. Pepys, about some Admiralty business, with so much solemnity that we hardly know him again.

It is Italy that seems (by her people) to have an air of child-ishness in our eyes to-day. I have to confess that when I hear an Italian say something to the purpose I always cry inwardly 'How intelligent!' But in those days England took frankly a lower place. It could not be otherwise, seeing that the late Renaissance as it was then in Rome had imposed law and taste upon the whole of Europe. Evelyn had nothing whatever to be proud of at home, inasmuch as he was ashamed of York Min-ster, Lincoln, Durham, and the rest; inasmuch, too, as Shake-speare's name occurs not once in his book. He never doubts that modern art had reached its culmination in St. Peter's and the Lateran, in Guido Reni and Domenichino.

He found all those splendours new, and it is no wonder if he was convinced that all this art in course of progress, as it was visibly, must be better integrally than what had gone before. He took no notice of the earlier masters of any of the schools, but admired precisely as Horace Walpole admired, and on the same scale and according to the same order. He was diligent in the galleries, but the student of to-day is dismayed to see no Botticelli up or down the page, and to find the polite English traveller in rapture before the blatant Bernini.

Englishmen, in a word, paid Italy the great compliment of taking her at the highest estimation as she was at the moment. There was no painful comparison with any period of the past, for we have evidence in his works that Bernini was not afraid of antiquity itself. In arts, in letters, in arms, in science especially, Italy was foremost in present action — *there* was her splendour, as we may find it hard to realize. Evelyn sent home preparations from her schools of anatomy to the Royal Society, to which such things were new.

And as to the gardens, happy was this traveller, who was soon after to plan the hedges and alleys of Wotton and of Sayes Court, in such a school of gardens. He had, in England, to contend with the perpetual inequalities which have hardly been sufficiently recognized as distinctive of our plains. In Italy he found the plains to be flat with that peculiar sub-alpine flatness, and the road straight. Most beautiful with the mountains for a distance — but he hardly had eyes for the mountains. It is rather difficult to forgive him for calling the rocks and bays of the coast 'horrid gaps' and 'dreadful mountains'; but 'Oh, the sweet Paradise!' he cries among the fountains and the vines.

His was a clear spirit. Wherever he journeyed he went upright; and if we desire to travel with him into Italy, it is not only for the sake of his Italy but for the sake of himself. Something we would have from him in exchange for our better instruction in the 'Gotiq ordonance'.

Venetian Girls

For some cause, perhaps referable to her own mere moderation of demeanour, beauty, and array, the Venetian woman of the people has had her portrait but ill done, though with a various kind of failure, by the generations of painters. The Venetian girl was presented in a light frock and yellow handkerchief, unlaced and untidy, fringed, strung with beads and set off with a flower, having her hair done in the open air, and gossiping, with gesture of the hands and play of expression.

Meanwhile the Venetian girls, giving no sign that they are aware of the tedious convention of the studios in regard to them, are pacing the city that is so much their own, often in black. Whatever the current fiction may be, they walk in that novelty and composure, surprise and harmony together, that (in fortunate countries and cities) are real life. The dress, if not always black, is always dark, trimly enough made, but quite indistinctive, neither short nor long; the stockings are always black, the shoes neat. And the universal open-air garment of the townswoman of all ages is the black shawl with a deep silken fringe, folded with a short point above and a long point below, that wraps the figure about from neck to foot. She does not fasten it at the throat, and when it slips off she has a way of gathering it upon one outstretched arm that is like the action of a dove stretching her wing.

Venice would be quite another Venice than that of the end of the nineteenth century if the Venetian girl should ever begin to wear a hat, but she shows no signs that she will ever be visited by such a desire. Evening is her time, for she is a girl of affairs; and where the band plays, she strolls. Groups of threes and fours of girls — how familiar is that association of light-linked figures in all towns where women are at work in shop or factory, in all villages where they take a share in labours of the field, meadow, or road! They laugh along so many highways in the dusk; and here it is a candid laugh, and there a giggle and a scream. But the Venetian girl knows no lapse of dignity. Never, early or late, nor on the Piazza, which she likes to tell you is a drawing-room, with the marble veins and edges of its pavement, nor in the darkest by-street, shall you hear these voices of leisure raised in any kind of discord, nor even so much as forced to an ill-bred pitch, or jangled by any untuning excitement, coarseness, or even gaiety or haste. Sweet bells of Venetian dialect — I mended my reading of Goldoni by listening for all their peculiar chimes, and got his *xè* precisely right. Coquettes these may be, but modest ones, who must be sought, who show nothing to the public but an easy and a sweet frigidity, whom no Venetian would have a dream, or desire, of engaging in that kind of gallantry to which the girls of a prouder race submit on their Bank-holidays — the approach by ways of burlesque, the provocative advance, in a word the irony, which is the strange popular form of the game further north.

Beauty is not frequent in the class that hears the band and walks under this Venetian moon. Twice or thrice a day you may see a head wearing the famous colour, the 'Titian red'; but the dark, straight hair is the rule, and there is almost the lack of height that prevails in France, but with somewhat more slenderness. The Venetian groups are not distinctly graceful, but with so much candour and composure they cannot be graceless. None of their painters seem to be aware of that peculiar reserve, nor of the look they all wear as conscious Venetians. Theirs is the incomparable city; theirs is St. Mark's, grave and fantastic; theirs the Lombard tower, plain and joyful; theirs are the two columns seaward; theirs the Gothic tracery and the Renaissance rectangle, the whole distinction of the city and the isles, and they put on their ownership visibly. There are no carriages to hustle them, no signs or shows of wealth, nothing to abash them—not that Venetian girls would be idly or vainly disconcerted, or of so mean a mind as to defy, to emulate, to deprecate, or even closely to observe, the shows of fortune. But the rich keep out of the way, or within doors, in the sea-city; and for the class that we call middle, or perhaps lower-middle, the palaces stand in the moonlight, the waters move, the splendid piazza is spread, polished and clean, the Gothic colonnade takes the shadows, the Saracenic colours of St. Mark's doorways front the late light; for them the square of little shops glows with the electric light, for them the band plays Wagner. Nowhere else may you see thus a great city in absolute self-possession. Or let the visitor boast that at any rate the coral-shops and bead-shops live by him. But the cafés live by the Venetians, and for them are set the hundreds of chairs, to-night on the Quadri side, to-morrow night on the Florian side, according to the pitching of the orchestra.

To Venice has long been awarded the lot of the rebuked, and the nations have taken upon themselves *le beau rôle* of the rebuker. Her greatness, her fall, her corruption — how many reproaches, how many lessons, how many confessions of the general justice of events, how many eloquent regrets, have closed each recital of the history of Venetia. Who that has told how her doge crowned a kneeling emperor of the East for the double jurisdiction, who that has rehearsed the successes of the Republic, but finds something to his hand for a warning, respectful and rhetorical, to ocean powers of a later age? No seaport too poor in history, too dull in aspect, too abject in the builded front it turns upon the wave, to moralize the tale of this city towards the east.

I know not from what vantage-ground of innocence the

nations impose their indignation and pity. But it is certain that Venice is not mentioned without her sins; you meet them in romances, ancient and new, even though we may import the crime in the dishonouring person of a popular poet. She is always, to the raconteur, the reproved city. Mrs. Thrale told a queer story of Venetian customs, and George Sand made matter for another. But, in fact, the rebuked city has innocent ways that would do any other city honour. Her streets are clean — the sea-streets and the stone. And much of this disregarded honour of Venice, and good report of her holiday and summer evenings, is to be ascribed to the young Venetians, those girls of dignity.

Bells

With mimicry, with praises, with echoes, or with answers, the poets have all but outsung the bells. The inarticulate bell has found too much interpretation, too many rhymes professing to close with her inaccessible utterance, and to agree with her remote tongue. The bell, like the bird, is a musician pestered with literature.

To the bell, moreover, men do actual violence. You cannot shake together a nightingale's notes, or strike or drive them into haste, nor can you make a lark toll for you with intervals to suit your turn, whereas wedding-bells are compelled to seem gay by mere movement and hustling. I have known some grim bells, with not a single joyous note in the whole peal, so forced to hurry for a human festival, with their harshness made light of, as though the Bishop of Hereford had again been forced to dance in his boots by a merry highwayman.

The clock is an inexorable but less arbitrary player than the bellringer, and the chimes await their appointed time to fly — wild prisoners — by twos or threes, or in greater companies. Fugitives — one or twelve taking wing — they are sudden, they are brief, they are gone; they are delivered from the close hands of this actual present. Not in vain is the sudden upper door opened against the sky; they are away, hours of the past.

Of all unfamiliar bells, those which seem to hold the memory most surely after but one hearing are bells of an unseen cathedral of France when one has arrived by night; they are no more to be forgotten than the bells in 'Parsifal'. They mingle with the sound of feet in unknown streets, they are the voices of an unknown tower; they are loud in their own language. The spirit of place, which is to be seen in the shapes of the fields and the manner of the crops, to be felt in a prevalent wind, breathed in the breath of the earth, overheard in a far street-cry or in the tinkle of some blacksmith, calls out and peals in the cathedral bells. It speaks its local tongue remotely, steadfastly, largely, clamorously, loudly, and greatly by these voices; you hear the sound in its dignity, and you know how familiar, how childlike, how lifelong it is in the ears of the people. The bells are strange, and you know how homely they must be. Their utterances are, as it were, the classics of a dialect.

Spirit of place! It is for this we travel, to surprise its subtlety; and where it is a strong and dominant angel, that place, seen once, abides entire in the memory with all its own accidents, its habits, its breath, its name. It is recalled all a lifetime, having been perceived a week, and is not scattered but abides, one living body of remembrance. The untravelled spirit of place — not to be pursued, for it never flies, but always to be discovered, never absent, without variation — lurks in the by-ways and rules over the towers, indestructible, an indescribable unity. It awaits us always in its ancient and eager freshness. It is sweet and nimble within its immemorial boundaries, but it never crosses them. Long white roads outside have mere suggestions of it and prophecies; they give promise not of its coming, for it abides, but of a new and singular and unforeseen goal for our present pilgrimage, and of an intimacy to be made. Was ever journey too hard or too long that had to pay such a visit? And if by good fortune it is a child who is the pilgrim, the spirit of place gives him a peculiar welcome, for antiquity and the conceiver of antiquity (who is only a child) know one another; nor is there a more delicate perceiver of locality than a child. He is well used to words and voices that he does not understand, and this is a condition of his simplicity; and when those unknown words are bells, loud in the night, they are to him as homely and as old as lullabies.

If, especially in England, we make rough and reluctant bells go in gay measures, when we whip them to run down the scale to ring in a wedding — bells that would step to quite another and a less agile march with a better grace — there are belfries that hold far sweeter companies. If there is no music within Italian churches, there is a most curious local immemorial music in many a campanile on the heights. Their way is for the ringers to play a tune on the festivals, and the tunes are not hymn tunes or popular melodies, but proper bell-tunes, made for bells. Doubtless they were made in times better versed than ours in the sub-divisions of the arts, and better able to understand the strength that lies ready in the mere little submission to the means of a little art, and to the limits — nay, the very embarrassments — of those means. If it were but possible to give here a real bell-tune — which cannot be, for those melodies are rather long — the reader would understand how some village musician of the past used his narrow means as a composer for the bells, with what freshness, completeness, significance, fancy, and what effect of liberty.

These hamlet-bells are the sweetest, as to their own voices, in the world. When I speak of their antiquity I use the word relatively. The belfries are no older than the sixteenth or seventeenth century, the time when Italy seems to have been generally rebuilt. But, needless to say, this is antiquity for music, especially in Italy. At that time they must have had foundries for bells of tender voices, and pure, warm, light, and golden throats, precisely tuned. The hounds of Theseus had not a more just scale, tuned in a peal, than a North Italian belfry holds in leash. But it does not send them out in a mere scale, it touches them in the order of the game of a charming melody. Of all cheerful sounds made by man this is by far the most light-hearted. You do not hear it from the great churches. Giotto's coloured tower in Florence, that carries the bells for Santa Maria del Fiore and Brunelleschi's silent dome, does not ring more than four contralto notes, tuned with sweetness, depth, and dignity, and swinging one musical phrase which softly fills the country.

The village belfry it is that grows so fantastic and has such nimble bells. Obviously it stands alone with its own village, and can therefore hear its own tune from beginning to end. There are no other bells in earshot. Other such dovecote-doors are suddenly set open to the cloud, on a *festa* morning, to let fly those soft-voiced flocks, but the nearest is behind one of many mountains, and our local tune is uninterrupted. Doubt-less this is why the little, secluded, sequestered art of composing melodies for bells — charming division of an art, having its own ends and means, and keeping its own wings for unfolding by law — dwells in these solitary places. No tunes in a town would get this hearing, or would be made clear to the end of their frolic amid such a wide and lofty silence.

Nor does every inner village of Italy hold a bell-tune of its own; the custom is Ligurian. Nowhere else as in Genoa did the nervous tourist complain of church bells in the morning, and in fact he was made to hear an honest rout of them betimes. But the nervous tourist had not, perhaps, the sense of place, and the genius of place does not signal to him to go and find it among innumerable hills, where one by one, one by one, the belfries stand and play their tunes. Variable are those lonely melodies, having a differing gaiety for the festivals; and a pitiful air is played for the burial of a villager.

As for the poets, there is but one among so many of their bells that seems to toll with a spiritual music so loud as to be unforgotten when the mind goes up a little higher than the earth, to listen in thought to earth's untethered sounds. This is Milton's curfew, that sways across one of the greatest of all the seashores of poetry — 'the wide-watered'.

Fireflies

COLD are the only living fires; for these are the little rhythmic flames that in so many thousands thread the country nights in the south. Fireflies are so true to summer that the tourist, and he who perversely chooses to winter in summer-lands, may well go through their career of travel and never once see the lighting and lapsing, lighting and lapsing, of those innumerable flights. Roses and blue skies are far less loyal to their liberal god, Summer, and more idly at the service of strange seasons. You may capture a show of flowers for a chilly winter garden, and persuade all the colours to lodge with you. But fireflies do not love travel — they baffle the collector by putting their soft lights out. For them you most rewardingly seek in the midst of the cultivated lands, where the little shining shuttles shoot in and out of vines and olives. They are most abundant in those homely lands, where narrow fields join hands in the monotonous order of a dance of little mulberry trees linked by vines.

It is small, encumbered scenery, full of unnumbered repetitions, and full also of the finest forms of leaf and classic plant, nowhere dense, nowhere impenetrable, and nowhere absorbent of the universal sun. In showers and showers the lights abound, and the earth is struck with sunshine at every point. The traveller may call this nothing else than a grievous lack of shade, if he be the usual traveller in search of something that is elsewhere appropriate. Shade there certainly is none in this Italian garden of small growth, but only delicate shadow, which is nothing else than the writing of the light — its thin pencil for drawing the hand of the fig tree or the vine, and the feather of maize. All the country has an inimitable unity rather because than despite of its small detail. No walls or hedges divide possession from possession or field from field; straight green grass paths give access far and near, and the whole land is interwoven all day by lights and by tendrils, all night by fireflies. They flit slowly, and do not baffle the tardy sight of man, which is so easily outrun, dazzled, eluded, set at naught, doubled upon, and abandoned by natural swift movement. Bees are quicker, and the perpetual alternate darkening and kindling of fireflies give to that shining flight in the night an effect of innumerable pauses. It is only when a firefly has come by some misfortune, and is injured and cannot fly, that it shines steadily.

In spite of the custom of poets to speak as though glow-worms were among the habitual beautiful things of a landscape as a night traveller sees it with his peering eyes, they are so rare that it is quite possible to know the English country for many years and in many places and characters, and to have seen perhaps three glow-worms all told, or perhaps none. Whereas, fireflies are in such multitudes as to be themselves the chief scenery, the foreground, and the distance of the deep night. Yet the poets have somewhat slighted them. No one, for example, who had ever really marked their intricate free flight, the beauty of movement, the length, the multiplicity, the universal presence and the difference of direction of all these little lights, would have thought of tangling them 'in a silver braid', to make an image of the Pleiades. Fireflies never swarm, they are never tangled, they do not glitter, no silver braid would add anything to their mystery or their brightness. Imagination had nothing to do with that similitude; but even as a rather common kind of fancy, it is surely something less than simple or just. In northern skies the Pleiades are too vague and dim for fireflies, and it is a little blur that tangles them without sparkle. In the south, where the Pleiades are pricked into keener starlight, and are to be counted clearly, you may see the ill-luck of the image, on the spot.

Elsewhere Tennyson has the simpler art to say merely that 'the firefly wakens', and with the firefly he names a palace garden, gold fins in a porphyry font, a cypress, a milk-white peacock, white and crimson petals asleep, and the glimmering of her who comes upon the garden walk like the ghost of Pope's or of Ben Jonson's unfortunate lady. It is a splendid night-piece. In such a palace garden, only marred or endeared, as the thing may seem to various fancies, by the realities of the south, the fireflies wakened summer after summer on the Ligurian coast. The finish and prosperity wherewith you are compelled to deck the garden of Tennyson were not there. There was nothing at all like a fine steel engraving; whereas, but for genius, the suggestion of a steel engraving 'soft' in effect, hard as nails in method, would be harassing in the Tennyson picture. Genius makes his garden noble and magical; but Italy made mine.

The palace of reality was out of repair, or if not precisely that, it was assuredly not what an Englishman would consider well 'kept up'. Its great loggia of arches showed no marble, but ancient plaster painted long ago in soft reds and yellows, after the local manner. It was long since gold fins had winked in the fountain, and the fountain had long forgotten to flow; maidenhair ferns cumbered the duct, and grass had broken the grey stones of the terraces. No flowers had been set in that garden for a hundred years, but tiny roses, yellow and white, had their way high and low, and random petunias and stocks breathed in the night.

Nevertheless, it is in the vineyards rather than in the garden that the fireflies are most truly in their own place, wandering interminably in interminable plantations. They fly close under village and city walls. Where the cultivated country begins abruptly there are they, and you may see them by ones and twos astray in the street, kindling and quenching their over-powered light under the electric lamps.

Not only for the infrequent glow-worm, but for the more infrequent will-o'-the-wisp are they slighted by poets. To hear these you would think every marsh to be lighted by the *ignus fatuus*, which was so dear a tradition of our childhood. Who has had the good luck to see such a thing? Humperdinck's opera 'Hansel und Gretel' was fairly lighted up with will-o'-the-wisps; they must have bored those wandering children with their per-sistent menaces. But neither wood nor bog yields an *ignis fatuus* to us once in a lifetime. Nor, after all, is that dance of fire the dance of life; it is only the dance of a proverb.

The firefly has the fire of actual life, and it is a cold fire, like that of the dead moon. All the beautiful eyes of the human race, which we feign to be luminous, do but 'lodge the light'. All the energetic red of our fires is less than this fire upon the wing — the little fly that can cast a shadow and is a living creature. It does not flit beyond its countries, nor is its season there long. A long midsummer sees its brilliant flight from beginning to end. The fruit is gathered without its company, and it does not light the vintage.

Giacinto Gallina

WHEN Giacinto Gallina died at the end of the nineteenth century, at the moment of the high tide of his work for the Venetian stage, English people were put into possession of some idea of his drama in the readiest way at hand. Gallina was said to be, more or less, a later Goldoni with a warmer heart. This was a brief description — or rather a mere sign — of an author whom few strangers would ever seek to know better. He is, indeed, so barred out of the knowledge of English readers by his frequent use of dialect that some such phrase was necessary as a first and final *mémoire*. It gave the news of his death with a first mention of his name and a compendious definition of his career, in one sentence.

Gallina certainly followed Goldoni in finding the arguments, action, and passions of his plays in the home life of the Venetians — a life more domestic than anything an English dramatist would have the courage to offer to a self-conscious public inclined to 'humour'. Although our countrymen are much afraid lest men should accuse them of exceeding domesticity, and are inclined to defend themselves with irony, they are in fact less domestic than any of their neighbours. You may hear two young Italian men, of what would be called among ourselves with some pride the frivolous world, exchange reports of the state and progress of their children (their babies really, but one hardly dares to say so, which is itself enough to denote the peculiar insular sense of dignities and indignities, the reserve, and the clowning that covers its hasty retreat). One hesitates, for fear of burlesque, to report in English a conversation that is in Italy quite simple, human, and unconnected with any kind of raillery.

If this almost majestic candour is found in 'the world', the home is at least equally important in the classes whereof Goldoni chiefly wrote, and Giacinto Gallina in succession to him. These middle classes are very homely, and also peculiarly Italian. Nothing quite so local is to be found among the very poor, whose customs are those of necessity all the world over, and whose manners are small; the rich also tend to resemble each other, luxury grows monotonous, and cookery, for example, is as French in a good hotel in Athens as in a good hotel in Rome. But the little professional world everywhere in Italy keeps deep and inner places wherein it is Italian, Italian beyond the ken of the traveller, and beyond the reach of alteration. The same thing that makes so much of Goldoni and of Gallina illegible to the rest of Europe encloses that sequestered home, and this is dialect. Business, especially if it be official, the business of an *impiegato*, is done in choice Italian, and all acquaintance with foreigners (which in these classes is not much) uses the same polite manner of speech. 'Toscaneggia' — 'he tuscanizes' — says one provincial of another, bantering the choice of words and the careful conjugations of verbs which he himself also will put on with the dignities of office.

But within the flat, within the palazzo, within the country villino alike, dialect has its nest of intimacy, and makes all speech homely with an intensity of homeliness that people without patois can hardly conceive. It sets up an understanding, it runs up a code of signals, it makes confidence, and is heard in a laugh. Habit has not blunted the people's sense of their locality of speech, even as it has left them the full consciousness of their sun. The barbarisms of local dialect are to the Italian citizens snug (as Swift would say) beyond descrip tion: their speech closes in their gossip, it prompts their allusions, it interprets, it understands, at close quarters. It is a kind of refuge from the generalities of literature; it consoles the heart from the threats of the preacher. But it scolds as no other kind of language can scold: scolds the servants with an equality of expression and a tyranny of oppression together that makes one of the curiosities of Italian domestic life; it scolds with the peculiar fury of the southern kitchen — a fury that casts itself implicitly upon the fellow-feeling of bystanders for excuse in the future time of calm. Dialect, in fine, sustains, comforts, winks, excludes the burden of the unintelligible world, deprecates, assuages; it keeps up the old, old habits of childhood, it knows the things that the citizen and the citizen's wife know best, it is aloof from politics.

Inasmuch as the little professional classes of the south do not live without society, their dialect associates them closely with their neighbours — closely yet without any defect of ceremony. The rites are as many, the farewells are as repeated, as though Tuscan were the language; and the speakers of a comparatively gross dialect, full of twang, are yet not people to spend their evenings in ungraceful isolation. Their domesticity is not of the English kind that is made by the habit of reading, and dialect dispenses them from none of the duties and dignities of entertainment. It is only that all is done within, within certain bonds of concentrated mutual understanding.

Indeed, the necessity of companionship for every evening causes a very courteous waiving of the differences of rank. The general asks the village druggist (who is also the barber), and all others of like condition, to his country house to play tombola, there being no other neighbours, or but few. The intercourse between them is that of perfectly equal and easy courtesy, the only sign of difference being the use of the address 'eccellenza' on one side only, but with the infrequence of natural good manners. Without dialect you could hardly have an understanding so close yet so decorous.

Even a remote dialect serves this intimate purpose. It was my fortune to know in childhood the inner interior of such a house. Genoese was my own tongue, and the barber's, and all the countryside's, and the General's was Modenese. His Modenese and his wife's had never abated a jot, for all their many years of dwelling in Liguria; as for their Italian, it was singularly exquisite (the General's recitation of Dante was the most perfect speech in the world), but it was not forthcoming for their tombola parties. Modenese met the quite alien Genoese in a kind of rivalry of historic provincialism. Hosts and guests understood each other barely, and the hard Modenese consonants snapped in reply to the Ligurian sing-song; but it was at any rate dialect, it was *noi altri*, it was the strong Italian home.

That the women should have their interests in these narrow things — narrow but not dull — is intelligible enough. Many of the older women remain indoors from Sunday noon to the next Sunday morning, in a jacket and slippers; not a few of the younger have their distractions, romances, emotions, at the window. Poverty, moreover, fosters these customs by forbidding much toilette, and thus the Italian woman of these middle classes, and of remote towns, who always dresses much, is content to dress seldom, and this perforce means a habit of home-keeping. But the men, with the slight alternative of the *caffè*, are equally absorbed by the things of the house. So does Goldoni show them to be in the whole series of his plays, and so must the men of his audience have been in the eighteenth century, or they would not have endured this perpetual comedy of domestic affairs, in the least exalted sense of the word domestic. Venetian men, and the citizens of other cities equally noble, sat to see the play that turns chiefly on the strife of a man's mother and his wife for the services of a single maid, and they sit to-day to see the same thing. Giacinto Gallina, too, has half a comedy occupied with that contention. He need hardly — but for its unflagging popularity — have taken the self-same motive, inasmuch as Goldoni is by no means out of date; he holds the stage as freshly as ever. Indeed, Italian women, except in the richer classes that have international examples more constantly before their eyes, alter little in a

matter of a hundred or two hundred years. In the women of
Goldoni and in the women of Giacinto Gallina you may see the
virtual contemporaries of Mrs. Samuel Pepys and of Mercer.

Ippolita

SHE who bore this name wore it also. It is a name to wear even
in Italy, where they use Hercules and Achilles with a more
week-day effect than we do here. And Hippolyta went about
as a visible and conscious remainder of the Renaissance. The
farmer's daughters are christened after the saints, and those
of the professional and civic classes are named out of the
History of Rome — Clelia and Cornelia, or something else
handsome and patriotic. But the father and mother of Hippo-
lyta had leisure and a little property in vineyards.

Little properties notoriously do not prosper under modern
Italy, but besides this cause of poverty something had gone
wrong with the *dote*; it was lost; and the daughter had not
married young. She had no contemporaries for companions —
her school friends were wives, and had given up reading the
poets. Under these circumstances Ippolita would have been
married to a cousin had there been a cousin at hand. Ecclesi-
astical law forbids the marriage of cousins, except for some
grave exceptional reasons; and the fact that a damsel has no
dote is held grave enough cause for anything. But there was no
docile young amateur tenor in the family (in the part of central
Italy where Ippolita dwelt, to say 'young man' is to say
'tenor' — the words are interchangeable). There were as many
as six tenors, one higher than another, in but one of the neigh-
bouring properties, and a great many more within easy reach.
They went about with guns among the vines all day in search
of small birds, and at night they sang to the guitar, but not with
any special reference to Ippolita. Nor did it occur to any one
that one among them might marry her, even though their own

choice was limited. The family of six, for instance, had never travelled out of the ancient former grand Duchy, which was their territorial 'country'.

Ippolita was exceedingly well brought up. She had never once been permitted to drop behind her mother in the street of the city near to which was their villa. The walk, within the walls, was always ordered thus: the mother of Ippolita took to herself a friend — another mother with a daughter; the two young girls walked a little in front, and the two ladies behind, talking incessantly but incessantly vigilant. After her school days were over she had a tutor — a gentle and swarthy ecclesiastic, who read with her the classics and the Italian poets. She was very well educated. With him she walked freely about the grass-grown paths, over-arched with perpetual roses, of the hill-side garden. This priestly tutor was a poet, as one is a poet in Italy — with a too willing language and a too rigid prosody. The phrase never resisted him, as it never resists any one in Italian, but he had the usual tussle with the metrical laws of the land; less happy, assuredly, than the English writer, whose diction confesses difficulty and strangeness and the beating of alien pulses full of life. Ippolita learned to write poetry, too, and her literary exercises under the care of so gentle and simple an enthusiast made this time of her life apparently the happiest she had known.

What made her case curious was the fact that nothing in her life had been intended to last. The unrelaxed watch of her mother, the reading of Dante (for, after all, some five years of the *Inferno* are more than enough to an Ippolita), the little parties among the neighbouring country houses, including a dance or two between Christmas and Lent, when she waltzed with the tenors, the unbroken companionship with her father and mother, her position in their home — all this was transitory in its nature. But she herself was not transitory. She had to abide in the fleeting conditions of a girl's life. Everything about her was on the wing, on the point of going. Some of the things seemed tolerable only because they were just off.

No one in Ippolita's world ever spent an evening alone, and

the nearest and easiest people with whom to exchange evenings were an exceedingly stout general and his wife, her parents' contemporaries. The two men played tric-trac every night. The general had no tenors, no family at all. Ippolita had to meet these two with an ever fresh effusion of delight. They all met with an almost ecstatic friendliness. The greetings were long, but the farewells were longer. And never an accent grew languid, brief, or inattentive. They saw each other out into the firefly nights, and renewed their farewells by volleys.

It never occurred to Ippolita to ask permission to stay at home; nor indeed would so sad an expedient as solitude have tempted her. But such evenings are obviously arranged on the understanding that young creatures are not likely to play the fifth in them for many years of life. There were no books to talk about, and there were no evening papers. The subjects of conversation simply came to an end, but the conversation went on. The phrases of ceremony, as in Japan, took up, fortunately, a good deal of the time.

It is not necessary to say that Ippolita never went away on a visit. It was not the local custom. Staying away on visits was a thing that implied a kind of deliberation, an acceptance of things as they were, and Ippolita could not settle down to her existence. She was not expected, as it were, after five-and-twenty. There was no precedent for her. She was nothing in the world but a belated little girl.

Her mother was considered to be a woman of masculine understanding. She conversed, and had read Byron and Scott; she liked to make general remarks on the distinctions of the various nations. She made an admirable mother for a girl of sixteen. She continued the mother of a girl of sixteen, being unprepared to be anything else. She was, moreover, the mother of a normal girl — a daughter with a portion; and she guarded year by year the daughter, whose *dote* had been lost, against tenors who would have desired the *dote* if it had not been lost.

Amid these conditions without precedent the two women, continuing all their futile habits because they knew no other habits, kept such a sweetness of temper as would have addi-

tionally adorned far gayer houses than theirs. It would be
impossible to call them happy. They were perfectly idle, and
they had no change of thoughts. And it is certain that their
perpetual gentleness and brilliance of manner was a matter of
domestic ceremony. Their voices never had an indifferent
tone. They never let a question fall unanswered or allowed a
platitude to pass without its due honours. They flattered one
another with the laugh and the quick reply. These voluble
maternal flatteries were all the compliments that Ippolita ever
received. She had never been alone with a tenor in her life.

She was a very stout girl. Her countrywomen have short
necks, but hers was hardly a neck at all. Her rather sentimental
head seemed to rise immediately from her shoulders, and when
she was dressed out (dress was her one little pleasure) in high
sleeves and tilted hat, she looked very modern. She seemed to
wear her accomplishments and her Christian name in addition,
as a last touch, on the summit of the other things. She had not
beauty, but she had fair hair and a full figure, and but for her
poverty there would have been no lack of tenors to claim
alliance with her family. There was no mystery in her, how-
ever, because she was sentimental, and had been trained to
avoid silence as the greatest of social offences.

Seeing her so cut off from young company (whether of men,
who were not permitted, or of girls, who had married away and
left her) two English damsels, who were passing a summer in
that country of cypress and vine, tried to teach Ippolita to walk
with them. Her mother let her go, out of sheer courtesy and
amiable feeling, on condition that the spinsters kept to the
high roads, and to the country, of course. It was not a great
success, for Ippolita took very short steps and so grew easily
tired. And her emancipation did not altogether delight her.
She was afraid of all the loiterers and all the dogs, and was not
dressed for dust. She wished to turn back from the beginning,
but was far too sweet to say so.

There is no end to the story of Ippolita. If there had been,
it would have been more of a story, but not worth telling. She
did not marry. She remained a stationary girl in a society

where there were no other stationary girls. Schoolgirls and young married women were all the other young women there were. She — remaining in her home — was the strangest and most unlooked-for of inmates. All other kinds of Italians are known according to their classes and kinds; Ippolita had no class and no kind.

At a Station

My train drew near to the Via Reggio platform on a day between two of the harvests of a hot September; the sea was burning blue, and there were a sombreness and a gravity in the very excesses of the sun as his fires brooded deeply over the serried, hardy, shabby, seaside ilex-woods. I had come out of Tuscany and was on my way to the Genovesato: the steep country with its profiles, bay by bay, of successive mountains grey with olive trees, between the flashes of the Mediterranean and the sky; the country through the which there sounds the twanging Genoese language, a thin Italian mingled with a little Arabic, more Portuguese, and much French. I was regretful at leaving the elastic Tuscan speech, canorous in its vowels set in emphatic *l*'s and *m*'s and the vigorous soft spring of the double consonants. But as the train arrived its noises were drowned by a voice declaiming in the tongue I was not to hear again for months — good Italian. The voice was so loud that one looked for the audience: Whose ears was it seeking to reach by the violence done to every syllable, and whose feelings would it touch by its insincerity? The tones were insincere, but there was passion behind them; and most often passion acts its own true character poorly, and consciously enough to make good judges think it a mere counterfeit. Hamlet, being a little mad, feigned madness. It is when I am angry that I pretend to be angry, so as to present the truth in an obvious and intelligible form. Thus even before the words were distinguishable it was

manifest that they were spoken by a man in serious trouble who
had false ideas as to what is convincing in elocution.

When the voice became audibly articulate, it proved to be
shouting blasphemies from the broad chest of a middle-aged
man — an Italian of the type that grows stout and wears
whiskers. The man was in *bourgeois* dress, and he stood with
his hat off in front of the small station building, shaking his
thick fist at the sky. No one was on the platform with him
except the railway officials, who seemed in doubt as to their
duties in the matter, and two women. Of one of these there
was nothing to remark except her distress. She wept as she
stood at the door of the waiting-room. Like the second woman,
she wore the dress of the shopkeeping class throughout Europe,
with the local black lace veil in place of a bonnet over her
hair. It is of the second woman — O unfortunate creature! —
that this record is made — a record without sequel, without
consequence; but there is nothing to be done in her regard
except so to remember her. And thus much I think I owe after
having looked, from the midst of the negative happiness that
is given to so many for a space of years, at some minutes of her
despair. She was hanging on the man's arm in her entreaties
that he would stop the drama he was enacting. She had wept
so hard that her face was disfigured. Across her nose was the
dark purple that comes with overpowering fear. Haydon saw
it on the face of a woman whose child had just been run over in
a London street. I remembered the note in his journal as the
woman at Via Reggio, in her intolerable hour, turned her head
my way, her sobs lifting it. She was afraid that the man would
throw himself under the train. She was afraid that he would
be damned for his blasphemies; and as to this her fear was
mortal fear. It was horrible, too, that she was humpbacked and
a dwarf.

Not until the train drew away from the station did we lose
the clamour. No one had tried to silence the man or to soothe
the woman's horror. But has any one who saw it forgotten her
face? To me for the rest of the day it was a sensible rather than
a merely mental image. Constantly a red blur rose before my

eyes for a background, and against it appeared the dwarf's head, lifted with sobs, under the provincial black lace veil. And at night what emphasis it gained on the boundaries of sleep! Close to my hotel there was a roofless theatre crammed with people, where they were giving Offenbach. The operas of Offenbach still exist in Italy, and the little town was placarded with announcements of *La Bella Elena*. The peculiar vulgar rhythm of the music jigged audibly through half the hot night, and the clapping of the town's-folk filled all its pauses. But the persistent noise did but accompany, for me, the persistent vision of those three figures at the Via Reggio station in the profound sunshine of the day.

LANDSCAPE

Waterfalls

'WE then went out to see a cascade. I trudged unwillingly, and was not sorry to find it dry.' Dr. Johnson was not often pleased, it seems, upon this tour in Wales in the company of 'my mistress' and her family, and the arid waterfall was no doubt a welcome incident, for the scenery had been tedious to his spirit. He made light of the mountains, and did not hesitate to propose a strange image to the fancy of his companions when he derided a river unlucky enough to come into the prospect: 'Why, sir, I could clear any part of it by a leap.' He rated very low the old house of Mrs. Thrale's family, though as a house it amused him more than any view. 'The addition of another storey would make an useful house, but it cannot be great.' The old parish clerk who, seeing Mrs. Thrale again, 'foolishly said that he was now willing to die', is no doubt justly rebuked; but so seems to be Mrs. Thrale herself: 'He had only a crown given him by my mistress.' Then there was that dispute on the Chester walls; and, first and last, Dr. Johnson was not found to be best of companions by the 'pretty woman' witty enough to 'add something to the conversation', with whom he himself would have been all content.

There is reason to think that scenery in those days was rather unfairly and dully insisted upon as a matter of taste. 'Dispositions of wood and water' were the subjects of a kind of expert study, and it is easy to understand what a bore a landscape might become under the eye of a judge. Miss Austen shows a distinct tendency to bring water, rising ground, and well-wooded slopes under review. If a modern mansion has been erected, with ignorance, in too low a situation, she has an instant eye for the barbarism. The shrubberies, the curving carriage drives, the conifers, the farm-buildings, if any, duly planted out, come under the rapid approval of an elegant mind, and so does the far prospect no less. The distance is declared to be in harmony with the demands of a lover of nature; and as you read you can hardly think of the scenery as thrilled with summer wind, or believe that its miles would mark human feet with dust, or would be measured by the wavering rods of human weariness, or subject to any incidents except those of a careful engraving. There is some charm in the false-classical landscape of that time, merely looked back upon; but it would be something less than interesting to be presently in the company of people who talked much of the dispositions of wood and water. There is a certain way of looking at a view that affects one almost with dismay to hear of. When a professor of scenery asks you to enjoy what he always calls a peep, with several kinds of fir trees coyly betraying the way to it, there is little delight there; nor are cottages so pleasant when they, too, are said to peep; but this is a later and even a duller fancy. Landscape a hundred years ago had more dignity, though no more 'spirit in the woods'.

If the dispositions of wood and water allowed of a waterfall, it is impossible to imagine a more welcome addition at that day to scenery constructed, like Mr. Pecksniff's younger daughter, upon good principles. The cascade had not yet been made quite a common convention, for the 'picturesque' had not then come and gone, making dull in its passage, at least in art and in letters, the sallies of nature. To find a waterfall, in the right place, was in those days an elegant and natural joy; and it must have been no small disappointment to see Dr. Johnson trudging unwillingly. But no doubt there had been too much said.

Taste, always so nearly in peril of derogation, and, in fact, so quickly, according to all experience, dimmed by habit, has done wrong, by its weak preferences, to all the flowers of scenery — not to the actual flowers of vegetation only, though these have long been turned to the basest uses of all decoration — but to the other outbreaks of the movement and vitality of earth. The white tops of mountains and the climax of storms, forests in their utmost leaf, waves at the crest, the clouds of sunset newly on fire, waters in haste — what a gathering of blossoms is this from the summits of the world, whether on heights or on plains! Light and sound seem to be set free by the mere resounding thought of so much fruition. But, for their all-intelligible beauty, these crowns of things were long tossed together for the use of any one who so much as knew their names, and not the less cheaply because the language of description grew to be more subtle, more expert, and more poetic. Soon that expert quality also became, as it were, the waste and refuse of literature.

Waterfalls, then have been too much in use. Not only by the travelling party of the Thrales have they been proposed too pressingly to admiration. They cannot be restored at second hand to their dignity. A very great man might restore them to his readers by a word, but no one of less authority than his need to begin to take the trouble to look for it. The right course is to see them where they are, and to let the literature of the matter rest. Any phrase written here in praise of waterfalls — if such should escape — is not intended to do more than point the way whither the traveller may trudge if he will. Norway and the Pyrenees keep for us the surprise of perpetually new waters drawing to the ancient fall.

The Alps, even, have many a slender stream, perhaps bearing no name, and certainly known by no names out of sight of their nearest peaks, that are remembered in their solitude, or at least recognized at each return of the traveller, where they drop, hushed by their distance as much as by the noisy train. There is one, for instance, seen for but a moment, that has so long a fall as to grow weak and to swing in all the light winds. The strong stem of the cascade springs from the bed of its upland stream; and as from a strong stem a sapling wavers upwards, entangled at last in all breezes, so the dropping brook wavers downwards to its last and lighter motion.

Waterfalls that are turned to torrents have not been so much the subject of the landscape of convention. Their wildness did not so take the general fancy when conventions were made; but they are the vitality of the mountains. Theirs is an expression of movement so great that all the Alpine region seems to manifest its life only by these noisy valleys. All communications, all signals and messages of the range, hasten in and out by these brilliant cataracts, one in the depth of every ravine.

They are not only the traffic and the mission of their mountains, the coursing of that cold blood and the pulse of the rock, but they carry the mountain spirit far out. There is no country under mountains but has its quietness awakened by wilder rivers than other lands are watered by. When the range is out of sight, the torrents are still hasty, cataract below cataract, shallow and clear, quick from the impulse of waterfalls. No loitering rivers in earthy beds keep level banks in those plains that have their horizon lifted by the line of great mountains; no silent rivers.

If the torrent runs dry, there is no one to be vexed by the silence. Dr. Johnson would not, perhaps, be asked to trudge for the sake of the rough charms of a mere torrent; but even if the disposition of wood and water comprised a torrent, he would have no revenge for his literary weariness in seeing his guide abashed. For a dry torrent is a most beautiful wreck, the ruin of a splendid progress and procession, of which the leader, when he went by, did not pass unknown. Such are the wide watercourses of the valleys in the Canton de Vaud, the colour of their innumerable stones a bright daylight grey, and the threads of water of their time of drought rippling just audibly by night.

Not all waterfalls make the conspicuous show of the cascades that take their leap from the rocks. In early autumn there is nothing fresher or sweeter than the minute, perpetual waterfall that hides in moss and undergrowth, and slips everywhere from the Alps. The air is nowhere silent, and hardly a blade of grass is unstirred by the delicate thrill of water. Without paths it drops minutely and invisibly into the lakes, the gentlest of all the signs of the barren and lofty snow.

The Lesson of Landscape

THE landscape, like our literature, is apt to grow and to get itself formed under too luxurious ideals. This is the evil work of that *little more* which makes its insensible but persistent additions to styles, to the arts, to the ornaments of life — to nature, when unluckily man becomes too explicitly conscious of her beauty, and too deliberate in his arrangement of it. The landscape has need of moderation, of that fast-disappearing grace of unconsciousness, and, in short, of a return towards the ascetic temper. The English way of landowning, above all, has made for luxury. Naturally the country is fat. The trees are thick and round — a world of leaves; the hills are round; the forms are all blunt; and the grass is so deep as to have almost the effect of snow in smoothing off all points and curving away all abruptness. England is almost as blunt as a machine-made moulding or a piece of Early Victorian cast-iron work. And on all this we have, of set purpose, improved by our invention of the country park. There all is curves and masses. A little more is added to the greenness and the softness of the forest glade, and for increase of ornament the fat land is devoted to idleness. Not a tree that is not impenetrable, inarticulate. Thick soil below and thick growth above cover up all the bones of the land, which in more delicate countries show brows and hollows resembling those of a fine face after mental experience. By a very intelligible paradox, it is only in a landscape made up for beauty that beauty is so ill achieved. Much beauty there must needs be where there are vegetation and the seasons. But even the seasons, in park scenery, are marred by the *little too much*: too complete a winter, too emphatic a spring, an ostentatious summer, an autumn too demonstrative.

'Seek to have less rather than more.' It is a counsel of perfection in *The Imitation of Christ*. And here, undoubtedly, is the secret of all that is virile and classic in the art of man, and of all in nature that is most harmonious with that art. Moreover, this is the secret of Italy. How little do the tourists and the poets grasp this latter truth, by the way — and the artists! The legend of Italy is to be gorgeous, and they have her legend by rote. But Italy is slim and all articulate; her most characteristic trees are those that are distinct and distinguished, with lines that suggest the etching-point rather than a brush loaded with paint. Cypresses shaped like flames, tall pines with the abrupt flatness of their tops, thin canes in the brakes, sharp aloes by the road-side, and olives with the delicate acuteness of the leaf — these make keen lines of slender vegetation. And they own the seasons by a gentle confession. Rather than be overpowered by the clamorous proclamation of summer in the English woods, we would follow June to this subtler south: even to the Campagna, where the cycle of the seasons passes within such narrow limitations that insensitive eyes scarcely recognize it. In early spring there is a fresher touch of green on all the spaces of grass, the distance grows less mellow and more radiant; by the coming of May the green has been imperceptibly dimmed again; it blushes with the mingled colours of minute and numberless flowers — a dust of flowers, in lines longer than those of ocean billows. This is the desert blossoming like a rose: not the obvious rose of gardens, but the multitudinous and various flower that gathers once in the year in every hand's-breadth of the wilderness. When June comes the sun has burnt all to leagues of harmonious seed, coloured with a hint of the colour of harvest, which is gradually changed to the lighter harmonies of winter. All this fine chromatic scale passes within such modest boundaries that it is accused as a monotony. But those who find its modesty delightful may have a still more delicate pleasure in the blooming and blossoming of the sea. The passing from the winter blue to the summer blue, from the cold colour to the colour that has in it the fire of the sun, the kindling of the sapphire of the Mediterranean — the significance of these sea-seasons, so far from the pasture and the harvest, is imperceptible to ordinary senses, as appears from the fact that so few stay to see it all fulfilled. And if the tourist stayed, he would no doubt violate all that is lovely and moderate by the insistence of his descriptions. He would find adjectives for the blue sea, but probably he would refuse to search for words for the white. A white Mediterranean is not in the legend. Nevertheless it blooms, now and then, pale as an opal; the white sea is the flower of the breathless mid-summer. And in its clear, silent waters, a few days, in the culmination of the heat, bring forth translucent living crea-tures, many-shaped jelly-fish, coloured like mother-of-pearl.

But without going so far from the landscape of daily life, it is in agricultural Italy that the *little less* makes so undesignedly and as it were so inevitably, for beauty. The country that is formed for use and purpose only is immeasurably the loveliest. What a lesson in literature! How feelingly it persuades us that all except a very little of the ornament of letters and of life makes the dullness of the world. The tenderness of colour, the beauty of series and perspective, and the variety of surface produced by the small culture of vegetables, are among the charms that come unsought, and that are not to be found by seeking — are never to be achieved if they are sought for their own sake. And another of the delights of the useful laborious land is its vitality. The soil may be thin and dry, but man's life is added to its own. He has embanked the hill to make little platforms for the growth of wheat in the light shadows of olive leaves. Thanks to the métayer land-tenure, man's heart as well as his strength, is given to the ground, with his hope and his honour. Louis Blanc's 'point of honour of industry' is a conscious impulse — it is not too much to say — with most of the Tuscan contadini; but as each effort they make for their master they make also for the bread of their children, it is no wonder that the land they cultivate has a look of life. But in all colour, in all luxury, and in all that gives material for picturesque English, this lovely scenery for food and wine and raiment has that *little less* to which we desire to recall a rhetorical world.

Wells

THE world at present is inclined to make sorry mysteries or unattractive secrets of the methods and supplies of the fresh and perennial means of life. A very dull secret is made of water, for example, and the plumber sets his seal upon the floods whereby we live. They are covered, they are carried, they are hushed, from the spring to the tap; and when their voices are released at last in the London scullery, why, it can hardly be said that the song is eloquent of the natural source of waters, whether earthly or heavenly. There is not one of the circumstances of this capture of streams — the company, the water-rate, and the rest — that is not a sign of the ill-luck of modern devices in regard to style. For style implies a candour and simplicity of means, an action, a gesture, as it were, in the doing of small things; it is the ignorance of secret ways; whereas the finish of modern life and its neatness seem to be secured by a system of little shufflings and surprises.

Dress, among other things, is furnished throughout with such fittings; they form its very construction. Style does not exist in modern arrayings, for all their prettiness and precision, and for all the successes — which are not to be denied — of their outer part; the happy little swagger that simulates style is but another sign of its absence, being prepared by mere dodges and dexterities beneath, and the triumph and success of the present art of raiment — 'fit' itself — is but the result of a masked and lurking labour and device.

The masters of fine manners, moreover, seem to be always

aware of the beauty that comes of pausing slightly upon the smaller and slighter actions, such as meaner men are apt to hurry out of the way. In a word, the workman, with his finish and accomplishment, is the dexterous provider of contemporary things; and the ready, well-appointed, and decorated life of all towns is now altogether in his hands; whereas the artist craftsman of other times made a manifestation of his means. The first hides the streams, under stress and pressure, in paltry pipes which we all must make haste to call upon the earth to cover, and the second lifted up the arches of the aqueduct.

The search of easy ways to live is not always or everywhere the way to ugliness, but in some countries, at some dates, it is the sure way. In all countries, and at all dates, extreme finish compassed by hidden means must needs, from the beginning, prepare the abolition of dignity. This is easy to understand, but it is less easy to explain the ill-fortune that presses upon the expert workman, in search of easy ways to live, all the ill-favoured materials, makes them cheap for him, makes them serviceable and effectual, urges him to use them, seal them, and inter them, turning the trim and dull completeness out to the view of the daily world. It is an added mischance. Nor, on the other hand, is it easy to explain the beautiful good luck attending the simpler devices which are, after all, only less expert ways of labour. In those happy conditions, neither from the material, suggesting to the workman, nor from the workman looking askance at his unhandsome material, comes a first proposal to pour in cement and make fast the underworld, out of sight. But fate spares not that suggestion to the able and the unlucky at their task of making neat work of the means, the distribution, the traffic of life.

The springs, then, the profound wells, the streams, are of all the means of our lives those which we should wish to see open to the sun, with their waters on their progress and their way to us; but, no, they are lapped in lead.

King Pandion and his friends lie not under heavier seals.

Yet we have been delighted, elsewhere, by open floods. The hiding-place that nature and the simpler crafts allot to the waters of wells are, at their deepest, in communication with the open sky. No other mine is so visited; for the noonday sun himself is visible there; and it is fine to think of the waters of this planet, shallow and profound, all charged with shining suns, a multitude of waters multiplying suns, and carrying that remote fire, as it were, within their unalterable freshness. Not a pool without this visitant, or without passages of stars. As for the wells of the Equator, you may think of them in their last recesses as the daily bathing-places of light; a luminous fancy is able so to scatter fitful figures of the sun, and to plunge them in thousands within those deeps.

Round images lie in the dark waters, but in the bright waters the sun is shattered out of its circle, scattered into waves, broken across stones, and rippled over sand; and in the shallow rivers that fall through chestnut woods the image is mingled with the mobile figures of leaves. To all these waters the agile air has perpetual access. Not so can great towns be watered, it will be said with reason; and this is precisely the ill-luck of great towns.

Nevertheless, there are towns, not, in a sense, so great, that have the grace of visible wells; such as Venice, where every *campo* has its circle of carved stone, its clashing of dark copper on the pavement, its soft kiss of the copper vessel with the surface of the water below, and the cheerful work of the cable.

Or the Romans knew how to cause the parted floods to measure their plain with the strong, steady, and level flight of arches from the watersheds in the hills to the arid city; and having the waters captive, they knew how to compel them to take part, by fountains, in this Roman triumph. They had the wit to boast thus of their brilliant prisoner.

None more splendid came bound to Rome, or graced captivity with a more invincible liberty of the heart. And the captivity and the leap of the heart of the waters have outlived their captors. They have remained in Rome, and have remained alone. Over them the victory was longer than empire, and their thousands of loud voices have never ceased to confess the conquest of the cold floods, separated long ago, drawn one by one, alive, to the head and front of the world.

Of such a transit is made no secret. It was the most manifest fact of Rome. You could not look to the city from the mountains or to the distance from the city without seeing the approach of those perpetual waters — waters bound upon daily tasks and minute services. This, then, was the style of a master, who does not lapse from 'incidental greatness', has no mean precision, out of sight, to prepare the finish of his phrases, and does not think the means and the approaches are to be plotted and concealed. Without anxiety, without haste, and without misgiving are all great things to be done, and neither interruption in the doing nor ruin after they are done finds anything in them to betray. There was never any disgrace of means, and when the world sees the work broken through there is no disgrace of discovery. The labour of Michelangelo's chisel, little more than begun, a Roman structure long exposed in disarray — upon these the light of day looks full, and the Roman and the Florentine have their unrefuted praise.

Solitudes

THE wild man is alone when he wills, and so is the man for whom civilization has been kind. But there are the multitudes to whom civilization has given little but its reaction, its rebound, its chips, its refuse, its shavings, sawdust, and waste, its failures; to them solitude is a right forgone or a luxury unattained; a right forgone, we may name it, in the case of the nearly savage, and a luxury unattained in the case of the nearly refined. Thus has the movement of the world thronged together into some blind by-way. Their share in the enormous solitude which is the common, unbounded, and virtually illimitable possession of all mankind has lapsed, unclaimed.

They do not know it is theirs. Of many of their kingdoms they are ignorant, but of this most ignorant. They have not guessed that they own for every man a space inviolate, a place of un-hidden liberty and of no obscure enfranchisement. They do not claim even the solitude of closed corners, the narrow privacy of lock and key. Nor could they command so much.

For the solitude that has a sky and a horizon they do not know how to wish. It lies in a perpetual distance. Eng-land has leagues of it, landscapes of it, verge beyond verge, a thousand thousand places in the woods, and on uplifted hills. Or rather, solitudes are not to be measured by miles; they are to be numbered by days. They are freshly and freely the dominion of every man for the day of his possession. There is loneliness for innumerable solitaries. As many days as there are in all the ages, so many solitudes are there for men. This is the open house of the earth. No one is refused. Nor is the space shortened or the silence marred because, one by one, men in multitudes have been alone there before. Solitude is separate experience. Nay, solitudes are not to be numbered by days, but by men themselves. Every man of the living and every man of the dead might have had his 'privacy of light'.

It needs no park. It is to be found in the merest working country; and a thicket may be as secret as a forest. It is not so difficult to get for a time out of sight and earshot. Even if your solitude be enclosed, it is still an open solitude, so there be 'no cloister for the eyes', and a space of far country or a cloud in the sky be privy to your hiding-place. But the best solitude does not hide at all. This the people who have drifted together into the streets live whole lives and never know. Do they suffer from their deprivation of even the solitude of the hiding-place? There are many who never have a whole hour alone. They live in reluctant or indifferent companionship, as people do in a boarding-house, by paradoxical choice, familiar with one another and not intimate. They live under careless observation and subject to a cold curiosity. There is the in-voluntary and perhaps the unconscious loss which is futile and barren.

One knows the men, and the many women, who have sacrificed all their solitude to the perpetual society of the school, the cloister, or the hospital-ward. They walk without secrecy, candid, simple, visible, without moods, unchangeable, in a constant communication and practice of action and speech. Theirs assuredly is no barren or futile loss, and they have a conviction, and they bestow the conviction, of solitude deferred.

Who has painted solitude so that the solitary seemed to stand alone and inaccessible? There is the loneliness of the shepherdess in many a drawing of Millet. The little figure is away, aloof. The girl stands so when the painter is gone. She waits so on the sun for the closing of the hours of pasture. Millet has her as she looks, out of sight.

And, although solitude is a prepared, secured, defended, elaborate possession of the rich, they too may deny themselves the natural solitude of a woman with a child. A newly born child is often so nursed and talked about, handled and jolted and carried about by aliens, and there is so much importunate service going forward, that a woman is hardly alone long enough to feel, in silence and recollection, how her own blood moves separately, beside her, with another rhythm and different pulses. All is commonplace until the doors are closed upon the two. This unique intimacy is a profound retreat, an absolute seclusion. It is more than single solitude, it is a multiplied isolation more remote than mountains, safer than valleys, deeper than forests, and further than mid-sea. That solitude partaken — the only partaken solitude in the world — is the Point of Honour of ethics. Treachery to that obligation and a betrayal of that confidence might well be held to be the least pardonable of all crimes. There is no innocent sleep so innocent as sleep shared between a woman and a child, the little breath hurrying beside the longer, as a child's foot runs. But a favourite crime of the modern sentimentalist is that of a woman against her child. Her power, her intimacy, her opportunity, that should be her accusers, excuse her.

A conventional park is by no means necessary for the preparation of a country solitude. Indeed, to make those far and wide and long approaches and avenues to peace seems to be a denial of the accessibility of what should be so simple. A step, a pace or so aside, is enough to lead thither. Solitude is not for a lifetime, but for intervals. A park insists too much, and, besides, does not insist very sincerely. In order to fulfil the apparent professions and to keep the published promise of a park, the owner thereof should be a lover of long seclusion or of a very life of loneliness. He should have gained the state of solitariness which is a condition of life quite unlike any other. The traveller who may have gone astray in countries where there is an almost life-long solitude possible is aware how invincibly apart are the lonely figures he has seen in desert places there. Their loneliness is broken by his passage, it is true, but hardly so to them. They look at him, but they are not aware that he looks at them. Nay, they look at him as though they were invisible. Their un-selfconsciousness is absolute; it is in the wild degree. They are solitaries, body and soul. Even when they are curious, and turn to watch the passer-by, they are essentially alone. Now, no one ever found that attitude in a squire's figure, or that look in any country gentleman's eyes. The squire is not a lifelong solitary. He never bore himself as though he were invisible. He never had the impersonal ways of a herdsman in the remoter Apennines, with a blind, blank hut in the rocks for his dwelling. Millet would not even have taken him as a model for a solitary in the briefer and milder sylvan solitudes of France. And yet nothing but a life-long, habitual, and wild solitariness would be quite proportionate to a park of any magnitude.

If there is a look of human eyes that tells of perpetual loneliness, so there is also the familiar look that is the sign of perpetual crowds. It is the London expression, and, in its way, the Paris expression. It is the quickly caught, though not interested look, the dull but ready glance of those who do not know of their forfeited place apart; who have neither the open secret nor the close, neither liberty nor the right of lock and key; no reserve, no need of refuge, no flight nor impulse of flight; no moods but what they may brave out in the street, no hope of news from solitary counsels. Even in many men and women who have all their rights over all the solitudes — solitudes of closed doors and territorial solitudes of sward and forest — even in these who have enough solitudes to fulfil the wants of a city, even in these is found, not seldom, the look of the street.

Walls

A SINGULAR love of walls is mine; perhaps because of long living in London, with its too many windows and too few walls, the city which of all capitals takes least visible hold upon the ground. Walls, blank and strong, reaching outward at the base, are a satisfaction to the eyes teased by the inexpressive peering of windows, by that weak lapse and shuffling which is the London 'area'. In a world where iron rails multiply and walls grow fewer it may be asked: has some early legend of affection — memory of the day when a wall, signed with seasons, visited by the alighting of seedlings and drift of sunny air, was known at close quarters to the eyes of a child — has such a tradition of antiquity much to do with the love of vanishing walls? For railings with their open-work are all unwelcome, although the season of spring has for one of its charms the translucent open-work of trees that lets the skies pass through, and fails to take them in its net. Spring threads increasing green with brightening skies, scatters the skies, leads them through the woods, shows them the way of the hollow lanes, and lets them walk the garden of the earth.

Needless perhaps to say, the new Italy and the new Rome hankered after railings. To have railings and *uno square* has not been the least among the national aspirations. And in nothing was the recasting of Rome achieved with a more definite purpose than in the demolition of walls. It is a painful thing to their constant lover to see them hewn down where they were wont to gather houses close in fortified village and hill town. Florentine walls — we have seen these fall; and not only the lofty and brown town walls that kept the fireflies out and were touched on the countryside by blossoms on the branch, but the lesser walls of narrow paths. No longer do these climb with cypresses, and toss the sunshine into the shade, so that the grey stones look clear as water, and all shadows shine. Even a northern summer bandies the hollow lights from red wall to red wall, and this inter-radiance is the beauty of all strait streets.

There is no kind of landscape, however busy, where the sun does not shine with a fine simplicity upon simple walls. White walls are the earthly clouds. They withstand the sun. For, as the sunshine that would go astray in the blue is brought to a halt upon a brilliant cloud, so the sunshine that would go wide into the distances of green landscape, turns against the barrier of the fort or town, the long sea-wall, or the wall of the small white house. They arrest the rays in ranks, turn them like a flying host, and show to the coloured world how white looks in the kindred light.

The masonry of man has strengthened some countries with those white boundaries. They make the simplicity of a ploughed and planted countryside. Where the land is a land of rocks the walls lay a strong and orderly grasp upon the peaks, and look calmer than eternal hills. Who has not felt the locks and bars of the simple horizontal walls of Monte Cassino, as you first see the hill from a distance, on the way to Naples? The height is lost, and the solitude gone, when you find the station at the foot; but from afar, among the fragments of Apennines, the unbroken long walls of man have an effect of mastery upon the sharp summits. Length rather than height seems always to be the proper beauty of a wall, and therewith thickness, which — in their measure — the door must have, the window-frame, the window-bar, and everything that man adds to the world. With a pardonable fanaticism I am inclined to answer when there is a question as to orders of architecture, 'Oh I am for the thick!' as though all history, shape, spirit, and evolution, height and aspect, were, beside thickness, of little moment.

Even little white walls have their strange and significant looks in the country in a summer early morning, or on the border of the woods. On the white side of a closed house to the east Corot shows the thrill of dawn as Wordsworth saw it there rather than on his hills. Even the darkened walls of the Thames side served that mysterious turn. 'Dear God! the very houses——' The familiar word never stood ready, in its place, in more transfiguring light. So stands many a white wall in all the lights of day. White are the walls that smoothly lock the broken hills; white was the 'peaceful citadel', white the little town by river or sea-shore. White are such towns in their bays upon the profound Adriatic, white as shells; and whiter yet are the walls of the roofless East. The Norwich painters — masters of the great School of English landscape — knew the value of walls. Crome, Cotman, Wilson set them in the east of their evening landscapes, their dusty roads, and upraised them opposite to the light, like clouds.

A wall is the safeguard of simplicity. It lays a long level line among the indefinite chances of the landscape. But never more majestic than in face of the wild sea, the wall, steadying its slanting foot upon the rock, builds in the serried ilex-wood and builds out the wave. The sea-wall is the wall at its best. And fine as it is on the strong coast, it is beautiful on the weak littoral and the imperilled levels of a northern beach.

That sea-wall is low and long; sea-pinks grow on the salt grass that passes away into shingle at its foot. It is at close quarters with the tempestuous sea, when, from the low coast with its low horizon, the sky-line of sea is jagged. Never from any height does the ocean-horizon show thus broken and battered at its very verge, but from the flat coast and the narrow world you can see the wave as far as you can see the water; and the stormy light of a clear horizon is seen to be mobile and shifting with the buoyant hillocks and their restless line. The Dutch dyke has not that English aspect of a lowly parapet against a tide; it springs with a look of haste and of height;

and when you first run upstairs from the encumbered Dutch fields to look at the sea, you are apt, because of old rivalries, to make comparisons with England. Even the Englishman of to-day is apt to share something of the old national perversity that was minded to cast derision upon the Dutch in their encounters with the tides.

It was against a seaport fortress,[1] profoundly walled, that some remembered winter storms lately turned their great artillery. It was a time of resounding nights; the sky was so clamorous and so close, up in the towers of the stronghold, that I seemed to be indeed admitted to the perturbed counsels of the winds. The gale came with an indescribable haste, hooting as it flew; it seemed to break itself upon the heights, yet passed unbroken out to sea; in the voice of the sea there were pauses, but none in that of the urgent gale with its hoo-hoo-hoo all night, that clamoured down the calling of the waves. This storm tossed the wave and the stones of the sea-wall up together. The next day it left the waters white with the thrilling whiteness of foam in sunshine. It was only the Channel; and in such narrow waters you do not see the distances, the wide levels of fleeting and floating foam, that lie light between long wave and long wave on a Mediterranean coast, regions of delicate and transitory brightness so far out that all the waves, near and far, seemed to be breaking at the same moment, one beyond the other, and league beyond league, into foam. But the Channel has its own strong, short curl that catches the rushing shingle up with the freshest of all noises and runs up with sudden curves, white upon the white sea-wall, under the random shadow of sea-gulls and the light of a shining cloud.

[1] Dover Castle.

The Horizon

To mount a hill is to lift with you something lighter and brighter than yourself or than any meaner burden. You lift the world, you raise the horizon; you give a signal for the distance to stand up. It is like the scene in the Vatican when a Cardinal, with his dramatic Italian hands, bids the kneeling groups to arise. He does more than bid them. He lifts them, he gathers them up, far and near, with the upward gesture of both arms; he takes them to their feet with the compulsion of his expressive force. Or it is as when a conductor takes his players to successive heights of music. You summon the sea, you bring the mountains, the distances unfold unlooked-for wings and take an even flight. You are but a man lifting his weight upon the upward road, but as you climb the circle of the world goes up to face you.

Not here or there, but with a definite continuity, the unseen unfolds. This distant hill outsoars that less distant, but all are on the wing, and the plain raises its verge. All things follow and wait upon your eyes. You lift these up, not by the raising of your eyelids, but by the pilgrimage of your body. 'Lift thine eyes to the mountains.' It is then that other mountains lift themselves to your human eyes.

It is the law whereby the eye and the horizon answer one another that makes the way up a hill so full of universal movement. All the landscape is on pilgrimage. The town gathers itself closer, and its inner harbours literally come to light; the headlands repeat themselves; little cups within the treeless hills open and show their farms. In the sea are many regions. A breeze is at play for a mile or two, and the surface is turned. There are roads and curves in the blue and in the white. Not a step of your journey up the height that has not its replies in the steady motion of land and sea. Things rise together like a flock of many-feathered birds.

But it is the horizon, more than all else, you have come in search of; that is your chief companion on your way. It is to uplift the horizon to the equality of your sight that you go high. You give it a distance worthy of the skies. There is no distance, except the distance in the sky, to be seen from the level earth; but from the height is to be seen the distance of this world. The line is sent back into the remoteness of light, the verge is removed beyond verge, into a distance that is enormous and minute.

So delicate and so slender is the distant horizon that nothing less near than Queen Mab and her chariot can equal its fineness. Here on the edges of the eyelids, or there on the edges of the world — we know no other place for things so exquisitely made, so thin, so small and tender. The touches of her passing, as close as dreams, or the utmost vanishing of the forest or the ocean in the white light between the earth and the air; nothing else is quite so intimate and fine. The extremities of a mountain view have just such tiny touches as the closeness of closing eyes shut in.

On the horizon is the sweetest light. Elsewhere colour mars the simplicity of light; but there colour is effaced, not as men efface it, by a blur or darkness, but by mere light. The bluest sky disappears on that shining edge; there is not substance enough for colour. The rim of the hill, of the woodland, of the meadowland, of the sea — let it only be far enough — has the same absorption of colour; and even the dark things drawn upon the bright edges of the sky are lucid, the light is among them, and they are mingled with it. The horizon has its own way of making bright the pencilled figures of forests, which are black but luminous.

On the horizon, moreover, closes the long perspective of the sky. There you perceive that an ordinary sky of clouds — not a thunder sky — is not a wall but the underside of a floor. You see the clouds that repeat each other grow smaller by distance; and you find a new unity in the sky and earth that gather alike the great lines of their designs to the same distant close. There is no longer an alien sky, tossed up in unintelligible heights.

Of all the things that London has forgone, the most to be regretted is the horizon. Not the bark of the trees in its right

colour; not the spirit of the growing grass, which has in some
way escaped from the parks; not the smell of the earth un-
mingled with the odour of soot; but rather the mere horizon.
No doubt the sun makes a beautiful thing of the London smoke
at times, and in some places of the sky; but not there, not where
the soft sharp distance ought to shine. To be dull there is to
put all relations and comparisons in the wrong, and to make the
sky lawless.

A horizon dark with storm is another thing. The weather
darkens the line and defines it, or mingles it with the raining
cloud; or softly dims it, or blackens it against a gleam of narrow
sunshine in the sky. The stormy horizon will take wing, and
the sunny. Go high enough, and you can raise the light from
beyond the shower, and the shadow from behind the ray. Only
the shapeless and lifeless smoke disobeys and defeats the
summons of the eyes.

Up at the top of the seaward hill your first thought is one of
some compassion for sailors, inasmuch as they see but little of
their sea. A child on a mere Channel cliff looks upon spaces
and sizes that they cannot see in the Pacific, on the ocean side
of the world. Never in the solitude of the blue water, never
between the Cape of Good Hope and Cape Horn, never be-
tween the Islands and the West, has the seaman seen anything
but a little circle of sea. The Ancient Mariner, when he was
alone, did but drift through a thousand narrow solitudes. The
sailor has nothing but his mast, indeed. And but for his mast
he would be isolated in as small a world as that of a traveller
through the plains.

A close circlet of waves is the sailor's famous offing. His
offing hardly deserves the name of horizon. To hear him you
might think something of his offing, but you do not so when
you sit down in the centre of it.

As the upspringing of all things at your going up the
heights, so steady, so swift, is the subsidence at your descent.
The further sea lies away, hill folds down behind hill. The
whole upstanding world, with its looks serene and alert, its
distant replies, its signals of many miles, its signs and com-

munications of light, gathers down and pauses. This flock of birds which is the mobile landscape wheels and goes to earth. The Cardinal weighs down the audience with his downward hands. Farewell to the most delicate horizon.

The Childish Town

SUMMER night in an English village has not yet been painted in its extraordinary delicacy of colour, or with one half of its own simplicity. Bright cottage lights under a dark sky we know in pictures well enough, and also the glows of a departing day full of the warmth of a fugitive sunset. But the beauty of one hour of late dusk has perhaps been somewhat hidden by its own ambiguity. Not all the windows are lighted; not all the light is gone from the sky, not all local colour is effaced. Not all the pollard trees have lost their dusky green, and you can see far enough to follow the subtle curve that chance long ago gave to the dwarfish street, deep-roofed, thick-walled, and warm.

The little town grew once, and the movement of life and growth is expressed in that wavering line of street, slight as the rudder tail of a swimming fish. Our eyes cannot take swift perspectives, for soon the tender curve brings the white of a little wall trending away to close up the distance. Everything is closed with the peculiar closeness of English life. All the people seem to be put away under white seals, and there is no sign of them, except the few weak and lovely lights of windows closed by blinds or by some other gentle shade. There is hardly one star of naked flame in this by-street, only here and there a square of the most delicate thin light, liquid and cool, far too pale to be called golden, made beautiful by its relation to the blue of the profound cloud travelling from the west.

For the night is full of movement, and it seems as though the west wind itself blew the last daylight back against the east, streaming by water and wood. Nevertheless, so trim is the little street that it shows no sign of wind. It is closed against storm, light, and life; it stands low, solid, white, warmly covered, and with its trees pollarded. Not a bough, not a shutter, not a bird, not a child flutters or breaks bounds under the volleys of the cloudy wind. Nothing in the village moves except the groups of unequal chimes setting forth eastward with the fragments of the broken day, as successive clouds blow light, blow dark. Violet-blue air, the soft, soft whiteness of the floor of the street, the more distinct whitewash, the dark roofs, the uncertain green, the tender lights and simple and square — these colours of the August evening of a country town are colours of beauty without splendour.

There are no other sounds so appropriate, in its daytime, to the childish country-town as the voices of children. School hours seem to mark its long dusty day. There is never so much noise of wheels but that the childish sounds — calling, crying, laughing, and footsteps — are free to float up in the buoyant silence. The stature of children is proper to every street, for whereas St. Peter's is but an indifferent big church for people twelve feet high and their appropriate angels, and cities are measured for men as they are, the country-town had for its unit of height and breadth and length that of the child's body. The proportion is a child's, and the large roofs look as though you might pat the little township on the head. How otherwise should every man and woman walking into the shops and looking out of the upper windows look too large?

The country-town has all a child's own acquaintance with the soil. It loves to dig, and sits in the dust of the country road. There is nothing in this brief street that is not near. As you go by the little windows you are one of the family within. You rub shoulders with the eaves of unguarded cottages. You could touch almost all you see, as the little blank walls close in with the slight windings of the street. It is no doubt this simplicity of low walls, white and near, that helps so much the look of childishness. The great city has too many eyes for any intelligible expression. The light there is a spy darting in at a thousand

thousand holes in search of paltry secrets, and the houses are too eager with their publicity of windows. Moreover, what gives light to the inmates makes a darkness for the scenery, so that London looks so dark a town not only because of its smoky colour, but because of its almost continuous windows. This village has few windows, and many low sides of house-wall softly bright with whitewash, the thick and simple wall low and long under the ruddy brown of roofs of tile.

Needless to say, the best thing in the childish town and the village, of every size alike, is the strong hold they all have on the earth. Without 'areas' and without large shop-windows, the steady little houses show none of the ignominious weaknesses of cities. This is what brings the street so near. As you sit at breakfast in the small bow-window of the inn parlour, the wire blind puts you on intimate terms with the freckles of the schoolboys hunting lazy flies outside in the sun. The shadows of their heads darken your morning paper. Never before were you quite so close to the white hair of any old shepherd. He — too large for the little panes — trudges the pavement talking slowly about the market into your very ear. The little theatre is cramped. You fancy that by putting forth your hand you could help yourself to the distinct toys in the opposite toy-shop, with their reds and blues; and the splendid roses in the shallow windows breathe close to your breath. More rare are the roses, however, than red geraniums, yellow calceolarias, and the cottager's dearer fuchsia. This last flower, with its unfashionable elegance, its drooping 1830 graces out of date, dangles genteelly in the lowlier windows, white, purple, and red.

But the field has now fewer colours than the little urban garden. Where poppies grow, indeed, they make August splendid, scarlet in dark fields as well as in the pale or golden. A few water-lilies are still afloat, and the moss in the woods has the ancient freshness that owns no season. But August has chiefly dim flowers that bear the scent of gentle burning — by no means the smell of fading nor the humid odour of October, but the breath of drought. Roadside clematis, though still in flower, has this scent, and so have the ashes of privet in the hedges. Sweet dust is sprinkled on the wild-rose bushes, and the principal wayfaring flowers are a little yellow snapdragon and camomile daisies. But the principal work of the sun is the gilding of the wheat-fields. The country has a sunburnt cheek, and is hooded in that humble colour like a young Elizabethan loved and reproached at once for her brownness, by her poet. She must look to it that she be useful and kind — *bonne comme le pain*, as the French say — or we know of roses and lilies to rebuke her with.

You may see the wheat, oats, and barley, not only at the two ends of the streets of a childish town, but straight through the little houses. In the daytime, before that early sealing up, there is a visible sunny way, clear through every cottage. Not one of them makes a secret of its loaded back-garden and the clattering red-brick path leading thereto. White pinafores passing to and fro flash lights into the transparent shadows of the narrow house; the roofs, so low to the street, stoop lower still in the red backyards until their moss touches the hollyhocks, and beyond the nearest paling is the August country, with half the grain now in sheaves.

In the Village of Oberammergau

WHEN the King of Bavaria, who was Wagner's 'genius', gave a marble Calvary to his 'artistic and faithful Oberammergauers', they promised in return a mystery play every Sunday in summer for a named number of years. I was there in the September of 1905 — the last month of the last year of this bond. Though the King's gift had been in memory of his visit to the Passion Play, the drama that I saw enacted was not that play, but 'The School of the Cross'. It is a series of scenes from the history of David, each one followed by a living picture of that passage in the life of Christ, of which it is held to be the type. The leader of the chorus introduces the acts by an exhortation; and this and the dialogue are written in blank verse, like the English, except that nearly every line has a dissyllabic ending. The versification is perfectly regular, the diction good. The clergy of the village have supplied this grave 'book of the words', and no one except an Englishman, possessor of King James's version of the Bible, need complain of the quality of the paraphrase and extension of the Scripture.

Much has been said of the beauty of the Passion Play presented by simple peasant men and women bred in a byway of Bavarian hills. But little has been reported of their simple resolution to be conventional and classical. The sign and proof of their candour is not rudeness, but a docile civility which inevitably tends to the Renaissance and to 'taste'. What seemed to me strange and interesting, and rather a pity, is to find these earnest villagers, who are a trans-alpine people and altogether German, making their hamlet subject to the tradition of a classic Italy. The proscenium is painted with a monochrome of Michelangelo's Moses; pediment and pilasters are Italian; the attitude of the groups within is after a Milanese picture or a Tuscan; the grace is that of Raphael. We are reluctantly reminded of the drawing-master in Alfred de Musset's 'Proverbe', who besought his pupil to make oppositions of action: 'Arrondissez-moi les bras, Mademoiselle; et ayez soin de faire des oppositions.' The head should be turned to the left whenever the feet skimmed to the right. Is not nearly the whole of Raphael there? The people of this hamlet were as convinced that art and taste dwelt beyond their dark highlands as though the second Decline and Fall — that of the art of the south — had never taken place.

Jeremy Taylor recommends to him who prays the observance of 'the essential and ornamental measures of address'; and with both are the actors provided at Oberammergau. Their church is of a rococo character that outdoes the flutter and posture of Italy; and their theatre, which is the outer court of their church, though of graver art, still puts its trust in Italy. And, the while, the chorus-leader and David, Jonathan, Absolom, and Saul, Abiathar the priest and Sadoc, and

Goliath — a noble figure — speak their deep-chested German; and over the top of the classical proscenium looks the black summit of a melancholy German mountain, clouded, and pricked with pines.

'The crucifix always enthrals me', wrote Wagner on the day of Corpus Christi in 1859. He had just seen one in a tinsel procession in the streets of Lucerne. He had also seen the crucifixes of art, painted and graven, in all the schools — the figure crucified, and the figure to be crucified — in the Manger, at the Jordan, or in the Judgment Hall. In the valleys of Bavaria the Crucifix stands on the approaches to the scanty fields; and on every pointed hill, set with pointed trees, stands a cross. Far to the south, where the Alps unfold, valley by valley, towards Italy, every fold enriched, and the tedious pointed trees giving place to the hand-holding, dancing mulberries and their vines; and where the mountains look to the sun, and the streams run to him; — there also, on the long road dropping, with foaming rivers, towards Italy, the new light, the cisalpine light, shines upon a thousand-fold crucifix, hooded in the hollows of the hills, and lifted as high as the eye can see.

But after the representation of the 'School of the Cross', at Oberammergau, the images that are not living seem made in vain; and no more need be painted or graven, since the German villager held his breath for a while, or took it stealthily, in order to look like a painting of Christ. There is no other image so well worth having. There is nothing in any of the schools that so 'enthrals', to use Wagner's word. The image at Oberammergau is a person of noble aspect. The hamlet has dedicated its most perfect man to the Passion Play and the 'School of the Cross'; and he, with the utmost simplicity, keeps his brown locks of the length chosen by the painters, and so goes about his daily work, closer to God than is the altar crucifix, and made by German nature and Italian art in the image of Christ.

Not only in the symmetry of the Crucifixion, but in the accidents of every day, shouldering a burden, footing a rough journey in these hard hills, turning his lathe, or gathering a child upon one arm, he carries this perpetual likeness, and turns towards the world this aspect unaltered, until his years shall pass those of the Saviour, when another will take his place. The beating heart, the tide of blood move to the divine purpose, so that the image veiled or scattered among the crowd, distributed, broken, shattered, or grown dull, is gathered up in him, in order and continual consciousness.

He lives down the image made by Rembrandt for Emmaus, and that made by Tintoretto for Calvary. The art is theirs, the more than actual beauty, and genius speaks in them. But 'Ah,' the pilgrim remembers, 'there was a wild breeze in the mountains, and I saw the hair of Christ lifted, and His cincture fluttered. I saw His tired breast rise upon a breath.'

THE CHILDREN

Real Childhood

THE world is old because its history is made up of successive childhoods and of their impressions. Your hours when you were six were the enormous hours of the mind that has little experience and constant and quick forgetfulness. Therefore when your mother's visitor held you so long at his knee, while he talked to her the excited gabble of the grown-up, he little thought what he forced upon you; what the things he called minutes really were, measured by a mind unused; what passive and then what desperate weariness he held you to by his slightly gesticulating hands that pressed some absent-minded caress, rated by you at its right value, in the pauses of his anecdotes. You, meanwhile, were infinitely tired of watching the play of his conversing moustache.

Indeed, the contrast of the length of contemporary time (this pleonasm is inevitable) is no small mystery, and the world has never had the wit fully to confess it.

You remembered poignantly the special and singular duration of some such space as your elders, perhaps, called half an hour — so poignantly that you spoke of it to your sister, not exactly with emotion, but still as a dreadful fact of life. You had better instinct than to complain of it to the talkative, easy-living, occupied people, who had the administration of time in their hands — your seniors. You remembered the duration of some such separate half-hour so well that you have in fact remembered it until now, and so now, of course, will never forget it.

As to the length of Beethoven, experienced by you on duty in the drawing-room, it would be curious to know whether it was really something greater than Beethoven had any idea of. You sat and listened, and tried to fix a passage in your mind as a kind of half-way mark, with the deliberate provident intention of helping yourself through the time during a future hearing; for you knew too well that you would have to hear it all again. You could not do the same with sermons, because, though even more fatiguing, they were more or less different each time.

While your elders passed over some particularly tedious piece of road — and a very tedious piece of road existed within short distance of every house you lived in or stayed in — in their usual state of partial absence of mind, you, on the contrary, perceived every inch of it. As to the length of a bad night, or of a mere time of wakefulness at night, adult words do not measure it; they hardly measure the time of merely waiting for sleep in childhood. Moreover, you were tired of other things, apart from the duration of time — the names of streets, the names of tradesmen, especially the *fournisseurs* of the household, who lived in them.

You were bored by people. It did not occur to you to be tired of those of your own immediate family, for you loved them immemorially. Nor were you bored by the newer personality of casual visitors, unless they held you, as aforesaid, and made you so listen to their unintelligible voices and so look at their mannered faces that they released you an older child than they took you prisoner. But — it is a reluctant confession — you were tired of your relations; you were weary of their bonnets. Measured by adult time, those bonnets were, it is to be presumed, of no more than reasonable duration; they had no more than the average or common life. You have no reason, looking back, to believe that your great-aunts wore bonnets for great and indefinite spaces of time. But, to your sense as a child, long and changing and developing days saw the same harassing artificial flowers hoisted up with the same black lace. You would have had a scruple of conscience as to really disliking the face, but you deliberately let yourself go in detesting the bonnet. So with dresses, especially such as had any little misfit about them. For you it had always existed, and there was no promise of its ceasing. You seemed to have been aware of it for years. By the way, there would be less cheap reproving of little girls for desiring new clothes if the censors knew how immensely old their old clothes are to them.

The fact is that children have a simple sense of the unnecessary ugliness of things, and that — apart from the effects of *ennui* — they reject that ugliness actively. You have stood and listened to your mother's compliments on her friend's hat, and have made your mental protest in very definite words. You thought it hideous, and hideous things offended you then more than they have ever offended you since. At nine years old you made people, alas! responsible for their faces, as you do still in a measure, though you think you do not. You severely made them answer for their clothes, in a manner which you have seen good reason, in later life, to mitigate. Upon curls, or too much youthfulness, in the aged, you had no mercy. To sum up the things you hated inordinately, they were friskiness of manner and of trimmings, and curls combined with rather bygone or frumpish fashions. Too much childish dislike was wasted so.

But you admired some things without regard to rules of beauty learnt later. At some seven years old you dwelt with delight upon the contrast of a white kid glove and a bright red wrist. Well, this is not the received arrangement, but red and white do go well together, and their distribution has to be taught with time. Whose were the wrist and glove? Certainly someone's who must have been distressed at the *bouquet* of colour that you admired. This, however, was but a local admiration. You did not admire the girl as a whole. She whom you adored was always a married woman of a certain age; rather faded, it might be, but always divinely elegant. She alone was worthy to stand at the side of your mother. You lay in wait for the border of her train, and dodged for a chance of holding her bracelet when she played. You composed prose in honour of her and called the composition (for reasons unknown to yourself) a 'catalogue'. She took singularly little notice of you.

Wordsworth cannot say too much of your passion for nature. The light of summer morning before sunrise was to you a spiritual splendour for which you wanted no name. The Mediterranean under the first perceptible touch of the moon, the calm southern sea in the full blossom of summer, the early spring everywhere, in the showery streets, in the fields, or at sea, left old childish memories with you which you try to evoke now when you see them again. But the cloudy dusk behind poplars on the plains of France, the flying landscape from the train, willows, and the last of the light, were more mournful to you then than you care to remember now. So were the black crosses on the graves of the French village; so were cypresses, though greatly beloved.

If you were happy enough to be an internationally educated child, you had much at heart the heart of every country you knew. You disliked the English accent of your compatriots abroad with a scorn to which, needless to say, you are not tempted now. You had shocks of delight from Swiss woods full of lilies of the valley, and from English fields full of cowslips. You had disquieting dreams of landscape and sun, and of many of these you cannot now tell which were visions of travel and which visions of slumber. Your strong sense of place made you love some places too keenly for peace.

The Child of Tumult

A POPPY bud, packed into tight bundles by so hard and resolute a hand that the petals of the flower never afterwards lose the creases, is a type of the child. Nothing but the unfolding, which is as yet in the non-existing future, can explain the manner of the close folding of character. In both flower and child it looks much as though the process had been the reverse of what it was — as though a finished and open thing had been folded up into the bud — so plainly and certainly is the future implied, and the intention of compressing and folding-close made manifest.

With the other incidents of childish character, the crowd of impulses called 'naughtiness' is perfectly perceptible — it would seem heartless to say how soon. The naughty child (who is often an angel of tenderness and charm, affectionate beyond the capacity of his fellows, and a very ascetic of penitence when the time comes) opens early his brief campaigns and raises the standard of revolt as soon as he is capable of the desperate joys of disobedience.

But even the naughty child is an individual, and must not be treated in the mass. He is numerous indeed, but not general, and to describe him you must take the unit, with all his incidents and his organic qualities as they are. Take then, for instance, one naughty child in the reality of his life. He is but six years old, slender and masculine, and not wronged by long hair, curls, or effeminate dress. His face is delicate and too often haggard with tears of penitence that Justice herself would be glad to spare him. Some beauty he has, and his mouth especially is so lovely as to seem not only angelic but itself an angel. He has absolutely no self-control and his passions find him without defence. They come upon him in the midst of his usual brilliant gaiety and cut short the frolic comedy of his fine spirits.

Then for a wild hour he is the enemy of the laws. If you imprison him, you may hear his resounding voice as he takes a running kick at the door, shouting his justification in unconquerable rage. 'I'm good now!' is made as emphatic as a shot by the blow of his heel upon the panel. But if the moment of forgiveness is deferred, in the hope of a more promising repentance, it is only too likely that he will betake himself to a hostile silence and use all the revenge yet known to his imagination. 'Darling mother, open the door!' cries his touching voice at last; but if the answer should be 'I must leave you for a short time, for punishment,' the storm suddenly thunders again. 'There (crash!) I have broken a plate, and I'm glad it is broken into such little pieces that you can't mend it. I'm going to break the 'lectric light.' When things are at this pass there is one way, and only one, to bring the child to an overwhelming change of mind; but it is a way that would be cruel, used more than twice or thrice in his whole career of tempest and defiance. This is to let him see that his mother is troubled. 'Oh, don't cry! Oh, don't be sad!' he roars, unable still to deal with his own passionate anger, which is still dealing with him. With his kicks of rage he suddenly mingles a dance of apprehension lest his mother should have tears in her eyes. Even while he is still explicitly impenitent and defiant he tries to pull her round to the light that he may see her face. It is but a moment before the other passion of remorse comes to make havoc of the helpless child, and the first passion of anger is quelled outright.

Only to a trivial eye is there nothing tragic in the sight of these great passions within the small frame, the small will, and, in a word, the small nature. When a large and sombre fate befalls a little nature, and the stage is too narrow for the action of a tragedy, the disproportion has sometimes made a mute and unexpressed history of actual life or sometimes a famous book; it is the manifest core of George Eliot's story of 'Adam Bede', where the suffering of Hetty is, as it were, the eye of the storm. All is expressive around her, but she is hardly articulate; the book is full of words — preachings, speeches, daily talk, aphorisms, but a space of silence remains about her in the midst of the story. And the disproportion of passion — the inner disproportion — is at least as tragic as that disproportion of fate and action; it is less intelligible, and leads into the intricacies of nature which are more difficult than the turn of events.

It seems, then, that this passionate play is acted within the narrow limits of a child's nature far oftener than in a nature adult and finally formed. And this, evidently, because there is unequal force at work within a child, unequal growth and a jostling of powers and energies that are hurrying to their development and pressing for exercise and life. It is this helpless inequality — this untimeliness — that makes the guileless comedy mingling with the tragedies of a poor child's day. He knows thus much — that life is troubled around him and that the fates are strong. He implicitly confesses 'the strong hours' of antique song. This same boy — the tempestuous child of passion and revolt — went out with quiet cheerfulness for a walk lately, saying as his cap was put on, 'Now, mother, you are going to have a little peace.' This way of accepting his own conditions is shared by a sister, a very little older, who, being of an equal and gentle temper, indisposed to violence of every kind and tender to all without disquiet, observes the boy's brief frenzies as a citizen observes the climate. She knows the signs quite well and can at any time give the explanation of some particular outburst, but without any attempt to go in search of further or more original causes. Still less is she moved by the virtuous indignation that is the least charming of the ways of some little girls. *Elle ne fait que constater.* Her equanimity has never been overset by the wildest of his moments, and she has witnessed them all. It is needless to say that she is not frightened by his drama, for Nature takes care that her young creatures shall not be injured by sympathies. Nature encloses them in the innocent indifference that preserves their brains from the more harassing kinds of distress.

Even the very frenzy of rage does not long dim or depress the boy. It is his repentance that makes him pale, and Nature here has been rather forced, perhaps — with no very good result. Often must a mother wish that she might for a few years govern her child (as far as he is governable) by the lowest motives — trivial punishments and paltry rewards — rather than by any kind of appeal to his sensibilities. She would wish to keep the words 'right' and 'wrong' away from his childish ears, but in this she is not seconded by her lieutenants. The child himself is quite willing to close with her plans, in so far as he is able, and is reasonably interested in the results of her experiments. He wishes her attempts in his regard to have a fair chance. 'Let's hope I'll be good all to-morrow,' he says with the peculiar cheerfulness of his ordinary voice. 'I do hope so, old man.' 'Then I'll get my penny. Mother, I was only naughty once yesterday; if I have only one naughtiness to-morrow, will you give me a halfpenny?' 'No reward except for real goodness all day long.' 'All right.'

It is only too probable that this system (adopted only after the failure of other ways of reform) will be greatly disapproved as one of bribery. It may, however, be curiously inquired whether all kinds of reward might not equally be burlesqued by that word, and whether any government, spiritual or civil, has ever even professed to deny rewards. Moreover, those who would not give a child a penny for being good will not hesitate to fine him a penny for being naughty, and rewards and punishments must stand or fall together. The more logical objection will be that goodness is ideally the normal condition, and that it should have, therefore, no explicit extraordinary result, whereas naughtiness, being abnormal, should have a visible and unusual sequel. To this the rewarding mother may reply that it is not reasonable to take 'goodness' in a little child of strong passions as the normal condition. The natural thing for him is to give full sway to impulses that are so violent as to overbear his powers.

But, after all, the controversy returns to the point of practice. What is the thought, or threat, or promise that will stimulate the weak will of the child, in the moment of rage and anger, to make a sufficient resistance? If the will were naturally as well developed as the passions, the stand would be soon made and soon successful; but as it is there must needs be a bracing by the suggestion of joy or fear. Let, then, the stimulus be of a mild and strong kind at once, and mingled with the thought of distant pleasure. To meet the suffering of rage and frenzy by the suffering of fear is assuredly to make of the little unquiet mind a battle-place of feelings too hurtfully tragic.

The penny is mild and strong at once, with its still distant but certain joys of purchase; the promise and hope break the mood of misery, and the will takes heart to resist and conquer.

It is only in the lesser naughtiness that he is master of himself. The lesser the evil fit the more deliberate. So that his mother, knowing herself to be not greatly feared, once tried to mimic the father's voice with a menacing, 'What's that noise?' The child was persistently crying and roaring on an upper floor, in contumacy against his French nurse, when the baritone and threatening question was sent pealing up the stairs. The child was heard to pause and listen and then to say to his nurse, '*Ce n'est pas Monsieur; c'est Madame,*' and then, without further loss of time, to resume the interrupted clamours.

Obviously, with a little creature of six years, there are two things mainly to be done — to keep the delicate brain from the evil of the present excitement, especially the excitement of painful feeling, and to break the habit of passion. Now that we know how certainly the special cells of the brain which are locally affected by pain and anger become hypertrophied by so much use, and all too ready for use in the future at the slightest stimulus, we can no longer slight the importance of habit. Any means, then, that can succeed in separating a little child from the habit of anger does fruitful work for him in the helpless time of his childhood. The work is not easy, but a little thought should make it easy for the elders to avoid the provocation which they — who should ward off provocations — are apt to bring about by sheer carelessness. It is only in childhood that our race knows such physical abandonment to sorrow and tears, as a child's despair; and the theatre with us must needs copy childhood if it would catch the note and action of a creature without hope.

The Child of Subsiding Tumult

THERE is a certain year that is winged, as it were, against the flight of time; it does so move, and yet withstands time's movement. It is full of pauses that are due to the energy of change, has bounds and rebounds, and when it is most active then it is longest. It is not long with languor. It has room for remoteness, and leisure for oblivion. It takes great excursions against time, and travels so as to enlarge its hours. This certain year is any one of the early years of fully conscious life, and therefore it is of all the dates. The Child of Tumult has been living amply and changefully through such a year — his eighth. It is difficult to believe that his is a year of the self-same date as that of the adult, the men who do not breast their days.

For them is the inelastic, or but slightly elastic, movement of things. Month matched with month shows a fairly equal length. Men and women never travel far from yesterday; nor is their morrow in a distant light. There is recognition and familiarity between their seasons. But the Child of Tumult has infinite prospects in his year. Forgetfulness and surprise set his east and west at immeasurable distance. His Lethe runs in the cheerful sun. You look on your own little adult year, and in imagination enlarge it, because you know it to be the contemporary of his. Even she who is quite old, if she have a vital fancy, may face a strange and great extent of a few years of her life still to come — his years, the years she is to live at his side.

Reason seems to be making good her rule in this little boy's life, not so much by slow degrees as by sudden and fitful accessions. His speech is yet so childish that he chooses, for a toy, with blushes of pleasure, 'a little duck what can walk'; but with a beautifully clear accent he greets his mother with the colloquial question, 'Well, darling, do you know the latest?' 'The *what*?' 'The latest: do you know the latest?' And then he tells his news, generally, it must be owned, with some reference to his own wrongs. On another occasion the unexpected little phrase was varied; the news of the war then raging distressed him; a thousand of the side he favoured had fallen. The child then came to his mother's room with the question: 'Have you heard the saddest?' Moreover the 'saddest' caused him several fits of perfectly silent tears, which seized him during the day, on his walks or at other moments of recollection. From such great causes arise such little things! Some of his grief was for the nation he admired, and some was for the triumph of his brother, whose sympathies were on the other side, and who perhaps did not spare his sensibilities.

The tumults of a little child's passions of anger and grief, growing fewer as he grows older, rather increase than lessen in their painfulness. There is a fuller consciousness of complete capitulation of all the childish powers to the overwhelming compulsion of anger. This is not temptation; the word is too weak for the assault of a child's passion upon his will That little will is taken captive entirely, and before the child was seven he knew that it was so. Such a consciousness leaves all babyhood behind and condemns the child to suffer. For a certain passage of his life he is neither unconscious of evil, as he was, nor strong enough to resist it, as he will be. The time of the subsiding of the tumult is by no means the least pitiable of the phases of human life. Happily the recovery from each trouble is ready and sure; so that the child who had been abandoned to naughtiness with all his will in an entire consent to the gloomy possession of his anger, and who had later undergone a haggard repentance, has his captivity suddenly turned again, 'like rivers in the south'. 'Forget it,' he had wept, in a kind of extremity of remorse; 'forget it, darling, and don't, don't be sad'; and it is he, happily, who forgets The wasted look of his pale face is effaced by the touch of a single cheerful thought, and five short minutes can restore the ruin, as though a broken little German town should in the twinkling of an eye be restored as no architect could restore it — should be made fresh, strong, and tight again, looking like a full box of toys, as a town was wont to look in the new days of old.

When his ruthless angers are not in possession the child shows the growth of this tardy reason that — quickened — is hereafter to do so much for his peace and dignity, by the sweetest consideration. Denied a second handful of strawberries, and seeing quite clearly that the denial was enforced reluctantly, he makes haste to reply, 'It doesn't matter, darling.' At any sudden noise in the house his beautiful voice, with all its little difficulties of pronunciation, is heard with the sedulous reassurance: 'It's all right, mother, nobody hurted ourselves!' He is not surprised so as to forget this gentle little duty, which was never required of him, but is of his own devising.

According to the opinion of his dear and admired American friend, he says all these things, good and evil, with an English accent; and at the American play his English accent was irrepressible. 'It's too comic; no, it's too comic,' he called in his enjoyment; being the only perfectly fearless child in the world, he will not consent to the conventional shyness in public, whether he be the member of an audience or of a congregation, but makes himself perceptible. And even when he has a desperate thing to say, in the moment of absolute revolt — such a thing as 'I *can't* like you, mother,' which anon he will recant with convulsions of distress — he has to 'speak the thing he will', and when he recants it is not for fear.

If such a child could be ruled (or approximately ruled, for inquisitorial government could hardly be so much as attempted) by some small means adapted to his size and to his physical aspect, it would be well for his health, but that seems at times impossible. By no effort can his elders altogether succeed in keeping tragedy out of the life that is so unready for it. Against great emotions no one can defend him by any forethought. He is their subject; and to see him thus devoted and thus wrung, thus wrecked by tempests inwardly, so that you feel grief has him actually by the heart, recalls the reluctance — the question — wherewith you perceive the interior grief of poetry or of a devout life. Cannot the Muse, cannot the Saint, you ask, live with something less than this? If this is the truer life, it seems hardly supportable. In like manner it should be possible for a child of seven to come through his childhood with griefs that should not so closely involve him, but should deal with the easier sentiments.

Despite all his simplicity, the child has (by way of inheritance, for he has never heard them) the self-excusing fictions of our race. Accused of certain acts of violence, and unable to rebut the charge with any effect, he flies to the old convention: 'I didn't know what I was doing,' he avers, using a great deal of gesticulation to express the temporary distraction of his mind. 'Darling, after nurse slapped me as hard as she could, I didn't know what I was doing, so I suppose I pushed her with my foot.' His mother knows as well as does Tolstoy that men and children know what they are doing, and are the more intently aware as the stress of feeling makes the moments more tense; and she will not admit a plea which her child might have learned from the undramatic authors he has never read.

Far from repenting of her old system of rewards, and far from taking fright at the name of a bribe, the mother of the Child of Tumult has only to wish she had at command rewards ample and varied enough to give the shock of hope and promise to the heart of her little boy, and change his passion at its height.

Toys

EVEN when we are about buying for a child the pretty toy, one thing we always say — 'And yet children love their ugly old toys best.' It is not true, however, that children love ugly toys; they like homely toys, toys that can be clasped very close; and though homely does mean ugly, in the American and the obsolete English languages (because we would hurt a word rather than our ugly fellow-creatures' feelings), yet what children like in homeliness is precisely homeliness, something not too bright or good. Ugliness is dreadful to a child, especially at first sight. He may learn to love it in a dear parent or dear nurse, as the little boy evidently loves the bottle-nosed man in Ghirlandajo's delightful picture, but ugliness in a stranger is, in the strict sense, frightful. We are imposing our own sense of humour on children (as usual), and in its most ignoble form, when we give them grotesque toys. And as for guys, whereby we invert the natural veneration of images, the Fifth of November is a date which — for the sake of Sylvia — we all dread.

When Sylvia was three, she wept and shuddered great part of a day, and some part of a night, because a guy had suddenly faced her on the pavement. Now she is four she cons the difficult task of assuring herself 'They are boys, they are only little boys.' You may watch through her delicate face the horrible misgiving, the resolute reply, succeeding each other in that innocent, faltering breast. She says little of her fear, but gently leads the talk that way; and, when she is told that the boy-guys have each received a penny, her dear effort is to establish a human relation with them in her thoughts. 'Pennies for them to buy nice sweets,' she says to herself. There is the thing in common with her own beauty and tenderness and her little appetites: sweets, then boys — not devils.

But if we wrong our children by the grotesque we do so more commonly by the gift of the worthless toy, a thing that will not last. The doll is perhaps as significant as the statue, the gargoyle, the coin; it is generally worse than even the statue. The manufactured image of mankind given to our little girls to play with is not only ill-designed, but so fragile as to cause more weeping than joy. The doll of commerce is very heartlessly made so that she often goes to pieces on the very day of presentation. Her brief arm comes off first; it had been ineffectually glued on. Piecemeal she comes apart. She does not preserve such poor individuality as she had, long enough to get a name. She is never named, never grows old, never gets the love of habit, never ratifies the rapture of possession, never justifies the first kiss. A little time — at the best it is not long — is all that we of larger than dolls' growth have for that ratification and for that proof. Well, it is hardly moral that the child and the doll should kiss but for an hour.

Why, the personality of an honest doll ought to outlast her head — nay, several (resembling) heads. It was so with the dolls of an elder day and a simpler country. When one head was unfortunately walked upon, the old cook took the trunk and the pieces into the town, and matched the type of beauty — he was very grave and intent, without condescension, over the business. The face was renewed, but the name and the affection held on with a persistence that was almost worthy of party politics.

There have been charming toys in literature, but none much dearer to the reader of goodwill than the little horse which Esther Summerson gave to Peepy after one of his misfortunes — Esther, contemned by the readers who think to crush Dickens by one word, 'Sentimentality' (albeit this is an emotion that would be good for the majority, and the majority includes those critics), and by another word, 'Caricature' (caricature being nevertheless a most admirable art). Dickens, of all the greater masters of our national Letters, has the most perfect memory of childhood. Not by his strangely overpraised 'little Nell' is this proved, nor by any but certain brief passages of Paul Dombey, but in his much less famous children, and in the little fists of these are toys.

The Stranger's Children

'Do you bite your thumb at us, Sir?' 'I do bite my thumb, Sir.'
'Do you bite your thumb at us, Sir?' 'No, Sir, I do not bite my
thumb at you, Sir; but I bite my thumb, Sir.'

Across the 'backy-garden', at the rear of the house where the Children dwelt — the child of tumult, his luminous little dark sister, and the somewhat older ones — and over the young poplars from George Meredith's garden, ran a small street with shops and lodgings. It was very full of children, and sometimes they leant so far out of the upper windows that the question arose in the Children's home, Would a neighbourly present of nursery window-bars be received with little or with much contempt, or perhaps declined, and if so with offended feelings or without? The Children themselves did not encourage the project. The children at the back were very proud, they said. And how did they show the passion? it was asked. 'Well, mother, they come to the window, and black their boots at us.'

Of all the many surprises of childish replies, this was not the least. It was given in great gravity and good faith. To these young observers the action of their opposite neighbours admitted no other interpretation, albeit there had been no exchange of covert verbal defiances, such as, 'Do you black your boots at us?' 'We do black our boots.' 'Do you black your boots at us?' 'We do not black our boots at you; but we black our boots.' The demonstration was not of battle, as 'I will frown as I pass by, and let them take it as they list' — but of sole, sufficient pride, silent, detached, lifted between heaven and earth, at the second-floor windows of its appropriate street. It was not for a mere grown-up person to introduce doubts, or to suggest how far from the usual manifestations of pride, how different from its customary pomps, is the symbolism of blacking and of boots. No doubt the children were right, and declined our symbolism on their own good authority.

Their conclusion as to the boots had probably its own obscure justification, and was not due to unworthy suspiciousness, for the Children were disposed to friendliness, and would have inclined rather to a lenient than to a severe interpretation of the act of demonstrative blacking, had there been room for doubt. At a taller and quite remote row of windows appeared the heads of other children, of whom Pride seemed to have made no victims. At least there appeared among them no signs of blacking. With these the more usually intelligible language of toys was the means of communication. At long range — so long that a walking duck could hardly be distinguished from a mechanical alligator, and dolls looked as much alike as the heroines of a year's novels — toy was held up for sympathetic and companionable rivalry with toy; and across intervening roofs, by means that yet remain a mystery, the pet names of both batches of children had been announced and exchanged. Never was so enterprising and prosperous a friendship on facilities so slender. The delays, hesitations, and reserves of acquaintances begun in the ordinary ways, in houses, in Kensington Gardens, or otherwise on point-blank terms, never troubled these mutual advances. Or so it seemed. But with some surprise the mother of the Children, walking with them, perceived that they cast looks askance, neither wholly strange nor in any wise intimate, at another walking group, equally lowering, gloomy with an equal kind of un-avowed intelligence, and with an equally embarrassed mother. The children of Pride, walking in the street perhaps with those very boots new-blacked, could hardly have been watched with more sombre or more cloudy eyes. Afraid lest her young ones should have committed the *grossièreté* of making enemies, the mother of the Children asked them, in their unwonted silence, who it was that they seemed to be cutting. With surprise she then heard that these strangers, seen at full length, were they whose distant eager heads were invested with so much childish friendship in the windows under the skies. Within an hour or so after that unfriendly encounter, with its shadowy strangeness and vigilance of eyes, all was restored at the high back-windows, and a London sunset showed the ambiguous toys — new ones, just bought in the course of that walk estranged — the signalling hands, and the jostling heads unequal of height, at their former intercourse, candid, clear, familiar, and full of spirit and drama.

Distance seemed to set these gallant little creatures free from some of the disadvantages of the world and from the uneasiness of crowds. They were released in a world barely sprinkled with people within hail of one another, glad of recognition, and made friends by intervening space, and liberty partaken.

Perhaps it was the childish solitude that made the window-communication so clear. Almost painful to the writer is still the memory of introductions in childhood. Ah, to be placed in front of three little natives in white embroidery, and bidden to talk with them in Genoese, or in any human tongue, with parents artificially listening in compliment to the stranger's children, but solicitous for their own! There are moments that are literally difficult to live through, and this was of them. Solitude and a garden hedge between, or some such other slight defence and distance, and Genoese no doubt would have flowed.

Nor can one easily forget the unexpressed misgivings at those invitations to play with the stranger's children in the gardens of the Tuileries. It was already depressing enough to stand on a counter to be fitted, and to hear the *modiste* tell one's mother that one ought to have the *petit jupon bouffant* which one had not, and that no coat could have justice without it. But to be accosted, under this visible disability, by the children of Paris, little girls obviously furnished with the *petit jupon bouffant* — this was the cause of a dumb shyness. '*Veux-tu venir jouer avec moi?*' So ran the invariable invitation of the charming Parisians, little citizens so well civilized as to need no defences, no barriers, no return to the space and the distances of birds in search of primitive confidence, or to the rarity of angels in quest of natural courage. The English child kept in the after years of life the sense of national defeat that attended the consent to that unequal game. If Waterloo was won upon the playing-fields of Eton, it has been many times avenged on the playing-grounds of the gardens of the Tuileries.

Otherwise, and the conditions being more free and more nearly equal, to play with strangers, to play internationally, was a great delight. The game, being all dramatic, did away with any need for close knowledge of the actor. Since yonder boy was a spirited horse of uncertain temper, his temper as a boy was of small importance. There was no need even for names when all the players alike were terra-cotta pipkins for sale, to be known as sound or cracked by their voices under a blow. Quarrels never arose in these encounters of an hour.

Our playfellows were toys of the liveliest animation, but without so much perceptible character as might chance to ruffle our own. The concert of Europe was undisturbed.

One only remembrance is fraught with some self-reproach. It is that of two little English girls, who chose to frighten all the children of an Italian village and sweep the hill of them. It was done without malice, but with a horrid sense of dominance; and without violence except that of mere running. The population — sad to remember — was so gentle that its full number of children, of several ages, were thus to be hunted down the slopes of the chestnut-woods, by the onset of a couple of capricious foreign girls. But so it was. The day was a *festa*, and the children, carrying their shoes, strolled on the hill-side, between the cypresses and the belfries. All things go in unequal groups on such an afternoon — little companies of church-bell tunes, young men playing at bowls, no one alone. The village children loitered principally about the steep avenues to the church. But when the two slender invaders began to give chase, the first group scattered, and then the next, perhaps not knowing how little formidable were the hunters; then a third broke, a fourth wheeled. Young Italians do not run without clamour, and the outcry of the dismay of all those children seemed the wilder that the two pursuers kept their breath for the hunting. One swept the wood, another charged down the narrow road. They joined, they closed upon the quarry, or in open order cut off the escape of scattered fugitives. Of the little villagers there was not found one to resist, or so much as to question the attack. They cried out to each other, pointing the probable way to safety as they ran. That they must run was the one thing they were sure of, and they sped over rough and smooth, heads down, so that the heights were presently clear of them, and their last clamours dropped as they reached the shelter of the street, like the cries of birds that wheel and settle after an alarm. The two representatives of the predominant race, who cannot have measured nine feet between them, sat down in the conquered district, flushed with success. Alas!

The Influential Child

LOVE is not a mystery in Japan. It would not have been a mystery in Europe if a child — Dante — had not been in love. For mystery, religious and passionate alike, has its source and sanction in the heart of childhood. In like manner the love of Nature — of the landscape and the heavens — was a spiritual mystery in the boyish hearts of Vaughan and Traherne (repeated in that of their son and brother Wordsworth, the boy whom the cataract haunted like a passion). By these boyhoods, remembered very seriously in after-life, European literature has been converted to two mystical passions which, century by century, are its very life. Without those boyhoods these two loves might have been fervent, exalting, poignant, but not mysterious, not spiritual with the 'golden purity', the ignorant spirituality of childhood.

It is said that our European manner of romantic love (strictly speaking romantic) is scandalous to the Japanese. They can have had no Dante. And, in spite of their pleasure in blossoms — their annual popular tryst with cherry and chrysanthemum — it is doubtful whether the love of Nature has ever taken an illustrious or mysterious form with these little people. Their landscape art is gay, observant, and arbitrary; but it is — as far as an Occidental student can interpret it — not passionate. For landscape that proves a passion for Nature and for mystery — both the legacies of man's dead childhood — we must look to the great painters of two countries, France and England; to Turner, Wilson, Crome, and Corot, and thus especially to the country that produced the boyhoods of Vaughan, Traherne, and Wordsworth. Many a child of our race has received that early inspiration, and these men of early genius not only received and remembered but put it on such record as to make it thenceforward a part of our literature. It is accepted, it is orthodox, it is expected of our poets. And this orthodoxy, due to these great men, is due originally to these great boys.

But for them these wonders of childhood would have been forgotten, or put away as childish things, by sensitive spirits who had likewise experienced them. They would not, at any rate, have gained this high literary honour and this literary authority. As it is, we are not ashamed to remember what midsummer early morning was to us at nine years old, because literature gives us authority. The light to our adult eyes is lovely still, but the magic of its quality is gone, the memory remaining, or the memory of the memory, or perhaps no more than the grace of knowing that there was once a memory —

Not to forget that I forget.

It is their own landscape, their own hour, that moves children not to words but to emotions. Great views, I think, give them a more ordinary and grown-up pleasure; they do not love formal gardens, even Italian formal gardens; and on this point certainly the child is not the father of the man. But hill-sides in wild flower, calm summer seas, and those aspects and phases of landscape to which Tennyson gave his perfect word in return for a perfect emotion — these are wonderful to children. When Tennyson is restored, after the indiscriminate honour and the indiscriminate disesteem that have befallen him, to his own place, it will be because his sense of landscape, his sense of light and of sun, is like a child's.

As to Dante's love, the presence of an adult sentiment in a boy's heart — one should rather say in his soul and in the topmost places of his soul — is a heavenly incident of human history and therefore may be subject to the worst parody. I find, for example, an exceeding vulgarity in the coquetting of boys and girls in certain kinds of American stories. It is not a corruption of things innocent to evil; but it is the corruption of an extreme and lofty wisdom, and that corruption, I think, is silly.

Let us place next to Dante's sacred love for a child the love of a man not sacred but profane — a man in fiction, as the great genius of Emily Brontë conceived him. Heathcliff's tempestuous love for Catherine remains throughout the

horrible story a child's fresh love, even though Heathcliff
is worse than a man. And, albeit Catherine dies a woman,
it is to her childish ghost that he cries out of that window on
the heights before his own death; the ghost of a child, and she
has been long a dead woman, and he is old.

Injustice

CHILDREN have a fastidiousness that time is slow to cure. It
is to be wondered, for example, whether if the elderly were
half as hungry as children are they would yet find so many
things at table to be detestable. It is this childish dislike of
many foods and drinks that makes the once general rule of
thwarting the tastes of children somewhat cruel and more than
a little unsalutary. For the omnivorous parent some discipline
of this kind might not be amiss; but for a critical and dis-
criminating child it was tyranny. Charles Dickens, to whom
four or five generations of children have owed a quite incalcu-
lable debt, shows us Pip at the breakfast-table of Mr. Pumble-
chook. Dickens remembered, or imagined perfectly, the
thoughts hidden in a child's heart at the sight of the meal of
an elderly *gourmand*, who asks questions in arithmetic between
his mouthfuls while the child, on a very ascetic diet, has to
guess the answers. Dickens was so dramatic that he could not
see the sombre children of discipline observing while the
grown-up people ate, without thinking their thoughts; he
comes to the rescue of the desperate insufficiency of their own
expression.

Not only once, or twice, does he make their stature, their
protest and their lowering little vigilance his own. He knew
what the deprived child thought of him and of the other guests,
and he was the only guest who cared. That no one else seemed
to have any sensitiveness as to the daily incident of those
times says much for the robust unconsciousness of the old, and

is really wonderful. How was it that people who cared at all for any opinion should care nothing for the opinion of children because it was disguised in the manners they were compelled to wear? Burns cared somewhat for the ill-opinion of a field-mouse.

What an insensibility, too, to the after-judgments, to the memories put away for the future! Ruskin who has a certain unavowed pride in his early hardships, seems to admire his mother for depriving him of toys, and for making him peel the walnuts (of which he might never eat) for his father's portly guests. Well, as to health, walnuts for the elderly who had just dined must needs be worse than walnuts for the child who had dined long before. But if Ruskin, remaining, in his greatness, so much the boy of his mother, the son of his father, even the child of his nurse, in his lifelong duty to them, respected their administration, there is another author who some years ago delighted to write of himself chiefly owing to rancour against his aunts, long dead. A. J. Hare was a child of that unjust time. Many scores of later wrongs must have been, we must hope, forgiven by him during all the years in which he remembered the oppressors of his early years. That he was really oppressed he has left us no room to doubt; his uncles and aunts have not been permitted to rest in the world's oblivion — he has made a close record of their tyrannies. But he does not seize the heart of the matter as Dickens seizes it, reading in the urchin hearts of the children of his friends. Neither Victor Hugo nor George Eliot has written quite like Dickens, from within the boundaries of a child's nature, from a child's stage of progress, and without the preoccupation and attitude of older experience.

That children have to be taught self-denial is a truth that the self-indulgent youth, middle-age, and old-age now alive, and having children in charge, would blush to publish. Example is a good way to teach them. Our immediate forefathers did not teach that way, if we may judge from these records. They seem to have taught that self-denial was good for the innocent but not for the more or less guilty. Let us suppose then that they reasoned in this comfortable way: 'Children have a keen pleasure in life — among other things a perpetual appetite.' Here is the injustice, for children have a thousand distastes; things are tedious to them. We have no right to attribute to them a belief in fairies or an unwearied delight in bread and milk, things which are alien to their simple hearts. We have now learnt that the children should have many and various pleasures; and we shall perhaps give them their own when we no longer grasp so many kinds of delights for ourselves, and when we thus gradually reverse the older order and correct the newer.

If the French share their days and their dinners — perhaps their too abundant dinners too abundantly — with their children more than we do even yet, they have this in their favour — that no French Mr. Hare has so dealt with his aunts, or has had so much unsalutary trouble, brought about with infinite pains and deliberation, to outgrow and outlive as a memory the bitter things of life.

St. Monica did not impose all the fasting on the little St. Augustine. She took her share of it, and more.

Near the Ground

We lose, by mere growing, something of the good habit of familiarity with the old and fresh earth — the familiarity, especially, of the eyes and hands — that is the child's amends for his neglect of the sky. We hold our heads up — or we should do so — and lift our eyes to the horizon, and upwards from it, and to the tops of steeples and towers; but a child hardly looks up at all, or no higher than his father's face. It seems that many a grazing and labouring animal feeds through its last long day and draws its last load without having ever looked aloft. Some kinds lift their heads a little when they utter calls or cries, but those are moments of preoccupation, and their attention is not in their eyes.

The eyes of a child, if not so long and so unconsciously bent away as the animals' from the sources of light and darkness and of the rains, are still so little interested in the heights as to need the rising of a bird to show them the way cloudward. The bird leaves a branch shaken, and the hurry of the leaves makes a child look, and, before he is aware that his eyes have taken flight, they are captured by the lark into that unwonted liberty, and beguiled into the manumission of blue sky. The child's sight hardly rises but as an arrow following the bird.

Otherwise the little gaze of those untravelled eyes is busy at close quarters with their own matters. It is not in vain that the senses of children in their simplicity are familiar with delicate shows and scents. While we walk, breathing at the levels of lilac trees and hawthorn, they have to breathe the fresh and strange odour of moss in the woods. Nor is there a breath of the breathing undergrowth that does not find its way to the spirit of a child, to create memories there. Either those wild and most homely scents that are close to the ground have in themselves more significance than have all the richer sweets that blossom breast-high, or else it is their direct communication with childhood that makes them magical. A child without a sense of the earth would miss as much as a child — if one could be — without a sense of the past.

Children poring over the ground make friends of a thousand little creatures that the elders have long ago forgotten. The child knows the spiritual-rustic scent of small daisies, though probably a great number of grown-up people have not been for many consecutive springs at the trouble of smelling a quite small wild daisy; one poet has had so short a memory as to call the daisies 'smell-less'; and so with other kinds of growth. There are ways of the clinging of ivy, many-footed, to be known only on the terms of childhood, and so with the little animals that find their way in the green twilight of blades of grass. Their fortunes are watched by children, who are so near them, and who would — if they might but know something of the work in hand — think themselves happy to use their superior strength and larger outlook in helping the industries of little ants and beetles. This may never be; the errands of the hurry of insects are not to be shared. And even in his consciousness of greater size and all other human conditions, the child is aware of his own one disproportionate disadvantage — he knows well that the ants and beetles are grown up. Only in the business of feeding he finds that he can come to an understanding with all kinds, or nearly all kinds, of small animals, and be useful.

He finds a city of ants most pleasantly responsive; there are no mistakes or misapprehensions. Dear were the ants in a wide stone *loggia* long ago, where they came up through the cracks to take their crumbs in the sunshine, until Benedetta swept them with a besom of destruction, and said in reply to the weeping (and, too probably, the fists) of the children that the ants were not Christians. The little ants — the little grown-up ants, who had something of our respect for aunts, and among whom we perceived differences of size and of manners, were involved in indiscriminate slaughter, like soldiers.

It is at close quarters, near the ground of gardens and fields, that children learn to know the countries, the counties, the north, the south, the orient, and the occident. The country that children pore over is surely the country of memories for which men afterwards die. For this, rather than for any distant plains, or valleys, or even mountains (for which armies have been said to be most willing to take the field). The country that sent the breath and spirit of its earth into the little nostrils of children, that was known in tiny detail, that was known in that low region of the earthy air through which the elders pass with their covered feet — this has always been *patria*.

It is a loss never to have lived young in countries so warm that a child is allowed to feel the grass there with naked feet. For the feet also ought to have communication with the fields; they have their own sensation of flowers. Even as all the senses are distinct and different, and as it were a separate conception of the mind, so also are the sensibilities. They are not merely added ways of communion, they are all unique ways. To lack the sensibility of feet that might have been acquainted with various Nature, but that had their tenderness touched by nothing save dead sand at the seaside, is a little loss that one wishes the civilized child had not to undergo.

Children in Midwinter

CHILDREN are so flower-like that it is always a little fresh surprise to see them blooming in winter. Their tenderness, their down, their colour, their fullness — which is like that of a thick rose or of a tight grape — look out of season. Children in the withering wind are like the soft golden-pink roses that fill the barrows in Oxford Street, breathing a southern calm on the north wind. The child has something better than warmth in the cold, something more subtly out of place and more delicately contrary; and that is coolness. To be cool in the cold is the sign of a vitality quite exquisitely alien from the common conditions of the world. It is to have a naturally, and not an artificially, different and separate climate.

We can all be more or less warm — with fur, with skating, with tea, with fire, and with sleep — in the winter. But the child is fresh in the wind, and awakes cool from his dreams, dewy when there is hoar-frost everywhere else; he is 'more lovely and more temperate' than the summer day and than the winter day alike. He overcomes both heat and cold by another climate, which is the climate of life; but that victory of life is more delicate and more surprising in the tyranny of January. By the sight and the touch of children, we are, as it were, indulged with something finer than a fruit or a flower in untimely bloom. The childish bloom is always rare. The fruit and flower will be common later on; the strawberries will be a matter of course anon, and the asparagus dull in their day. But a child is a perpetual *primeur*.

Or rather he is not in truth always untimely. Some few days in the year are his own season — unnoticed days of March or April, soft, fresh and equal, when the child sleeps and rises with the sun. Then he looks as though he had his brief season, and ceases for a while to seem so strange.

It is no wonder that we should try to attribute the times of the year to children; their likeness is so rife among annuals. For man and woman we are naturally accustomed to a longer rhythm; their metre is so obviously their own, and of but a single stanza, without repetition, without renewal, without refrain. But it is by an intelligible illusion that we look for a quick waxing and waning in the lives of young children — for a waxing that shall come again another time, and for a waning that shall not be final, shall not be fatal. But every winter shows us how human they are, and how they are little pilgrims and visitants among the things that look like their kin. For every winter shows them free from the east wind; more perfectly than their elders, they enclose the climate of life. And, moreover, with them the climate of life is the climate of the spring of life; the climate of a March that is sure to make a constant progress, and of a human April that never hesitates. The child 'breathes April and May' — another April and his own May.

The winter child looks so much the more beautiful for the season as his most brilliant uncles and aunts look less well. He is tender and gay in the east wind. Now more than ever must the lover beware of making a comparison between the beauty of the admired woman and the beauty of a child. He is indeed too wary ever to make it. So is the poet. As comparisons are necessary to him, he will pay a frankly impossible homage, and compare a woman's face to something too fine, to something it never could emulate. The Elizabethan lyrist is safe among lilies and cherries, roses, pearls, and snow. He undertakes the beautiful office of flattery, and flatters with courage. There is no hidden reproach in the praise. Pearls and snow suffer, in a sham fight, a mimic defeat that does them no harm, and no harm comes to the lady's beauty from a competition so impossible. She never wore a lily or a coral in the colours of her face, and their beauty is not hers. But here is the secret: she is compared with a flower because she could not endure to be compared with a child. That would touch her too nearly. There would be the human texture and the life like hers, but immeasurably more lovely. No colour, no surface, no eyes of woman have ever been comparable with the colour, the surface, and the eyes of childhood. And no poet has ever run the risk of such a defeat. Why, it is defeat enough for a woman to have her face, however well-favoured, close to a child's even if there is no one by who should be rash enough to approach them still nearer by a comparison.

This, needless to say, is true of no other kind of beauty than that beauty of light, colour, and surface to which the Elizabethans referred, and which suggested their flatteries in disfavour of the lily. There are, indeed, other adult beauties, but those are such as make no allusions to the garden. I do but aver that the beautiful woman, widely and wisely likened to the flowers, which are inaccessibly more beautiful, must not, for her own sake, be likened to the always accessible child.

Besides light and colour, children have a beauty of finish which is much beyond that of more finished years. This gratuitous addition, this completeness, is one of their unlooked for advantages. Their beauty of finish is the peculiarity of their first childhood, and loses, as years are added, that little extra character and that surprise of perfection. A bloom disappears, for instance. In some little children the whole face, and especially all the space between the growth of the eyebrows and the growth of the hair, is covered with hardly perceptible down as soft as bloom. Look then at the eyebrows themselves. Their line is as definite as in later life, but there is in the child the finish given by the exceeding fineness of the delicate hairs. Moreover, what becomes, afterwards, of the length and the curl of the eyelash? What is there in growing up that is destructive of a finish so charming as this?

Queen Elizabeth forbade any light to visit her face 'from the right or from the left' when her portrait was a-painting.

She was an observant woman, and liked to be lighted from the front. It is a light from the right or from the left that marks an elderly face with minute shadows. And you must place a child in such a light, in order to see the finishing and parting caress that infancy has given to his face. The down will then be found even on the thinnest and clearest skin of the middle red of his cheek. His hair, too, is imponderably fine, and his nails not much harder than petals.

But another word of the child in January. It is his month for the laying up of dreams. No one can tell whether it is so with all children, or even with a majority, but with some children of passionate fancy there occurs now and then a children's dance, or a party of any kind, which has a charm and glory mingled with uncertain dreams. Never forgotten, and yet never certainly remembered as a fact of this life, is such an evening. When many and many a later pleasure, about the reality of which there never was any kind of doubt, has been long forgotten, that evening — as to which all is doubt — is impossible to forget. In a few years it has become so remote that the history of Greece derives antiquity from it. In later years it is still doubtful, still a legend.

The child never asked how much was fact. It was always so immeasurably long ago that the sweet party happened — if indeed it happened. It had so long taken its place in that past wherein lurks all the antiquity of the world. No one would know, no one could tell him, precisely what occurred. And who can know whether — if it be indeed a dream — he has dreamt it often, or has dreamt once that he had dreamt it often? That dubious night is entangled in repeated visions during the lonely life a child lives in sleep; it is intricate with allusions. It becomes the most mysterious and the least worldly of all memories, a spiritual past. The word pleasure is too trivial for such a remembrance. A midwinter long gone by contained the suggestion of such dreams. And the midwinter of every year must doubtless prepare for the heart of many an ardent young child a like legend and a like antiquity. For us it is a mere present.

INTRODUCTIONS
AND REVIEWS

Robert Herrick

A CERTAIN time of the seventeenth century is Herrick's, but Herrick is also the time's. He occurs, with his genius and simplicity, precisely when the language was simple and full of genius. It is as though English, in those few decades of years, had but to speak in order to say something exquisite; but then it must be with Herrick's tongue. His time is virtually between the Elizabethan age and that seventeenth century which fulfilled the promise of ages, and with its close brought a whole literature to an end. At times Herrick is purely, freshly, an Elizabethan, then again there is the riper and richer phrase of the mellower day. The silver sunshine of morning changes to the golden sunshine of afternoon, of the westering hours. 'Rise and put on your foliage!' he cries to Corinna in that poem which has so cool and so clear an Elizabethan note in its many lines, and the sentence has the conscious richness of the somewhat later time. This is but one example of the fuller, if not deeper, fancy of this riper time. Corinna's apparel — her foliage — may represent for us that more abundant fancy; but, to continue the similitude, there may be also for us a suggestion of regret for the slender leafage of the fresher Elizabethan reign, the time when some of the leaves were still in bud, and when the green was light.

Herrick follows generally the convention of his time, and writes of love, of beauty, of the country, of his own approaching old age, of his death, as did his contemporaries; we hardly know how much the clear poetic sincerity owed to his experience as a man. He certainly loved town, and he hated Devonshire, which was probably as far as he ever went from it; and he bravely breaks from the convention to tell us so. But soon he is back again at play with the praise of a country life, making a little ready-made boast of his frugal table and his content; but 'His Noble Numbers' surely carry a truer as well as a graver burden. In these fine poems he exerts himself to think; — always very simply, but still to think; he is no longer content with that mere utterance which with him is almost always so enchanting. He has thought out his plain religious position, and has undergone something in the change of thoughts. Here and everywhere in the several regions of his to-and-fro, limited, and repeated, little poetic walks, he has his own proper dignity, the dignity of his fortunate lyrical language.

For it is to the lyrical language — the vintage of a happy year, Herrick's year, that we return. It was a language not overcharged by the poets of the past, but charged to the right point. It bore the significance of the sixteenth century and earlier; it was capable of the 'golden pomp' of the late seventeenth, but the capacity was not yet filled. When Herrick speaks to his lady of 'the babies in her eyes', he uses a delightful phrase of which the sweetness is both his and the time's; and, we may add, the modern reader's in his place. 'Babies' are in sixteenth and seventeenth centuries what we call dolls. Shakespeare's 'baby of a girl' is merely a little girl's doll. If Herrick meant to give to the images in clear eyes, the name of dolls, we know not precisely; but we find the word babies exquisite and innocent; we refer the word to the lovelier poem of a modern poet, in which Coventry Patmore writes of eyes:

> In whose brown shade
> Bright Venus and her baby played.

This is the line of imagination and Herrick was perhaps not this — not more than the poet of fancy, but of poets of fancy the sprightliest, and — the word is not too great — the noblest.

The Mystical Lyric

ENGLISH literature, rich in love, in terror, in compassion, in gaiety, in sweetness, in human tragedy, is rich also in the divine comedy of the religious lyric. One of the truest poets of the nineteenth century has denied, in one destructive phrase, to the religious poet his high place not only in England, but in the world:

> From David unto Dante none,
>   And none since him.

But this must be heard with indulgence; for even so majestic a poet as Coventry Patmore does himself some wrong and has to take some pardon at our hands for too angry or even too indignant a judgment. English lyrists have not in truth lacked the love, the contrition, the mystery, or the mirth of religious poetry. They have not failed in this, wherein failure is most fatal; they have not been content with the easy successes of the despair of love; with the foregone conclusion of death; with the good reasons assigned for the gathering of rosebuds while there is time; with the song sung to the cradle 'endlessly rocking', or keeping time to the march; with the annual welcome to the spring; with the alternate mood now of Euphrosyne, and now of solitary Saturn. They have put their diviner fortunes to the touch, they have had what the French call an *échappée* towards the yonder side of things; have beheld and fingered with spiritual senses those symbols and similitudes which are the matters of daily life. They have remembered by day the night-mind of man, at customary noon the freshness of sunrise, and in adult days the first seven years. The skies, suns, and landscapes in their verse are rather restored than borrowed; they have repaid Nature, replaced man, and reinstated the antitype.

I have used the word religious rather than mystical, not because the terms are precisely equivalent, but because the first is the safer. It is ominous to hear the name of mysticism so

easily used, given and taken, without a thought of its cost.
It is not long since an interesting novel appeared of which the
motive and the whole subject was Mysticism. Visions were
easy to come by; and revelations, and such extreme things as
'the unitive life' — things for which the Saints thought fifty
years of self-conquest and self-abandonment a paltry price —
were discussed as incidents of well-read aspiration. There was
no mention of the first step, there was much chatter of the last.
No one in the band of confident people engaged in this story
in artistic work for a celestial end seemed to have entered upon
the indispensable beginnings, to have overcome anything
within, to have shut his mouth upon a hasty word, to have
dismissed a worldly thought, to have compelled his heart to a
difficult act of pardon, to have forgone beloved sleep, cherished
food, conversation, sharp thoughts, or darling pride. The
Saints, on the other hand, gave themselves to that spade-work
before permitting themselves so much as one credible dream.

Now it may be that the poets are to be held excused from
the greater part of this saintly discipline. There is a certain
measure of indulgence to be dispensed to them in requital of
their song. One of the greatest of them has placed himself at
the gate of a 'glad palace' — a beggar with leave to look within
and sing the pomp he sees. We may remember (certainly not
with pride) that all kinds of impunity, if not immunity, have
been proposed by critics and biographers, and the world in
general, for admired poets. The cruelties of one poet, the
random licence of another, the treacheries of yet another, his
breaking of bonds that left a fellow-creature broken — all this
and more has been pardoned for the sake of a lyric; to the
degradation, at any rate, of the pardoner. It is a far lesser
degree of excuse that we propose in the case of our mystic
poets; we hold them dispensed from the long and rigorous
experience of their brothers, the Saints. Personal perfection
of life shall be remitted to them; they who are apt to boast of
the sufferings of poetry shall be spared the infinitely greater
sufferings of sanctitude. They become mystics by their genius
and the divinity of their imagination.

Religious poetry had never been altogether silent; simple hearted allusions occur and recur throughout the Elizabethan drama. But it is in the later seventeenth century — the ripe age, the rich, the sweet and flavorous, the age of honey and fruit following the blossom — that the mystical lyric uncloses. Shall I be forgiven for omitting Milton, in his own age, from the number of mystical poets? It is difficult to account 'Paradise Lost' a mystic poem, treasury as it is of august thoughts and sentences; and the exquisite lyrical Milton — more rightly of the seventeenth century — touches mysticism only in a passage of 'Lycidas'. It is through the somewhat less conspicuous poets, who would be called 'minor' by our journalists, that the seventeenth century breathes its fragrant breath and shows its visionary lights. Crashaw, Cowley (cold, unfired, but yet alight), Herbert (rather exclusively religious than inclusively mystical, yet he is of them), Donne, Vaughan, Traherne, Marvell (who is a mystic of natural rather than preternatural things), and Lovelace were among those who brought poetry and sanctity to meet.

The seventeenth century, it may be said in passing, which saw the world, 'flown with insolence and wine', exalted at Versailles and at Whitehall, saw the world renounced, denied flouted, set at naught, in the hiding-places of obscure holy ones, mystics but by no means poets, grown more numerous as the age grew garish and triumphant. They had never been lacking. In every background of the battles of the Middle Ages, when war was in the streets of cities that were in themselves so many divided nations; in every background of the pageants of the Renaissance, lurked a mystic Saint. The famous families might possess one of their own: a man of seraphic soul, insatiable of labour, who bore the abominable name of Borgia; a woman insatiable of righteousness, who bore the turbulent name of Pazzi; a cousin, niece, aunt cloistered within the very heart of intrigue, revelry, and strife to whom man and woman fled for pity or for comfort when fortune rebuked them, or their loves and hates were too tangled for release. In outer darkness and inner light, bound hand and oot by inexplicable distress and disease, but wandering the heights and abysses in ecstasy and trance, these sacred creatures hide themselves in penance and fast and poverty in the middle of the gold and beauty and song of those resplendent ages; little sequestered oracles of God. They never fail, throughout the riotous centuries; but in the seventeenth, when sins and crimes grow more flippant than passionate, and rather ironical than tragic, they — withdrawn from a laughing world — increase in numbers and redouble in sanctity. They are no longer, as in the Middle Ages, in danger of honour. They are allowed to hide themselves in very truth. Their feats, the terrible successes of their sufferings, no longer greatly interest the world in the pauses of its loves and wars. Safe in disrespect, secluded and secure in oblivion, these mystics are recorded; they lived alone in pain and died of joy, alone, and little note was taken of them except by subsequent canonizations. In Italy, in Spain, in France, in Belgium, the hasty survey made by Huysmans in his 'Sainte Lydwine' shows us seventeen of these (he is considering women only) in the century of Vaughan and Crashaw — far more than in the age of Chaucer — against four in the age of Pope and of Gray; and then again fourteen in the age of Shelley and Wordsworth. Nation answers nation; and while these great experimentalists the Saints underwent the life of self-conquest, slowly attaining at last to that 'unitive life' which seems about to become the slang of studios; while they grew perfect in difficulty and earned their visions through dereliction and spoliation of the heart — superstitious nuns of Latin race, let us call them if we can — the English poets broke through time and were excused a novitiate, and made free at once to see and sing 'the pomp' of spiritual pleasures. The Restoration needed the Saints and the poets it did not greatly value. George Herbert left his lovely MSS. long unprinted; Vaughan succeeded in hiding himself so well that makers of some of the best anthologies of English lyrical poetry in the later middle of the nineteenth century were hardly aware of him. Where did Wordsworth make that great spiritual acquaintance? For the 'Ode on the

Intimations of Immortality' is the work of Vaughan as much as of Wordsworth, or more than of Wordsworth. Vaughan not only set the sun of dreams in the heavens, he also set the child in the midst of humankind.

In Vaughan's life and in Traherne's we find two most important boyhoods, conscious of the joys of their innocence, conscious of the landscape and of the afterwards unrecoverable illumination of early heavens in childish eyes. These conditions they remembered, and such memories cannot be cherished but in seclusion. Traherne so sequestered his tender genius that we have only now become the heirs of his riches and of their usufruct. Some lesson of the sanctitude of saints these two at least had learnt. It is not to Crashaw, Herbert, Traherne, or Vaughan that the dispensation here suggested needs to be assigned. Let us keep that evasion and excuse for more modern men, and recognize in the profane poet who is also a 'mystic' an advantage granted him in the counsels of the generosity of God.

The mystical spirit manifests itself in the love-poems and nature-poems of that luminous century. To us, in our dailiness and common degree of spiritual health, there seems to be something of slight delirium in the visionary mind and visionary eyes, in the exaltation of all the senses, especially this of sight, in the poetry of the seventeenth-century mystics. If it is the quality of delirium or of dreams, it is yet strangely evident in the very commonplaces of their poems. The rehearsal of the customary reproach to an inconstant mistress takes an august tone in Campion's solemn verse:

> When thou must home to shades of underground,
> And there arrived, a new-admired guest —

and the same much-accustomed rebuke sounds thus majestic and mysterious in the stanza of Carew beginning:

> When thou, poor Excommunicate
> From all the joys of love —

Here is the mystic spirit fallen in love, and brooding solemnly

and sullenly in the lights and glooms of passionate dreams.
And here again is the noble and mystical Marvell:

> My love is of a birth as rare
> As 'tis, for object, strange and high.
>
> .   .   .   .   .   .
>
> Magnanimous despair alone
> Could show me so divine a thing.

Elsewhere it is the mystical spirit in love with Nature. We
have to acknowledge this slight delirium to be the wildness
not of disease, but of a further, more delicate, and more
rapturous health. Marvell's garden offers him not only the
nectarine and curious peach, but a garden-ecstasy:

> Casting the body's vest aside
> My soul into the boughs does glide
> There, like a bird it sits and sings,
> Then whets and claps its silver wings,
> And, till prepared for longer flight,
> Waves in its plumes the various light.

Even the Cavalier poet, Lovelace, is a mystical poet in the
lovely lines 'To Lucasta paying her obsequies to the chaste
memory of my dearest cousin, Mrs. Bowes Barne', and in
those to 'A guiltless Lady penanced'. It is perhaps the ardent
love of chastity that gives to these two poems the transcendence
so separating them from all ignoble life. It is to the tenderness
yet the austerity of morning that Crashaw offers his 'Satisfac-
tion [as we should say his excuse or apology] for Sleep'. He has
neglected his muse,

> Whose feet can walk the Milky Way and choose
> Her starry throne;
>
> .   .   .   .   .   .
>
> But O thou,
> Bright lady of the morn, pity doth lie
> So warm in thy soft breast, it cannot die.

And all these are but poems upon human or natural things, and not, in the stricter sense of the beautiful collection before me,[1] religiously mystical poems. In citing them my object has, I think, been clear. I have led the reader on the seventeenth-century road from the bower of Campion's love to the forest and the heavens of Traherne's adoration, from glow to glow, and from tenderness to tenderness; from the body earlier called 'the soul's dark cottage' to the risen body of Vaughan's immortal childhood. For it is of the later seventeenth century that mystery and mysticism in the religious sense are so clearly characteristic. The earlier years of that age have the Elizabethan quality, the single-heartedness, a kind of adult innocence even in the savage tragedies of almost inconscient passion, a simplicity of intellect. It is as the age warms and sweetens, is reddened and gilded, towards the wheat-harvest and the apple-harvest, that the great consciousness of mysticism transforms the world, all its colours and all its lights; but this only for a little time. Although Vaughan and Traherne lived to the verge of the eighteenth century, that age last named had virtually set in before the signature of the centuries changed. The Milton of the lyrics is a seventeenth-century poet albeit not a mystic; the Milton of the epics is, except in a few passages, prophetically an eighteenth-century poet; Dryden — it is difficult to realize — lived only to see the new age appear, but he was of that new age. Addison, from head to feet a representative of the eighteenth century, its own man, yet lived no more than nineteen years of it. Therefore, with Elizabeth at one hand and Anne at the other, we have to concentrate our most glorious and most spiritual seventeenth century upon not many years, not many men. About those years, about those men, there is no question; they are virtually the canonized ones of our literature.

Let it stand, however, as a sign of the irony of human things that those great mystics — I had almost written those greater mystics — the authors of the Scottish and Border ballads, have neither name nor date. In making an anthology of the most

[1] *The Mount of Vision*, an anthology of mystical poems chosen by Adeline Cashmore.

perfect poetry of our language, and having to place those wonderful mystical poems, 'The Lyke-wake Dirge' and the 'Wife of Usher's Well', and the others almost their equals, according to some chronological system, I gathered them into the seventeenth-century fold at a venture, but left that great song of insanity, 'Tom o' Bedlam', to career outside, between the sixteenth century and the seventeenth.

And after the seventeenth century the mystical poetry vanishes so quickly and so completely that our wonder is great to find the temper of a national literature thus almost suddenly altered. Mystery and mysticism fly on a sudden from poetry and prose, and, between Vaughan and Blake, hide who knows in what childish and inarticulate hearts, for our poetry has no more of them. The wonder of the passing of nearly a century so vacuous of mystical meaning is less than the wonder of the passing of Prior, the passing of Johnson, of Gray—the world, whether flippant, or reasonable, or rhetorical, the alien world, between the last note of Vaughan and the first note of Wordsworth. These two virtually touch one another so nearly. The eighteenth century was not without poetic aspiration. It excited itself to a 'noble rage'; and 'madness' and 'madding' were words of its poetic vocabulary. Its eye rolled, and it put straws in its hair — nay, straws in its periwig — but it had no delirium of rapturous health.

Blake, Wordsworth, Coleridge—in whose 'Ancient Mariner' the exaltation of the senses has a seventeenth-century delicacy and transcendence and excess — Shelley, Tennyson, Browning — in exceedingly few pages — Rossetti, Christina Rossetti — in a page or two — Patmore pre-eminently, Francis Thompson, Meredith — these are the principal mystical poets of the age just closed. It is too great a company not to leave to us a sense of solitude when they have passed. Poetry has not died with them, nor talent, nor genius, but miracles have ceased for a while.

Cowper

THE ideal of poetry in Cowper's age was plain good sense, in perfect metre and diction of a 'modern' elegance. These things, already polite, the more polish they received from the educated hand, the better poetry they were accounted. It was not so — though scores of critics have thought it was — throughout the century. In the earlier years the poets of England were ambitious in another manner. It was not good sense they desired, it was delirium. They aimed at ecstasy, or what they called 'madness'; it was gone with the seventeenth century, but they invoked its stilted and self-conscious spectre. In Cowper's day they did so no more. The very memory of ecstasy had at last passed away. And we must read him with the fact present to our minds that no passion was then looked for in poetry, that no half-thought, no speculation, no groping, no hesitancy would have been tolerated, that no word not in the best epistolary or conversational use would have been admitted, that the language of the sixteenth and seventeenth centuries, ever fresh in our ears to-day, was in Cowper's day 'antiquated', and that he apologized for the pleasure he took in the piety of George Herbert, the expression of which, he allowed, was 'barbarous'. Then we shall be able better to understand the genius that speaks with an unmistakable voice in that immortal poem, 'On the receipt of my Mother's Picture'. The stepping couplet, the taste, the temper, the polish, the rejections and denials of the time, the dull limitations, controlled indeed but did not alter the profound emotion of that poem. It speaks for itself in its own inimitable voice, and wants no exterior proof. But if proof were needed, Cowper's tragic history would be the most affecting and convincing sign of his all-involving sincerity and — in every full sense of that terrible word — his passion. It is a deeply significant fact — it may seem at the first glance disproportionate or even grotesque to say so, but it is said very gravely — that Cowper was not saved from the passion of grief by the measured latinized diction, and was not rescued from despair by the heroic couplet. The heart within the moderate phrase, the heart within the balanced rhythm, was the human heart; it was wrung. The fashionable words were no defence; 'to evince', 'to convey', 'to peruse' did not protect him. He suffered as much as reason could endure, until reason could endure no more. He underwent the extremity, and passed through the narrow door of conscious despair into the dreadful liberty of the insane; and as civilized man suffers consciously in words (as he thinks in words) Cowper suffered all things in the most modern and the politest. We are sometimes tempted to think that eighteenth-century English was able to keep the more urgent emotions at arm's length; but we know that grief did reach to the living centre of Cowper's heart, for it finally destroyed him.

In the case of the lines on his mother's picture, it is not by this exterior proof, to be found in his history, that we know of the pang in the poem. We are aware of it in the lines; their moderate and gentle phrase conveys it; how we are so touched, so moved, and so convinced, we hardly know. But through the following changes of the language of English poetry — the real reform, the new life, the exaggeration, the Teutonism, the tatters, the destruction, the reconstruction, the violence, the defeat — Cowper's regret for his mother and for the past speaks a tongue that no man can at any time misinterpret; and so doubtless it will be when our English is undergoing phases that we do not now foresee.

Cowper would doubtless have been continuously a better poet in an age less well satisfied than was his with good commonplace, 'polished'. As it is, we have nothing else throughout his works that touches the beauty of the poem already named and the vigour of the 'Boadicea'. Here and there, besides, we find a moment of original thought and feeling, as when he has the courage to look at the hero in the light of morals and intellect, and to speak of his puny hands. Rarely his line has a higher nobility — something more than the dignity to which he not seldom rises as where he names

The unambiguous footsteps of a God.

The poet of this one line might have been consistently great. The once-popular rhetorical passage beginning 'Slaves cannot breathe in England', is far less significant of Cowper's peculiar power.

Cowper's life is the history of a long disease. That his melancholy settled upon religious misgiving was the inevitable accident; his sorrow chose for herself the deepest place; he had all his life a boundless leisure, so that there was time for the terrible choice, and nothing to hinder it. But until it was finally made, any other anxiety would serve the turn of his disease. The first attack of acute insanity was brought about by his agony at the prospect of a formal appearance before the House of Lords. He narrowly escaped the alternative suicide. The anticipation of a little safe journey by stage-coach or post with a friend caused fear and distress too sharp for sleep; and so on with the other insignificant incidents of a sheltered life. But though his melancholia ceased for no more than eight happy years after the first outbreak, and for the rest of his life did not wholly pass away, it is impossible to read his delightful letters and not be assured that Cowper was often and often a happy man. He did not live in the inconsolable place; it was behind him; often he did not look round. Human friendship in its most devoted, most vigilant, and most selfless activity was at his service all his life. It could not comfort his despair, but it made the intervals pleasant, made them gay, filled his days with the sweet talk of Mrs. Unwin, the sweeter laughter of Lady Hesketh. His ghostly friend, Mr. Newton, did not foster his fears, but encouraged his confidence. He loved nature, and his hares and his kitten charmed 'the sense of pain' out of his willing heart. That he died not out of his distress, but in it, is one of the facts that darken our vision of the history of the past. One voice has been raised above the grave to which he went in desolation — the voice of heavenly compassion. Elizabeth Barrett Browning divined the secret of his painful life, explained it, shed her tears over his earthly destiny, but 'saw his rapture in a vision'.

The Seven Lamps of Architecture

THIS memorable book appeared in 1849, during the course of the production of *Modern Painters*, six years later than the first volume of that great work and eleven years earlier than the fifth and last. The original edition of *The Seven Lamps* was the first of Ruskin's works that he published with his own drawings. The plates were etchings of architectural detail, done in haste, and bitten in haste by the author, who had made his studies from windows, lofts, and ladders. Nor was that haste uncalled for. When, for *Modern Painters*, he drew the outline of cloud — the loftier and the nearer flights of vapour — and the strong timbers of old pine trees, the cloud-shape fled from him, swiftly in the lower regions of air, slowly in the higher, on the wings of wild or delicate winds; every landscape-painter knows that he must not loiter in drawing clouds; while the old pine stood for his masterly portraiture, and he could take his time. But the beautiful stone that Ruskin loved, which was as strong as the tree, was passing out of his reach as surely as the cloud. The destroyer was at hand; the pick-axe was demolishing one side of some arch or fountain whilst he was drawing the other side, so as to save at least its image. When he was outlining primroses (the work to which, he tells us in another place, he was most naturally called) he had no need to dispatch; primroses abound and repeat each other, and if he was at work on the last of a season the primroses of another spring would repeat the pattern of their forms. He would not be at a loss in his studies. But the Gothic tracery, once destroyed, would never be renewed, and each fragment was unique. Ruskin worked urgently to commit it in time to the keeping of his pages. This book, then, which is one of the most orderly in the whole of Ruskin literature, was produced under stress of time and in much grief of heart. It was an architectural interlude in the study of landscape and landscape-painting, and takes its place in the forefront of the architectural series that have done so much for history and for art in the education of

England. Ruskin withdrew the overbitten and technically un-
successful plates in subsequent editions, but the labour with
the point should be remembered in connection with the
influential and perdurable labour of the pen.

The Seven Lamps of Architecture is a book resembling a
fortress-palace built, with a system of approaches and defences,
around a little court of special honour and security. This place
of perfection is represented by a certain half-century — fifty
fortunate years set between the rise and the decline of the art
of that great Gothic incident, the window. That historical half-
century is the dominant centre of the book, and the author's
thoughts are ranged and ranked about it in a high perfection
of order. The medieval stone-mason of those fifty years —
Ruskin's stone-mason, for we must lend him Ruskin's eye, or
lend his eye to Ruskin — opening a window from within his
church outward to the sky, saw two things equally — the shape
of the light and the shape of his stone, the form of the tracery
and the pattern of the light it enclosed; saw them with an equal
regard, designed them with an equal attention and delight.
His predecessor had thought more about the design of the
carved sky, his successor was to think more about the design
of the carved stone. The stone-sculptor of the brief time set
between two imperfections designed a star of sky and a starred
stone in equal and equivalent dignity, beauty, and invention;
thus he achieved the noblest window in history, and the noblest
window implies the noblest Gothic. The reader will do well
to pause upon this historical discovery of Ruskin's, for it is not
only greatly instructive, it is also exceedingly Ruskinian. He
has elsewhere commended the artist who preserves the inno-
cence of the eye. And his was the innocence as well as the
wisdom of the eye when, looking skyward from the shadows
of the church, he appraised now the shaping light and now the
shaping stone, and now both interlaced and locked together.
Every child awake in a room where there is a patterned paper
lies staring at it, arranging it now this way, now that, as a
pattern of design or as a pattern of intervals. And no doubt
every man is aware of a like alternative in the Gothic window,

but Ruskin assumed the mind of the man who branched the stone and enclosed the sky; he travelled back and thought with him, adopted his traditions, stepped with him out of the preceding time, grew with him, achieved with him the short-lived perfection of art in this moving world, and bequeathed, with him, that perfection to be inevitably marred in the time succeeding. Other students of the past keep their station in the present, but Ruskin thinks over again the thoughts that he records.

The author of *The Seven Lamps of Architecture* was still a young man, and in some most characteristic respects a far younger man than any other man of his thirty years. He was, for example, still much the son of his father, the boy of his mother, nay, the nursling of his nurse, the member of his family, the child of his home. Ruskin, known to us as a teacher, was long a scholar, a disciple, giving the name of 'master' in later years to more than one whom he tutored. But it is with another kind of docility that he was charged — adorned or oppressed, and perhaps indeed both graced and hampered — in those days when he was still obedient to his parents, albeit already a commander if ever there was one in our literature. Now, Ruskin could not be the child of his parents in architecture, for he was here seeking his own adventures; but in the prejudices of his theology, his literature, and his ethics, he was obviously the one son, the companion-child, the beloved but disciplined young one, not only under subjection, but willingly so, heartily so, and with eager conviction. It is only in the later years, when father and mother were long since dead, and Ruskin stood entirely solitary in a world of which he had begun, only after youth was passed, to perceive the sadness and the wrongs, that he looked back upon that sheltered life of prolonged boyhood, and condemned its ease as selfish and its comfort as luxurious. Living in the order, and at the orders, of father and mother, he had not questioned the justice of such a life. And the influence of home, and of fashions in literature obviously paternal, is perceptible in Ruskins' literary habits, the disproportionate love of Scott, the disproportionate love of

Byron. It was an old fashion, inherited by the most original man of his century. Moreover, the savage theology of *The Seven Lamps*, as it was in the original edition, unmitigated by notes and refutations, and the untenable doctrine as to the virtue of truth, are certainly records of the illogical things taught to a child, and by this child grappled to his growing soul. It was with a kind of shock of departure, of loss, and of spoliation, that — almost an old man — Ruskin found himself stripped of these maxims. Let us take the passage upon the virtue of truth. It occurs in the section of 'The Lamp of Sacrifice', which it closes as it were with a lock. Ruskin here satisfies the common human passion for one inverified, august, irresponsible doctrine, a doctrine which, as the Italians say, 'imposes itself'. At any rate Ruskin, the learner and the teacher of the doctrine, would impose it on the willing and the unwilling, with no uncertain hand. Truth, he professes, is the single virtue that owns no borderlands, no venialities. 'Truth regards with the same severity the lightest and the boldest violations of its law'; it is the one quality 'of which there are no degrees'; whereas 'there are some faults light in the sight of love, some errors slight in the estimate of wisdom, truth forgives no insult and endures no stain'. Who will fail to hear, in this thunderous adult voice, a repetition of the unreasoned imposition on the child's mind? Little John Ruskin, imposed upon, accepted and retained the teaching with all his heart, and in after life is thus content to assert it in balanced rhetoric, with no thought of the angler that deceives a fish. For it is not necessary to cite the showy case of the physician who deceives a homicidal lunatic to prevent murder. Ruskin had called on the 'lightest violation', and the lightest he shall have. He shall damn the angler who deceives a fish. But assuredly we have all to learn that truth is by no means to be thus separated from the other virtues, her proper company, or to be relieved from her share in the difficulty and doubt that besets them all.

It is hardly to be wondered at that, having delivered his message, so long unquestionable, Ruskin should find himself called to reassure his readers, lest they might be visited by scruples of the moral conscience in regard to art that might look more or less like nature, and thus partake of the nature of deceit. It is worth noting in regard to this matter that Ruskin abates nothing of his estimate of England, 'a nation distinguished for its general uprightness and faith', albeit the English 'admit into their architecture more of prudence, concealment and deceit than any other [people] of this or of past times'. The English fault is thus treated somewhat arbitrarily, as a mere inconsistency; but the Italian fault — the paltry 'exhibitory' mock art of the modern Italian — is charged with important implications and reflections upon character.

A son of the home, then, and a most enterprising traveller of the mind, at once, Ruskin, at the date of the writing of this book, abounded with thought, with principles, with monitions, and with a towering sincerity. He is a thousand times convinced, convinced as a child, but with a great man's capacity for conviction. He brings a large intellect and, more, a large will into order. It is difficult for him (and he uses the difficulty for the making of majestic sentences) to satisfy his indignation in the passage wherein he menaces the English nation with retributions, to bear heavily upon her arts, her commerce, and her honour, because an office in her legislature had been 'impiously conceded to a Romanist'. In after years he disclaimed, he shuddered, he looked askance, at that young presumption; but he did not smile at it. It had been the remains of his boyhood.

Throughout *The Seven Lamps* his work is anxious. He labours the thought in the 'Lamp of Sacrifice', for example — the difference between sacrifice and waste, the difference between the manifestation and the mere exhibition — and the reader is inclined to think that Ruskin himself, amongst others, has so improved, quickened, and exercised the modern mind that we need less instruction, less urging, and less exposition than did they for whom the book was first written. Yet on one point we stand more than they did in need of Ruskin's warning against a certain excess of simplicity. In 1849 the love of Gothic was still young and eager. To-day our

eyes are so accustomed that we begin to be too fond, in fine
architecture, of a plain wall, so it be thick, a wide surface, an
undecorated arch. It is a negative merit that is growing too
dear to us; and we, rather than our fathers, need to be told
that such simplicities 'are but the rests and monotones of the
art; it is to its far happier, far higher exultation that we owe
those fair fronts of variegated mosaic, charged with wild
fancies and dark hosts of imagery, ... those vaulted gates
trellised with close leaves, those window-labyrinths of twisted
tracery'.

As the historian of Gothic — that is, chiefly of the window —
Ruskin gives us in this book another brief lesson, which, like
that on the equipoised half-century, is equal, for its sight and
insight, to the great pages of instruction in *Stones of Venice*.
The wayfarer in London has often wondered why the Perpen-
dicular style was chosen for the Houses of Parliament, and has
generally heard, in reply, that the suggestion of Henry VII's
Chapel, over against the entrances of the house, gave the note
and secured the date. But Perpendicular Gothic was, in fact,
chosen because it was the distinctively English manner of
architecture, and marked the division of the national way of
England from the national way of France. And it is of the
moment of parting that Ruskin makes himself the masterly
historian. The student cannot do better, whether in regard to
Gothic, in regard to Ruskin, or in regard to English prose-
thought, than return to the page of *The Seven Lamps* which
records one of Ruskin's vigilant perceptions, one of his greatly
wise and alert watchings of the changes of the world; and is
besides a most perfect passage of exactly beautiful diction. It
begins with 'At the close of the period of pause, the first sign
of serious change was like a low breeze, passing through the
emaciated tracery, and making it tremble'. Note what follows
— the delicate words describing, with so much solid feeling,
that frail alteration, and the implicit reprobation of the too
slender tracery which, though still severe and pure, was ready
for this disastrous inflection. The reference is to the French
Gothic, which wavered when the English grew rigid, the one

like flame and the other like frost. The English change — we must call it the English corruption — drew away from the French, leaving far behind the great thirteenth century in its international and liberal interchange. Thus modern Westminster is a monument of division, of scattering, of the diversities of declension from the high phase which cannot last on earth.

Another of the noblest passages in the book is that which teaches the architect the custom of thinking in shadow. 'Let him cut out the shadows, as men dig wells in unwatered plains.' Let him see that the light 'is bold enough not to be dried up by twilight', and the shadow 'deep enough not to be dried like a shallow pool by a noonday sun'. These images are as full of delight as any in Ruskin's work. His thought is itself a pool of freshness, clearness and mystery, holding not the darkness only but also reflected suns.

Another example of Ruskin's historical apprehension is his exposition of the Gothic of rejection — the Venetian which began in the luxuriance whereto other architectures have declined and wherein they have expired, which put away Byzantine ornaments one by one, ruled itself 'by laws more and more severe', and 'stood forth at last, a model of domestic Gothic, so grand, so complete, so nobly systematized, that, to my mind, there never existed an architecture with so stern a claim to our reverence'. I think Ruskin partly renounced this extreme judgment later, in favour of early Lombard building.

The student will fathom *The Seven Lamps* in search of the utmost that is to be learnt and loved in Ruskin's teaching on two distinct characters — or rather two sanctions — of architecture: one, the impression that the art received from human power, and the other the image it carries of the natural creation. We know how Ruskin has laboured elsewhere this insistent reference of art to natural form; and in what wilful — nay, obstinate, nay, perverse ways he led and compelled his thought to walk. In *The Two Paths*, for example, he draws a famous contrast between India and Scotland. The two nations — the two races — were to be judged, according to the plan of the book, by their art. And India was judged to be corrupt by the sign of her art, which had neglected or despised natural form. The Hindoo, we are told, 'draws no plant, but only a spiral'. Therefore not his art only, but he, his race, his child, his nation fell. His art, parted from nature, and devoted to cruelty in the sword-hilt, to sensuality in the girdle, and to superstition in the temple, involved his East in degradation. We may accept this, with some hesitation, perhaps, in regard to the temple, albeit remembering something of philosophic, pure, oriental creeds; in regard to the girdle, albeit bearing in mind the chaste Indian woman in the silks and gold of her seclusion; in regard to the sword, albeit knowing the fact of universal war. But we cannot do otherwise than withstand our teacher, and resist him, when he reproaches India with Scotland, and the Hindoo with the Scot, and the Buddhist with the Calvinist, and the lover of the sacred bride with the lover of Jean Armour, because these contrasts are involved in his judgment of Indian art. For what has Ruskin wherewith to confront the Indian design, the Indian colour, but only — the plaid? And where is natural form here, where natural colour? The corrupt Hindoo has at least a curve, and nature is full of curves; and at any rate a gradation, and nature is full of gradations. But the pure Scot defies nature, and denies the curve, and disdains gradation in the design and colour of his one national work of art. Yet hear the ethical difference according to Ruskin's judgment: 'Out of the peat cottage came faith, courage, self-sacrifice, purity, piety . . . ; out of the ivory palace came treachery, cruelty, cowardice, idolatry, bestiality.' And if it were so — but with what a half-hearted pause do we pass the words 'purity', 'piety', thinking of Burns and the national lyrism! But if it were so, what would become of the argument from art? Alas, what? In *The Stones of Venice* we have the necessity of natural form illustrated far better to the purpose, the necessity of life taught by no such disastrous paradox as that of *The Two Paths*. Ruskin takes, in the earlier book, that delightful illustration of the ribbon and the seaweed or grass which no reader who has ever enjoyed it will forget: the ribbon an indeterminate length having 'no strength, no languor. It cannot wave, but only flutter; it cannot bend, but only turn and be wrinkled'; whereas the grass and the seaweed have parts, gradation, direction, and an allotted size. We are called upon to denounce the ribbons of Raphael, and we do so cordially; as we do even the ribbons that tie 'Ghiberti's glorious bronze flowers', and all the foolish ends of bows, and scrolls used for decoration.

Great as has been, and is, and will be, the influence of this noble book, it is certain that to one of its instructions the English world has proved indifferent, sceptical, negligent, or defiant — at any rate altogether indocile. It was so at the date of the book, it is so now after sixty years. Ruskin's counsel was that 'things belonging to purposes of active and occupied life', as distinct from architectural structures properly so called, should be left undecorated. Even as we are chidden for too much love of simplicity in a Gothic façade, we are chidden for ornament in our factories. The railway-station, the factory chimney, the shop-front and the shop, the warehouse, the workroom, and the office should be plain. None the less have we the tedious and the habitual decoration — tedious even in a place of comparative honour, and twice dishonoured, twice paltry and wearisome where it even does not suggest an outworn pleasure — besetting our business in the iron of a station and the moulding of a factory-shaft. In his youth, Ruskin tells us, he could have been glad to go 'through the streets of London, pulling down the brackets and friezes and large names, restoring to the tradesmen the capital they had spent in architecture, and putting them on honest and equal terms, each with his name in black letters over his door'. In the matter of restoration, also, *The Seven Lamps* and its warnings and menaces have been little heeded. 'Do not let us talk of Restoration. The thing is a lie from beginning to end.' The passage is famous; its inhibition has frighted very few.

Because of this and other disobediences, it is to be supposed that the respect paid to this great work of Ruskin's early prime is offered to his art of words rather than to his art of thought.

It is much to be wished that the two were not thus put asunder. But it must be confessed that Ruskin himself distinguishes them — distinguishes, though he never separates, them — somewhat too much by an excessive eloquence. And the injudicious reader seizes on the slight occasion afforded him by this trespass of the master's early eagerness and urgency, to make an unlawful and disastrous division, expressed a thousand times by the 'admirers' of Ruskin who repeat one another to say that they love him little for the things he says but much for his manner of saying them.

And as to this praised manner, now over-studious of the ear, now as perfect in the ornament of diction as — in its place — the Gothic window of the best half-century, this book may go far to persuade us that, at this date of writing, Ruskin was a better master of description in regard to architecture than in regard to landscape. The page of Alpine landscape, with all its splendour, its resolute endeavour, its impassioned desire to communicate that majestic vision of nature to the reader, is less successful (let the unworthy and inadequate word be allowed) than the page of architecture in which Giotto's tower is praised: 'coloured like a morning cloud and chased like a sea shell', with what follows.

When Ruskin names the 'Lamp of Life' in architecture, we see it lighted in this beautiful and impassioned work of litera-ture. One thing he never lacks, never flags in, and that is an invincible vitality. Compared with his great vitality, the viva-city of other authors is little more than an insignificant or ineffectual agitation. 'No inconsiderable part of the essential character of beauty depends on the expression of vital energy in organic things, or on the subjection to such energy of things naturally passive and powerless.' Ruskin's own drawing of the pine, his own drawing of the rock, his own animation and re-animation of the language, are all the expression of vital energy such as he taught the workers with stone, that it might give power to the plan, and deal the chisel mighty blows. And this Lamp — this one of the Seven — was destined to remain unquenched in that lofty spirit to the last of his days, when for him the Lamp of Memory was flickering, and the Lamp of Beauty was untended, and the Lamp of Obedience — that wonderful obedience to what his fathers had told him — was quenched. In the last writings of that noble pen, when there was no more artifice of balanced eloquence, no more delight in phrase, no more dogmatic security, no more sure or certain hope, the light of life never lapsed, and the fire of life was never lowered.

The Poetry of George Meredith

GEORGE MEREDITH as a poet teaches explicitly; as a novelist implicitly, or with a word indirect, a look askance, and by means of a lesson rehearsed for our observation rather than spoken for our conning. But in prose and verse he teaches, and in verse emphatically, with reiteration, and insistence, and the announcement of a law: 'Thou shalt love thy mother Nature with all thy heart, and with all thy mind, and with all thy soul, and with all thy strength. Thou shalt put thy whole trust in her. She is benign even when she seems cruel, albeit she loves thee not at all.' This is the first and great commandment. And the second is like unto it: 'Thou shalt not love thyself.' It is chiefly in poetry that this law can be delivered; for in poetry personification is not only permitted, it is prescribed. Meredith proclaims a personal Nature, and predicates of her the 'intention', the 'wish', the 'aim', the 'care', the 'will'. We are compelled to ask ourselves, How much is philosophy, and how much is poetry? Would Meredith, in prose, attribute this foresight, this intention *à parte ante* to the lawgiver — Nature, who made the law of the survival of the fittest, for example? All men recognize and confess the law in action and after action; Meredith, the poet, recognizes it as a design, as it

343

were, before action. Paley's is not a more respectful recognition; but Paley does not use the feminine pronoun. Now the question, How much is philosophy, and how much is poetry? is obviously very important to the students of Meredith's philosophy, less momentous to the readers of his poetry; let me be allowed to cite one personal recollection in this case. This is that Mr. Meredith habitually used the same forms of speech and of thought in the prose of conversation: Nature 'does not care', and 'Nature's intention', 'Nature's only wish', and phrases of like significance.

Honouring the personality of a law-giver, Meredith observes the law of the lives of animals and vegetables upon earth, submits his intellect to all that seems unkind or imperfect there, accepts all, loves all, and gives back to all his own blessing as a creature. It is when he professes to draw from Nature the tables of the moral law that we question the poet who limits himself, who circumscribes himself, by the art of poetry, who takes refuge, as it were, in its imagery, who encloses himself within the boundaries of the art, and also gives himself the liberties of the fancy without which poetry is not poetry. Meredith professes, in verse and rhyme and imagery, to find all moral law in the Earth, our only visible friend, our only teacher, the only revelation of whatever Power —

The great Unseen, never the dark Unknown —

is above and beyond her. 'Never the dark unknown', because that Power has revealed itself in Nature. I say 'professes' advisedly. I cannot see that he does more. Meredith loved the unit — the child, the friend; the Nature he adored loves only the species much, the genus more, the unit not at all. An inexplicable love — for love, personal love, he predicates of her — which enthusiastically and aforethought provides for the multiplication of units she cares nothing for! The question of revelation is all. The definite religions are for another system; asserting that morality — if it does not begin where Nature leaves off — develops, corrects, alters, chastises the revelation

344

of the earth and her laws. They aver that Meredith's 'great
Unseen' is not 'the dark Unknown' because when the con-
sciousness of moral good and evil was established — established
for ever — in man, and in man alone, a direct appeal to that
consciousness, now become conscience, became the chief
necessity of the world, and — in several forms — took place.
Morality is assuredly the greatest fact on Earth; but, as
assuredly, Earth does not suffice for it. In our human kind
we have all seen some foolish little mother looking with un-
intelligent wonder upon an illustrious son. If Earth is, as
Meredith will have her, the mother of Morality, then is
Morality such an alien son.

To his love of the Earth — the heart-whole, all-trusting,
optimistic, courageous, submissive love he bore her — we owe
Meredith's most wonderful poems. To the woods, on the
moss, on the track of wild life, with exquisite tenderness, with
joy such as human happiness fails to inspire in hearts less
exquisite than his, with rapture of heart, without a 'whimper'
for the pain he found there, but with a valorous pity, this great
poet betook himself. He counted all the cost of his love and
his creed. Much that is human he overcame within himself,
or thought that he overcame. The peace he found was not
without an agonizing novitiate. Some solitary crucifixion of
the heart, such as his great contemporary, Coventry Patmore,
underwent in a man's love for women, Meredith underwent in
his love of the woods. Patmore's poem — the struggle over —
is of heavenly grief, Meredith's, of earthly rapture. And both
were spiritual men, and knew man to be a spirit. With a heart
so subdued at once and so ennobled, Meredith faced the facts
of Nature, using the incomparable alertness and sweetness of
his observation, and using it with a strange delicacy; for the
urbanity of his character, so constant in his letters, so charming
in his manners, was his in the enchanted woods. Urbanity is
a pleasantly paradoxical word to use in regard to one who
dared thus to trust his own mind with the problem of wild
life. But George Meredith was the most civilized of men.
'Civilized' was with him a favourite word in commendation of

his friends. No professed lover of country life, having half Meredith's love for it, has had half his urbanity. And he knew — and conquered his grief in knowing — that the wild thing must go down before the cultivated. He compelled himself to acquiesce in the killing of the young fox; though, for my part, I think he need not have so subdued his heart as to consent to 'sport'. And his own bearing observed the perfection of manners; it belonged to the time, gone by now, when it was permissible to speak of manners; he practised even the little tricks of that time — worth remembering because they were significant — and had an obvious dislike of the more modern bearing and address in which manners are, as it were, negative; with him they were positive. And even thus he cherished the worm, the snake, the bird, the seasons, and the wildest of all the winds.

It is rightly that the true student of this great poet gives almost his whole attention to the philosophy — 'my philosophy' he called it with grave appropriation — for the sake of which nearly all his poetry was written. Nearly, but not all. Outside of this persistent 'Reading of Earth', and sermon on the text of the reading, are the great dramatic poems, 'Attila', 'Napoléon', and other 'Poems of Tragic Life', in which action and passion brandish a vitality of words altogether amazing; and the quieter but no less vital drama of 'Modern Love', 'Love in a Valley', and their kind. And here, and throughout, appears, conspicuous, not fantastic, not habitual, not disproportionately exhibited, a marvellous vocabulary. Perhaps no reader pauses necessarily upon Meredith's vocabulary, for there is no obvious research in its high distinction (let us except some of the Odes on French history). It is to what I dare to call the pocket vocabulary of such poets as Swinburne that our unwilling attention is compelled. So with Meredith as a metrist. There are refinements in the mere mechanism of his verse — the punctual relation of syllables, for example, at the conclusion of one line and the beginning of the next — such as I have not found in any other poet, Shakespeare always excepted. To make an unwilling comparison of different arts, the 'music' of Swinburne seems a tune, while Meredith's is a melody. It is, therefore, as a singer of words, among other and greater qualities, that George Meredith stands among the score of major poets of our incomparable literature.

Ada Negri

OUR own unpardoning English language, though it does not altogether daunt the futile rash writer, because he will not be daunted, yet helps time to defeat him. There is little charm of sweet sound and of self-graceful phrase (phrase that is graceful to any man's hand who uses it) to remain when living poetry is proved to be absent from the work of an Englishman. The French will tell you that to write accurate verse in their language is to be a poet, so difficult are the rules of their prosody; and the saying, by the way, seems to show a singular lack of the perception of poetic quality. But there would be more excuse for anyone who should aver that to write musically (really musically) in English is to be proved a poet, if not a fine one. The music of an English line is a better and more severe test than the correctness of a French one; but no such brief proof, needless to say, is really possible.

Of the Italian poet no similar nonsense can be spoken, even by the way of hyperbole; for hyperbolic is the Frenchman's phrase. It is but intended to make his hearer understand that Alexandrines are not child's play. The very different difficulty in Italian is to distinguish and to detach the special grace of a phrase from the inevitable grace of its kind and its like. It is the difficulty of an easy and indulgent language, and even the ready, the officious, music is less dangerous than the easy antithesis which seems to play, ready-turned and ready-balanced, within the sentences rather than within the poet's fancy and wit.

Nor, in fact, can an Italian poet, using the language in its rather unbraced, languid state of modern ease, entirely evade the peril of its all too accessible dignities and graces. In any case, it is imagery that loses. The old phrase takes the place of the new image, and though the verse may be decorated now and then with a similitude, yet entire imagery, corporate imagery, such as that which brings about the transfiguration of the substance of a fine poem or a fine passage in the English of Keats or Coleridge, is not within the hope or scope of the Italian. The mechanical suspension of a similitude (if I may allow myself that illustration) is the most that is to be achieved by the Italian poet, while English poetry has it in chemical solution.

But as every difficulty serves distinction, so does this most subtle difficulty of too much ease. A language relaxed in meanings and musical in sound is too ready and, as has just been said, indulgent. It is easy for the many, that is, and difficult for the few; charged with excuses and dispensations for those who desire them, and, therefore, disheartening for the severe. To make that beautiful which is beautiful already is a work that needs not a beautiful touch merely but a strong one: and to constrain the customary grace to be singly graceful is an act that cannot be accomplished but by a muse nobly intent upon graver things than graces.

Perhaps an Italian poet who should inspire himself with a northern sense of imagery might solve the clinging, curving, and intricate knots of this poetic 'situation', and might make Italian new by a change. But this is not what has been done by Ada Negri, the poet of 'Tempeste' and 'Fatalità'. She has taken the hardest of many hard methods, and has made her Italian new in Italian ways. She gives the costliest life, which is her own, to her poems, and she is throughout Italian. She uses the language in its conventional poetic form, with all the familiar conditions of Italian literature, and uses it for the purposes of Italian thought. With all this, she is a free woman, and proves her freedom.

It is not merely that her subjects are from her own redeemed

348

experience. They are indeed so, for she writes, according to what she has seen and known, the verses that have been called 'socialistic' (with the angriest of all anger — vague anger — in the charge), but are no more nor less than human. This is not what would distinguish her in the choice of her themes. What she does in that choice has been abundantly done by others: it is a mere platitude to say that the subjects of grave human literary history have been greatly multiplied of late, not in the direction of the past, but by attention to contemporary things. It is even possible that actual things will, at this rate, soon make us long for distances, as in the encumbered Belgian plains. She has rather suffered than gained by the vogue of the street. If it were worth while to be salient by the choice of subject, which it is not, she would be at no advantage by her 'socialism'; she would be effaced rather than made salient by her poems about the poor as they are. But she is distinct, in spite of the old convention of her instrument, and in spite of the new popularity of her theme, because of the mere vitality of her own spirit. She has impulse more than sufficient to disengage her sweetness from the sweetness of words, her passion from the passion of language, and her sympathy from the sympathy of panic and contagion.

Ada Negri is no sentimental singer. She begins a love-song only to excuse herself, to dispense herself, to explain her distractions by the real ardour of her absent heart, struck by a 'Roman thought' of less smooth things. She is without regret for the violet, myrtle, and cypress of the north Italian country when she welcomes the factory and the devastation, fire, and blight of 'industry' displacing labour. One might have a word with her on that point, perhaps; and she must be aware that the suffering of which she writes is much oftener the suffering of the street, the workshop of machines, the mine, and the hospital, than the privation of the fields, even the injured, despoiled, and outraged fields, vineyards, and plantations of modern Italy. Even when she is singing a song of pity, it is not a helpless impulse that moves her; she is not without love, anger or defiance. There seems to be no entirely unfruitful pain in her poetry, even when she mourns over her 'Birichino di Strada', the street child, the rascal, with his inevitable future. Nor is there anything more impassioned than the verse in which she — his sister in solitude — wishes that she could give him 'all her kisses'. Nothing in the gentler and tenderer pages of her books is so entire in its avowal as this, nor does the love of lovers move her with so close a pang as does this sisterly despair.

She does not fear the dreadful scenes of life and death, of which one might wish that weaker poets had a natural fear, and her audacity is justified by those strong verses called 'Autopsia' and by her conception of the cold anger she attributes to the dead under the surgeon's hand. She must assuredly have taken a lesson here from the terrors of mourners' dreams. For among the dreams that are told by the bereaved there is one they do not tell — the dream of the anger of the dead, a dream hidden in the human mind by who knows what prehistoric fright and primitive misgiving in the men of the early world, who were children, a dream that is the most intolerable when it visits the mind of the civilized and the adult with an increased, a multiplied and spiritualized, yet still pure and primitive distress. If the mind of the poet was ever touched by such a dream of the anger of the dead, she had the genius to hale her captured tremor to the light and keep it there.

There are other latent things she has the force to tell: one of them is sweetly expressed in the word *disamata*. But she is no more a melancholy singer than the antique poets were melancholy singers. Her defiance of fortune is itself a happiness: and the fact that she did set aside the menace of a gloomy life of almost desperate poverty, and did take her part in the national history of her time (she has done no less), is but the least testimony to her invincibility. 'Success' is almost a detraction from her courage, for she needed no visible approval and proof, and her secret defeat and her obscure failure of which men would not have been aware, as they are not aware of the overthrown, would have been a still more secret conquest, for they would have proved her a creature independent.

Italian cannot yet well be quoted, as French can be, in an evening paper, and not even French in a morning one; therefore, we have to be content with the translation of a phrase or two. This is the lover from the factory running upstairs to the factory girl, 'black with dust, magnificent with love'. 'Mother,' she sings with all her art, 'I wish I might forget I am a poet, and become again a *bambino*.' When she left the little hut she was 'rich with dreams'; she calls the skylark an 'audacious angel'. This is enough and too much — it does Ada Negri little service to turn these scraps out alone in an alien world. I should like to try one or two entire translations for another week.

The above was printed in the *Pall Mall Gazette* of November 17th, 1897. Punctually one week later appeared three translations by Alice Meynell of which this is one:

MISFORTUNE

Armed, and with lightning eyes that clove the dark,
    One stood at midnight near me,
Told me her daunting name, and claimed me: 'Hark!
    I am Misfortune. Fear me!

'I shall not leave thy pathway, nor forsake,
    Young one, thy timorous side;
Shall watch thy sleep, and on thy grave shall wake.'
    'Let me alone,' I cried.

Yet she kept near: 'By unrebuked decrees
    Thou art made a flower of snow,
A dusty flower, a flower of cypress trees,
    Of mire, of fire, of woe.'

I cried, 'I am for life, for joy, for one,
    Only one fear — love's own.
I want the kiss of genius and the sun;'
    I wept, 'Let me alone!'

'Glory,' she said, 'is of my gift; renown
Closes my troubled day.
I crush and I proclaim, I wound, I crown.'

I said: Misfortune, stay!

Elizabeth Barrett Browning

I. HER LETTERS

ELIZABETH BARRETT BROWNING's letters to a stranger or one of slight acquaintance are much unlike those into the privacy whereof we were admitted when her correspondence with her husband was made public. Her letters to Mr. Horne, for example, were written from her seclusion to a man hardly known to her — one at least who was never a near witness to her life; and from behind such a veil, from within that singular security, from the dark room upstairs and the sofa, out of the confidence of timidity unspied and of diffidence denied, she did much the same as Charlotte Brontë when she too wrote to strangers. There is with both an ill-suited flourish of the phrase. *Mutatis mutandis* (the alterable things, let it be granted, are many) the two women out of sight write not unlike Byron when, conspicuous, he wrote to Moore. This swaggering — nay, this strutting — of the gentle is an unlooked-for outbreak of the day-dreaming love of adventure. Then does the nimble fancy flit from the little room or from the parsonage to the outer world, and imagine a brilliant and fluent Charlotte Brontë, a dauntless Elizabeth Barrett, as the secluded creature might be guessed at from afar, and then does that nimble fancy flit back to dress the reality by that conjectural image. Such a double journey as that is taken in the twinkling of an eye by the young imagination of a woman which would indeed make little of a flight redoubled and far more intricate. Here, for the prisoner is freedom; for the unsunned, change; here is a frolic for the demure; here is a swashing and a martial style for the cloistered one who yet does not quit her cloister; here, in a word, is dash — the dash of the hesitating, the thoughtful and the reluctant. Here, without alteration of the monotonous facts, is a part to be played. This is the work and the power of letters, as letters are sent from the hooded shadow of the authoress's shyness out into the various world.

Perhaps there was something in the reflex influence of the author of 'Orion' that provoked in Elizabeth Barrett an assertion and an emphasis of style in no true sense her own; for her simpler letters, those to her nearer friends, are delicately natural. They keep the sensitive line of her actual thought, somewhat as the spirit-level observes the horizon with a kind of mobile constancy. The violence of 'Lady Geraldine' and of the letters to Horne gives place to the recollection — the *receuillement* — of the gentle 'Sea-Mew' — that lovely poem — and to the inward, attentive, candid, and equal spirit of these exquisite messages to her chosen friends. Mrs. Browning's gentleness is the most delicate thing in all her manifold but not intricate nature. You look for that quality to and fro in her poetry and find it not often, and only in the poems that an otherwise eager popularity has been willing to let slip by. An uneasy force, an anxious decisiveness, a spurred impulsiveness, a very habit and trick of violence, once acquired as an assertion of strength, and then renewed perforce because the tense effort would otherwise have left the language stretched and lax — these are obvious characteristics of Mrs. Browning, even in her most beautiful and admirable work; but with her they were not natural signs of weakness. They were probably first a challenge thrown in the way of the critics who rewarded her with 'a high place amongst our female poets'. If so, it was a futile strife; for years the praises of her reviewers never failed to finish with the comfortable anti-climax.

But it is by her gentleness that she speaks to the judicious ear. And for the love of that lovely virtue we forgive its excess — Mrs. Browning's too much tolerance and generosity. She venerated her friends, so that Miss Martineau is written of as 'a woman exercised in high logic'. Was it not Miss

Martineau who once complained of some writer that he argued 'in a circle'? Nay, she mended the phrase, persuaded that if to argue in a circle was futile, how much more faulty must it be to argue 'in a segment of a circle'. This is a mere incident, but it illustrates Mrs. Browning's hasty humility.

Her letters prove that she endured with perhaps too much patience the strange judgments and praises astray that wronged her work. There can hardly be a doubt, with judicious and deliberate students of poetry, that 'Geraldine' is the one of all her mature poems that has the least dignity and control, and is most explosive and full of reiterated extremities, untempered. Yet the conscious author is tolerant of such a fact as this: 'Both Carlyle and Miss Martineau select as favourite "Lady Geraldine's Courtship".' And of the same opinion was 'Mr. Eagles, one of the first writers in *Blackwood*, and a man of very refined taste'.

By the gentleness of her true nature, and by the gentleness of her little health, she possessed her husband's violent heart in peace. He held her, subject to the annual threat of death, and at a price he was not permitted to forget. With every winter the common price of human love was counted over and over again before his eyes. It was paid a thousand times by actual anticipation, and in many a night of illness had she repeated to him in secret 'the harrowing praise' of the dying. In Robert Browning's care Elizabeth, winter by winter, 'only did not die'. She had to die at last, as also the unloved die, alone, although she was in his arms. 'Then came,' he says of her last moments, 'what my heart will keep till I see her again and longer — the most perfect expression of her love to me within my whole knowledge of her. And in a few minutes she died in my arms, her head on my cheek.'

II. THE CENTENARY OF HER BIRTH

A poet's birthday is well kept. The saints are commemorated on their death, but poets enter their paradise on earth. An English poet's birthday should be a festival for the whole world, and perhaps it will be so when the other peoples and tongues teach themselves to give that liberal and generous attention to our incomparable literature which we pay to the letters of the stranger. As it is, Elizabeth Barrett Browning's centenary is a local feast — or would be, but for the more than equal, more than dutiful or adequate, love of America for English poets. At any rate, the sixth of March in this year, 1906, is a day famous within the language.

More than two centuries ago Dryden, called to sing the death of Mrs. Anne Killigrew, sang her birth rather than her death. But he held an earthly commemoration to be merely local; we have to be content with English-speaking nations; Dryden was not content with the globe. Let us hear how greatly his high sincerity and composed emotion speak through the convention of his verse as it appeals to Heaven:

> Thy brother-angels at thy birth
>   Strung each his lyre, and tuned it high,
>   That all the people of the sky
> Might know a poetess was born on earth.
>
> .   .   .   .   .   .
>
> Hear then a mortal muse thy praise rehearse
>   In no ignoble verse;
> But such as thy own voice did practise here, . . .
>   While yet a young probationer
>   And candidate of Heaven.

To the later and more illustrious poetess belongs also rightly Dryden's lovely eloquence in this phrase:

> Her wit was more than man, her innocence a child.

Her wit — in the language of to-day her intellect. Elizabeth Barrett Browning was an intellectual poet. The quality of her poetry is somewhat misdescribed when called chiefly emotional. It is not, indeed, as is Robert Browning's, an exposure of the process or procedure of the thought. Browning, we know, compelled the grinding and hammering and riveting of his argument to take the reluctant measure of verse, the reluctant music of rhyme, and he was therefore less exclusively a poet. On the other hand, we must deplore the later criticism that shuts out from poetry (the noblest kingdom of man) his noblest attribute, his reason. Intellect is poetic, but intellect convinced, intellect in the morning of a secluded night, and in the subsidence of a remote tempest. The waves may be high, but the winds should be at rest. Mrs. Browning is a poet of abundant thoughts. From the rugged pages of *Aurora Leigh* much matter be quarried by poorer wits. We are fond of epigrams to-day; Mrs. Browning could furnish them.

About the poets whose place is on the summit — on one of the two summits — of the Muses' mountain there is no quarrel of opinion. We do not relate them to inferiors. But those who are on the splendid but lower heights we refer to one another. They are not the greatest, but they are the greater. Such as this gentle poetess are measurably, not immeasurably, great. But there can be no man or woman capable of the love of poetry, and insensible to hers.

However unequal may be her poetry, it is the breath of a spiritual creature, the beat of an ardent heart. It is moved by every generous passion. It has profuse beauties and no ignoble faults. Her husband wrote of her that 'her glories would never fade', and she lives possessed of no less than glory. Weeping on Cowper's grave she saw his glory, his rapture, 'in a vision'. On her grave we do not weep. We do not cast back upon the day of her birth any sadness of subsequent life. The advantage of time gives us no threat to hold above her cradled head. She was happy; that newborn head was to wear a poet's laurel, to lie upon a poet's heart, to yield its last breath in the arms of his tenderness. And we commemorate her to-day as one of those majestic babes whose births mark our country's centuries.

ALICE MEYNELL AET: 64
A photograph (1912) by Sherril Schell

SELECTED POEMS

In Early Spring

O SPRING, I know thee! Seek for sweet surprise
    In the young children's eyes.
But I have learnt the years, and know the yet
    Leaf-folded violet.
Mine ear, awake to silence, can foretell
    The cuckoo's fitful bell.
I wander in a grey time that encloses
    June and the wild hedge-roses.
A year's procession of the flowers doth pass
    My feet, along the grass.

And all you wild birds silent yet, I know
  The notes that stir you so,
Your songs yet half devised in the dim dear
  Beginnings of the year.
In these young days you meditate your part;
  I have it all by heart.
I know the secrets of the seeds of flowers
  Hidden and warm with showers,
And how, in kindling Spring, the cuckoo shall
  Alter his interval.
But not a flower or song I ponder is
  My own, but memory's.
I shall be silent in those days desired
  Before a world inspired.
O all brown birds, compose your old song-phrases,
  Earth, thy familiar daisies!

A poet mused upon the dusky height,
  Between two stars towards night,
His purpose in his heart. I watched, a space,
  The meaning of his face:
There was the secret, fled from earth and skies,
  Hid in his grey young eyes.
My heart and all the Summer wait his choice,
  And wonder for his voice.
Who shall foretell his songs, and who aspire
  But to divine his lyre?
Sweet earth, we know thy dimmest mysteries,
  But he is lord of his.

To the Beloved

OH, not more subtly silence strays
    Amongst the winds, between the voices,
Mingling alike with pensive lays,
    And with the music that rejoices,
Than thou art present in my days.

My silence, life returns to thee
    In all the pauses of her breath.
Hush back to rest the melody
    That out of thee awakeneth;
And thou, wake ever, wake for me!

Thou art like silence all unvexed,
    Though wild words part my soul from thee.
Thou art like silence unperplexed,
    A secret and a mystery
Between one footfall and the next.

Most dear pause in a mellow lay!
    Thou art inwoven with every air.
With thee the wildest tempests play,
    And snatches of thee everywhere
Make little heavens throughout a day.

Darkness and solitude shine, for me.
    For life's fair outward part are rife
The silver noises; let them be.
    It is the very soul of life
Listens for thee, listens for thee.

O pause between the sobs of cares;
    O thought within all thought that is;
Trance between laughters unawares:
    Thou art the shape of melodies,
And thou the ecstasy of prayers!

A Letter from a Girl to her own Old Age

L ISTEN, and when thy hand this paper presses,
O time-worn woman, think of her who blesses
What thy thin fingers touch, with her caresses.

O mother, for the weight of years that break thee!
O daughter, for slow time must yet awake thee,
And from the changes of my heart must make thee!

O fainting traveller, morn is grey in heaven.
Dost thou remember how the clouds were driven?
And are they calm about the fall of even?

Pause near the ending of thy long migration,
For this one sudden hour of desolation
Appeals to one hour of thy meditation.

Suffer, O silent one, that I remind thee
Of the great hills that stormed the sky behind thee,
Of the wild winds of power that have resigned thee.

Know that the mournful plain where thou must wander
Is but a grey and silent world, but ponder
The misty mountains of the morning yonder.

Listen: —the mountain winds with rain were fretting,
And sudden gleams the mountain-tops besetting.
I cannot let thee fade to death, forgetting.

What part of this wild heart of mine I know not
Will follow with thee where the great winds blow not,
And where the young flowers of the mountain grow not.

Yet let my letter with my lost thoughts in it
Tell what the way was when thou didst begin it,
And win with thee the goal when thou shalt win it.

Oh, in some hour of thine my thoughts shall guide thee.
Suddenly, though time, darkness, silence, hide thee,
This wind from thy lost country flits beside thee, —

Telling thee: all thy memories moved the maiden,
With thy regrets was morning over-shaden,
With sorrow, thou hast left, her life was laden.

But whither shall my thoughts turn to pursue thee?
Life changes, and the years and days renew thee.
Oh, Nature brings my straying heart unto thee.

Her winds will join us, with their constant kisses
Upon the evening as the morning tresses,
Her summers breathe the same unchanging blisses.

And we, so altered in our shifting phases,
Track one another 'mid the many mazes
By the eternal child-breath of the daisies.

I have not writ this letter of divining
To make a glory of thy silent pining,
A triumph of thy mute and strange declining.

Only one youth, and the bright life was shrouded.
Only one morning, and the day was clouded.
And one old age with all regrets is crowded.

Oh, hush, Oh, hush! Thy tears my words are steeping.
Oh, hush, hush, hush! So full, the fount of weeping?
Poor eyes, so quickly moved, so near to sleeping?

Pardon the girl; such strange desires beset her.
Poor woman, lay aside the mournful letter
That breaks thy heart; the one who wrote, forget her:

The one who now thy faded features guesses,
With filial fingers thy grey hair caresses,
With morning tears thy mournful twilight blesses.

Builders of Ruins

WE build with strength the deep tower wall
    That shall be shattered thus and thus.
And fair and great are court and hall,
    But *how* fair — this is not for us,
Who know the lack that lurks in all.

We know, we know how all too bright
    The hues are that our painting wears,
And how the marble gleams too white; —
    We speak in unknown tongues, the years
Interpret everything aright,

And crown with weeds our pride of towers,
    And warm our marble through with sun,
And break our pavements through with flowers,
    With an Amen when all is done,
Knowing these perfect things of ours.

O days, we ponder, left alone,
    Like children in their lonely hour,
And in our secrets keep your own,
    As seeds the colour of the flower.
To-day they are not all unknown,

The stars that 'twixt the rise and fall,
    Like relic-seers, shall one by one
Stand musing o'er our empty hall;
    And setting moons shall brood upon
The frescoes of our inward wall.

And when some midsummer shall be,
   Hither will come some little one
(Dusty with bloom of flowers is he),
   Sit on a ruin i' the late long sun,
And think, one foot upon his knee.

And where they wrought, these lives of ours,
   So many-worded, many-souled,
A North-west wind will take the towers,
   And dark with colour, sunny and cold,
Will range alone among the flowers.

And here or there, at our desire,
   The little clamorous owl shall sit
Through her still time; and we aspire
   To make a law (and know not it)
Unto the life of a wild briar.

Our purpose is distinct and dear,
   Though from our open eyes 'tis hidden.
Thou, Time to come, shalt make it clear,
   Undoing our work; we are children chidden
With pity and smiles of many a year.

Who shall allot the praise, and guess
   What part is yours and what is ours? —
O years that certainly will bless
   Our flowers with fruits, our seeds with flowers,
With ruin all our perfectness.

Be patient, Time, of our delays,
   Too happy hopes, and wasted fears,
Our faithful ways, our wilful ways;
   Solace our labours, O our seers
The seasons, and our bards the days;

And make our pause and silence brim
  With the shrill children's play, and sweets
Of those pathetic flowers and dim,
  Of those eternal flowers my Keats,
Dying, felt growing over him!

Regrets

A s, when the seaward ebbing tide doth pour
    Out by the low sand spaces,
The parting waves slip back to clasp the shore
  With lingering embraces, —

So in the tide of life that carries me
  From where thy true heart dwells,
Waves of my thoughts and memories turn to thee
  With lessening farewells;

Waving of hands; dreams, when the day forgets;
  A care half lost in cares;
The saddest of my verses; dim regrets;
  Thy name among my prayers.

I would the day might come, so waited for,
  So patiently besought,
When I, returning, should fill up once more
  Thy desolated thought;

And fill thy loneliness that lies apart
  In still, persistent pain.
Shall I content thee, O thou broken heart,
  As the tide comes again,

And brims the little sea-shore lakes, and sets
    Seaweeds afloat, and fills
The silent pools, rivers and rivulets
    Among the inland hills?

The Young Neophyte

Who knows what days I answer for to-day?
    Giving the bud I give the flower. I bow
This yet unfaded and a faded brow;
Bending these knees and feeble knees, I pray.
Thoughts yet unripe in me I bend one way,
    Give one repose to pain I know not now,
    One check to joy that comes, I guess not how.
I dedicate my fields when Spring is grey.

O rash! (I smile) to pledge my hidden wheat.
    I fold to-day at altars far apart
Hands trembling with what toils? In their retreat
    I seal my love to-be, my folded art.
I light the tapers at my head and feet,
    And lay the crucifix on this silent heart.

Song of the Night at Daybreak

All my stars forsake me,
    And the dawn-winds shake me.
Where shall I betake me?

Whither shall I run
Till the set of sun,
Till the day be done?

To the mountain-mine,
To the boughs o' the pine,
To the blind man's eyne,

To a brow that is
Bowed upon the knees,
Sick with memories?

Renouncement

I MUST not think of thee; and, tired yet strong,
  I shun the thought that lurks in all delight —
    The thought of thee — and in the blue Heaven's height,
And in the sweetest passage of a song.
Oh, just beyond the fairest thoughts that throng
  This breast, the thought of thee waits hidden yet bright;
    But it must never, never come in sight;
I must stop short of thee the whole day long.

But when sleep comes to close each difficult day,
  When night gives pause to the long watch I keep,
    And all my bonds I needs must loose apart,
Must doff my will as raiment laid away, —
  With the first dream that comes with the first sleep
    I run, I run, I am gathered to thy heart.

A Song of Derivations

I COME from nothing; but from where
Come the undying thoughts I bear?
  Down, through long links of death and birth,
  From the past poets of the earth,
My immortality is there.

I am like the blossom of an hour.
But long, long vanished sun and shower
  Awoke my breath i' the young world's air;
  I track the past back everywhere
Through seed and flower and seed and flower.

Or I am like a stream that flows
Full of the cold springs that arose
  In morning lands, in distant hills;
  And down the plain my channel fills
With melting of forgotten snows.

Voices, I have not heard, possessed
My own fresh songs; my thoughts are blessed
  With relics of the far unknown.
  And mixed with memories not my own
The sweet streams throng into my breast.

Before this life began to be,
The happy songs that wake in me
  Woke long ago and far apart.
  Heavily on this little heart
Presses this immortality.

Veni Creator

SO humble things Thou hast borne for us, O God,
  Left'st Thou a path of lowliness untrod?
Yes, one, till now, another Olive-Garden.
For we endure the tender pain of pardon, —
One with another we forbear. Give heed,
Look at the mournful world Thou hast decreed.
The time has come. At last we hapless men
Know all our haplessness all through. Come, then,
Endure undreamed humility: Lord of Heaven,
Come to our ignorant hearts and be forgiven.

'I am the Way'

THOU art the Way.
  Hadst Thou been nothing but the goal,
      I cannot say
If Thou hadst ever met my soul.

    I cannot see —
I, child of process — if there lies
      An end for me,
Full of repose, full of replies.

    I'll not reproach
The road that winds, my feet that err.
      Access, Approach
Art Thou, Time, Way, and Wayfarer.

'Why wilt thou Chide?'

WHY wilt thou chide,
    Who hast attained to be denied?
    O learn, above
All price is my refusal, Love.
    My sacred Nay
Was never cheapened by the way.
Thy single sorrow crowns thee lord
Of an unpurchasable word.

    O strong, O pure!
As Yea makes happier loves secure,
    I vow thee this
Unique rejection of a kiss.
    I guard for thee
This jealous sad monopoly.
I seal this honour thine; none dare
Hope for a part in thy despair.

The Lady Poverty

THE Lady Poverty was fair:
    But she has lost her looks of late,
With change of times and change of air.
Ah slattern! she neglects her hair,
Her gown, her shoes; she keeps no state
As once when her pure feet were bare.

Or — almost worse, if worse can be —
She scolds in parlours, dusts and trims,
Watches and counts. Oh, is this she
Whom Francis met, whose step was free,
Who with Obedience carolled hymns,
In Umbria walked with Chastity?

Where is her ladyhood? Not here,
Not among modern kinds of men;
But in the stony fields, where clear
Through the thin trees the skies appear,
In delicate spare soil and fen,
And slender landscape and austere.

At Night

To W. M.

Home, home from the horizon far and clear,
    Hither the soft wings sweep;
Flocks of the memories of the day draw near
    The dovecote doors of sleep.

Oh, which are they that come through sweetest light
    Of all these homing birds?
Which with the straightest and the swiftest flight?
    Your words to me, your words!

The Two Poets

WHOSE is the speech
That moves the voices of this lonely beech?
Out of the long west did this wild wind come —
O strong and silent! And the tree was dumb,
    Ready and dumb, until
The dumb gale struck it on the darkened hill.

    Two memories,
Two powers, two promises, two silences
Closed in this cry, closed in these thousand leaves
Articulate. This sudden hour retrieves
    The purpose of the past,
Separate, apart — embraced, embraced at last.

    'Whose is the word?
Is it I that spake? Is it thou? Is it I that heard?'
'Thine earth was solitary, yet I found thee!'
'Thy sky was pathless, but I caught, I bound thee,
    Thou visitant divine.'
'O thou my Voice, the word was thine.' 'Was thine.'

The Rainy Summer

THERE's much afoot in heaven and earth this year;
The winds hunt up the sun, hunt up the moon,
Trouble the dubious dawn, hasten the drear
    Height of a threatening noon.

No breath of boughs, no breath of leaves, of fronds,
    May linger or grow warm; the trees are loud;
The forest, rooted, tosses in her bonds,
    And strains against the cloud.

371

No scents may pause within the garden-fold;
  The rifled flowers are cold as ocean-shells;
Bees, humming in the storm, carry their cold
  Wild honey to cold cells.

The Unknown God

ONE of the crowd went up,
  And knelt before the Paten and the Cup,
Received the Lord, returned in peace, and prayed
Close to my side. Then in my heart I said:

'O Christ, in this man's life —
This stranger who is Thine — in all his strife,
All his felicity, his good and ill,
In the assaulted stronghold of his will,

'I do confess Thee here,
Alive within this life; I know Thee near
Within this lonely conscience, closed away
Within this brother's solitary day.

'Christ in his unknown heart,
His intellect unknown — this love, this art,
This battle and this peace, this destiny
That I shall never know, look upon me!

'Christ in his numbered breath,
Christ in his beating heart and in his death,
Christ in his mystery! From that secret place
And from that separate dwelling, give me grace!'

A General Communion

I saw the throng, so deeply separate,
    Fed at one only board —
The devout people, moved, intent, elate,
    And the devoted Lord.

O struck apart! not side from human side,
    But soul from human soul,
As each asunder absorbed the multiplied,
    The ever unparted, whole.

I saw this people as a field of flowers,
    Each grown at such a price
The sum of unimaginable powers
    Did no more than suffice.

A thousand single central daisies they,
    A thousand of the one;
For each, the entire monopoly of day;
    For each, the whole of the devoted sun.

In Manchester Square

In Memoriam T. H.

THE paralytic man has dropped in death
    The crossing-sweeper's brush to which he clung,
One-handed, twisted, dwarfed, scanted of breath,
    Although his hair was young.

373

I saw this year the winter vines of France,
    Dwarfed, twisted goblins in the frosty drouth —
Gnarled, crippled, blackened little stems askance
    On long hills to the South.

Great green and golden hands of leaves ere long
    Shall proffer clusters in that vineyard wide.
And Oh, his might, his sweet, his wine, his song,
    His stature, since he died!

The Courts

A Figure of the Epiphany

THE poet's imageries are noble ways,
    Approaches to a plot, an open shrine,
Their splendours, colours, avenues, arrays,
    Their courts that run with wine;

Beautiful similes, 'fair and flagrant things,'
Enriched, enamouring, — raptures, metaphors
Enhancing life, are paths for pilgrim kings
    Made free of golden doors.

And yet the open heavenward plot, with dew,
Ultimate poetry, enclosed, enskied,
(Albeit such ceremonies lead thereto)
    Stands on the yonder side.

Plain, behind oracles, it is; and past
All symbols, simple; perfect, heavenly-wild,
The song some loaded poets reach at last —
    The kings that found a Child.

The Launch

FORTH, to the alien gravity,
Forth, to the laws of ocean, we,
    Builders on earth by laws of land,
    Entrust this creature of our hand
Upon the calculated sea.

Fast bound to shore we cling, we creep,
And make our ship ready to leap
    Light to the flood, equipped to ride
    The strange conditions of the tide —
New weight, new force, new world: the Deep.

Ah thus — not thus — the Dying, kissed,
Cherished, exhorted, shriven, dismissed;
    By all the eager means we hold
    We, warm, prepare him for the cold,
To keep the incalculable tryst.

To the Body

THOU inmost, ultimate
Council of judgement, palace of decrees,
Where the high senses hold their spiritual state,
    Sued by earth's embassies,
And sign, approve, accept, conceive, create;

    Create — thy senses close
With the world's pleas. The random odours reach
Their sweetness in the place of thy repose,
    Upon thy tongue the peach,
And in thy nostrils breathes the breathing rose.

To thee, secluded one,
The dark vibrations of the sightless skies,
The lovely inexplicit colours, run;
　　The light gropes for those eyes.
O thou august! thou dost command the sun.

Music, all dumb, hath trod
Into thine ear her one effectual way;
And fire and cold approach to gain thy nod,
　　Where thou call'st up the day,
Where thou awaitest the appeal of God.

The Unexpected Peril

UNLIKE the youth that all men say
　　They prize — youth of abounding blood,
In love with the sufficient day,
　　And gay in growth, and strong in bud;

Unlike was mine! Then my first slumber
　　Nightly rehearsed my last; each breath
Knew itself one of the unknown number.
　　But Life was urgent with me as Death.

My shroud was in the flocks; the hill
　　Within its quarry locked my stone;
My bier grew in the woods; and still
　　Life spurred me where I paused alone.

'Begin!' Life called. Again her shout,
　　'Make haste while it is called to-day!'
Her exhortations plucked me out,
　　Hunted me, turned me, held me at bay.

But if my youth is thus hard pressed
    (I thought) what of a later year?
If the end so threats this tender breast,
    What of the days when it draws near?

Draws near, and little done? Yet lo,
    Dread has forborne, and haste lies by.
I was beleaguered; now the foe
    Has raised the siege, I know not why.

I see them troop away; I ask
    Were they in sooth mine enemies —
Terror, the doubt, the lash, the task?
    What heart has my new housemate, Ease?

How am I left, at last, alive,
    To make a stranger of a tear?
What did I do one day to drive
    From me the vigilant angel, Fear?

The diligent angel, Labour? Ay,
    The inexorable angel, Pain?
Menace me, lest indeed I die,
    Sloth! Turn; crush, teach me fear again!

Christ in the Universe

WITH this ambiguous earth
  His dealings have been told us. These abide:
The signal to a maid, the human birth,
The lesson, and the young Man crucified.

377

But not a star of all
The innumerable host of stars has heard
How He administered this terrestrial ball.
Our race have kept their Lord's entrusted Word.

Of His earth-visiting feet
None knows the secret, cherished, perilous,
The terrible, shamefast, frightened, whispered, sweet,
Heart-shattering secret of His way with us.

No planet knows that this
Our wayside planet, carrying land and wave,
Love and life multiplied, and pain and bliss,
Bears, as chief treasure, one forsaken grave.

Nor, in our little day,
May His devices with the heavens be guessed,
His pilgrimage to thread the Milky Way,
Or His bestowals there be manifest.

But, in the eternities,
Doubtless we shall compare together, hear
A million alien Gospels, in what guise
He trod the Pleiades, the Lyre, the Bear.

Oh, be prepared, my soul!
To read the inconceivable, to scan
The million forms of God those stars unroll
When, in our turn, we show to them a Man.

Beyond Knowledge

'Your sins . . . shall be white as snow.'

INTO the rescued world newcomer,
   The newly-dead stepped up, and cried,
'Oh, what is that, sweeter than summer
   Was to my heart before I died?
Sir (to an angel), what is yonder
   More bright than the remembered skies,
A lovelier sight, a softer splendour
   Than when the moon was wont to rise?
Surely no sinner wears such seeming
   Even the Rescued World within?'

'Oh, the success of His redeeming!
   O child, it is a rescued sin!'

A Thrush before Dawn

A VOICE peals in this end of night
   A phrase of notes resembling stars,
Single and spiritual notes of light.
   What call they at my window-bars?
      The South, the past, the day to be,
      An ancient infelicity.

Darkling, deliberate, what sings
   This wonderful one, alone, at peace?
What wilder things than song, what things
   Sweeter than youth, clearer than Greece,
      Dearer than Italy, untold
      Delight, and freshness centuries old?

And first first-loves, a multitude,
   The exaltation of their pain;
Ancestral childhood long renewed;
   And midnights of invisible rain;
         And gardens, gardens, night and day,
         Gardens and childhood all the way.

What Middle Ages passionate,
   O passionless voice! What distant bells
Lodged in the hills, what palace state
   Illyrian! For it speaks, it tells,
         Without desire, without dismay,
         Some morrow and some yesterday.

All-natural things! But more — Whence came
   This yet remoter mystery?
How do these starry notes proclaim
   A graver still divinity?
         This hope, this sanctity of fear?

         O innocent throat! O human ear!

A Father of Women

AD SOROREM E. B.

'Thy father was transfused into thy blood.'
         DRYDEN: *Ode to Mrs. Anne Killigrew*

OUR father works in us,
   The daughters of his manhood. Not undone
Is he, not wasted, though transmuted thus,
   And though he left no son.

Therefore on him I cry
To arm me: 'For my delicate mind a casque,
A breastplate for my heart, courage to die,
Of thee, captain, I ask.

'Nor strengthen only; press
A finger on this violent blood and pale,
Over this rash will let thy tenderness
A while pause, and prevail.

'And shepherd-father, thou
Whose staff folded my thoughts before my birth,
Control them now I am of earth, and now
Thou art no more of earth.

'O liberal, constant, dear,
Crush in my nature the ungenerous art
Of the inferior; set me high, and here,
Here garner up thy heart!'

Like to him now are they,
The million living fathers of the War —
Mourning the crippled world, the bitter day —
Whose striplings are no more.

The crippled world! Come then,
Fathers of women with your honour in trust,
Approve, accept, know them daughters of men,
Now that your sons are dust.

To Tintoretto in Venice

The Art of Painting had in the Primitive years looked with the light, not towards it. Before Tintoretto's date, however, many painters practised shadows and lights, and turned more or less sunwards: but he set the figure between himself and a full sun. His work is to be known in Venice by the splendid trick of an occluded sun and a shadow thrown straight at the spectator.

MASTER, thy enterprise,
    Magnificent, magnanimous, was well done,
Which seized the head of Art, and turned her eyes —
The simpleton — and made her front the sun.

    Long had she sat content,
Her young unlessoned back to a morning gay,
To a solemn noon, to a cloudy firmament,
And looked upon a world in gentle day.

    But thy imperial call
Bade her to stand with thee and breast the light,
And therefore face the shadows, mystical,
Sombre, translucent vestiges of night,

    Yet the glories of the day.
Eagle! we know thee by thy undaunted eyes
Sky-ward, and by thy glooms; we know thy way
Ambiguous, and those halo-misted dyes.

    Thou Cloud, the bridegroom's friend
(The bridegroom sun)! Master, we know thy sign:
A mystery of hues world-without-end;
And hide-and-seek of gamesome and divine;

Shade of the noble head
Cast hitherward upon the noble breast;
Human solemnities thrice hallowèd;
The haste to Calvary, the Cross at rest.

Look sunward, Angel, then!
Carry the fortress-heavens by that hand;
Still be the interpreter of suns to men;
And shadow us, O thou Tower! for thou shalt stand.

The Two Shakespeare Tercentenaries

OF BIRTH, 1864; OF DEATH, 1916

TO SHAKESPEARE

L ONGER than thine, than thine,
Is now my time of life; and thus thy years
Seem to be clasped and harboured within mine.
Oh, how ignoble this my clasp appears!

Thy unprophetic birth,
Thy darkling death: living I might have seen
That cradle, marked those labours, closed that earth.
O first, O last, O infinite between!

Now that my life has shared
Thy dedicated date, O mortal, twice,
To what all-vain embrace shall be compared
My lean enclosure of thy paradise:

To ignorant arms that fold
A poet to a foolish breast? The Line,
That is not, with the world within its hold?
So, days with days, my days encompass thine.

Child, Stripling, Man — the sod.
Might I talk little language to thee, pore
On thy last silence? O thou city of God,
My waste lies after thee, and lies before.

The Poet and his Book

HERE are my thoughts, alive within this fold,
  My simple sheep. Their shepherd, I grow wise
As dearly, gravely, deeply I behold
      Their different eyes.

O distant pastures in their blood! O streams
  From watersheds that fed them for this prison!
Lights from aloft, midsummer suns in dreams,
      Set and arisen.

They wander out, but all return anew,
  The small ones, to this heart to which they clung;
'And those that are with young,' the fruitful few
      That are with young.

The Wind is Blind

'Eyeless, in Gaza, at the mill, with slaves'
MILTON'S Samson

THE wind is blind.
　　The earth sees sun and moon; the height
　　Is watch-tower to the dawn: the plain
Shines to the summer; visible light
　　Is scattered in the drops of rain.

　　　The wind is blind.
The flashing billows are aware;
　　With open eyes the cities see;
Light leaves the ether, everywhere
　　Known to the homing bird and bee.

　　　The wind is blind,
Is blind alone. How has he hurled
　　His ignorant lash, his aimless dart,
His eyeless rush, upon the world,
　　Unseeing, to break his unknown heart!

　　　The wind is blind,
And the sail traps him, and the mill
　　Captures him; and he cannot save
His swiftness and his desperate will
　　From those blind uses of the slave.

Time's Reversals

A Daughter's Paradox

To his devoted heart*
  Who, young, had loved his ageing mate for life,
In late lone years Time gave the elder's part,
  Time gave the bridegroom's boast, Time gave a younger
    wife.

A wilder prank and plot
  Time soon will promise, threaten, offering me
Impossible things that Nature suffers not —
  A daughter's riper mind, a child's seniority.

Oh, by my filial tears
  Mourned all too young, Father! On this my head
Time yet will force at last the longer years,
  Claiming some strange respect for me from you, the dead.

Nay, nay! Too new to know
  Time's conjuring is, too great to understand.
Memory has not died; it leaves me so —
  Leaning a fading brow on your unfaded hand.

The Threshing-Machine

No 'fan is in his hand' for these
  Young villagers beneath the trees,
  Watching the wheels. But I recall
  The rhythm of rods that rise and fall,
Purging the harvest, over-seas.

* Dr. Johnson outlived by thirty years his wife, who was twenty years his
senior.

No fan, no flail, no threshing-floor!
And all their symbols evermore
   Forgone in England now — the sign,
   The visible pledge, the threat divine,
The chaff dispersed, the wheat in store.

The unbreathing engine marks no tune,
Steady at sunrise, steady at noon,
   Inhuman, perfect, saving time,
And saving measure, and saving rhyme —
And did our Ruskin speak too soon?

'No noble strength on earth' he sees
'Save Hercules' arm'; his grave decrees
   Curse wheel and steam. As the wheels ran
   I saw the other strength of man,
I knew the brain of Hercules.

To Sleep

DEAR fool, be true to me!
  I know the poets speak thee fair, and I
    Hail thee uncivilly.
Oh, but I call with a more urgent cry!

    I do not prize thee less,
I need thee more, that thou dost love to teach —
    Father of foolishness —
The imbecile dreams clear out of wisdom's reach.

Come and release me; bring
My irresponsible mind; come in thy hours;
Draw from my soul the sting
Of wit that trembles, consciousness that cowers.

For if night comes without thee
She is more cruel than day. But thou, fulfil
Thy work, thy gifts about thee —
Liberty, liberty, from this weight of will.

My day-mind can endure
Upright, in hope, all it must undergo.
But Oh, afraid, unsure,
My night-mind waking lies too low, too low.

Dear fool, be true to me!
The night is thine, man yields it, it beseems
Thy ironic dignity.
Make me all night the innocent fool that dreams.

'Lord, I owe Thee a Death'

Richard Hooker

IN TIME OF WAR

MAN pays that debt with new munificence,
Not piecemeal now, not slowly, by the old:
Not grudgingly, by the effaced thin pence,
But greatly and in gold.

The Voice of a Bird

'He shall rise up at the voice of a bird' — ECCLESIASTES

Who then is 'he'?
 Dante, Keats, Shakespeare, Milton, Shelley; all
Rose in their greatness at the shrill decree,
 The little rousing inarticulate call.

 For they stood up
At the bird-voice, of lark, of nightingale,
Drank poems from that throat as from a cup.
Over the great world's notes did these prevail.

 And not alone
The signal poets woke. In listening man,
Woman, and child a poet stirs unknown,
Throughout the Mays of birds since Mays began.

 He rose, he heard —
Our father, our St. Peter, in his tears —
The crowing, twice, of the prophetic bird,
The saddest cock-crow of our human years.

To Silence

'Space, the bound of a solid': Silence, then, the form of a melody

Not, Silence, for thine idleness I raise
 My silence-bounded singing in thy praise,
But for thy moulding of my Mozart's tune,
Thy hold upon the bird that sings the moon,
 Thy magisterial ways.

Man's lovely definite melody-shapes are thine,
Outlined, controlled, compressed, complete, divine.
Also thy fine intrusions do I trace,
Thy afterthoughts, thy wandering, thy grace,
      Within the poet's line.

Thy secret is the song that is to be.
Music had never stature but for thee,
Sculptor! strong as the sculptor Space whose hand
Urged the Discobolus and bade him stand.

    ·   ·   ·   ·   ·   ·

Man, on his way to Silence, stops to hear and see.

'Rivers Unknown to Song'

JAMES THOMSON

Wide waters in the waste; or, out of reach,
    Rough Alpine falls where late a glacier hung;
Or rivers groping for the alien beach,
    Through continents, unsung.

Nay, not these nameless, these remote, alone;
    But all the streams from all the watersheds —
Peneus, Danube, Nile — are the unknown
    Young in their ancient beds.

Man has no tale for them. O travellers swift
    From secrets to oblivion! Waters wild
That pass in act to bend a flower, or lift
    The bright limbs of a child!

For they are new, they are fresh; there's no surprise
  Like theirs on earth. O strange for evermore!
This momen't Tiber with his shining eyes
  Never saw Rome before.

Man has no word for their eternity —
  Rhine, Avon, Arno, younglings, youth uncrowned:
Ignorant, innocent, instantaneous, free,
  Unwelcomed, unrenowned.

The Poet to the Birds

You bid me hold my peace,
  Or so I think, you birds; you'll not forgive
My kill-joy song that makes the wild song cease,
  Silent or fugitive.

Yon thrush stopt in mid-phrase
  At my mere footfall; and a longer note
Took wing and fled afield, and went its ways
  Within the blackbird's throat.

Hereditary song,
  Illyrian lark and Paduan nightingale,
Is yours, unchangeable the ages long;
  Assyria heard your tale;

Therefore you do not die.
　But single, local, lonely, mortal, new,
Unlike, and thus like all my race, am I,
　Preluding my adieu.

My human song must be
　My human thought. Be patient till 'tis done.
I shall not hold my little peace; for me
　There is no peace but one.

BIBLIOGRAPHICAL NOTE

The essays and poems in this collection are here assigned to the books in which they first appeared. When a later version has been chosen, the source of the revised text is also given, in italics.

THE RHYTHM OF LIFE: Elkin Mathews and John Lane, 1893
The Rhythm of Life (*Essays*, 1914)
A Remembrance
At a Station [By a Railway Side]
The Lesson of Landscape
Composure (*Essays*, 1914)
THE COLOUR OF LIFE: Elkin Mathews and John Lane, 1896
The Colour of Life (*Essays*, 1914)
A Woman in Grey
Eyes
THE CHILDREN: John Lane, 1897
Children in Midwinter
Real Childhood
THE SPIRIT OF PLACE: John Lane, 1898
Wells
Marceline Valmore
The Horizon (*Essays*, 1914)
Mrs. Dingley (*Essays*, 1914)
Bells [The Spirit of Place] (*Wayfaring*, 1928)
Solitudes (*Wayfaring*, 1928)
The Lady of the Lyrics (*Essays of Today and Yesterday*, 1926)
CERES' RUNAWAY: Constable, 1909
A Vanquished Man
A Northern Fancy (*Essays*, 1914)
Anima Pellegrina! (*Essays*, 1914)
The Little Language (*Essays*, 1914)
Harlequin Mercutio (*Essays*, 1914)
The Child of Tumult (*Essays*, 1914)
The Child of Subsiding Tumult (*Essays*, 1914)
MARY THE MOTHER OF JESUS: Philip Lee Warner, 1912
The Mother

CHILDHOOD: Batsford, 1913
Toys
The Stranger's Children
The Influential Child
Injustice
Near the Ground
ESSAYS: Burns and Oates, 1914
Steele's Prue
Mrs. Johnson
HEARTS OF CONTROVERSY: Burns and Oates, 1917
Tennyson
Dickens
Swinburne
Charmian
The Century of Moderation
THE SECOND PERSON SINGULAR: Oxford University Press, 1921
Superfluous Kings
An Elizabethan Lyrist
Arabella Stuart [A Modern Poetess]
To Italy with Evelyn
Waterfalls
A Corrupt Following
The Swan of Lichfield
Joanna Baillie
A Hundred Years Ago
Coventry Patmore
Poetry and Childhood
Giacinto Gallina
The Second Person Singular
ESSAYS OF TODAY AND YESTERDAY: Harrap, 1926
Elizabeth Inchbald
Mary Wollstonecraft's Letters
The Brontës
Christina Rossetti

BIBLIOGRAPHICAL NOTE

WAYFARING: Jonathan Cape, 1928

Walls

Fireflies

Venetian Girls

The Roaring Moon

The Childish Town

In the Village of Oberammergau

'Heroines' is from *A Book of Homage to Shakespeare*: Oxford University Press, 1916; 'Robert Browning' is from *The Pen*, 1880; 'The New Helena', 'Hester', 'In a South Alpine Castle', 'Ippolita', 'Ada Negri', 'Elizabeth Barrett Browning's Letters' and 'The Centenary of Mrs. Browning's Birth' are all from the *Pall Mall Gazette*, 1893-1900; 'The Poetry of George Meredith' is from *The Bookman*, 1912.

The Introductions are from *Herrick*: Blackie, 1904; *Cowper*: Blackie, 1904; *The Seven Lamps of Architecture* by John Ruskin: Routledge, 1910; 'The Mystical Lyric' is from *The Mount of Vision*, edited by Adeline Cashmore: Chapman & Hall, 1910.

PRELUDES by A. C. Thompson: H. S. King & Co., 1875

In Early Spring

To the Beloved

A Letter from a Girl to her own Old Age

Builders of Ruins

Regrets

The Young Neophyte

Song of the Night at Daybreak

POEMS: Elkin Mathews and John Lane, 1893

Renouncement

A Song of Derivations

Veni Creator

OTHER POEMS: Privately printed, 1896

'I am the Way'

'Why wilt Thou Chide'

The Lady Poverty

At Night

LATER POEMS: John Lane, 1902

The Two Poets

COLLECTED POEMS: Burns and Oates, 1913

The Rainy Summer

The Unknown God

A General Communion

In Manchester Square

The Courts

The Launch

To the Body

The Unexpected Peril

Christ in the Universe

Beyond Knowledge

TEN POEMS, 1913-15: Privately printed, Romney St. Press, 1915

A Thrush before Dawn

A FATHER OF WOMEN, AND OTHER POEMS: Burns and Oates, 1917

A Father of Women

To Tintoretto in Venice

The Two Shakespeare Tercentenaries

LAST POEMS: Burns and Oates, 1923

The Poet and His Book

The Wind is Blind

Time's Reversals

The Threshing-Machine

To Sleep

'Lord, I owe Thee a Death'

The Voice of a Bird

To Silence

'Rivers unknown to Song'

The Poet to the Birds

The editors of this book are Frederick Page, Viola Meynell, Olivia Sowerby and Francis Meynell. The device on the title page is by Reynolds Stone

08-053749-1   HUM   824
                    M614

18.25

MEYNELL, ALICE CHRISTIANA
PROSE AND POETRY

RO1106 49131

824
08-053749-1   HUM   M614

HOUSTON PUBLIC LIBRARY

CENTRAL LIBRARY
500 MCKINNEY

INDEXED IN Ebli